Jo's Girls

Jo's Girls

EDITED BY

CHRISTIAN McEWEN

TOMBOY TALES

OF HIGH

ADVENTURE,

TRUE GRIT,

AND REAL LIFE

BEACON PRESS

Boston

BEACON PRESS
25 Beacon Street
Boston, Massachusetts 02108-2892

Beacon Press books
are published under the auspices of
the Unitarian Universalist Association of Congregations.

Text design by Lucinda L. Hitchcock

LIBRARY OF CONGRESS CATALOGING-IN-PUBLICATION DATA
Jo's girls : tomboy tales of high adventure, true grit, and real life
    / edited by Christian McEwen.
        p.   cm.
    Includes bibliographical references.
    ISBN: 0-8070-6211-1 (pbk.)
    1. Girls—Literary collections.   2. Sex role—Literary
collections.   3. American literature—Women authors.   I. McEwen,
Christian. 1956–   .
PS509.G57J67   1997
810.8'0352042—DC21   96-47124

For my Sister, Isabella

Contents

Acknowledgments

THIS ANTHOLOGY COULD NEVER HAVE BEEN COMPLETED WITHOUT A great deal of help. I would especially like to thank Judy Willis of the Buckland Public Library for tracking down so many books and references; Ron Bosch, my neighbor up the hill, for unlimited access to his (superb!) computer; my stalwart editor, Deanne Urmy; and my partner, Nina Newington, for her love and clarity and great good sense. I would also like to thank the following people for their letters, suggestions, and inspired conversation: Malaga Baldi, Iris Bloom, Ruthie Bosch, Karen Braziller, Sarah Buttenwieser, Amy Caldwell, Roz Calvert, Elizabeth Rose Campbell, Louise Chouinard, Edite Cunha, Pamela Christie, Margo Culley, Meg Davis, Susan Davis, Anna Demska, Charlene Ellis, Rachel Ganz, Bea Gates, Gail Griffin, Caroline Harcourt, Adrienne Harris, Rachel Hass, Andrea Hawkes, Annie Hole, Parker Huber, Pat Hynes, Terry Iacuzzo, Kim Jessor, Marion Kelner, Irena Klepfisz, Anne LaBastille, Joan Larkin, Linda Marks, Elizabeth McMahan, Katherine McNamara, Bernice Mennis, Pamela Meyer, Jane Miller, Lisa Miller, Aina Niemela, Theo Oktenberg, Paula Panich, Elaine Parker, Roz Parr, Diane Pieri, Jan Raymond, Amy Reiser, Leonie Rushforth, Christina Schlesinger, Elizabeth Segel, Gabrielle Silver, Michelle Spark, Edith Sullwold, and Hazel Wolf.

Introduction

There are times when girls are inspired, when they want the risks to go on and on. They want to be heroines, regardless. They want to take a joke beyond where anybody has ever taken it before. To be careless, dauntless, to create havoc — that was the lost hope of girls.

—Alice Munro, OPEN SECRETS

I.

I WAS EIGHT WHEN I MET MY FIRST TOMBOY. HER NAME WAS SUSAN Meldrum. She had dirty-blonde hair and bold white knees which stood out sharply under her regulation tunic. I remember the sound of her heels on the wooden floor and the scuffed toes of her heavy lace-up shoes. I remember too the way she flung herself across a room, swerving and skidding and crashing into things, with utter disregard for her own safety. How I marvelled at her! She was only six, but she seemed to be afraid of nothing.

I was a different sort of child myself, more anxious, more self-critical. I could climb a tree all right, but I found it hard to get down again. I hated netball and hockey, and was never any good at judo. Still, I knew myself to be a tomboy, with my longing for dungarees and close-cropped hair, and my determination never to get married. The word "tomboy" itself seemed magical to me: fiery, disobedient, gloriously untidy. "Girl," by comparison, was flat and uninspiring.

Half a lifetime later, nudging forty, I put together a series of tomboy writing workshops in New York City and began to gather material for this anthology. It was a wonderful project. I only had to mention it to provoke a flare-up of excited talk and storytelling. I sent out a call for submissions, and for weeks my mailbox was jammed with tomboy stories and reminiscences, drawings of hidden tree-houses and secret dens, of bows-and-arrows, catapults, and knives. Almost every woman I approached had a tomboy story she wanted to tell.

The range of such stories was enormous, from the girls who always wanted to be boys, to the girls who wanted not to be girls as "girl" was then understood, to the girls who despised all such distinctions and wanted simply to be free and genderless. For some, solitude was crucial: "wanting to be free-in-the-country-having-adventures."[1] For others, company was an integral part of the dream.

But in almost all cases, such company was male. The notion that *another girl* might also be a tomboy seemed almost unimaginable.

Perhaps because tomboy friendships had been (relatively) so rare, the telling of these early stories brought with it a powerful sense of release. It was as if a long-locked door had finally been broken open. Behind that door huge issues lay compacted: issues of power and danger, of sex and sexuality, of anger and ambition and passionate, unresolved resentment. Clearly "tomboy," both as word and theme, was far more freighted than I had originally thought.

2.

I looked up "tomboy" in my *Chambers Twentieth Century Dictionary.* "A high spirited romping girl," it said. But in the *Oxford English Dictionary* I found layers of more complicated meanings. Before the tomboy was a girl, she was a boy, and a "rude, boistrous and forward" one at that. She was a woman too, for a while, "bold or immodest," unchaste, a prostitute. The judgments echoed down the centuries. *Tomboy:* "a girle or wench that leaps up and down like a boy" (1656); "a ramping frolicsome rude girl" (1730–1736). It was not until 1876 that the word began to take on more positive connotations. What Charlotte M. Yonge meant by tomboyism, she said, was "a wholesome delight in rushing about at full speed, playing at active games, climbing trees, rowing boats, making dirt-pies and the like." [2]

It is a definition Jo March would have approved. Tall and thin and brown, with long coltish limbs, a decided mouth, and a "fly-away look to her clothes," Jo (of Alcott's *Little Women*) is, of course, the quintessential tomboy. She likes "boys' games and work, and manners," hates to think that she has to grow up and be Miss March, and declares fiercely that she "can't get over [her] disappointment in not being a boy." [3]

When I asked people if they remembered any literary tomboys, Jo's name was almost always the first to come to mind. A couple cited George Eliot's Maggie Tulliver (in *The Mill on the Floss*), or Carson McCullers's Frankie (in *The Member of the Wedding*), and there were some oddball European examples too, among them Astrid Lindgren's *Pippi Longstocking,* and the redoubtable Maria in *Mistress Masham's Repose* by T. H. White. But most of the other references were to North American children's books: very white, very upper middle class, almost all written in the seventy years between 1866 and 1936. They included the *Gypsy Breynton* books by Elizabeth Stuart Phelps; the *Katy*

books by Susan Coolidge; *Merrylips* by Beaulah Marie Dix; *Roller Skates* by
Ruth Sawyer; *Caddie Woodlawn* by Carol Ryrie Brink; *Middl'un* by Elizabeth
Burleson; and the *Little House* books by Laura Ingalls Wilder.[4]

Long before I had agreed to edit *Jo's Girls*, I stumbled quite by chance upon
Gypsy Breynton in a secondhand bookstore in Vermont.[5] I'd never heard of it
before, but I knew the author's name, and the book itself was tempting: a
handsome hardbound copy in the palest olive, with the title embossed in red
and gold. Inside, a preface by Elizabeth Stuart Phelps introduced me to the
tomboy heroine: "A lively girl in pretty short dresses and very long stockings.
. . . She paddles a raft, she climbs a tree, she skates and tramps and coasts, she
is usually very muddy, and a little torn. . . . Wherever there is mischief, there is
Gypsy."[6]

In her ardor, her disorder, her perpetual good intentions, Gypsy is the first
in a long line of tomboy heroines, most of whom share her love of the outdoors
and her impatience with the usual female trappings. While her brother Tom can
toss on his cap and be ready, "Gypsy Breynton Esq." is hampered by the
"complication of garments necessary to the feminine adventurer if she so much
as crosses the yard."[7] She resents this fiercely, and would have sympathized
with Katy, in *What Katy Did*, whose gowns are "always catching on nails and
tearing themselves."[8] She would have understood too the scene in *Roller Skates*
where Lucinda Wyman (note the tiny pun!) cuts off the legs of her underdrawers
so she can skate more freely. Such scenes are by no means always fictional. My
mail last year included a wonderful letter from a self-designated "tom-old-lady"
who as a girl had been so infuriated by her brand new shoes that she went to the
shed, "took up the ax, and chopped off both heels."[9] A few years later, when
her mother bought her a corset, she broke the ribs off bit by bit, finally abandoning the hated garment altogether.

This battle between the harassed mother and her rebellious tomboy daughter
remains a staple of almost all the tomboy books I've read, whether fiction or
nonfiction, written for children or for adults. Again and again the mother
struggles to get her daughter to *behave:* to wash her hands and comb her hair,
and dress like all the other girls. Again and again, the tomboy disobeys. "When
are you going to begin making a young lady out of this wild Indian?" the
Circuit Rider asks Mrs. Woodlawn, in a question that splits the choices very
tidily along racist lines.[10] Either Caddie is obedient, "civilized," well-dressed,
or she is a little savage. There is no room for *both/and*. An energetic, disobedient
young woman is as unimaginable as a civilized Indian.

Elizabeth Segel has written usefully about this,[11] pointing out how often the dark tomboy heroine (Maggie Tulliver, Gypsy Breynton, Jo March, Lucinda Wyman, Laura Ingalls Wilder) is contrasted with the ladylike girl, the blonde one, the sister or cousin or friend, and how the tomboy's "darkness" in turn connects her to other "dark" people, leading her to identify with them or befriend them in some way. Lucinda and her friend Tony share a picnic with old Rags-an'-Bottles, the man who drives the rubbish cart. Gypsy shocks her cousin Joy by rescuing a crying beggar-child on the streets of Boston. Caddie Wood-lawn rides off into the dark to warn Indian Jo that the settlers are plotting a massacre.

Meanwhile the mothers and aunts and guardians persist in their efforts to turn their harum-scarum charges into women like themselves. Laura's mother scolds her for yelling like an Indian, and constantly urges her to wear her sunbonnet. Caddie turns twelve, and Mrs. Woodlawn thinks that is "time to begin to be a young lady."

"When I was her age, I could make bread and jell and six kinds of cakes, including plum, not to mention all the samplers I had stitched. . . . And what does Caddie know how to do?"

"I can plow," said Caddie, with a twinkle in her eye . . .

"Plow!" exclaimed Mrs. Woodlawn, rolling her eyes and holding up her hands. "Yes, my daughter knows how to plow!"[12]

Plowing is, of course, no kind of occupation for a lady. But then, what tomboy wants to be a lady in the first place? If these books are any evidence, most tomboys would rather not be girls at all.[13] The extraordinary *Merrylips* (set at the time of the English Civil War), is actually dedicated, "To every little girl who has wished for an hour to be a little boy." Its central character dreams for years that she might somehow escape the strictures of biology, and grow up to be a boy. "To be a boy meant to run and play with no hindering petticoats to catch the heels and trip the toes. It meant to go away to school or to camp. It meant to be a soldier and have adventures."[14]

Girls, alas, are not supposed to have adventures. They are supposed to stay at home and do what they are told: to sit on a cushion and sew a fine seam. When Merrylips goes to war, she goes disguised as a boy. It is as if she cannot even conceive of courage or adventure in female terms. Sadly she lays aside her boy's clothes at the end of the book. "Fare thee well!" she tells them. "I'm a lass – godmother's lass – henceforth!" And she bids farewell to her boy self too. "Fare thee well, Tibbott Venner, forever and ever."[15]

This yearning for boys' freedom and achievement, boys' adventures (and then the renunciation of those things), is a painfully constant theme throughout children's tomboy literature. Few authors succeed in imbuing female achievements with the same glamour, though Susan Coolidge does her best. Here, for example, Katy Carr draws on half-remembered images of Grace Darling and Joan of Arc as she struggles to articulate her future career: "Perhaps . . . it will be rowing out in boats, and saving people's lives, like that girl in the book. Or perhaps I shall go and nurse in the hospital, like Miss Nightingale. Or else I'll head a crusade and ride on a white horse, with armor and a helmet on my head, and carry a sacred flag. Or if I don't do that, I'll paint pictures, or sing, or scalp – sculp – what is it? Anyhow, it shall be *something*."[16]

Jo March, too, dreams of doing "something very splendid," something heroic or wonderful that won't be forgotten after she's dead. She doesn't know what it is yet, but declares she's "on the watch for it," and means to astonish her family some day. "I think I shall write books, and get rich and famous."[17]

But as the plots unfold, neither girl achieves success in quite the terms she'd hoped. Katy falls from the barn-swing and lies crippled for four long years. Her Cousin Helen (herself a long-suffering invalid) takes her in hand, talking to her about "God's School," which is "The School of Pain"[18] with its lessons of Patience, Cheerfulness, and Making the Best of Things. Katy learns these lessons all too well. Although she does, eventually, learn to walk again, by the end of the book the naughty, awkward, impulsive heroine has completely disappeared. In her place we have a new Katy, whose "gentle expression . . . womanly look . . . pleasant voice . . . politeness" bespeak not a spark of quirkiness or originality.[19]

Jo, too, changes enormously over the course of *Little Women*. She publishes several of her stories, it is true, but is then urged to give up her writing, so she can take better care of her family.[20] By the time Mr. March comes back from the wars he finds not his "son Jo," but instead, "a young lady who pins her collar straight, laces her boots neatly, and neither whistles, talks slang, nor lies on the rug."[21] He claims to miss his "wild girl," but declares that if he gets a "strong, helpful, tender-hearted woman" in her place, he'll be quite satisfied.

Hannah's father (in *Middl'un*) and Caddie's father (in *Caddie Woodlawn*) make similar statements, designed to coax their errant daughters across the border into traditional womanhood. "I want you to be a woman with a wise and understanding heart," says Mr. Woodlawn, "healthy in body and . . . in mind." For a moment this seems reasonable enough. But the attentive reader will hear a certain insistence in the words that follow: "Do you think you would like to be growing up into that woman *now?*"[22]

As a committed tomboy of whatever age, it is hard not to rage against these speeches, especially as they are almost always made not by the mother/aunt/guardian figure, against whom the tomboy has been pitted throughout the story, but by the one grown-up she trusts: the beloved father (or in Merrylips's case, the beloved godmother), whom she has tried so hard to please. It is exactly this love, this loyalty, that traps her in the end, a pressure more effective than all the women's chivying and scolding.

Of the books I have looked at here, not one includes a tomboy who remains untamed into adulthood. Gypsy Breynton, that bright spirit, promises well in the first books of the series. *She* is not going to get married, she declares. *She* is not going to stay at home and keep house and look sober with her hair tied up behind. "I'd rather be an old maid and have a pony, and run round in the woods."[23] But by the third book, Gypsy, too, has suffered a sea change. When her brother Tom falls into bad ways, it is she who rescues him, becoming in the process "such a model of a little sister" as to astonish him beyond measure.[24] He calls her a "firstrate fellow," and his later achievements at college are attributed entirely to her.

In the fourth and final book, Gypsy leaves home for boarding school, where she makes friends with another tomboy, Jo. But Gypsy's mother disapproves, for Jo is "loud of laughter and noisy of speech; she shouted on the street; she sang at the window when boys were going by."[25] Worst of all, "Jo inclined to being a boy. . . . She was sorry that she was made a woman. She wished she were a man."[26] And although Gypsy herself does not share this trait,[27] it is Mrs. Breynton who is given the last word. "If you decide to be a woman, be a woman. It may be as brave and strong and bright and learned, and independent a woman as it chooses, but *it must not degrade itself by aping something which it was never destined to be, and never can be, try as hard as it may.*"[28] Biology, in other words, will always triumph. Every tomboy must grow up and be a woman.

In Ruth Sawyer's *Roller Skates*, this requirement is suspended, at least for the duration of the story. The book is, in fact, framed as a kind of childhood sabbatical, a hymn of praise to tomboy liberty and independence. Lucinda's parents are away in Italy, and her brothers are conveniently disposed of elsewhere. For Lucinda, this "year of being an orphan" is "the very loveliest year of all."[29] She has no idea what might lie on the other side of it, and no real desire to find out. Instead, she imagines staying on alone, skating in Central Park for ever and ever. "Somebody else could have it – could be eleven who wanted to. She didn't." [30]

In real life, of course, no one gets to stay on in the park for ever and ever. And in Ruth Sawyer's sequel, *The Year of Jubilo,* Lucinda, too, is forced to do some growing up. Her father has just died, and she and her brothers are catapulted up to Maine, along with their helpless mother. The boys literally divide the world between them: one fishing, one planting a garden, one working in the woods beyond the house. As the only girl, Lucinda is left in charge of the kitchen, even though she can't really cook. Her efforts to join in the boys' adventures are often thwarted, and not even the boistrous emphasis on "Wyman solidarity," or her friendship with an independent-minded Irish girl, take away the sad, sour feeling that in this book, Lucinda, too, has been betrayed. [31]

But if good-girl capitulation were the only theme, no tomboy book would have survived past its first printing. Despite the conscious intentions of their authors, books like *Little Women* and *What Katy Did* (and *Roller Skates* and the *Little House* series) also carry a very different and more subversive message. "Copy me!" they say. "Watch what I do! See, you can do it too!" Again and again, it is as if some truth were being vouched for, some celebration of physical exuberance and daring, of delicious disobedience and ambition. Perhaps because so many tomboy books are, in fact, surreptitious portraits of their author, such ambition is often framed in literary terms.[32]

For Simone de Beauvoir, *Little Women* was the "one book in which I believed I had caught a glimpse of my future self." She identified passionately with Jo. "Brusque and bony, Jo clambered into trees when she wanted to read; she was much more tomboyish and daring than I was, but I shared her horror of sewing and housekeeping and her love of books. She wrote: in order to imitate her more completely, I composed two or three short stories." [33] Cynthia Ozick, too, has described how Jo erupted into her consciousness. "I read *Little Women* a thousand times. Ten thousand! I am no longer incognito, not even to myself. I am Jo in her 'vortex'; not Jo exactly, but some Jo-of-the-future. I am under an enchantment: who I truly am must be deferred, waited for and waited for." [34]

Both Ozick and de Beauvoir did, of course, become writers when they grew up. Nor were they the only ones. Carolyn Heilbrun has written brilliantly on this. In her view, Jo is "the daimon, the unique girl who dared to speak as [the aspiring writers] felt. . . . In fiction her children were boys. [But in life] her true children were girls who grew up and went to Paris and did wonderful things." [35]

3.

But however beloved and inspiring, there are issues that the tomboy classics never raise, exactly because they were always meant as children's books. Despite the age range of their various heroines (from Merrylips's eight or so to Jo March's fifteen), the atmosphere of most is a perpetual twelve. Rereading them at thirty-nine, I found myself asking what was missing – what an unabashed adult collection might look like. What if the tomboy were free, for once, from the moral straitjacket of the Young Adult plot, the painfully predictable ending? What if she were not just white and North American, but Black and Hispanic and European and Asian? What if she were allowed to exist in all her ages, from fierce little girlhood and on past puberty into adulthood, and the full late flowering of tom-old-ladyhood? What kind of life might she invent for herself? Would she get married? Would she become a lesbian? How would she meet the challenges of middle and old age?

As my project gathered momentum, I began to look seriously for such stories, turning first to adult classics like *Orlando* and *The Member of the Wedding,* and moving on to more recent books like *The Woman Warrior* by Maxine Hong Kingston, *Sacred Country* by Rose Tremain, and *Stone Butch Blues* by Leslie Feinberg. Soon I had a new list of tomboy heroines, drawn not from children's books this time, but from adult novels and short stories and autobiography. It included Leslie Feinberg's Jess, Carson McCullers's Frankie, Rose Tremain's Mary/Martin, and Toni Morrison's Sula. There were also such real-life examples as Anne LaBastille and Teresa Jordan; Colette's mother, Sido; and (stretching the definition to its furthest) the girl gangsters in Maria Hinojosa's *Crews.*

I took certain risks in deciding what kinds of writing to include. None of the books I drew from (except, perhaps, *The Member of the Wedding*) came with a tag marked, "Tomboy Literature: Essential Text!" But by then I was so immersed in the genre that it was easy for me to define what I was looking for: a certain liveliness and fervor in my tomboy heroine, a certain authenticity of spirit. I looked, too, for the hallmarks of gender disobedience and physical courage, the deliberate flouting of traditional feminine behavior. But as I organized my findings (arranging them chronologically, from "Tombabies" and "Tomboys" through "Tomboys Resurgent"), it was always that feisty tomboy spirit I returned to, watching in delight as it emerged again and again from its shackles, "independent, actively willing, original." [36]

The youngest tomboys – my "tombabies" – are lively little girls of four and five and six, full of energy and wild imagination. As the adult world presses upon them (most usually in the person of their mothers), some are able to switch easily between roles. Catherine Petroski's girlchild, for example, believes herself to be a horse, perhaps the last mustang. "When there are girl things to do . . . like read . . . or go in the car . . . for ice cream, I have to be a girl, but when there are hillsides of grass and forests . . . I am a horse."

Other tombabies insist more fiercely on their own imaginative truth. Linda Smukler's narrator, for instance, declares that she is "really a drummer." She drums most of the day and on through family dinner. "If I drum, all dinners will be done, and I can take off my skirt." Soon her drumming knocks over a glass, drenching her in milk. Gladly she escapes upstairs. "I take off my skirt full of milk and leave it on the floor. I find my jeans and put them on."

Again and again, contemporary tomboys take off their "skirts full of milk," replacing their culturally defined girl selves, their incipient woman selves, with the outfit that for them is magical. Smukler's child imagines herself in lederhosen and a purple shirt, carrying a stick with a red bandanna on the end. Everything she owns is tied up in that bandanna: "A metal plate. A knife. A flint. A fishing line and a hook. One pair of socks and an extra shoelace." This joyous minimalism, this undressing to dress again in the *right* clothes, this gathering together of the *right* equipment, is a scene that recurs throughout the anthology.

In her flight from femininity, her passion for escape, Smukler's narrator is one of a vast company of rebel girls. See, for example, the excerpt from Sandra Cisneros's *The House on Mango Street*, where Esperanza of the dusty hair and dirty blouse declares that she will not "grow up tame like the others." She will be different. Already she has begun her own quiet war. Already she "leaves the table like a man, without putting back the chair or picking up the plate."

The sense that men, in their selfishness, can provide a liberating role model appears again in the excerpt from Nadezhda Durova's *The Cavalry Maiden* and in Nina Newington's short story "Man." More often, however, tomboys model themselves on boys, in particular their older brothers and boy-cousins. With some exceptions (I think of the protagonist in Lara Cardella's *Good Girls Don't Wear Trousers*), the issue is not maleness per se. Most tomboys do not actually want to *be* boys. Rather, they covet a boy's freedom and independence: the opportunity to explore and have adventures, the acceptance of physical risk. For the girls in Ursula K. Le Guin's "Horse Camp," "freedom is to run. Freedom is galloping." For Simone de Beauvoir's best friend, Zaza, it is permission to do "the cartwheel, the splits and all other kinds of tricks," to climb trees and hang down from the branches by her hands.

But as tomboys approach puberty, their stories begin to change, becoming less innocent, less blithely exuberant. Major discoveries are made, about love or lust or sex or menstruation, the enormous grown-up facts of life and death. Carson McCullers's Frankie (in *The Member of the Wedding*), feels especially disoriented and overwhelmed. She is quite literally terrified of growing up: "This August she was twelve and five-sixth years old. She was five feet and three-quarter inches tall, and she wore a number seven shoe. . . . If she reached her height on her eighteenth birthday, she had five and one-sixth growing years ahead of her. Therefore, according to mathematics, and unless she could somehow stop herself, she would grow to be over nine feet tall. And what would be a lady who is over five feet tall? She would be a Freak."

Frankie is hardly the first lanky literary tomboy. Jo March and Katy Carr were both unusually tall. Jo "had the uncomfortable appearance of a girl who is rapidly shooting up into a woman and *didn't like it*"[37], and Katy was "the *longest* girl that was ever seen . . . all legs and elbows, and angles and joints."[38] But Frankie is one of the first tomboys whose horror and panic at her changing body is actually given space on the page.[39] She is also one of the first to carry her tomboy curiosity into the sexual arena. See, for example, the scene with the young soldier, which she escapes only by biting down hard (on his tongue!) and braining him with a glass pitcher.[40]

Still, Frankie, too, is tamed in the end, and in classic style. She drops her tomboy moniker (and all variants thereof) and returns to her given name, the flat and ladylike "Frances." She becomes best friends with a plump "marshmal-low white" girl called Mary Littlejohn, someone her old self would have heartily despised. Her tomboy ambitions flare up from time to time – Frances plans to be "a great poet – or else the foremost authority on radar." But they are soon submerged.[41]

Frankie's story is not the only one, however. Contemporary tomboys have a wider range of options than their predecessors. The narrator in Maxine Hong Kingston's *The Woman Warrior* tells of a mythical warrior apprenticeship. Becky Birtha's Johnnieruth sets her sights on "being different," and is inspired by her encounter with her first lesbian couple. Meanwhile, Cora Sandel's "child who loved roads," an incipient artist, like so many tomboy narrators, fights hard to preserve her childhood energy and authenticity. "No one should grow up," she thinks. "Children should stay children and rule the whole world."

Most classic tomboy books abandon their protagonist in her middle teens, just over the border into puberty. Their entire plot unfolds in four or five years. No mention is made of what comes after that – of the ways in which a tomboy girlhood impinges upon adolescence, or, indeed, upon later adult life.[42] What happens to that energy and ambition, that courage, that insistent curiosity? Is the tomboy really tamed, as all the old books say? Or does she somehow find a way to survive?

It is clear from the stories that some tomboys do indeed go into a kind of hibernation around puberty. Susan Moon, for example, was a joyously self-confident tomboy child. Then puberty hit, "like a curtain coming down," and for years she felt ashamed, "claimed by [her] tribe, marked irrevocably as a second-class citizen. . . . Physical exuberance was gone."

Other tomboys, less inhibited or vulnerable, somehow manage to translate that physical exuberance into sexual terms. Alice Munro's Del, for instance, in *Lives of Girls and Women*, does her best to explore sex and sexuality in whatever ways she can, in the hopes that she too, like the men, will be able to "take on all sorts of experience . . . shuck off what [she doesn't] want, and come back proud." Forty years ago, Del would have been called a "hoyden."[43] Nowadays, her transgressions seem touchingly mild. Compare, for example, the Puerto Rican girl gangsters in Maria Hinojosa's *Crews*. All week long, they do what they are told, obey their parents, go to school, do their homework, and clean house. But when Friday comes, they burst out onto the streets. "We . . . hang out and act like there wasn't no law. . . . We . . . throw garbage cans . . . throw ice when it snows, we . . . chase guys. We . . . beat up guys."

It is not usual to label such girls "tomboys" – or "hoydens" either, for that matter. And yet after all, why not? Does a tomboy cease to be a tomboy because she puts on lipstick and gold earrings, because she finds herself pregnant? Is age and sexuality the issue here, or ethnicity and class? Are all tomboys still assumed to be prepubescent white girls? And if so, how does one categorize these street-wise warrior girls? How honor their ability to fight, their fierce loyalty to their friends? "We don't want to see our sisters get hurt," says one of the girls in *Crews*. And again, "I trust the crew more than I trust any guy."[44]

If one version of the tomboy adolescent is the heterosexual "bad girl," carrying her physical liveliness and daring into the forbidden realm of sex and sexuality, another is the girl who grows up to be a lesbian. Once again, the barrier of puberty is crucial. What is seen as charming in a nine-year-old tomboy (her boyish ways, her adventurous spirit) becomes in the adolescent "freakish" or "perverted."[45] Such epithets are painful even for the heterosexual teenager. For the young lesbian, they can be genuinely life-threatening. Bia Lowe has written powerfully of her own experience: "Teendom was a setup for failed assimilation. I was bullied into forfeiting the things I did best. . . . I was called a lez." The word itself was terrifying. "*Lez* lodged inside me like a burr. It had come to name me, to claim the longing I was supposed to outgrow."

Other tomboys have a yet harder battle, struggling to create the physical self that feels right to them, and then to come out as transgendered or transsexual. The fictional Mary/Martin in Rose Tremain's *Sacred Country* is a case in point. From the age of six, Mary is convinced that there's been a mistake. "I am not a girl," she thinks. "I am a boy." When breasts appear, she treats them like intruders, "as if something had laid two eggs under her skin, and now these parasites were growing on her."

The sense of incongruity persists, and by the age of twenty-one, Mary is desperate. Then a friend directs her to the help she needs, and she embarks upon a course of hormone treatment. Soon her outward appearance begins to match her inner sense of herself. When a boat attendant addresses her as "lad," she is delighted. "The word 'lad' stabbed me with pleasure."

But not everyone is so strongly male-identified. For Jess Goldberg, semi-autobiographical protagonist of Leslie Feinberg's novel, *Stone Butch Blues,* the anguish has a less obvious solution. "I don't feel like a man trapped in a woman's body," says Jess. "I just feel trapped."

Like Virginia Woolf's Orlando, Jess Goldberg is both man and woman: s/he "know[s] the secrets, share[s] the weaknesses of each." But unlike Orlando, Jess cannot move unnoticed or unscathed across the sexual divide. There is punishment for confusing people, punishment for "being different," for insisting that clothes, genitals, and pronouns need not always match. As Minnie Bruce Pratt has written about her real-life relationship with Leslie Feinberg, most people don't know what to do with a world in which "gender and sex are fluid." Such "bothness" seems freakish to them, deeply troubling. It calls to mind the "women-men of the sideshow at the circus . . . tawdry, pitiful, hidden, wasted."

Pratt's words remind me of Frankie Addams, and her horror of the Freaks at the county fair, her terror of their long Freak eyes. Such feelings are familiar ones: powerful and well-ensconced. While they're left unexamined, there will be little compassion or generosity for the grown-up tomboy. Those like Jess who insist on male clothes, male appearance and accomplishments, while at the same time maintaining a visible female "otherness," will be seen as especially threatening.

But even the heterosexual white woman, seen as "ordinary" or "acceptable" by the dominant culture, may not find it so easy to carry that feisty tomboy spirit on into adulthood and early middle age. Raised on the classic plot, with its handful of prepubescent adventures, she may scarcely recognize the "tomboy trajectory" as it extends through time, or value those few women who model it successfully. For her, tomboyhood will be a lost thing, shrouded in nostalgia. Gail Griffin, for example, writes yearningly of her long-ago summer camp: "a place out of time, stretching from little-girlhood across the great divide into womanhood . . . a place where girls could be strong and weak, stupid and smart, silly and serious . . . could learn and take chances and fail and triumph, all of it apart from the gender-police, the sexual straitjacketing of Real World adolescence. . . . Was it the first time in my life I felt free? It was certainly the last."

Other women, such as Susan Moon, abandon their tomboy selves in adolescence or early adulthood, only to recover them (with gusto!) later on. Moon, now in her fifties, is clearly delighted by the tomboy's return. "My nine-year-old self thinks it would be a good idea for me to join a friend in Maine . . . to photograph the blueberry barrens. . . . She says I never have to brush my hair again, unless I want to. She says it's not too late to learn to play the drums."

This recovery of the "lost" or "inner" tomboy can be a powerfully transformative experience. Pamela Meyer, another tom-old-lady correspondent, wrote to me of the "exciting psycho/spiritual journey" which exploded in her forties, and through which she was able to connect with her own "inner masculine." This male self became for her a tremendous friend and ally, and (movingly to me) she called him Tom. "He brought me back, in many ways, to the twelve-year-old tomboy I'd lost and mourned without ever quite knowing it." [46]

For a rare few, however, the tomboy doesn't need to be recovered. She is alive and well throughout a woman's life. [47] Anne LaBastille, for instance, grew up in the New Jersey suburbs, with a mother who wanted her to become a young lady. Lonely and rebellious, she buried herself in boys' adventure stories, built herself a tree-house, and spent hours there reading. Those early tomboy years helped fuel a lifetime of gorgeous risk-taking, from building a cabin in the wilderness – with no road, electricity, phone, or indoor plumbing – to back-packing alone across the six-million-acre Adirondack Park, and later travelling 4,000 miles up and down the Amazon River.

In Colette's memoir of her mother, Sido, that same indomitable spirit flares up again. Sido is in her seventies, old and sick; she can no longer do her chores as she once did. And yet, again and again, she insists on doing them: on hauling the heavy bucket up from the well, on splitting the firewood on the oaken block, on rescuing the dizzy cat from the rooftop. Youthful and mischievous, sturdy, disobedient, she is a tom-old-lady to the last, "her little gray septuagenarian's plait of hair turning up like a scorpion's tail at the nape of her neck," her back bent to the task, sawing her wood in her own backyard.

Coda

At the front of my copy of *Gypsy Breynton,* there is a bookplate made out in the name of Hilda Rice Ayer. It shows a powerful black stallion leaping a high stone wall. Inside the wall is a beautiful white house surrounded by a well-kept garden. It is a spacious, pleasant house, with a long, glassed-in conservatory, the sort of house that people envy. But the horse does not envy it. The horse only wants to get away.

As I gathered stories for this anthology, I thought often of that horse: its energy and determination, its sheer physical exuberance. It seemed natural to identify it with the tomboy spirit in the girl. Nor was I the first to make such an analogy. "I was born with a boy's spirit under my bib and tucker," wrote Louisa May Alcott in her memoirs. "I always thought I must have been a deer or a horse in some former state, because it was such a joy to me to run. No boy could be my friend till I had beaten him in a race, and no girl if she refused to climb trees, leap fences and be a tomboy."[48]

There it is again, that crucial word. Word of ardor, word of freedom and disobedience. It is easy to believe we don't need such a word anymore, that the bad old days are gone, that girls (and by extension women too) are free to do anything they want in life.[49] After all, some women have achieved immense success. I think of track-and-field star Jackie Joyner-Kersee, the only person to have won back-to-back gold medals in the Olympic heptathlon. I think of Barbara McClintock, winning the Nobel Prize for a lifetime's research in molecular biology. I think of women artists and writers and politicians: of Georgia O'Keeffe and Toni Morrison and Bella Abzug and Mary Robinson, of all those who (like Anne LaBastille) have hewn so persistently to their own chosen interests that they have opened a way for others to follow.

But the fact remains that most girls have little hope of fulfilling their potential in such lavish terms. Often they are deprived *even of the knowledge* that there are those who have.[50] Small wonder that while seven- to eleven-year-olds (my "tombabies" and "tomboys") are lively and irreverent and bold, girls in ninth grade ("On the Threshold") have already begun to lose themselves. Their IQ scores are plummeting, they have become deferential, self-critical, depressed; they're abandoning their questing, energetic selves.[51]

All the more crucial, then, to provide what role models we can, whether through books or radio, television, video, or film. All the more crucial to unlock the stable-door and let that tomboy horse run free, forward into her own untrammelled days.

---

1. Pamela Meyer, personal communication.
2. The definitions are taken from *The Oxford English Dictionary* (New York: Oxford University Press, 1971) and from *Chambers Twentieth Century Dictionary* (Edinburgh: W & R Chambers, 1972).
3. Louisa May Alcott, *Little Women* (1868; edited and with an introduction by Elaine Showalter, New York: Penguin Books, 1989, p. 3). Compare Nigel Nicolson's remark about his mother, Vita Sackville-West, in his introduction to her book *Challenge:* "Not to have been born a boy was her lifelong regret" (New York: Avon Books, 1975), p. 11.
4. See the bibliography for publishers and dates of these books.
5. The *Gypsy* books came out in 1866 and 1867, just before *Little Women* (1868) and *What Katy Did* (1872). They were written in haste (all four within a year), at $150 apiece, and published by the Massachusetts Sabbath Society. See Elizabeth Stuart Phelps, *Chapters from a Life* (Boston: Houghton Mifflin, 1896), p. 85. See also Elizabeth Segel's "The *Gypsy Breynton* Series: Setting the Pattern for American Tomboy Heroines," *Children's Literature Association Quarterly*, vol. 14, no. 2 (summer 1989), pp. 67–71.
6. Elizabeth Stuart Phelps, *Gypsy Breynton* (1866; New York: Dodd, Mead and Co., 1894).
7. Elizabeth Stuart Phelps, p. 70. The author herself felt strongly about this, arguing, for example, that the phrase "dressed to kill" had ceased to be a metaphor. "I believe," she wrote in her memoir, *Chapters from a Life*, "that the methods of dress practiced among women are a marked hindrance to the realization of [their own best] possibilities, and should be scorned or persuaded out of society." See Elizabeth Stuart Phelps, *Chapters from a Life*, pp. 250–251.
8. Susan Coolidge [Pseud. Sarah Chauncey Woolsey], *What Katy Did* (1872; Boston: Little, Brown & Co., 1938), p. 12.
9. Hazel Wolf, personal communication.
10. Carol Ryrie Brink, *Caddie Woodlawn* (1935; New York: Collier Books, 1970), p. 12.
11. Elizabeth Segel, p. 68. See, too, *The Mill on the Floss*, in which George Eliot compares Maggie Tulliver to her delicate cousin Lucy. "It was like the contrast between a rough, dark,

overgrown puppy and a white kitten." George Eliot, *The Mill on the Floss* (1860; New York: W. W. Norton & Co., 1994), p. 52.

12. Carol Ryrie Brink, pp. 98 – 99. Compare the remark of Gwen Raverat's granddaughter, Anne, quoted in *Period Piece:* "Grandmamma, when I am grown up, I think I shall be a witch. There are too many ladies, don't you think?" Gwen Raverat, *Period Piece: A Cambridge Childhood* (London: Faber & Faber, 1952), p. 75.

13. See, for example, thirteen-year-old Hannah in Elizabeth Burleson's *Middl'un,* who, like Jo March, is her father's "son" and proud of it. When her sister Lissa tells her she should "act her age," Hannah is outraged. "Act my age? Why, I can ride all day with Pa and help as good as a – " But Lissa doesn't let her finish. "Act your *girl* age!" she emphasizes. "And you know very well what that means. You're a girl whether you want to be or not." Elizabeth Burleson, *Middl'un* (Chicago: Follett Publishing Co., 1968), p. 34.

Once again, the fictional tomboy is wonderfully corroborated by her real-life counterpart. Elizabeth McMahan, a retired termite specialist at the University of Chapel Hill, and a tom-old-lady in her own right, was told at age six or seven that if a girl could kiss her elbow she would turn into a boy. "I nearly dislocated my arm in the attempt, calling on Aunt Mary and Aunt Mag to witness my success. But they always said no, I hadn't quite done it, and anyway, what was wrong with being a girl?" (Elizabeth McMahan, personal communication)

14. Beaulah Marie Dix, *Merrylips* (London: Macmillan Publishers, 1906), p. 6. See also Lois Lenski's *Texas Tomboy* (Philadelphia: J. B. Lippincott Co., 1950), with its poignant dedication, "For Mary, who was never allowed to be a tomboy."

15. Beaulah Marie Dix, p. 307. Only towards the very end of the book does Merrylips begin to recognize that her beloved godmother is herself a hero. Hannah in *Middl'un* learns the same lesson. "Pa had always been first with me, a hero to worship, a model to live up to. Now, slowly, the idea began to take shape in my mind that Ma was a sort of hero too." Elizabeth Burleson, p. 98.

16. Susan Coolidge, p. 26.

17. Louisa May Alcott, p. 143.

18. Susan Coolidge, pp. 172–173.

19. Susan Coolidge, p. 270.

20. Louisa May Alcott, p. 446. It is as if Alcott believes that it would somehow be wrong or dangerous for Jo to admit her own ambition. Alcott herself built a successful career as a literary spinster, glorying in her professionalism and independence. Travelling in Europe after the success of *Little Women,* she signed her letters "spinsterhood forever," and wrote of the "sweet independence of the spinster's life." See Carolyn G. Heilbrun, "Alcott's *Little Women,*" in *Hamlet's Mother and Other Women* (New York: Ballantine Books, 1990), p. 170. But it is not until Jo is long married, and responsibly ensconced in her community, that she is allowed to fulfill her dreams of literary success. For a hilarious account of the consequences see Chapter 3, "Jo's Last Scrape," in *Jo's Boys,* the third book of the *Little Women* series. Louisa May Alcott, *Jo's Boys* (1886: Boston: Little, Brown & Co., 1942), pp. 37–59.

For further discussion of these issues, see, too, Elizabeth Segel, "Tomboy Taming and Gender-Role Socialization: The Evidence of Children's Books," in *Gender Roles Through the Life Span: A Multidisciplinary Perspective,* edited by Michael R. Stevenson (Muncie, Ind., Ball State University, 1994), p. 58.

21. Louisa May Alcott, p. 223. Alcott, too, was known as her father's son.

22. Carol Ryrie Brink, p. 216. My emphasis. See also Elizabeth Burleson, p. 182.

23. Elizabeth Stuart Phelps, *Gypsy's Cousin Joy* (1866; New York: A. D. Porter Co., 1894), p. 200.

24. Elizabeth Stuart Phelps, *Gypsy's Sowing and Reaping* (1866; New York: A. D. Porter Co., 1894), p. 217.

25. Elizabeth Stuart Phelps, *Gypsy's Year at the Golden Crescent* (1867; New York: Dodd, Mead & Co., 1876), p. 198.

26. Elizabeth Stuart Phelps, *Gypsy's Year at the Golden Crescent*, p. 199.

27. "Why I wouldn't be a boy for anything in the world," Gypsy says. "I think they're horrid!" See Elizabeth Stuart Phelps, *Gypsy's Year at the Golden Crescent*, p. 202.

28. Elizabeth Stuart Phelps, *Gypsy's Year at the Golden Crescent*, p. 197. My emphasis.

29. Ruth Sawyer, *Roller Skates* (1936; New York: Puffin, 1986), p. 5.

30. Ruth Sawyer, p. 185

31. This feeling is exacerbated at intervals throughout the book; for instance, when Lucinda's brother, Duncan, favors her with the usual lecture on womanly compliance. "You've reached the point where the poet says childhood and womanhood meet. . . . You can grow more cantankerous, or you can grow gentle. You can stay a fighting, disagreeable hoyden, or you can grow in understanding, in a gentle giving-in that won't hurt you." Ruth Sawyer, *The Year of Jubilo* (New York: Viking Press, 1940), p. 25.

32. Jo and Katy, Lucinda and Laura, are all voracious readers, and Jo and Lucinda see themselves as writers too. Lucinda keeps a daily diary (a delight to read!) crammed with her own, ever-expanding enthusiasms. Jo scribbles away in her beloved attic, "her papers spread out upon a trunk before her, while Scrabble, the pet rat, promenaded the beams overhead." See Louisa May Alcott, p. 147. Scenes like these combine to imply that the richest, most satisfying adventure is, after all, the author's own: growing up to write the story of her girlhood self, and like Jo, signing her name with a gorgeous flourish at the end.

    Another, more recent literary tomboy is, of course, Louise Fitzhugh's *Harriet the Spy*. Harriet is determined to be a writer when she grows up, and never goes anywhere without her notebook. See Louise Fitzhugh, *Harriet the Spy* (New York: Harper & Row, Publishers, 1964).

33. Simone de Beauvoir, *Memoirs of a Dutiful Daughter* (New York: Harper & Row, Publishers, 1959), pp. 89, 90.

34. Cynthia Ozick, "A Drugstore in Winter," in *Art & Ardor* (New York: Alfred A. Knopf, 1983), p. 303.

35. Carolyn G. Heilbrun, pp. 173–174.

36. Adrienne Rich, quoted in Carolyn G. Heilbrun, p. 171.

37. Louisa May Alcott, p. 4. My emphasis.

38. Susan Coolidge, p. 12.

39. See, too, Stephen's outcry in *The Well of Loneliness:* "It's my face . . . something's wrong with my face." Stephen hates parties, and for years is afraid that people will laugh at her. Radclyffe Hall, *The Well of Loneliness* (1928; New York: Doubleday, 1990), p. 73.

40. Carson McCullers, *The Member of the Wedding* (1946; New York: Bantam Books, 1950), p. 130. This scene is not included in my excerpt.

41. Carson McCullers, p. 150. Again, this scene is not included here.

42. *Little Women* is an exception to this, of course, as are its sequels, *Little Men* (1871; Boston: Little, Brown & Co., 1943) and *Jo's Boys* (1886; Boston: Little, Brown & Co., 1942), in which "Mrs. Jo" is seen to flourish well into comfortable middle age. See, too, Laura Ingalls Wilder's account of a tomboy's early married life with its all-too-real adventures: its hailstorms and house fires and domestic tragedies, all occurring between the ages of eighteen and twenty-two. Laura Ingalls Wilder, *The First Four Years* (New York: Harper & Row, Publishers, 1971).

43. "Hoyden" is an interesting word, thought to have come from the Dutch *heiden*, a heathen or gypsy. It is often used as a synonym for "tomboy." But there is a sexual connotation too, which "tomboy" has long since lost.

44. Compare other tomboy friendships included here: the live-wire electricity between Sula and Nel in the excerpt from Toni Morrison's *Sula;* the passionate alliance between Lizzie and the narrator in the short story "Lizzie Higgins." Such accounts are still rare, perhaps because so many tomboys have been understood as solitary: awkward exceptions to the usual girlish rule. Homophobia may also be an issue, especially for the authors of children's books.

45. I think here of Frankie's horror that she herself may be a "Freak"; and also of Gypsy Breynton's mother, and her outrage at girls like Jo who "ape what they were never destined to be." See Elizabeth Stuart Phelps, *Gypsy's Year at the Golden Crescent*, p. 202.

46. Pamela Meyer, personal communication.

47. Compare, too, the following from an old friend in New Mexico, currently running a real estate business in Santa Fe, "Do you know that tomboys have all the fun? If I hadn't been one I wouldn't have nearly the life I have today – tree forts became spec houses, romping in the woods became treks to Nepal and the South San Juans. Wrestling with boys became hot foreplay . . . [and] learning to cuss with the guys has stood me well in business." (Pamela Christie, personal communication.)

48. Louisa May Alcott, quoted in *Louisa May Alcott: Her Life, Letters and Journals*, edited by Edriah D. Cheney (Boston: Roberts Brothers, 1892).

49. See, for example, a discussion that takes place in *Tomboy*, a contemporary children's book by Norma Klein. A group of ten-year-old girls are talking over who or what they'd like to be (a boy, a horse, a dog), when the mother of one of them walks in. "I used to want to be a boy," she admits. "How come you stopped?" asks one of the girls. "Well . . ." answers the mother. "I don't know exactly when . . . I guess when I began to feel there wasn't anything I could do as a boy that I couldn't do as a girl."

    "But that's not true," exclaims her daughter, Libby. "Boys can do more things!"

    "Phoeey," the mother answers. "That's just an excuse." Norma Klein, *Tomboy* (New York: Simon & Schuster, 1978), p. 73.

50. In the average classroom, girls are exposed to almost three times as many boy-centered stories as girl-centered stories; they read six times as many biographies of men as of women. Even in animal stories, the animals are twice as likely to be males. See "How Schools Shortchange Girls," quoted in Mary Pipher, *Reviving Ophelia: Saving the Selves of Adolescent Girls* (New York: Grosset Books, 1994), p. 62.

51. This self-loss has been documented over and over. See, for example, Barbara A. Kerr's *Smart Girls, Gifted Women* (Columbus, Ohio: Ohio Publishing Co., 1985), Mira and David Sadker's *Failing at Fairness: How America's Schools Shortchange Girls* (New York: Charles Scribner's Sons and Maxwell Macmillan International Publishing Co., 1994), and numerous books by Carol Gilligan and others.

PART ONE

Tombabies

Catherine Petroski

Beautiful My Mane in the Wind

Catherine Petroski was born in St. Louis in 1939. She is the author of Gravity and Other Stories *(1981) and* Beautiful My Mane in the Wind *(1983). She has taught at the University of North Carolina at Chapel Hill and at Duke University.*

I AM A HORSE, PERHAPS THE LAST MUSTANG.

This is my yard, this is my pasture. And I told her I hate her. My dam-mother. She does not understand horses. She doesn't even try. There are many things she doesn't notice about me.

Horses move their feet like this.

Horses throw their heads like this, when they are impatient, about to dash away to some shady tree. See how beautiful my mane in the wind.

Horses snort.

Horses whinny.

Horses hate her.

I am a girl horse. I am building a house under the loquat tree. It is taking me a long time.

My house is made of logs, logs that Daddy doesn't want. That is because our fireplace goes nowhere. It is just a little cave in the wall because this is Texas and it is mostly hot here. Our fireplace has a permanent fake log. I am six.

I will be six next month.

Anyway that is why I got the real logs when our weeping willow died and Mama pushed it over one Sunday afternoon. The bottom of the trunk was rotten and the tree just fell over and Mama laughed and the baby laughed and I didn't laugh. I hate her.

I hate also the baby who is a Botherboy.

Daddy cut the willow tree into pieces I could carry and gave them to me and now I am building a horsehouse under the loquat and waiting for a man horse to come along, which is the way it is supposed to happen.

I saw a picture of one and its name was Centaur.

OF A SUNDAY AFTERNOON, IN HER STABLE

My room I also hate. Bother loves it best and squeals when he gets to its door, because he thinks it's nicer than his own room, nicer than the bigroom, nicer than anyplace at all. He likes best all the blocks and the toy people. I build temples and bridges sometimes but then he comes along. He throws blocks when he plays because he's just a baby. And a boy. And not a horse.

What I hate most about this room is picking up pieces of the lotto game when he throws it all over, picking up pieces of jigsaw puzzles that he has thrown all over. Picking up the spilled water, the blocks, the people. I hate his messes. I know that horses are not this messy. Mama says it is our fate to be left with the mess, but I don't think she likes it any more than I do.

She pays very little attention to me actually. She thinks I just read and I'm pretty sure she doesn't realize about the change. To a horse. She acts as though I'm still a girl. She doesn't observe closely.

ADMINISTERING HERSELF FIRST AID

The fact is there is a fossil in my hoof.

At school we have a hill that is called Fossilhill because there are a lot of fossils to be found there. Actually the fossils are very easy to find. You just pick up a handful of dirt and you come up with fossils. The trick is to find big fossils. I can always find the biggest fossils of anybody, snails and funny sea snakes and shells of all kinds.

The boys run up and down Fossilhill and don't look where they're going. It's no wonder they don't find many fossils. They come and pull Horse's mane. They scuff through where Horse is digging with her hoof. They sometimes try to capture Horse, since she is perhaps the last mustang and of great value. But mostly they are silly, these boys. They don't make much sense, just a mess.

Today I was trotting on the side of the hill and found the biggest fossil I have ever found in my life, which in horse is I think twelve or maybe twenty-four years old. Then I found more and more fossils and other children came to the hill, even the girlygirls who never look for fossils because they always play games I don't know how to play. House and Shopping and Bad Baby. But they tried to find fossils today and asked me if this was a fossil or that, and they found many, many fossils. And we all had a good time. And when we had found all the fossils we had time to find, our teacher said, Put them in your pockets, children, and if you don't have pockets put them in your socks. And we did, and that's why there is a fossil in my hoof.

GIRLYGIRLS VS. BOYANNOYS VS. HORSE

In my kindergarten there is a girl whose name is Larch. It is a funny name for a girl. It might not be such a funny name for a horse, but Larch isn't a horse because she is in fact the girl leader because she decides what games are going to be played and will let the boys tie her up. And the other girls too. When they tie people up they don't use real rope because our teacher wouldn't allow that. If they tie me up with their pretend rope it doesn't work. They think I just don't want to play, but the truth is I'm a horse and stronger than a girl and can break their girlygirl rope.

It's more fun being a horse. More fun than being a girl too, because they just play Housekeeping Area and none of them really knows yet how to read even though they pretend to. I can tell because they can't get the hard words. So they don't let me play with them. My mother says it's all right because they wish they could enjoy stories themselves and next year they will all read and everything will be all right.

The reading is the real problem between the horse and the girls, I guess. But sometimes they do let me play with them, if they need a victim or a hostage or an offering.

HERSELF AMONG THE OTHERS

Horses are I think lucky. They do not seem to have friends, such as people, you know, for they do not seem to need friends. They have enemies – the snakes, the potholes, the cougars, the fancy-booted cowboys who don't know the difference between a canter and a hand gallop. What friends they have are on a very practical basis. Other horses with the same problems.

The wind.

A TALK WITH HERSELF

If I tell her what I am she will not believe me.

If I tell the others what I am they may rope me and tell me to pull their wagon.

If I tell a boy what I am he will invade my loquat house, and maybe it will be good and maybe it will be bad.

If I tell Daddy what I am he will act interested for a minute and then drink some beer and start reading again.

And if I tell Bother he will not understand even the words but will grab my mane and pull it until he has pulled some of it out.

What does it matter? What does it all matter? I will whinny and run away.

Who could blame me? Horses should not be abused, ignored, or made fun of.

DISCUSSING THE WEATHER OR NOTHING AT ALL

Just a little while ago, when I needed to go out to race a bit and throw my head in the wind, she stopped me, my dam-mother, and asked me who I thought I was. A girl? A horse? My name? I know what she's thinking. The others at school ask me the same question.

So I said, A girl, because I know that's what I'm supposed to think. One thing I know, not a girlygirl, which would be stupid playing games talking teasing being tied to the junglegym. I won't. Sometimes it's hard not telling her what I really think, what I know. That sometimes I'm a girl, sometimes I'm a horse. When there are girl-things to do, like read, which a horse never does, or go in the car to the stockshow or for ice cream or any of those things, I have to be a girl, but when there are hillsides of grass and forests with lowhanging boughs and secret stables in loquat trees, I am a horse.

Maybe someday there will be no changing back and forth and I will be stuck a horse. Which will be all right with me. Because horses think good easy things, smooth green and windy things, without large people or Bothers or other kids or school, and they have enough grass to trot in forever and wind to throw their manes high to the sky and cool sweet stream water to drink, and clover.

Emily Hiestand

By Great Good Fortune

Emily Hiestand is a poet, essayist, and visual artist. Her books include Green the Witch-Hazel Wood *(1989),* The Very Rich Hours *(1992), and* Travels at Home *(1997). She lives in Cambridge, Massachusetts, with her husband, the musician and writer Peter Niels Dunn.*

Hiestand's maternal grandmother, Frances Webb Callahan Watkins, was a tomboy in her day. As a girl, she and her brothers played a game called "Squirrel," which involved climbing high up into trees. None of Frances's four sisters joined in this game.

THE FATTEST WOMAN IN THE WORLD (CIRCA 1953) LIVED ON MY street, Gordon road, in the small East Tennessee town where I grew up. She had a daughter named Alice who was nine years old, three years older than me at the time of which I speak. One day I asked Alice why her mother was so fat. "She's not fat," said Alice, indignantly. "She is *pregnant.*"

I could tell from Alice's tone that this was an explanation, but it was the first time the word "pregnant" had been used in my presence and it failed to signify – a triumph that was the product of a long tradition. Late into the twentieth century, the women of my mother's family in Alabama used the phrase "in a family way," and the men simply did not mention it.

Alice and her family, about whom I have no further memory whatsoever, lived next door to an elderly lady named Mrs. Bayliss. Because Mrs. Bayliss's house sat on the crest of a hill and at the extreme edge of what my brothers and I considered known territory, I had the impression that Mrs. Bayliss lived on a cliff. Looked at in later years, and strictly topographically, the land only sloped rather gently at Mrs. Bayliss's yard, descending into a thicket of paw-paw and persimmon trees. The grove exuded the pungent, sweet smell of persimmons in late summer, and more strongly in fall when the fruits had dropped and matted the slope in slicks of overripe, rotting pulp and skin.

Our house stood on flat, sunny ground, about nine houses away from Mrs. Bayliss and the cliff. One very hot August afternoon, as Ellen Jane Warne and I were playing with the hose in my front yard, Mrs. Bayliss appeared – walking along the low privet hedge that divided our yard from the sidewalk. She was wearing a silk print dress, and a close-fitting hat, and gloves, and she carried a patent leather purse over her arm in the way that the Queen of England did. She dressed this way whenever she walked the half-mile to the A&P grocery store in Jackson Square.

I had the garden hose in my hand as Mrs. Bayliss passed in front of our yard – and when the thought came into my mind to point the hose at Mrs. Bayliss and soak her, nothing intervened. It was a pure, instantaneous, intuitive act. I did know that it was considered wicked to squirt a jet of water at a grownup, most especially at a frail old widow, but something strong in me overrode this feeble teaching. The sensation of abandoned, transcendent joy that came to me – even as the water arched toward Mrs. Bayliss, and especially as it landed, in a great whoosh directly in the middle of her body – was unparalleled. I had willfully crossed a line, and known the ecstasy of dissolving an absolute rule – in this case, Decency. By great good fortune, silk turns very dark when it is wet, and Mrs. Bayliss not only was wet, she looked wet.

For a moment, all three of us stood frozen, staring at each other, unsure if we believed what had actually happened. Mrs. Bayliss's dress was sopping wet and water ran down her face and plopped onto her black patent purse. She must have said something to us at this juncture, but I cannot remember any words, only watching her come slowly to her senses, turn herself around and go back home. Ellen Jane and I played now in the yard in the same frame of mind that bank robbers must be in after they have pulled off the heist, and are back safely in the compound, running their hands excitedly through piles of gold, and listening to the radio for police reports.

In about twenty minutes Mrs. Bayliss reappeared, again walking along the low hedge in front of our house. She had put on a new silk dress and the same hat, and she had dried off her purse and face. Then – this is a true story – I squirted her again, same as before. The inward, guiding voice spoke again, suggesting that once over the line, you might as well linger there a while. Mrs. Bayliss did speak to us this time – in sharp, high, and memorable if not fathomable sounds. Then, she turned around, went home, changed her clothes, came back a third time in a different silk dress, and – *Yes!* Three times she appeared before us, trusting in our basic goodness, three times she tempted us, and three times we soaked her to the skin. Times two and three Ellen Jane and I fought over who would do it. But it had been my brilliant idea, and when the blade came down, Ellen Jane was the one who had been "led on," and I was the ghastly child. The fourth time she set out for the grocery, Mrs. Bayliss turned left at the fork in Gordon Road, rather than right toward our yard (where we waited poised), and she went the long way down Georgia Avenue to Jackson Square to shop.

She called my mother the next day. After replacing the heavy receiver in its cradle – her arm and whole body moving in a strange, calm way – my mother used my full name, and told me to come into her room.

Language is greatly a tonal affair, and no one could have failed to tremble at the eschatological timbre now flowing abundantly in my mother's voice. She said that I should sit down on the ottoman by the window – a low, round thing covered in a rose fabric, which had only a rare functionality. During the "very serious talk, young lady" that ensued, my mother's own sunny nature was replaced by the scorches of Presbyterian Hell. Afterwards, my mother helped me to dress in one of my Sunday School outfits. We practiced my apology several times and then my mother walked with me up the road to Mrs. Bayliss's house on the edge of the cliff. We knocked on the door.

Mrs. Bayliss had always been kind (in a syrupy way) to all the children in the neighborhood, including me. Now, as we waited at the door, I felt not precisely remorse for my action (the feeling my mother had done her level best to arouse), but rather a dim sense that Nature had chosen me to redress this goo of kindness. It was far too subtle and dangerous an idea of Justice to explore in the moment. I hung my head in Mrs. Bayliss's dark, musty house, offered my whispered apology, and then we sat in her living room parlor and ate butter cookies. Mrs. Bayliss forgave me and continued being sugary and frail. The only lesson I learned at the time, if you can call it a lesson, was that for an exquisite joy, the ineffable feeling of surety, of being perfectly in tune with Nature and the gods, there will be a price to pay – and that it will be worth it.

Recently I asked my mother, now aged seventy-four, about this long-ago event, and what her point of view was at the time. "My point of view," she replied, the incident coming rather easily to mind, "was the point of view of a mother who wants to crawl under the foundation of the house and never show her face again." My mother also claims that Mrs. Bayliss was neither old nor frail at the time of her soaking. In fact, she was not much older than my mother herself, which would have put Mrs. Bayliss in her early forties. Nor was she a widow; there was a *Mr.* Bayliss! "And," my mother continues, the ripples of corrective memory sweeping her on, "the dress – [she means *dresses*] – could *not* have been silk. In summer, dear, Mrs. Bayliss would have been wearing *voile.*" About these variances: I doubt neither my mother's memory nor her greater apperception of the victim's character; I can only say that the person she describes is simply not the person I squirted, though I grant that the dresses were very likely voile.

The savage glee of that afternoon lodged in mind and body, where it seems to contrast completely with the tenets of my present moral life – with the patient work of compassion and courtesy. I am often these days trusted with not only hoses but hearts, and good causes, and tender mercies. Recently I traveled from my home in New England south to the East Tennessee mountains of my youth. I walked in that yard, touched the fir tree planted for my birth, and leaned against the sugar maple under which Ellen Jane and I so often played. Mrs. Bayliss, I learned, had died, only the year before. How I would like to have visited her once more. By her person and sublimely misplaced trust in one child's nature, the lady provided me a pristine happiness, undimmed across four decades.

Linda Smukler

Drummer

Linda Smukler is the author of Normal Sex *(1994), from which this excerpt is taken, and* Home in Three Days, Don't Wash, *a multimedia project with accompanying CD-ROM (1996). She has been nominated for a Lambda Literary Award, and has received fellowships in poetry from the New York Foundation for the Arts and the Astraea Foundation. She is co-author, with Susan Fox Rogers, of* Portraits of Love *(1997).*

I DREAM I'M IN A FIELD. THERE'S A DOG BARKING. IT'S TAMMY. she's come to walk with me. The sky carries us up. It's summer in my dreams. Last summer when I was a bare-chested Indian boy and saw the devil's paintbrush.

Paintbrush in the linoleum. I sit on the floor in the kitchen. My mother is making dinner. Dinner smells in the stove and on the roof. The cabinets are high above. The specks in the linoleum are beetles. A swarm of bugs that eat houses. They eat and eat until their eating is a roar and my father walks in the door. He's big. He has on a suit and tie. He's left his car outside even though it's small enough to fit under the table. That's what my mother says. Dad kisses Mom. The dishes in Mom's hands are heavy. She can't let go to kiss him back. Dad walks over to me. "Hello little girl," he says. Hello little boy is what I hear. Suddenly I'm up in the air. My father smells like trucks. The floor is upside down. Bugs crawl up my father's legs and stomach. My sister walks in and my father swings me down into a chair. He pulls my sister up like he did me, only my sister laughs. She likes it. She dances. Mom's lips get thin. "That's enough," she says. "It's dinnertime now."

Everyone's at the table. "What did you do today?" Dad asks Mom. Mom serves the lima beans. There's a table in the middle of a big room. I'm on one side with my sister. The baby's in a high chair on the other side. Mom sits at one end and Dad at the other. "What did you do today?" Dad asks again. Mom's not angry anymore. She cuts up pieces of light brown meat for the baby and tells me to

[11

start eating. I have to finish everything on my plate. My plate's not full, but I don't like any of it. I look up and watch my father's face talk and eat at the same time. There's food under his lip. I look down at my plate and push the potato over the meat so it looks like I've eaten something. I do eat a lima bean and that tastes good and clean. Mom tells Dad what she did in school today, that her teacher said her paper was excellent. I think my mother is learning things I'll learn someday. Then I think that's not true. I'm making it up.

I'm really a drummer. I drum most of the day. If I drum, dinner will be over. My mother tells me to stop drumming. If I drum, all dinners will be done and I can take off my skirt. I hit the glasses with my knife. The baby stops eating to listen. I drum better than the man in the orchestra with the big bowls. The glasses bang and bang. Bang. Mom stops talking. She stares at me. My sister looks sad. Dad grabs my hand and the knife knocks over a glass. I try to catch it but I push my plate off the table instead. "Look what you've done! Look what you've – " Mom yells. She swings her arm over the table at me but catches herself before anything happens. My hand freezes around the knife. Mom gets up and walks into the kitchen for paper towels. She won't look at me while she helps me wipe up the mess. I'm not doing it right. I've got my skirt full of milk. Mom tries to clean the baby's tray and the baby throws a piece of potato at her. I slide out the door into the hall and up the blue stairs to my room. I take off my skirt full of milk and leave it on the floor. I find my jeans and put them on.

I walk to the closet. I take down some hangers and rip the ends of the wire parts out of the cardboard tubes. I have real drumsticks now. I play the cardboard tubes on the bedspread so they can't hear downstairs. I play in all the patterns and all the flowers like Harry Belafonte. Sometimes Dad listens to Harry Belafonte. There's a fence in the bedspread. I play in that fence. I bounce over it and there's a stream. I walk in the stream and the trees tower over me. They stand naked for a long time before they reach their full and leafy tops. I throw rocks in the water. One sound is like a bell. The next like my drum. There are frogs too. Green and portly frogs like the hearts of bears. I have on lederhosen and a purple shirt. I walk. One bare knee, then the other. I follow my knees all the way down the stream. I walk with a stick on my shoulder. At the end of the stick there's a red bandanna tied around all my belongings. A metal plate. A knife. A flint. A fishing line and a hook. One pair of socks and an extra shoelace. I need very little. I walk with the fish. The stream runs through my head and out my feet. I throw my hair in and out of the water and raise my arms and bring them down again. I hear a rooster and a clap. Someone is coming up the stairs. I hide my sticks under the pillow and run into the bathroom. I turn the water on in the sink and listen. I'm hidden in a waterfall. A one-eyed bandit. The one with the patch and the German Shepherd dog. My dog will tell me when it's safe to come out. Just be quiet and wait, I think. Just be quiet and be.

How Lars Porsena of Clusium Got Opal into Trouble

Opal Whiteley was born in Colton, Washington, in 1897, and grew up in a number of logging communities in Oregon. She kept a journal from the age of six, written on whatever scraps of paper she could find.

Years later that journal was published in serial form in the Atlantic Monthly *and then as a book, under the title* The Story of Opal: The Journal of an Understanding Heart *(1920). It was a resounding success. Skeptics, however, called it a hoax. Sales dropped, and the book fell out of print. Shortly afterwards Whiteley left America for England, where, apart from a 9,000-mile journey across India, and two years in a Viennese convent, she was to remain for the rest of her life. She died in a British mental hospital in 1992.*

In the excerpt that follows, Aristotle, Plato, and Pliny are Bats, Brave Horatius is the family dog, Sadie McKibben is a friendly neighbor, and Thomas Chatterton Jupiter Zeus is a "most dear velvety woodrat."

TO-DAY WAS A WARM, HOT DAY. IT WAS WARM IN THE MORNING AND hot at noon. Before noon and after noon and after that, I carried water to the hired men in the field in a jug. I got the water out of the pump to put into the jug. I had to put water in the pump before any would come out. The men were glad to have that water in the jug.

While I was taking the water in the jug to the men in the field, from her sewing-basket Lars Porsena of Clusium took the mamma's thimble, and she didn't have it and she couldn't find it. She sent me to watch out for it in the house and in the yard and everywhere. I know how Lars Porsena of Clusium has a fondness for collecting things of bright colors, like unto my fondness for collecting rocks; so I ran to his hiding-place in the old oak tree. There I found the mamma's thimble; but she said the pet crow's having taken it was as though I had taken it, because he was my property; so I got a spanking with the hazel switches that grow near unto our back steps. Inside me I couldn't help feeling she ought to have given me thanks for finding the thimble.

Afterwards I made little vases out of clay. I put them in the oven to bake. The mamma found my vases of clay. She threw them out the window. When I went to pick them up, they were broken. I felt sad inside. I went to talk things over with my chum, Michael Angelo Sanzio Raphael. He is that most tall fir tree that grows just back of the barn. I scooted up the barn door. From there I climbed onto the lower part of the barn roof. I walked up a ways. Up there I took a long look at the world about. One gets such a good wide view of the world from a barn roof. After, I looked looks in four straight ways and four corner ways. I said a little prayer. I always say a little prayer before I jump off the barn into the arms of Michael Angelo Sanzio Raphael, because that jump is quite a long jump, and if I did not land in the arms of Michael Angelo Sanzio Raphael, I might get my leg or neck broken. That would mean I'd have to keep still a long time. Now I think that would be the most awful thing that could happen, for I do so love to be active. So I always say a little prayer and do that jump in a careful way. To-day, when I did jump, I did land right proper in that fir tree. It is such a comfort to nestle up to Michael Angelo Sanzio Raphael when one is in trouble. He is such a grand tree. He has an understanding soul.

After I talked with him and listened unto his voice, I slipped down out of his arms. I intended to slip into the barn corral, but I slid off the wrong limb in the wrong way. I landed in the pig-pen on top of Aphrodite, the mother-pig. She gave a peculiar grunt. It was not like those grunts she gives when she is comfortable.

I felt I ought to do something to make up to her for having come into her home out of the arms of Michael Angelo Sanzio Raphael instead of calling on her in the proper way. I decided a good way to make it up to her would be to pull down the rail fence in that place where the pig-pen is weak, and take her for a walk. I went to the wood-shed. I got a piece of clothes-line rope. While I was making a halter for the mother-pig, I took my Sunday-best hair-ribbon – the blue ribbon the Uncle Henry gave to me. I made a bow on that halter. I put the bow just over her ears. That gave her the proper look. When the mamma saw us go walking by, she took the bow from off the pig. She put that bow in the trunk; me she put under the bed.

By-and-by – some time long it was – she took me from under the bed and gave me a spanking. She did not have time to give me a spanking when she put me under the bed. She left me there until she did have time. After she did it she sent me to the ranch-house to get milk for the baby. I walked slow through the oak grove, looking for caterpillars. I found nine. Then I went to the pig-pen. The chore boy was fixing back the rails I had pulled down. His temper was quite warm. He was saying prayer words in a very quick way. I went not near unto him. I slipped around near Michael Angelo Sanzio Raphael. I peeked in between the fence-rails. Aphrodite was again in the pig-pen. She was snoozing, so I tiptoed over to the rain-barrel by the barn. I raised mosquitoes in the rain-barrel for my pet bats. Aristotle eats more mosquitoes than Plato and Pliny eat.

On my way to the house I met Clementine, the Plymouth Rock hen, with her family. She only has twelve baby chickens now. The grandpa say the other one she did have died of new monia because I gave it too many baths for its health. When I came to the house one of the cats, a black one, was sitting on the doorstep. I have not friendly feelings for that big black cat. Day before the day that was yesterday I saw him kill the mother hummingbird. He knocked her with his paw when she came to the nasturtiums. I didn't even speak to him.

Just as I was going to knock on the back door for the milk, I heard a voice on the front porch. It was the voice of a person who has an understanding soul. I hurried around to the front porch. There was Sadie McKibben with a basket on her arm. She beamed a smile at me. I went over and nestled up against her blue gingham apron with cross stitches on it. The freckles on Sadie McKibben's wrinkled face are as many as are the stars in the Milky Way, and she is awful old – going on forty. Her hands are all brown and cracked like the dried-up mud-puddles by the roadside in July, and she has an understanding soul. She always has bandages ready in her pantry when some of my pets get hurt. There are cookies in her cookie-jar when I don't get home for meals, and she allows me to stake out earthworm claims in her back yard.

She walked along beside me when I took the milk home. When she came near the lane, she took from her basket wrapping-papers and gave them to me to print upon. Then she kissed me good-bye upon the cheek and went her way to her home. I went my way to the house we live in. After the mamma had switched me for not getting back sooner with the milk, she told me to fix the milk for the baby. The baby's bottle used to be a brandy bottle, but it evoluted into a milk bottle when they put a nipple onto it.

I sit here on the doorstep printing this on the wrapping-paper Sadie McKibben gave me. The baby is in bed asleep. The mamma and the rest of the folks is gone to the ranch-house. When they went away, she said for me to stay in the doorway to see that nothing comes to carry the baby away. By the step is Brave Horatius. At my feet is Thomas Chatterton Jupiter Zeus. I hear songs – lullaby songs of the trees. The back part of me feels a little bit sore, but I am happy listening to the twilight music of God's good world. I'm real glad I'm alive.

Suniti Namjoshi

Bird Woman

Suniti Namjoshi was born in Bombay, India, in 1941, and now lives in the south of England with her partner, Gillian Hanscombe. Among her books are Feminist Fables *(1981), from which this excerpt is taken,* Aditi and the One-Eyed Monkey *(1986),* The Mothers of Maya Dup *(1989), and* Building Babel *(1996). The last chapter of* Building Babel *will appear on the Home Page of Spinifex Press, Melbourne, with an invitation to contribute: that is, to enact the process of building Babel. Namjoshi says, "Alas, I've never done anything particularly tomboyish. I once shot a gecko with an airgun, but I had intended to* miss!"

ONCE THERE WAS A CHILD WHO SPROUTED WINGS. THEY SPRANG FROM her shoulder blades, and at first they were vestigial. But they grew rapidly, and in no time at all she had a sizable wing span. The neighbours were horrified. "You must have them cut," they said to her parents. "Why?" said her parents. "Well, it's obvious," said the neighbours. "No," said the parents, and this seemed so final that the neighbours left. But a few weeks later the neighbours were back. "If you won't have them cut, at least have them clipped." "Why?" said the parents. "Well, at least it shows that you're doing something." "No," said the parents, and the neighbours left. Then for the third time the neighbours appeared. "On at least two occasions you have sent us away," they informed the parents, "but think of that child. What are you doing to the poor little thing?" "We are teaching her to fly," said the parents quietly.

PART TWO

Tomboys

Sandra Cisneros

Beautiful and Cruel

Sandra Cisneros was born in Chicago in 1954, the only girl in a family of six boys. She identifies strongly as a Mexican-American, and has published poems, short stories, and children's books. The following excerpt is from The House on Mango Street *(1984), which is widely used in both grade schools and college classes. The narrator's name is Esperanza, and Nenny is her younger sister. Minerva is a neighbor, who "already has two kids and a husband who left."*

Cisneros is also the author of Woman Hollering Creek and Other Stories *(1991). She lives in San Antonio, Texas.*

I AM AN UGLY DAUGHTER. I AM THE ONE NOBODY COMES FOR.
Nenny says she won't wait her whole life for a husband to come and get her, that Minerva's sister left her mother's house by having a baby, but she doesn't want to go that way either. She wants things all her own, to pick and choose. Nenny has pretty eyes and it's easy to talk that way if you are pretty.

My mother says when I get older my dusty hair will settle and my blouse will learn to stay clean, but I have decided not to grow up tame like the others who lay their necks on the threshold waiting for the ball and chain.

In the movies there is always one with red red lips who is beautiful and cruel. She is the one who drives the men crazy and laughs them all away. Her power is her own. She will not give it away.

I have begun my own quiet war. Simple. Sure. I am one who leaves the table like a man, without putting back the chair or picking up the plate.

from *An American Childhood*

Annie Dillard was born in Pittsburgh in 1945. In 1975 she won a Pulitzer prize for a book of essays, Pilgrim at Tinker Creek. *Since then, she has been best known for her nature writing, though she has also published a novel,* The Living *(1992), and several other books, including* An American Childhood *(1987),* Living by Fiction *(1982), and* Teaching a Stone to Talk *(1982).*

SOME BOYS TAUGHT ME TO PLAY FOOTBALL. THIS WAS FINE SPORT. You thought up a new strategy for every play and whispered it to the others. You went out for a pass, fooling everyone. Best, you got to throw yourself mightily at someone's running legs. Either you brought him down or you hit the ground flat out on your chin, with your arms empty before you. It was all or nothing. If you hesitated in fear, you would miss and get hurt: you would take a hard fall while the kid got away, or you would get kicked in the face while the kid got away. But if you flung yourself wholeheartedly at the back of his knees – if you gathered and joined body and soul and pointed them diving fearlessly – then you likely wouldn't get hurt, and you'd stop the ball. Your fate, and your team's score, depended on your concentration and courage. Nothing girls did could compare with it.

Boys welcomed me at baseball, too, for I had, through enthusiastic practice, what was weirdly known as a boy's arm. In winter, in the snow, there was neither baseball nor football, so the boys and I threw snowballs at passing cars. I got in trouble throwing snowballs, and have seldom been happier since.

On one weekday morning after Christmas, six inches of new snow had just fallen. We were standing up to our boot tops in snow on a front yard on trafficked Reynolds Street, waiting for cars. The cars traveled Reynolds Street slowly and evenly; they were targets all but wrapped in red ribbons, cream puffs. We couldn't miss.

I was seven; the boys were eight, nine, and ten. The oldest two Fahey boys were there – Mikey and Peter – polite blond boys who lived near me on Lloyd

Street, and who already had four brothers and sisters. My parents approved Mikey and Peter Fahey. Chickie McBride was there, a tough kid, and Billy Paul and Mackie Kean too, from across Reynolds, where the boys grew up dark and furious, grew up skinny, knowing, and skilled. We had all drifted from our houses that morning looking for action, and had found it here on Reynolds Street.

It was cloudy but cold. The cars' tires laid behind them on the snowy street a complex trail of beige chunks like crenellated castle walls. I had stepped on some earlier; they squeaked. We could have wished for more traffic. When a car came, we all popped it one. In the intervals between cars we reverted to the natural solitude of children.

I started making an iceball – a perfect iceball, from perfectly white snow, perfectly spherical, and squeezed perfectly translucent so no snow remained all the way through. (The Fahey boys and I considered it unfair actually to throw an iceball at somebody, but it had been known to happen.)

I had just embarked on the iceball project when we heard tire chains come clanking from afar. A black Buick was moving toward us down the street. We all spread out, banged together some regular snowballs, took aim, and, when the Buick drew nigh, fired.

A soft snowball hit the driver's windshield right before the driver's face. It made a smashed star with a hump in the middle.

Often, of course, we hit our target, but this time, the only time in all of life, the car pulled over and stopped. Its wide black door opened; a man got out of it, running. He didn't even close the car door.

He ran after us, and we ran away from him, up the snowy Reynolds sidewalk. At the corner, I looked back; incredibly, he was still after us. He was in city clothes: a suit and tie, street shoes. Any normal adult would have quit, having sprung us into flight and made his point. This man was gaining on us. He was a thin man, all action. All of a sudden, we were running for our lives.

Wordless, we split up. We were on our turf; we could lose ourselves in the neighborhood backyards, everyone for himself. I paused and considered. Everyone had vanished except Mikey Fahey, who was just rounding the corner of a yellow brick house. Poor Mikey, I trailed him. The driver of the Buick sensibly picked the two of us to follow. The man apparently had all day.

He chased Mikey and me around the yellow house and up a backyard path we knew by heart: under a low tree, up a bank, through a hedge, down some snowy steps, and across the grocery store's delivery driveway. We smashed through a gap in another hedge, entered a scruffy backyard and ran around its back porch and tight between houses to Edgerton Avenue; we ran across Edgerton to an alley and up our own sliding woodpile to the Halls' front yard; he kept coming. We ran up Lloyd Street and wound through mazy backyards toward the steep hilltop at Willard and Lang.

He chased us silently, block after block. He chased us silently over picket fences, through thorny hedges, between houses, around garbage cans, and across streets. Every time I glanced back, choking for breath, I expected he would have quit. He must have been as breathless as we were. His jacket strained over his body. It was an immense discovery, pounding into my hot head with every sliding, joyous step, that this ordinary adult evidently knew what I thought only children who trained at football knew: that you have to fling yourself at what you're doing, you have to point yourself, forget yourself, aim, dive.

Mikey and I had nowhere to go, in our own neighborhood or out of it, but away from this man who was chasing us. He impelled us forward; we compelled him to follow our route. The air was cold; every breath tore my throat. We kept running, block after block; we kept improvising, backyard after backyard, running a frantic course and choosing it simultaneously, failing always to find small places or hard places to slow him down, and discovering always, exhilarated, dismayed, that only bare speed could save us – for he would never give up, this man – and we were losing speed.

He chased us through the backyard labyrinths of ten blocks before he caught us by our jackets. He caught us and we all stopped.

We three stood staggering, half blinded, coughing, in an obscure hilltop backyard: a man in his twenties, a boy, a girl. He had released our jackets, our pursuer, our captor, our hero: he knew we weren't going anywhere. We all played by the rules. Mikey and I unzipped our jackets. I pulled off my sopping mittens. Our tracks multiplied in the backyard's new snow. We had been breaking new snow all morning. We didn't look at each other. I was cherishing my excitement. The man's lower pants legs were wet; his cuffs were full of snow, and there was a prow of snow beneath them on his shoes and socks. Some trees bordered the little flat backyard, some messy winter trees. There was no one around: a clearing in a grove, and we the only players.

It was a long time before he could speak. I had some difficulty at first recalling why we were there. My lips felt swollen; I couldn't see out of the sides of my eyes; I kept coughing.

"You stupid kids," he began perfunctorily.

We listened perfunctorily indeed, if we listened at all, for the chewing out was redundant, a mere formality, and beside the point. The point was that he had chased us passionately without giving up, and so he had caught us. Now he came down to earth. I wanted the glory to last forever.

But how could the glory have lasted forever? We could have run through every backyard in North America until we got to Panama. But when he trapped us at the lip of the Panama Canal, what precisely could he have done to prolong the drama of the chase and cap its glory? I brooded about this for the next few years. He could only have fried Mikey Fahey and me in boiling oil, say, or dismembered us piecemeal, or staked us to anthills. None of which I really wanted, and none of which any adult was likely to do, even in the spirit of fun. He could only chew us out there in the Panamanian jungle, after months or years of exalting pursuit. He could only begin, "You stupid kids," and continue in his ordinary Pittsburgh accent with his normal righteous anger and the usual common sense.

If in that snowy backyard the driver of the black Buick had cut off our heads, Mikey's and mine, I would have died happy, for nothing has required so much of me since as being chased all over Pittsburgh in the middle of winter – running terrified, exhausted – by this sainted, skinny, furious redheaded man who wished to have a word with us. I don't know how he found his way back to his car.

Lara Cardella

translated from the Italian by Diana Di Carcaci

from *Good Girls Don't Wear Trousers*

Lara Cardella was born in Licata, Sicily, in 1969, and was educated at Palermo University. She wrote Good Girls Don't Wear Trousers *at the age of nineteen, and, like her heroine, Annetta, was banished from her hometown after its publication. The book has since sold more than two million copies.*

BUT WHO, OR RATHER WHAT, WAS A MAN? I HAD OFTEN HEARD MY parents or the aunts and uncles saying, "Now, now, boys don't cry," or "Boys shouldn't play with girls," or even, "Oh, look, he'll be shaving soon." Men, I soon realized, were a race apart; coarse, strong, brave, and ruthless. I had lived what felt like a lifetime with a boy in the house and had always had to endure the burden of tradition and convention. My brother was some years older, which seemed to make him think he could be the man of the house, bossing me around, when our father was out working in the fields.

Antonio and I had never been close. I was too different, too female, for any communication to be possible, and anyway he was hardly ever at home. He usually helped Dad with his work in the fields, then came home and went straight out again. Often, he came back drunk and very late, blundering against the furniture before collapsing on his bed, still fully clothed and with his shoes on. I did not hate him; I did not hate anyone, but he was not what I felt a brother should be. At bottom, the only thing we shared was that we happened to have been born to the same woman. I often wondered what my life would have been like if she had not been my mother, if I had been conceived in another womb or lived in another part of the world or if on the night I was conceived my father had been too exhausted to lift so much as a finger . . . I don't suppose it would have changed much. After all, there would have been countless other nights when he would not have been too tired to switch off the light and deposit me in her uterus. And then my mother would have said, "Aren't you done yet?" and nine months later out I'd have popped, or some other me with the same name, who would have lived like me and had the same thoughts I'm having now, like, "What if that evening . . . ?"

In order to set about my grand project of being a man, I embarked on minute observations of that alien species, especially my cousin Angelo. He was thirteen, with pitch-black hair and eyes and a perennial suntan from working outdoors helping Uncle Giovanni, whose nickname was "Hairy" and who was living proof of Darwin's theories. Angelo was solid, with lascivious eyes and nimble hands, everyone's stock image of a Sicilian teenager. He did not go to school because he didn't need to. He was clever, lively, and masculine without macho posturing.

I used to follow him around the countryside like a lost lamb. I would stand over him when he milked the scrawny, muddy goats and watch while he sucked a raw, new-laid egg with one gulp or when he shut himself away in the stable to smoke the cigarette butts discarded by his father. I would be close on his heels when he deliberately walked through the horse droppings because he thought it brought good luck and when he looked in the mirror to check the progress of his stubble. I copied everything he did, so, while my peers were lining up to paint their faces, I was locked in the bathroom, learning how to shave. I would lather my face expertly, then take the razor and very slowly (not for fear of nicking myself but because it seemed more stylish) remove the layer of foam from my cheeks. While the other girls were using up mountains of Kleenex and wiggling their hips, I spent much of my time scratching a gravely underendowed crotch. And while they maintained decorous composure even when sitting on the toilet, I surreptitiously practiced peeing standing up and spitting out of windows. My classmates made it a point of honor to swoon at the sight of a spider while I was enthusiastically capturing and dissecting them.

I made several attempts at chewing tobacco and soon, after a few initial difficulties, was managing to smoke up to thirty cigarette butts a day; I learned how to inhale and exhale nonchalantly through my nose. By this time, I was trailing Angelo like a shadow. I didn't let him out of my sight and spied on all his activities. He only had to turn around and presto, there I was. Though he objected at first ("This is man's work, Annetta"), he was won over in the end. He was the only person I confided my secret to, not, you'll understand, voluntarily, but because once he peeped through the keyhole and caught me peeing standing up. There was no possible explanation without a full confession. Predictably, he greeted my announcement with gales of mirth, but when he saw I was completely serious, he appointed himself as my instructor.

From then on, he took me with him everywhere, even to the bathroom, where, standing shoulder to shoulder, we peed together. He taught me how to lob stones at tin cans, first with my eyes open, then blindfolded. He showed me how to spit through clenched teeth, head tipped back so the spittle would fall in an elegant curve, and how to dissect frogs and set mouse-traps. He taught me how to fool the guard dogs when we were stealing plump tomatoes from Uncle Vincenzo's orchard, how to strut like a boy and shake hands like a man. Then he showed me his father's dirty comic books. This was a complete eye-opener: during my religious phase I hadn't even been able to look at the illustrations of naked men in my science book. Too horrified even to touch the page, I would cover it with an exercise book or another of my text books. The comic Angelo had selected for me was *Snow White and the Seven Dwarfs*. I was rather taken aback by the fact that it seemed to have very little to do with the fairy tale. By page 5 I was flabbergasted: there was Snow White on all fours with her dress hitched up over her bare bottom and the kindly huntsman with his trousers around his knees and something very odd sticking out between his legs. involuntarily, I found myself gazing at Angelo's crotch, then raised my eyes to his face. He was reveling in my discomfiture.

"Don't tell me you didn't know what men look like down there," he smirked. Well, okay, I had observed the way boys seemed to scratch between their legs all the time and naturally I had wondered why. Moreover, it hadn't escaped my notice that Angelo always turned his back on me when we peed together, so all I ever saw was his shoulder or, at the very most, a glimpse of bare bottom.

My apprenticeship had lasted barely two months, but it had been a time of hopes and dreams. Now I saw that it had been pointless, that I would never be able to have that "thing," that without it I could never become a man, and that never, ever, would I be able to wear trousers.

Simone de Beauvoir

translated from the French by James Kirkup

from *Memoirs of a Dutiful Daughter*

Simone de Beauvoir (1908–1980) was born in Paris and educated at the Sorbonne. It was there she met Jean-Paul Sartre, who was to become her lifelong companion. Together they developed the philosophical system known as existentialism, which would inform de Beauvoir's novels and philosophical essays, as well as her classic feminist study, The Second Sex *(1952).*

Until 1943, de Beauvoir earned her living as a secondary-school teacher. Her first novel, L'Invitee, *was published in that year. Thereafter, she published a considerable number of novels and essays, as well as five volumes of autobiography, including* Memoirs of a Dutiful Daughter *(1958). The following excerpt describes the amazing exploits of her tomboy best friend, Zaza.*

THE DAY I ENTERED THE FOURTH-FIRST FORM — I WAS THEN RISING ten – the seat next to mine was occupied by a new girl: she was small, dark, thin-faced, with short hair. While we waited for Mademoiselle to come in, and when the class was over, we talked together. She was called Elizabeth Mabille, and she was the same age as myself. Her schooling, begun with a governess, had been interrupted by a serious accident: in the country, while roasting some potatoes out in the open, her dress had caught fire; third-degree burns on her thighs had made her scream with agony for night after night; she had had to remain lying down for a whole year; under her pleated skirt, her flesh was still puffed up. Nothing as important as that had ever happened to me; she at once seemed to me a very finished person. The manner in which she spoke to the teachers astounded me; her natural inflexions contrasted strongly with the stereotyped expressionless voices of the rest of the pupils. Her conquest of me was complete when, a few days later, she mimicked Mademoiselle Bodet to perfection; everything she had to say was either interesting or amusing.

Despite certain gaps in her knowledge due to enforced inactivity, Elizabeth soon became one of the foremost in the class; I only just managed to beat her at composition. Our friendly rivalry pleased our teachers: they encouraged our association. At the musical and dramatic performance which was given every year round about Christmas, we played in a sketch. I, in a pink dress, my hair all in ringlets, impersonated Madame de Sévigné as a little girl; Elizabeth took the part of a high-spirited boy cousin; her young man's costume suited her, and she enchanted the audience with her vivacity and ease. The rehearsals, our repeated conversations in the glow of the footlights drew us closer and closer together; from then on we were called "the two inseparables."

My father and mother had long discussions about the different branches of various families they had heard of called Mabille; they decided that there was some vague connexion between Elizabeth's parents and themselves. Her father was a railway engineer, and held a very high post; her mother, *née* Larivière, belonged to a dynasty of militant Catholics; she had nine children and was an active worker for charity. She sometimes put in an appearance at our school in the rue Jacob. She was a handsome woman of about forty, dark-haired, with flashing eyes and a studied smile, who wore a black velvet ribbon adorned with an old-fashioned piece of jewellery round her neck. She softened her regal bearing with a deliberate amiability of manner. She completely won Mama over by addressing her as *"petite madame"* (my dear lady) and by telling her that she could easily have mistaken her for my elder sister. Elizabeth and I were allowed to go and play in each other's homes.

On my first visit to her home in the rue de Varennes my sister went with me and we were both scared out of our wits. Elizabeth – who was known in the family circle as Zaza – had an elder sister, a grown-up brother, six brothers and sisters younger than herself, and a whole horde of cousins and friends. They would run and jump about, clamber on the tables, overturn the furniture and shout all the time at the tops of their voices. At the end of the afternoon, Madame Mabille entered the drawing-room, picked up a fallen chair and smilingly wiped perspiring brows; I was astonished at her indifference to bumps and bruises, stained carpets and chair covers and smashed plates; she never got cross. I didn't care much for those wild games, and often Zaza too grew tired of them. We would take refuge in Monsieur Mabille's study, and, far away from the tumult, we would talk. This was a novel pleasure for me. My parents used to talk to me, and I used to talk to them, but we never talked together; there was not sufficient distance between my sister and myself to encourage discussion. But with Zaza I had real conversations, like the ones Papa had in the evenings with Mama. We would talk about our school work, our reading, our common friends, our teachers, and about what we knew of the world: we never talked about ourselves.

We never exchanged girlish confidences. We did not allow ourselves any kind of familiarity. We addressed each other formally as *"vous"* (never *"tu"*) and, excepting at the ends of letters, we did not give each other kisses.

Zaza, like myself, liked books and studying; in addition, she was endowed with a host of talents to which I could lay no claim. Sometimes when I called at the rue de Varennes I would find her busy making shortbread or caramels; or she would spike on a knitting-needle quarters of orange, a few dates, and some prunes, and immerse the lot in a saucepan full of a syrupy concoction smelling of warm vinegar: her imitation fruits looked just as delicious as those made by a real confectioner. Then she used to hectograph a dozen or so copies of a *Family Chronicle* which she edited and produced herself each week for the benefit of grandmothers, uncles, and aunts who lived outside Paris. I admired, as much as the liveliness of her tales, her skill in making an object which resembled very closely a real newspaper. She took a few piano lessons with me, but very soon became much more proficient and moved up into a higher grade. Puny-armed and skinny-legged, she nevertheless was able to perform all sorts of contortions; when the first fine days of spring came along, Madame Mabille would take us out to a grassy, wildflower suburb – I believe it was Nanterre – and Zaza would run into a field and do the cartwheel, the splits, the crab, and all kinds of other tricks; she would climb trees and hang down from branches by her heels. In everything she did, she displayed an easy mastery which always amazed me. At the age of ten she would walk about the streets on her own; at the Cours Désir she showed no signs of my own awkwardness of manner; she would talk to the ladies of the establishment in a polite but nonchalant way, almost as if she were their equal. One year at a music recital she did something while she was playing the piano which was very nearly scandalous. The hall was packed. In the front rows were the pupils in their best frocks, curled and ringleted and beribboned, who were awaiting their turn to show off their talents. Behind them sat the teachers and tutors in stiff black silk bodices, wearing white gloves. At the back of the hall were seated the parents and their guests. Zaza, resplendent in blue taffeta, played a piece which her mother thought was too difficult for her; she always had to scramble through a few of the bars: but this time she played it perfectly, and, casting a triumphant glance at Madame Mabille, put out her *tongue* at her! All the little girls' ringlets trembled with apprehension and the teachers' faces froze into disapproving masks. But when Zaza came down from the platform her mother gave her such a light-hearted kiss that no one dared reprimand her. For me this exploit surrounded her with a halo of glory. Although I was subject to laws, to conventional behaviour, to prejudice, I nevertheless liked anything novel, sincere, and spontaneous. I was completely won over by Zaza's vivacity and independence of spirit.

I did not immediately consider what place this friendship had in my life; I was still not much cleverer than I was as a baby at realizing what was going on inside me. I had been brought up to equate appearances with reality; I had not learned to examine what was concealed behind conventions of speech and action. It went without saying that I had the tenderest affection for all the members of my family, including even my most distant cousins. For my parents and sister I felt love, a word that covered everything. Nuances and fluctuations of feeling had no claim to existence in my world. Zaza was my best friend: and that was all. In a well-regulated human heart friendship occupies an honourable position, but it has neither the mysterious splendour of love, nor the sacred dignity of filial devotion. And I never called this hierarchy of the emotions into question.

Ursula K. Le Guin

Horse Camp

Ursula K. Le Guin was born in Berkeley, California, in 1929, the youngest in a family of three brothers. She now lives in Portland, Oregon. She has published short stories, essays, and numerous works of science fiction. Among her best-known books are The Left Hand of Darkness *(1969),* Always Coming Home *(1985), and* Dancing at the Edge of the World *(1989).*

ALL THE OTHER SENIORS WERE OVER AT THE STREET SIDE OF THE parking lot, but Sal stayed with her sister Norah while they waited for the bus drivers. "Maybe you'll be in the creek cabin," Sal said, quiet and serious. "I had it second year. It's the best one. Number Five."

"How do they – when do you, like, find out what cabin?" asked Norah.

"They better remember we're in the same cabin," Ev said, sounding shrill. Norah did not look at her. She and Ev had planned for months and known for weeks that they were to be cabinmates, but what good was that if they never found their cabin, and also Sal was not looking at Ev, only at Norah. Sal was cool, a tower of ivory.

"They show you around as soon as you get there," she said, her quiet voice speaking directly to Norah's dream last night of never finding the room where she had to take a test she was late for and looking among endless thatched barracks in a forest of thin black trees growing very close together, like hair under a hand lens. Norah had told no one the dream, and now remembered and forgot it. "Then you have dinner, and First Campfire," Sal said. "Kimmy's going to be a counsellor again. She's really neat. Listen, you tell old Meredy . . ."

Norah drew breath. In all the histories of Horse Camp which she had asked for and heard over and over for three years – the thunderstorm story, the horse-thief story, the wonderful Stevens Mountain stories – in all of them Meredy the handler had been: Meredy said, Meredy did, Meredy knew . . .

"Tell him I said hi," Sal said, with a shadowy smile, looking across the parking lot at the far, insubstantial towers of downtown. Behind them the doors of the Junior Girls bus gasped open. One after another the engines of the four buses roared and spewed. Across the asphalt, in the hot morning light, small figures were lining up and climbing into the Junior Boys bus. High, rough, faint voices bawled. "O.K., hey, have fun," Sal said. She hugged Norah and then, keeping a hand on her arm, looked down at her intently for a moment from the tower of ivory. She turned away. Norah watched her walk, light-foot and buxom, across the black gap to the others of her kind, who enclosed her, greeting her, "Sal! Hey, Sal!"

Ev was twitching and nickering, "Come on, Nor, come on. We'll have to sit way at the back. Come on!" Side by side, they pressed into the line below the gaping doorway of the bus.

In Number Five cabin, four iron cots, thin-mattressed, gray-blanketed, stood strewn with bottles of insect repellent and styling mousse, T-shirts lettered "UCSD" and "I ♥ Teddy Bears," a flashlight, an apple, a comb with hair caught in it, a paperback book open face down: "The Black Colt of Pirate Island." Over the shingle roof huge second-growth redwoods cast deep shade, and a few feet below the porch the creek ran out into sunlight over brown stones streaming bright-green weed. Behind the cabin Jim Meredith, the horse-handler, a short man of fifty who had ridden as a jockey in his teens, walked along the well-beaten path, quick and a bit bow-legged. Meredith's lips were pressed firmly together. His eyes, narrow and darting, glanced from cabin to cabin, from side to side. Far through the trees high voices cried.

The counsellors know what is to be known. Red Ginger, blond Kimmy, and beautiful black Sue: they know the vices of Pal, and how to keep Trigger from putting her head down and drinking for ten minutes from every creek. They strike the great shoulders smartly: "Aw, get over, you big lunk!" They know how to swim underwater, how to sing in harmony, how to get seconds, and when a shoe is loose. They know where they are. They know where the rest of Horse Camp is. "Home Creek runs into Little River here," Kimmy says, drawing lines in the soft dust with a redwood twig that breaks. "Senior Girls here, Senior Boys across there, Junior Birdmen about here."

"Who needs 'em?" says Sue, yawning. "Come on, who's going to help me walk the mares?"

They were all around the campfire on Quartz Meadow after the long first day of the First Overnight. The counsellors were still singing, but very soft, so soft you almost couldn't hear them, lying in the sleeping bag listening to One Spot stamp and Trigger snort and the shifting at the pickets, standing in the fine, cool alpine grass listening to the soft voices and the sleepers shifting and, later, one coyote down the mountain singing all alone.

"Nothing wrong with you. Get up!" said Meredy, and slapped her hip. Turning her long, delicate head to him with a deprecating gaze, Philly got to her feet. She stood a moment, shuddering the reddish silk of her flank as if to dislodge flies, tested her left foreleg with caution, and then walked on, step by step. Step by step, watching, Norah went with her. Inside her body there was still a deep trembling. As she passed him, the handler just nodded. "You're all right," he meant. She was all right.

Freedom, the freedom to run, freedom is to run. Freedom is galloping. What else can it be? Only other ways to run, imitations of galloping across great highlands with the wind. Oh, Philly, sweet Philly, my love! If Ev and Trigger couldn't keep up she'd slow down and come round in a while, after a while, over there, across the long, long field of grass, once she had learned this by heart and knew it forever, the purity, the pure joy.

"Right leg, Nor," said Meredy. And passed on to Cass and Tammy.

You have to start with the right fore. Everything else is all right. Freedom depends on this, that you start with the right fore, that long leg well balanced on its elegant pastern, that you set down that tiptoe middle fingernail, so hard and round, and spurn the dirt. High-stepping, trot past old Meredy, who always hides his smile.

Shoulder to shoulder, she and Ev, in the long heat of afternoon, in a trance of light, across the home creek in the dry wild oats and cow parsley of the Long Pasture. I was afraid before I came here, thinks Norah, incredulous, remembering childhood. She leans her head against Ev's firm and silken side. The sting of small flies awakens, the swish of long tails sends to sleep. Down by the creek, in a patch of coarse grass, Philly grazes and dozes. Sue comes striding by, winks wordless, beautiful as a burning coal, lazy and purposeful, bound for the shade of the willows. Is it worth getting up to go down to get your feet in the cool water? Next year Sal will be too old for a camper, but can come back as a counsellor, come back here. Norah will come back a second-year camper, Sal a counsellor. They will be here. This is what free-

dom is, what goes on – the sun in summer, the wild grass, coming back each
year.

Coming back from the long pack trip to Stevens Mountain, weary and dirty,
thirsty and in bliss, coming down from the high places, in line, Sue jogging just
in front of her and Ev half asleep behind her – some sound or motion caught
and turned Norah's head to look across the alpine field. On the far side, under
dark firs, a line of horses, mounted and with packs: "Look!"

Ev snorted. Sue flicked her ears and stopped. Norah halted in line behind
her, stretching her neck to see. She saw her sister going first in the distant line,
the small head proudly borne. She was walking light-foot and easy, fresh, just
starting up to the high passes of the mountain. On her back a young man sat
erect, his fine, fair head turned a little aside, to the forest. One hand was on his
thigh, the other on the reins, guiding her. Norah called out and then broke from
the line, going to Sal, calling out to her. "No, no, no, no!" she called. Behind
her, Ev and then Sue called to her, "Nor! Nor!"

Sal did not hear or heed. Going straight ahead, the color of ivory, distant in
the clear, dry light, she stepped into the shadow of the trees. The others and
their riders followed, jogging one after the other till the last was gone.

Norah had stopped in the middle of the meadow, and stood in grass in
sunlight. Flies hummed.

She tossed her head, turned, and trotted back to the line. She went along it
from one to the next, teasing, chivying, Kimmy yelling at her to get back in
line, till Sue broke out of line to chase her and she ran, and then Ev began to
run, whinnying shrilly, and then Cass and Philly and all the rest, the whole
bunch, cantering first and then running flat out, running wild, racing, heading
for Horse Camp and the Long Pasture, for Meredy and the long evening
standing in the fenced field, in the sweet dry grass, in the fetlock-shallow water
of the home creek.

from *Sula*

Toni Morrison was born in Lorain, Ohio, in 1931. She is the author of six novels, including The Bluest Eye *(1970),* Song of Solomon *(1977),* Beloved *(for which she won the Pulitzer prize for fiction in 1988), and* Jazz *(1992). She has also published a book of literary criticism,* Playing in the Dark: Whiteness and the Literary Imagination *(1992). She was awarded the Nobel Prize for Literature in 1993.*

The following charts the friendship of two women, Sula Peace and Nel Wright, here introduced as twelve-year-old girls. Mrs. Wright is Nel's mother, Hannah is Sula's, and Eva is Sula's grandmother.

NEL WRIGHT AND SULA PEACE WERE BOTH TWELVE IN 1922, WISHBONE thin and easy-assed. Nel was the color of wet sandpaper – just dark enough to escape the blows of the pitch-black truebloods and the contempt of old women who worried about such things as bad blood mixtures and knew that the origins of a mule and a mulatto were one and the same. Had she been any lighter-skinned she would have needed either her mother's protection on the way to school or a streak of mean to defend herself. Sula was a heavy brown with large quiet eyes, one of which featured a birthmark that spread from the middle of the lid toward the eyebrow, shaped something like a stemmed rose. It gave her otherwise plain face a broken excitement and blue-blade threat like the keloid scar of the razored man who sometimes played checkers with her grandmother. The birthmark was to grow darker as the years passed, but now it was the same shade as her gold-flecked eyes, which, to the end, were as steady and clean as rain.

Their friendship was as intense as it was sudden. They found relief in each other's personality. Although both were unshaped, formless things, Nel seemed stronger and more consistent than Sula, who could hardly be counted on to sustain any emotion for more than three minutes. Yet there was one time when that was not true, when she held on to a mood for weeks, but even that was in defense of Nel.

Four white boys in their early teens, sons of some newly arrived Irish people, occasionally entertained themselves in the afternoon by harassing black schoolchildren. With shoes that pinched and woolen knickers that made red rings on their calves, they had come to this valley with their parents believing as they did that it was a promised land – green and shimmering with welcome. What they found was a strange accent, a pervasive fear of their religion and firm resistance to their attempts to find work. With one exception the older residents of Medallion scorned them. The one exception was the black community. Although some of the Negroes had been in Medallion before the Civil War (the town didn't even have a name then), if they had any hatred for these newcomers it didn't matter because it didn't show. As a matter of fact, baiting them was the one activity that the white Protestant residents concurred in. In part their place in this world was secured only when they echoed the old residents' attitude toward blacks.

These particular boys caught Nel once, and pushed her from hand to hand until they grew tired of the frightened helpless face. Because of that incident, Nel's route home from school became elaborate. She, and then Sula, managed to duck them for weeks until a chilly day in November when Sula said, "Let's us go on home the shortest way."

Nel blinked, but acquiesced. They walked up the street until they got to the bend of Carpenter's Road where the boys lounged on a disused well. Spotting their prey, the boys sauntered forward as though there were nothing in the world on their minds but the gray sky. Hardly able to control their grins, they stood like a gate blocking the path. When the girls were three feet in front of the boys, Sula reached into her coat pocket and pulled out Eva's paring knife. The boys stopped short, exchanged looks and dropped all pretense of innocence. This was going to be better than they thought. They were going to try and fight back, and with a knife. Maybe they could get an arm around one of their waists, or tear . . .

Sula squatted down in the dirt road and put everything down on the ground: her lunchpail, her reader, her mittens, her slate. Holding the knife in her right hand, she pulled the slate toward her and pressed her left forefinger down hard on its edge. Her aim was determined but inaccurate. She slashed off only the tip of her finger. The four boys stared open-mouthed at the wound and the scrap of flesh, like a button mushroom, curling in the cherry blood that ran into the corners of the slate.

Sula raised her eyes to them. Her voice was quiet. "If I can do that to myself, what you suppose I'll do to you?"

The shifting dirt was the only way Nel knew that they were moving away; she was looking at Sula's face, which seemed miles and miles away.

But toughness was not their quality – adventuresomeness was – and a mean determination to explore everything that interested them, from one-eyed chickens high-stepping in their penned yards to Mr. Buckland Reed's gold teeth, from the sound of sheets flapping in the wind to the labels on Tar Baby's wine bottles. And they had no priorities. They could be distracted from watching a fight with mean razors by the glorious smell of hot tar being poured by roadmen two hundred yards away.

In the safe harbor of each other's company they could afford to abandon the ways of other people and concentrate on their own perceptions of things. When Mrs. Wright reminded Nel to pull her nose, she would do it enthusiastically but without the least hope in the world.

"While you sittin' there, honey, go 'head and pull your nose."

"It hurts, Mamma."

"Don't you want a nice nose when you grow up?"

After she met Sula, Nel slid the clothespin under the blanket as soon as she got in the bed. And although there was still the hateful hot comb to suffer through each Saturday evening, its consequences – smooth hair – no longer interested her.

Joined in mutual admiration they watched each day as though it were a movie arranged for their amusement. The new theme they were now discovering was men. So they met regularly, without even planning it, to walk down the road to Edna Finch's Mellow House, even though it was too cool for ice cream.

Then summer came. A summer limp with the weight of blossomed things. Heavy sunflowers weeping over fences; iris curling and browning at the edges far away from their purple hearts; ears of corn letting their auburn hair wind down to their stalks. And the boys. The beautiful, beautiful boys who dotted the landscape like jewels, split the air with their shouts in the field, and thickened the river with their shining wet backs. Even their footsteps left a smell of smoke behind.

It was in that summer, the summer of their twelfth year, the summer of the beautiful black boys, that they became skittish, frightened and bold – all at the same time.

In that mercury mood in July, Sula and Nel wandered about the Bottom barefoot looking for mischief. They decided to go down by the river where the boys sometimes swam. Nel waited on the porch of 7 Carpenter's Road while Sula ran into the house to go to the toilet. On the way up the stairs, she passed the kitchen where Hannah sat with two friends, Patsy and Valentine. The two women were fanning themselves and watching Hannah put down some dough, all talking casually about one thing and another, and had gotten around, when Sula passed by, to the problems of child rearing.

"They a pain."

"Yeh. Wish I'd listened to mamma. She told me not to have 'em too soon."

"Any time atall is too soon for me."

"Oh, I don't know. My Rudy minds his daddy. He just wild with me. Be glad when he growed and gone."

Hannah smiled and said, "Shut your mouth. You love the ground he pee on."

"Sure I do. But he still a pain. Can't help loving your own child. No matter what they do."

"Well, Hester grown now and I can't say love is exactly what I feel."

"Sure you do. You love her, like I love Sula. I just don't like her. That's the difference."

"Guess so. Likin' them is another thing."

"Sure. They different people, you know . . ."

She only heard Hannah's words, and the pronouncement sent her flying up the stairs. In bewilderment, she stood at the window fingering the curtain edge, aware of a sting in her eye. Nel's call floated up and into the window, pulling her away from dark thoughts back into the bright, hot daylight.

They ran most of the way.

Heading toward the wide part of the river where trees grouped themselves in families darkening the earth below. They passed some boys swimming and clowning in the water, shrouding their words in laughter.

They ran in the sunlight, creating their own breeze, which pressed their dresses into their damp skin. Reaching a kind of square of four leaf-locked trees which promised cooling, they flung themselves into the four-cornered shade to taste their lip sweat and contemplate the wildness that had come upon them so suddenly. They lay in the grass, their foreheads almost touching, their bodies stretched away from each other at a 180-degree angle. Sula's head rested on her arm, an undone braid coiled around her wrist. Nel leaned on her elbows and worried long blades of grass with her fingers. Underneath their dresses flesh

tightened and shivered in the high coolness, their small breasts just now beginning to create some pleasant discomfort when they were lying on their stomachs.

Sula lifted her head and joined Nel in the grass play. In concert, without ever
meeting each other's eyes, they stroked the blades up and down, up and down.
Nel found a thick twig and, with her thumbnail, pulled away its bark until it
was stripped to a smooth, creamy innocence. Sula looked about and found one
too. When both twigs were undressed Nel moved easily to the next stage and
began tearing up rooted grass to make a bare spot of earth. When a generous
clearing was made, Sula traced intricate patterns in it with her twig. At first Nel
was content to do the same. But soon she grew impatient and poked her twig
rhythmically and intensely into the earth, making a small neat hole that grew
deeper and wider with the least manipulation of her twig. Sula copied her, and
soon each had a hole the size of a cup. Nel began a more strenuous digging and,
rising to her knee, was careful to scoop out the dirt as she made her hole deeper.
Together they worked until the two holes were one and the same. When the
depression was the size of a small dishpan, Nel's twig broke. With a gesture of
disgust she threw the pieces into the hole they had made. Sula threw hers in too.
Nel saw a bottle cap and tossed it in as well. Each then looked around for more
debris to throw into the hole: paper, bits of glass, butts of cigarettes, until all of
the small defiling things they could find were collected there. Carefully they
replaced the soil and covered the entire grave with uprooted grass.

Neither one had spoken a word.

In the Night

Jamaica Kincaid was born Elaine Potter Richardson in 1949. She grew up in Antigua, and moved to New York City at the age of sixteen, where she worked as a freelance journalist. Later she became a regular contributor to The New Yorker, *which published many of her early stories. Her books include* At the Bottom of the River *(1978), from which this story is taken, and the novels* Annie John *(1985),* Lucy *(1991), and* Autobiography of My Mother *(1996). She has also written a nonfiction study of Antigua, entitled* A Small Place *(1988).*

Jamaica Kincaid lives with her husband and children in Vermont.

IN THE NIGHT, WAY INTO THE MIDDLE OF THE NIGHT, WHEN THE night isn't divided like a sweet drink into little sips, when there is no just before midnight, midnight, or just after midnight, when the night is round in some places, flat in some places, and in some places like a deep hole, blue at the edge, black inside, the night-soil men come.

They come and go, walking on the damp ground in straw shoes. Their feet in the straw shoes make a scratchy sound. They say nothing.

The night-soil men can see a bird walking in trees. It isn't a bird. It is a woman who has removed her skin and is on her way to drink the blood of her secret enemies. It is a woman who has left her skin in a corner of a house made out of wood. It is a woman who is reasonable and admires honeybees in the hibiscus. It is a woman who, as a joke, brays like a donkey when he is thirsty.

There is the sound of a cricket, there is the sound of a church bell, there is a sound of this house creaking, that house creaking, and the other house creaking as they settle into the ground. There is the sound of a radio in the distance – a fisherman listening to merengue music. There is the sound of a man groaning in his sleep. There is the sound of a woman disgusted at the man groaning. There is the sound of the man stabbing the woman, the sound of her blood as it hits the floor, the sound of Mr. Straffee, the undertaker, taking her body away. There is the sound of her spirit back from the dead, looking at the man who used to groan; he is running a fever forever. There is the sound of a woman writing a letter; there is the sound of her pen nib on the white writing paper;

there is the sound of the kerosene lamp dimming; there is the sound of her head aching.

The rain falls on the tin roofs, on the leaves in the trees, on the stones in the yard, on sand, on the ground. The night is wet in some places, warm in some places.

There is Mr. Gishard, standing under a cedar tree which is in full bloom, wearing that nice white suit, which is as fresh as the day he was buried in it. The white suit came from England in a brown package: "To: Mr. John Gishard," and so on and so on. Mr. Gishard is standing under the tree, wearing his nice suit and holding a glass full of rum in his hand – the same glass full of rum that he had in his hand shortly before he died – and looking at the house in which he used to live. The people who now live in the house walk through the door backward when they see Mr. Gishard standing under the tree, wearing his nice white suit. Mr. Gishard misses his accordion; you can tell by the way he keeps tapping his foot.

In my dream I can hear a baby being born. I can see its face, a pointy little face – so nice. I can see its hands – so nice, again. Its eyes are closed. It's breathing, the little baby. It's breathing. It's bleating, the little baby. It's bleating. The baby and I are now walking to pasture. The baby is eating green grass with its soft and pink lips. My mother is shaking me by the shoulders. My mother says, "Little Miss, Little Miss." I say to my mother, "But it's still night." My mother says, "Yes, but you have wet your bed again." And my mother, who is still young, and still beautiful, and still has pink lips, removes my wet nightgown, removes my wet sheets from my bed. My mother can change everything. In my dream I am in the night.

"What are the lights in the mountains?"

"The lights in the mountains? Oh, it's a jablesse."

"A jablesse! But why? What's a jablesse?"

"It's a person who can turn into anything. But you can tell they aren't real because of their eyes. Their eyes shine like lamps, so bright that you can't look. That's how you can tell it's a jablesse. They like to go up in the mountains and gallivant. Take good care when you see a beautiful woman. A jablesse always tries to look like a beautiful woman."

No one has ever said to me, "My father, a night-soil man, is very nice and very kind. When he passes a dog, he gives a pat and not a kick. He likes all the parts of a fish but especially the head. He goes to church quite regularly and is always glad when the minister calls out, 'A Mighty Fortress Is Our God,' his favorite hymn. He would like to wear pink shirts and pink pants but knows that this color isn't very becoming to a man, so instead he wears navy blue and brown, colors he does not like at all. He met my mother on what masquerades as a bus around here, a long time ago, and he still likes to whistle. Once, while running to catch a bus, he fell and broke his ankle and had to spend a week in hospital. This made him miserable, but he cheered up quite a bit when he saw my mother and me, standing over his white cot, holding bunches of yellow roses and smiling down at him. Then he said, 'Oh, my. Oh, my.' What he likes to do most, my father the night-soil man, is to sit on a big stone under a mahogany tree and watch small children playing play-cricket while he eats the intestines of animals stuffed with blood and rice and drinks ginger beer. He has told me this many times: 'My dear, what I like to do most,' and so on. He is always reading botany books and knows a lot about rubber plantations and rubber trees; but this is an interest I can't explain, since the only rubber tree he has ever seen is a specially raised one in the botanic gardens. He sees to it that my school shoes fit comfortably. I love my father the night-soil man. My mother loves my father the night-soil man. Everybody loves him and waves to him whenever they see him. He is very handsome, you know, and I have seen women look at him twice. On special days he wears a brown felt hat, which he orders from England, and brown leather shoes, which he also orders from England. On ordinary days he goes barehead. When he calls me, I say, 'Yes, sir.' On my mother's birthday he always buys her some nice cloth for a new dress as a present. He makes us happy, my father the night-soil man, and has promised that one day he will take us to see something he has read about called the circus."

In the night, the flowers close up and thicken. The hibiscus flowers, the flamboyant flowers, the bachelor's buttons, the irises, the marigolds, the whitehead-bush flowers, the lilies, the flowers on the daggerbush, the flowers on the turtleberry bush, the flowers on the soursop tree, the flowers on the sugar-apple tree, the flowers on the mango tree, the flowers on the guava tree, the flowers on the cedar tree, the flowers on the stinking-toe tree, the flowers on the dumps tree, the flowers on the papaw tree, the flowers everywhere close up and thicken. The flowers are vexed.

Someone is making a basket, someone is making a girl a dress or a boy a shirt, someone is making her husband a soup with cassava so that he can take it to the cane field tomorrow, someone is making his wife a beautiful mahogany chest, someone is sprinkling a colorless powder outside a closed door so that someone else's child will be stillborn, someone is praying that a bad child who is living prosperously abroad will be good and send a package filled with new clothes, someone is sleeping.

Now I am a girl, but one day I will marry a woman – a red-skin woman with black bramblebush hair and brown eyes, who wears skirts that are so big I can easily bury my head in them. I would like to marry this woman and live with her in a mud hut near the sea. In the mud hut will be two chairs and one table, a lamp that burns kerosene, a medicine chest, a pot, one bed, two pillows, two sheets, one looking glass, two cups, two saucers, two dinner plates, two forks, two drinking-water glasses, one china pot, two fishing strings, two straw hats to ward the hot sun off our heads, two trunks for things we have very little use for, one basket, one book of plain paper, one box filled with twelve crayons of different colors, one loaf of bread wrapped in a piece of brown paper, one coal pot, one picture of two women standing on a jetty, one picture of the same two women embracing, one picture of the same two women waving goodbye, one box of matches. Every day this red-skin woman and I will eat bread and milk for breakfast, hide in bushes and throw hardened cow dung at people we don't like, climb coconut trees, pick coconuts, eat and drink the food and water from the coconuts we have picked, throw stones in the sea, put on John Bull masks and frighten defenseless little children on their way home from school, go fishing and catch only our favorite fishes to roast and have for dinner, steal green figs to eat for dinner with the roast fish. Every day we would do this. Every night I would sing this woman a song; the words I don't know yet, but the tune is in my head. This woman I would like to marry knows many things, but to me she will only tell about things that would never dream of making me cry; and every night, over and over, she will tell me something that begins, "Before you were born." I will marry a woman like this, and every night, every night, I will be completely happy.

Alexis De Veaux

Adventures of the Dread Sisters

Alexis De Veaux was born and raised in New York City. Among her books are Spirits in the Street *(1973), a memoir;* Don't Explain *(1980), a biography of jazz singer Billie Holiday; and two award-winning children's books. De Veaux has also published a number of poems, short stories, and essays, and her plays have been produced on television, off Broadway, and in regional theatres.*

She says that she has always embraced her tomboy self, and fully expects to grow old with her.

WE CROSSING THE BROOKLYN BRIDGE. TRAFFIC IS SLOW GOING. Bumper to bumper. And cars everywhere. Taxis blowing horns. It's Saturday morning. Everybody making it to Manhattan. Us too. We got to get there soon. Before the snow. Threatening to cover the city. Any minute now. We going to the RALLY AGAINST GOVERNMENT TRUCKS HAULING NUCLEAR WASTE THROUGH HARLEM. Every day for a week they been saying on the radio

> *don't worry folks*
> *don't worry*
> *don't worry it's safe*

I might be only 15 but even I know ain't nothing safe. Not on no city street. Anything could happen. So I don't believe nothing the government says. Personally, I'm through with the government. Too many people ain't got jobs. And whole families be living in the streets. I'm for get rid of the government, give life back to the people.

We stuck on this bridge. We got 25 minutes to get uptown.

> *Is that soot or snow I see*
> *falling up ahead*

46]

Hope it ain't snow
The windshield wipers don't work
too tough
Nigeria says.

Nigeria and me, we call ourselves The Dread Sisters. We're not real sisters. She's not my real mother neither. But she raised me. So we are definite family. We even look alike. Both of us short and got big eyes. Both of us got dreadlocks. Just like the Africans in the pictures in Nigeria's books.

We got twenty minutes before the rally start. We slow dragging our wheels over the bridge's skin. Our blue Pinto crammed between two screaming-yellow taxis. The East River below us. The gray sky above. Manhattan coming slowly nearer. I stare at Nigeria out the corner of my eye. She sucking her teeth. Mashing on the brakes. She hate to be late. She catch me staring. Winks. Locks her eyes back on the road.

My sister Toni and me been living with Nigeria ever since we was little. She adopted us. Then moved us to a house on Adelphi Street. Got a backyard and a attic. Got my own room and so do Toni. Got a home. Nigeria be like our mother and father. And for my money, I wouldn't have it no other way. But Toni ain't like me and Nigeria. Toni be liking boys. She don't like books. She like to straighten her hair cause she in high school. Toni be the last person to get up before noon on a Saturday. Don't care whether it's a life and death thing like a rally or not. The whole planet could blow up it wouldn't wake Toni up.

Nigeria
What
I don't want to die in no nuclear war
Ain't gonna be no nuclear war pumpkin

she says in her Colored and Progressive Peoples' Campaign office-voice

God won't allow it

People who make bombs
don't believe in God

I fires back at her. And she don't say nothing but roll down her window. December hit us slap in the face.

Nigeria got a profile like a African sculpture. She be looking carved outta black wood. Her lips be chiseled. And she got a mole above her right cheek. Like somebody dotted her eyebrow. Ain't nothing moving on this bridge.

It's what you *believe that counts*

she finally says

> *never play the game by the enemy's*
> *rules fight back*
> *Whether it's bullets or bombs*
> *do the unexpected*

then she pokes her head out the window. The red leather Nefertiti-shaped crown holding her dreads falls to one side. Three lanes of cars plug up the bridge. From one end to the other. We move a little bit. Stop go. Stop. I open up my sketchbook. Flip through the drawings. Till I get to the ones I'm doing on Afa Tu Twelve. Which is this made-up planet. Where all the females become Ebabas, the hooded blueblack women who fly.

Nigeria gave me my first sketchbook. And taught me how to draw. She's a painter. Used to work summers on the boardwalk in Atlantic City. Doing charcoal portraits. One for 3 dollars or two for 5. Me and Toni used to go with her. I remember one day a old Black lady came by Nigeria's stall. She was old but she was beautiful. All dressed in black. With a black hat and veil. Black summer gloves. Some medals pinned to the lapel of her dress. She walked with a military step. She had watched Nigeria draw all summer. And now she wanted her picture done. So Nigeria sat the old lady down and started drawing. It took nearly 3 hours. To do a job that usually takes 20 minutes. By the time she finished there was a crowd of people standing around *oooi*ng and *aaah*ing. Everybody was saying how the old woman had jumped into Nigeria's eyes. Poured herself through Nigeria's fingers. Liquefied on the paper. The picture shimmered when it was finished. It made the old lady happy.

Daughter

she said to Nigeria

these is God's hands you got

and she kissed Nigeria's fingers and pressed a brand-new 20 dollar bill in Nigeria's hand. And walked away. Humming "Lift Every Voice and Sing." Nigeria still got that 20 dollar bill. Which she keep in a black silk handkerchief. Tied with a red string and a little piece of paper, "1967" written on it.

The year Langston Hughes
died

she's in the habit of reminding me because he was her favorite poet.

Anyway we caught in this no-moving traffic. Nigeria not mashing so hard on the brakes now. We stop and go some more. It is cold inside the car. She leans forward. Rolls up her window. Sits back. I ask before I think not to.

How come you never had no kids
of your own Nigeria
I didn't want any of my own
I wanted some that belonged to the world

Then she don't say no more. Look like she thinking. I'm thinking too. I wonder if there's gonna be a world.

Over our heads the sky is thick with the threat of snow. We stuck on the bridge. Nothing's moving. And it's 5-to-the-rally. Nigeria reaches into the back seat. Grabs a bunch of flyers. Gives me some.

If you can't get to the rally
when it starts
start the rally wherever you are

she says. And jumps out the car. Her yellow wool coat whipped by the wind. And I'm right behind her. Snuggled up in my big jacket. My neck wrapped twice with cloth from Kenya. We leave Miss Pinto in a herd of cars. Nigeria take one lane. I take the other. We passing out flyers when sure enough here we are in another adventure cause here comes the snow.

THE END

PART THREE

On the Threshold

Toni Cade Bambara

Gorilla, My Love

Toni Cade Bambara (1939-1995) was born and brought up in New York City. She was one of the first writers to address the issue of Black awareness and feminism, in her book-length anthologies The Black Woman *(1970) and* Tales and Stories for Black Folk *(1971). These were followed by two collections of short stories,* Gorilla, My Love *(1972) and* The Sea Birds Are Still Alive *(1977), as well as a novel,* The Salt Eaters *(1980). Bambara's last book,* Deep Sightings and Rescue Missions: Stories, Essays and Conversation, *appeared posthumously in 1996.*

THAT WAS THE YEAR HUNCA BUBBA CHANGED HIS NAME. NOT A CHANGE up, but a change back, since Jefferson Winston Vale was the name in the first place. Which was news to me cause he'd been my Hunca Bubba my whole lifetime, since I couldn't manage Uncle to save my life. So far as I was concerned it was a change completely to somethin soundin very geographical weatherlike to me, like somethin you'd find in a almanac. Or somethin you'd run across when you sittin in the navigator seat with a wet thumb on the map crinkly in your lap, watchin the roads and signs so when Granddaddy Vale say "Which way, Scout," you got sense enough to say take the next exit or take a left or whatever it is. Not that Scout's my name. Just the name Granddaddy call whoever sittin in the navigator seat. Which is usually me cause I don't feature sittin in the back with the pecans. Now, you figure pecans all right to be sittin with. If you thinks so, that's your business. But they dusty sometime and make you cough. And they got a way of slidin around and dippin down sudden, like maybe a rat in the buckets. So if you scary like me, you sleep with the lights on and blame it on Baby Jason and, so as not to waste good electric, you study the maps. And that's how come I'm in the navigator seat most times and get to be called Scout.

So Hunca Bubba in the back with the pecans and Baby Jason, and he in love. And we got to hear all this stuff about this woman he in love with and all. Which really ain't enough to keep the mind alive, though Baby Jason got no better sense than to give his undivided attention and keep grabbin at the photograph which is just a picture of some skinny woman in a countrified dress with her hand shot up to her face like she shame fore cameras. But there's a movie house in the background which I ax about. Cause I am a movie freak from way back, even though it do get me in trouble sometime.

Like when me and Big Brood and Baby Jason was on our own last Easter and couldn't go to the Dorset cause we'd seen all the Three Stooges they was. And the RKO Hamilton was closed readying up for the Easter Pageant that night. And the West End, the Regun and the Sunset was too far, less we had grownups with us which we didn't. So we walk up Amsterdam Avenue to the Washington and *Gorilla, My Love* playin, they say, which suit me just fine, though the "my love" part kinda drag Big Brood some. As for Baby Jason, shoot, like Granddaddy say, he'd follow me into the fiery furnace if I say come on. So we go in and get three bags of Havmore potato chips which not only are the best potato chips but the best bags for blowin up and bustin real loud so the matron come trottin down the aisle with her chunky self, flashin that flashlight dead in your eye so you can give her some lip, and if she answer back and you already finish seein the show anyway, why then you just turn the place out. Which I love to do, no lie. With Baby Jason kickin at the seat in front, egging me on, and Big Brood mumblin bout what fiercesome things we goin do. Which means me. Like when the big boys come up on us talkin about Lemme a nickel. It's me that hide the money. Or when the bad boys in the park take Big Brood's Spaudeen way from him. It's me that jump on they back and fight awhile. And it's me that turns out the show if the matron get too salty.

So the movie come on and right away it's this churchy music and clearly not about no gorilla. Bout Jesus. And I am ready to kill, not cause I got anything gainst Jesus. Just that when you fixed to watch a gorilla picture you don't wanna get messed around with Sunday School stuff. So I am mad. Besides, we see this raggedy old brown film *King of Kings* every year and enough's enough. Grownups figure they can treat you just anyhow. Which burns me up. There I am, my feet up and my Havmore potato chips really salty and crispy and two jawbreakers in my lap and the money safe in my shoe from the big boys, and here comes this Jesus stuff. So we all go wild. Yellin, booin, stompin and carryin on. Really to wake the man in the booth up there who musta went to sleep and put on the wrong reels. But no, cause he holler down to shut up and then he turn the sound up so we really gotta holler like crazy to even hear ourselves good. And the matron ropes off the children section and flashes her light all over the place and we yell some more and some kids slip under the rope and run up and down the aisle just to show it take more than some dusty ole velvet rope to tie us down. And I'm flingin the kid in front of me's popcorn. And Baby Jason kickin seats. And it's really somethin. Then here come the big and bad matron, the one they let out in case of emergency. And she totin that flashlight like she gonna use it on somebody. This here the colored matron Brandy and her friends call Thunderbuns. She do not play. She do not smile. So we shut up and watch the simple ass picture.

Which is not so simple as it is stupid. Cause I realize that just about anybody in my family is better than this god they always talkin about. My daddy wouldn't stand for nobody treatin any of us that way. My mama specially. And I can just see it now, Big Brood up there on the cross talkin bout Forgive them Daddy cause they don't know what they doin. And my Mama say Get on down from there you big fool, whatcha think this is, playtime? And my Daddy yellin to Granddaddy to get him a ladder cause Big Brood actin the fool, his mother side of the family showin up. And my mama and her sister Daisy jumpin on them Romans beatin them with they pocketbooks. And Hunca Bubba tellin them folks on they knees they better get out the way and go get some help or they goin to get trampled on. And Granddaddy Vale sayin Leave the boy alone, if that's what he wants to do with his life we ain't got nothin to say about it. Then Aunt Daisy givin him a taste of that pocketbook, fussin bout what a damn fool old man Granddaddy is. Then everybody jumpin in his chest like the time Uncle Clayton went in the army and come back with only one leg and Granddaddy say somethin stupid about that's life. And by this time Big Brood off the cross and in the park playin handball or skully or somethin. And the family in the kitchen throwin dishes at each other, screamin bout if you hadn't done this I wouldn't had to do that. And me in the parlor trying to do my arithmetic yellin Shut it off.

Which is what I was yellin all by myself which make me a sittin target for Thunderbuns. But when I yell We want our money back, that gets everybody in chorus. And the movie windin up with this heavenly cloud music and the smart-ass up there in his hole in the wall turns up the sound again to drown us out. Then there comes Bugs Bunny which we already seen so we know we been had. No gorilla my nuthin. And Big Brood say Awwww sheeet, we goin to see the manager and get our money back. And I know from this we business. So I brush the potato chips out of my hair which is where Baby Jason like to put em, and I march myself up the aisle to deal with the manager who is a crook in the first place for lyin out there sayin *Gorilla, My Love* playin. And I never did like the man cause he oily and pasty at the same time like the bad guy in the serial, the one that got a hideout behind a push-button bookcase and play "Moonlight Sonata" with gloves on. I knock on the door and I am furious. And I am alone, too. Cause Big Brood suddenly got to go so bad even though my Mama told us bout goin in them nasty bathrooms. And I hear him sigh like he disgusted when he get to the door and see only a little kid there. And now I'm really furious cause I get so tired grownups messin over kids just cause they little and can't take em to court. What is it, he say to me like I lost my mittens or wet on myself or am somebody's retarded child. When in reality I am the smartest kid P.S. 186 ever had in its whole lifetime and you can ax anybody. Even them teachers that don't like me cause I won't sing them Southern songs or back off when they tell me my questions are out of order. And cause my Mama come up there in a minute when them teachers start playin the dozens behind colored folks. She stalk in with her hat pulled down bad and that Persian lamb coat draped back over one hip on account of she got her fist planted there so she can talk that talk which gets us all hypnotized, and teacher be comin undone cause she know this could be her job and her behind cause Mama got pull with the Board and bad by her own self anyhow.

So I kick the door open wider and just walk right by him and sit down and tell the man about himself and that I want my money back and that goes for Baby Jason and Big Brood too. And he still trying to shuffle me out the door even though I'm sittin which shows him for the fool he is. Just like them teachers do fore they realize Mama like a stone on that spot and ain't backin up. So he ain't gettin up off the money. So I was forced to leave, takin the matches from under his ashtray, and set a fire under the candy stand, which closed the raggedy ole Washington down for a week. My Daddy had the suspect it was me cause Big Brood got a big mouth. But I explained right quick what the whole thing was about and I figured it was even-steven. Cause if you say Gorilla, My Love, you suppose to mean it. Just like when you say you goin to give me a party on my birthday, you gotta mean it. And if you say me and Baby Jason can go South pecan haulin with Granddaddy Vale, you better not be comin up with no stuff about the weather look uncertain or did you mop the bathroom or any other trickified business. I mean even gangsters in the movies say My word is my bond. So don't nobody get away with nothin far as I'm concerned. So Daddy put his belt back on. Cause that's the way I was raised. Like my Mama say in one of them situations when I won't back down, Okay Badbird, you right. Your point is well-taken. Not that Badbird my name, just what she say when she tired arguin and know I'm right. And Aunt Jo, who is the hardest head in the family and worse even than Aunt Daisy, she say, You absolutely right Miss Muffin, which also ain't my real name but the name she gave me one time when I got some medicine shot in my behind and wouldn't get up off her pillows for nothin. And even Granddaddy Vale – who got no memory to speak of, so sometime you can just plain lie to him, if you want to be like that – he say, Well if that's what I said, then that's it. But this name business was different they said. It wasn't like Hunca Bubba had gone back on his word or anything. Just that he was thinkin bout gettin married and was usin his real name now. Which ain't the way I saw it at all.

So there I am in the navigator seat. And I turn to him and just plain ole ax him. I mean I come right on out with it. No sense goin all around that barn the old folks talk about. And like my mama say, Hazel – which is my real name and what she remembers to call me when she bein serious – when you got somethin on your mind, speak up and let the chips fall where they may. And if anybody don't like it, tell em to come see your mama. And Daddy look up from the paper and say, You hear your mama good, Hazel. And tell em to come see me first. Like that. That's how I was raised.

So I turn clear round in the navigator seat and say, "Look here, Hunca Bubba or Jefferson Windsong Vale or whatever your name is, you gonna marry this girl?"

"Sure am," he say, all grins.

And I say, "Member that time you was baby-sittin me when we lived at four-o-nine and there was this big snow and Mama and Daddy got held up in the country so you had to stay for two days?"

And he say, "Sure do."

"Well. You remember how you told me I was the cutest thing that ever walked the earth?"

"Oh, you were real cute when you were little," he say, which is suppose to be funny. I am not laughin.

"Well. You remember what you said?"

And Granddaddy Vale squintin over the wheel and axin Which way, Scout. But Scout is busy and don't care if we all get lost for days.

"Watcha mean, Peaches?"

"My name is Hazel. And what I mean is you said you were going to marry *me* when I grew up. You were going to wait. That's what I mean, my dear Uncle Jefferson." And he don't say nuthin. Just look at me real strange like he never saw me before in life. Like he lost in some weird town in the middle of night and lookin for directions and there's no one to ask. Like it was me that messed up the maps and turned the road posts round. "Well, you said it, didn't you?" And Baby Jason lookin back and forth like we playin ping-pong. Only I ain't playin. I'm hurtin and I can hear that I am screamin. And Granddaddy Vale mumblin how we never gonna get to where we goin if I don't turn around and take my navigator job serious.

"Well, for cryin out loud, Hazel, you just a little girl. And I was just teasin."

" 'And I was just teasin,' " I say back just how he said it so he can hear what a terrible thing it is. Then I don't say nuthin. And he don't say nuthin. And Baby Jason don't say nuthin nohow. Then Granddaddy Vale speak up. "Look here, Precious, it was Hunca Bubba what told you them things. This here, Jefferson Winston Vale. And Hunca Bubba say, "That's right. That was somebody else. I'm a new somebody."

"You a lyin dawg," I say, when I meant to say treacherous dog, but just couldn't get hold of the word. It slipped away from me. And I'm crying and crumplin down in the seat and just don't care. And Granddaddy say to hush and steps on the gas. And I'm losin my bearins and don't even know where to look on the map cause I can't see for cryin. And Baby Jason cryin too. Cause he is my blood brother and understands that we must stick together or be forever lost, what with grownups playin change-up and turnin you round every which way so bad. And don't even say they sorry.

Nina Newington

Woman, Man, and *Trousers*

Nina Newington was born in Hong Kong in 1958. She is English by nationality, and has lived in the United States since 1981. As a child she called herself Mike and planned to go to sea. These days she works as a writer and garden designer in the hills of western Massachusetts. The excerpts included here are from her first novel, Harvest of Ghosts. *Other excerpts have appeared in* The American Voice *and* Resurgent: New Writings by Women *(1992).*

WOMAN

Dave never tells me stories, she makes cartoons instead. All the people have square jaws. The boys have slicked back hair and the girls have ponytails. She gave me a cartoon of my father. I keep it in the chest. First he is holding a golf club, ready to swing. He is looking straight ahead. Then he is running and his knee is very sharp and almost up to his chin, the other leg points straight out behind him toward the swarm of bees which chase him like a long black cloud. Then he is lying in a ditch of water with only his feet sticking up and the cloud is passing over him and there is a frog sitting on a log with its mouth open. Then there is a big picture of the frog with its mouth so wide it looks like it is laughing. The frog has spots on its back and if you look close the spots are really bees.

She hands me the one she just made. There is a boy with a stick sticking out in front of his jeans. He is whistling. In the next frame there is a girl. Her eyes are big and round and her eyebrows look like question marks. Her mouth is an O and inbetween her legs is another O. Then there is a car. Then the boy and the girl are standing opposite each other. The little lines behind their legs say they are walking towards each other. Then the boy's stick is in the girl's O. Where the stick sticks through the O it is drawn in dots. The girl's feet don't touch the ground anymore and the boy isn't whistling.

I look at it for a long time. "Where does it go?" My cheeks feel so big and red I can see them out of the bottom of my eyes. I have to know. My stomach hurts.

"It goes inside the girl," says Dave.

[59

"But where?" I want to cry. "There isn't room."

Dave goes in her closet and puts her hand in one of her sneakers. She brings out a piece of paper which she unfolds and spreads on her knee. There, against a blue background, is a woman, all white. She is cut in half. She has long pointy fingernails. It is a diagram. She is pushing a small stick up a gap which leads to something that looks like a catcher's mitt only it has more fingers. It looks like something that grows on the bottom of the ocean. "Where did you get this?"

"The trash. I found something else in the trash too. It's a secret."

I look at her. "We're brothers, remember."

She takes this piece of paper out of her other sneaker. It is bigger and shinier. She starts to unfold it. One side is jagged like it was torn out of a book. First I see the beach and then I see her shoes. They are black and shiny with pointy toes and long thin heels which sink down in the sand. Then we go up her legs which are long too and far apart. Dave stops. She goes to the door and listens then she unfolds it another time and where her legs meet there is hair, it is yellow and glinty except in the middle where something pinky brown sticks down like a tongue.

"That's her pussy," says Dave.

"I know," I say because I need to hear my voice sound big and strong but it doesn't and then I say, "It's yellow" which doesn't make any sense to me either.

Dave keeps going. The woman has sharp red fingernails. She holds her waist in and her nails point down like little neon lights. I want to say stop but then there is her bosom.

"Titties," says Dave.

They are like balloons full of water with the knots sticking out. Her arms stick out from her body so you can see the beach and the sea and on the right side there is a palm tree only I can't see the top of it yet. Then there is the rest of the tree and her neck is long like the tree. It goes up and up to her chin which is tipped back. Right by her neck the paper is torn.

"Who is it?" I say to Dave.

"I don't know. It's just someone in a magazine."

Her mouth is huge and red and shining. It is an O too only I can see the tip of her tongue in the corner of her mouth. It is curled around like a snake's tail and her teeth are very big and white. I am afraid to see her eyes, I know they will be hard and black but they aren't, they are half covered with eyelids, and her eyelashes are so long it is like she is looking through tall grass at me. I can see the wind in her hair and the sky is blue. At the very top in little black letters it says, "Playboy July 1967." Dave whistles. I take the piece of paper and hold it in front of me. The way she is standing is weird, it is like she is pinned out on a board, like the seahorse in Peg's house. "I don't get it."

"You're not supposed to get it dummy."

"What's it for?"

"It's for men to look at. Sailors do it all the time."

"Oh."

"That's what they do when it's too dark to fish."

Dave knows she knows something I don't. I don't care. My head feels crowded. I keep thinking how she couldn't go anywhere in the sand with those shoes. It is a thought which keeps the other thoughts back.

"You wanna take it?"

"What?"

"Her, dummy."

"Why?"

"You could put it in your marine chest with the equipment."

"Why don't you keep it?"

"Because it's better in your chest. You can lock it."

I know Dave's mom snoops a lot. "O.K."

"Take the other picture too."

"No, throw that in the trash." I fold her up and put her in my pocket. When I get home I'll put her inside my flashlight wrapped around the batteries.

MAN

I am grown, a tall and handsome man. Nothing will be wrong. My mother leans her head on my shoulder. We stroll in the garden. I am wearing corduroys. Muscle stretches across the boney plate of my chest. My forearms fill the tweed jacket I wear. I could lift her, carry her across any river. I feel no pressure, only the gathering together of muscle in my shoulders. It is as if I have wings. Nothing is wrong. Her fingers are touching my wrist. In the distance I see my father. He is a thin giant. Stooped. He is the dried skin of a melon. I have scooped the seeds, the juice runs sweet in my veins. At any step my toes could push my mother and me from the ground. In one enormous stride we might be anywhere. A tiger looks at me. His stripes ripple like a catspaw on water. I look in his yellow eyes. He is gone. I am a man. I run the marathon. My bronzed body oiled, I run. In Sparta I am a hero. My body coils and hurls the javelin. The people cheer and then are silent as the javelin travels up up toward the sun.

A thin dark pole it will pierce the sun. The people are afraid. When I swim I swim at night. I follow the path of the moon. Lightning plays in my hair and I am not afraid. At the end of every race I run my mother kneels before me. She anoints my feet. She kisses the place where I am a man. From a great height I watch her head bobbing like a ball on the waves. My eyes have flown up to the sky. I watch. I will call out her name. I must. I must follow the road to its end.

TROUSERS

I hear footsteps in the hall. I lie with my arms by my side and my eyelids don't move. I am asleep. Bill went to sleep a long time ago. The door opens. She turns on the light.

"Goodnight," she says. Her voice is thin.

I won't look. She walks to the chair. My father is away. He's away. He isn't here. He went away. He went away to look at war. The war. He's away. She picks up something. She's in the middle of the room. I want to go away. Everywhere in my body I want to go away. I want to go away anywhere. I want to go. She's standing still. She's looking at me. I won't look. I can feel her eyes sucking on my cheeks.

"If you want to be a man, you have to learn to fold your trousers properly. Look at this, a crumpled mess."

I won't. She knows. I won't. I won't look.

"If you want to be a man you have to learn to fold your trousers properly. IF. YOU. WANT. TO. BE. A. MAN. YOU. HAVE. TO. LEARN. TO. FOLD. YOUR. TROUSERS. PROPERLY."

I open my eyes. Bill will wake up. She is standing by the chair. She is holding my jeans in front of her. She holds them upside down so the belt buckle dangles down. She pinches together the two legs so the seam is on the side. Her eyes don't have anything in the middle. I feel sick. She shouldn't know. I don't want her to know anything. I live on an island.

"LOOK. AT. ME."

She is still holding them by the bottom. Now she flips them up over her arm. They lie over her arm with the seam facing me.

"There," she says. "There." She smiles at them. "Do you see? DO. YOU. SEE."

"Yes."

"Yes what?"

"Yes thank you."

"Yes what thank you?"

"Yes Mum thank you."

She goes to the closet and gets out a hanger. I can't breathe. She hangs up the jeans and she slides the closet door shut. I close my eyes. I am asleep. I think she can hear my heart.

"Goodnight." She is near the door.

"G'night." I mumble it. She shuts the door. The light is still on. She's gone. I think about her fingers on my jeans. It makes me sick. It. Makes. Me. Sick. Bill hasn't moved at all. I don't know if he is asleep. I wish Dad would come home. I send him a thought in the air. To Biafra. He's flying in a plane with Prince Richard. It is dark except for the green light of the instrument panel. They are sitting close together in the little airplane. Prince Richard is steering. It is too dark to see except when a gun fires and then the ground is covered in dead bodies and the animals are taking legs and arms away in the bush to eat and the animals' eyes are green and shining. Prince Richard and my father fly back and forth. Nobody can shoot them. I get up and turn out the light.

Becky Birtha

Johnnieruth

Becky Birtha was born in Virginia in 1948. She is the author of two collections of short stories, both of which foreground African-American women, For Nights Like This One: Stories of Loving Women *(1983) and* Lovers' Choice *(1987), from which "Johnnieruth" is taken. She has also published a poetry collection entitled* The Forbidden Poems *(1991).*

Birtha's stories have been anthologized in more than twenty college textbooks, and have appeared in such trade anthologies as Woman on Woman *(1990) and* Daughters of Africa *(1991). She lives in Philadelphia.*

THERE WAS ONE SUNDAY WHEN I MUSTA BEEN AROUND EIGHT. I REMEMber it was before my sister Corletta was born, cause right around then was when I put my foot down about that whole sanctimonious routine. Anyway, I was dragging my feet along Twenty-fifth Street in back of Mama and Vincent and them, when I spied this lady. I only seen her that one time but I still remember just how she look. She don't look like nobody I ever seen before. I *know* she don't live around here. She real skinny. But she ain't no real young woman, neither. She could be old as my mama. She ain't nobody's mama – I'm sure. And she ain't wearing Sunday clothes. She got on blue jeans and a man's blue working shirt, with the tail hanging out. She got patches on her blue jeans, and she still got her chin stuck out like she some kinda African royalty. She ain't carrying no shiny pocketbook. It don't look like she care if she got any money or not, or who know it, if she don't. She ain't wearing no house-shoes, or stockings or high heels neither.

Mama always speak to everybody, but when she pass by this lady she make like she ain't even seen her. But I get me a real good look, and the lady stare right back at me. She got a funny look on her face, almost like she think she know me from some place. After she pass on by, I had to turn around to get another look, even though Mama say that ain't polite. And you know what? She was turning around, too, looking back at me. And she give me a great big smile.

I didn't know much in them days, but that's when I first got to thinking about how it's got to be different ways to be, from the way people be around my way.

It's got to be places where it don't matter to nobody if you all dressed up on Sunday morning or you ain't. That's how come I started saving money. So, when I got enough, I could go away to some place like that.

Afterwhile I begun to see there wasn't no point in waiting around for handouts, and I started thinking of ways to earn my own money. I used to be running errands all the time – mailing letters for old Grandma Whittaker and picking up cigarettes and newspapers up the corner for everybody. After I got bigger, I started washing cars in the summer, and shoveling people sidewalk in the wintertime. Now I got me a newspaper route. Ain't never been no girl around here with no paper route, but I guess everybody got it figured out by now that I ain't gonna be like nobody else.

The reason I got me my Peugeot was so I could start to explore. I figured I better start looking around right now, so when I'm grown, I'll know exactly where I wanna go. So I ride around every chance I get.

Last summer, I used to ride with the boys a lot. Sometimes eight or ten of us'd just go cruising around the streets together. All of a sudden my mama decide she don't want me to do that no more. She say I'm too old to be spending so much time with boys. (That's what they tell you half the time, and the other half the time they worried cause you ain't interested in spending more time with boys. Don't make much sense.) She want me to have some girl friends, but I never seem to fit in with none of the things the girls doing. I used to think I fit in more with the boys.

But I seen how Mama might be right, for once. I didn't like the way the boys was starting to talk about girls sometimes. Talking about what some girl be like from the neck on down, and talking all up underneath somebody clothes and all. Even though I wasn't really friends with none of the girls, I still didn't like it. So now I mostly just ride around by myself. And Mama don't like that neither – you just can't please her.

This boy that live around the corner on North Street, Kenny Henderson, started asking me one time if I don't ever be lonely, cause he always see me by myself. He say don't I ever think I'd like to have me somebody special to go places with and stuff. Like I'd pick him if I did! Made me wanna laugh in his face. I do be lonely, a lotta times, but I don't tell nobody. And I ain't met nobody yet that I'd really rather be with than be by myself. But I will someday. When I find that special place where everybody different, I'm gonna find somebody there I can be friends with. And it ain't gonna be no dumb boy.

I found me one place already, that I like to go to a whole lot. It ain't even really that far – by bike – but it's on the other side of the Avenue. So I don't tell Mama and them I go there, cause they like to think I'm right around the neighborhood someplace. But this neighborhood too dull for me. All the houses look just the same – no porches, no yards, no trees – not even no parks around here. Every block look so much like every other block it hurt your eyes to look at, afterwhile. So I ride across Summit Avenue and go down that big steep hill there, and then make a sharp right at the bottom and cross the bridge over the train tracks. Then I head on out the boulevard – that's the nicest part, with all them big trees making a tunnel over the top, and lightning bugs shining in the bushes. At the end of the boulevard you get to this place call the Plaza.

It's something like a little park – the sidewalks is all bricks and they got flowers planted all over the place. The same kind my mama grow in that painted-up tire she got out front masquerading like a garden decoration – only seem like they smell sweeter here. It's a big high fountain right in the middle, and all the streetlights is the real old-fashion kind. That Plaza is about the prettiest place I ever been.

Sometimes something going on there. Like a orchestra playing music or some man or lady singing. One time they had a show with some girls doing some kinda foreign dances. They look like they were around my age. They all had on these fancy costumes, with different color ribbons all down they back. I wouldn't wear nothing like that, but it looked real pretty when they was dancing.

I got me a special bench in one corner where I like to sit, cause I can see just about everything, but wouldn't nobody know I was there. I like to sit still and think, and I like to watch people. A lotta people be coming there at night – to look at the shows and stuff, or just to hang out and cool off. All different kinda people.

This one night when I was sitting over in that corner where I always be at, there was this lady standing right near my bench. She mostly had her back turned to me and she didn't know I was there, but I could see her real good. She had on this shiny purple shirt and about a million silver bracelets. I kinda liked the way she look. Sorta exotic, like she maybe come from California or one of the islands. I mean she had class – standing there posing with her arms folded. She walk away a little bit. Then turn around and walk back again. Like she waiting for somebody.

Then I spotted this dude coming over. I spied him all the way cross the Plaza. Looking real fine. Got on a three-piece suit. One of them little caps sitting on a angle. Look like leather. He coming straight over to this lady I'm watching and then she seen him too and she start to smile, but she don't move till he get right up next to her. And then I'm gonna look away, cause I can't stand to watch nobody hugging and kissing on each other, but all of a sudden I see it ain't no dude at all. It's another lady.

Now I can't stop looking. They smile at each other like they ain't seen one another in ten years. Then the one in the purple shirt look around real quick – but she don't look just behind her – and sorta pull the other one right back into the corner where I'm sitting at, and then they put they arms around each other and kiss – for a whole long time. Now I really know I oughtta turn away, but I can't. And I know they gonna see me when they finally open they eyes. And they do.

They both kinda gasp and back up, like I'm the monster that just rose up outta the deep. And then I guess they can see I'm only a girl, and they look at one another – and start to laugh! Then they just turn around and start to walk away like it wasn't nothing at all. But right before they gone, they both look around again, and see I still ain't got my eye muscles and my jaw muscles working right again yet. And the one lady wink at me. And the other one say, "Catch you later."

I can't stop staring at they backs, all the way across the Plaza. And then, all of a sudden, I feel like I got to be doing something, got to be moving.

I wheel on outta the Plaza and I'm just concentrating on getting up my speed. Cause I can't figure out what to think. Them two women kissing and then, when they get caught, just laughing about it. And here I'm laughing too, for no reason at all. I'm sailing down the boulevard laughing like a lunatic, and then I'm singing at the top of my lungs. And climbing that big old hill up to Summit Avenue is just as easy as being on a escalator.

Edith Konecky

from *Allegra Maud Goldman*

Edith Konecky was born in Brooklyn, New York, and, like Allegra in the excerpt included here, lived there for most of her childhood. She was dubbed a tomboy as a child because she was always furiously active, loved climbing trees, and never played with the dolls she was unfailingly given for her birthdays. She never felt that "tomboy" was derogatory; rather that it was her due.

Edith Konecky has published two novels, Allegra Maud Goldman *(1976) and* A Place at the Table *(1989), as well as numerous short stories. She lives in New York City and is currently finishing a new novel.*

David, in the following excerpt, is, of course, Allegra's brother.

EVERYONE WAS ALWAYS SAYING HOW PRECOCIOUS I WAS, THOUGH they never said it as though it were anything good to be. Still, I didn't really hear about sex until the summer when I was almost nine. I knew about parts of the body, and about babies coming out of them, but I had pushed away all of the "how" questions, perhaps because I sensed that I wouldn't be ready for the answers. Naturally, I couldn't help suspecting that there was something afoot. After all, I read books. And my father, in his mellower moods, when he was being his idea of jolly, was not above making certain innuendoes in mixed company, at which my mother would usually veil her eyes and feign a yawn.

It took my cousin Sonia to deliver me from ignorance. My cousin Sonia was my age but an entirely different type, so that although we saw a lot of each other, we never really became friends. Sonia was shorter than I and more feminine, with a pile of gold hair and a nose that wrinkled when she smiled. I mean it deliberately wrinkled. Sonia was making a career of being cute. She was bright but not particularly intelligent, and our interests couldn't have been more dissimilar.

"They call it intercause," she said.

We were at Zimmerman's Silver Birch Colony, a family-type summer resort on a big lake in Sullivan County, New York. We were there for the whole summer: our family, two sets of aunts and uncles, and three of my mother's buddies: Jennie, Ann and Ethel, with their broods. Our crowd filled half the place, so my mother had a game every minute, though she did find time for nine holes of golf every day and a swim afterwards.

"Intercause?" I said. "Don't be silly. I'd have heard of it."

I had never gotten anything good from my cousin Sonia. I had gotten whooping cough from her, and measles, and a certain amount of jealousy, but that was it.

"Anyhow," I said, "who would do anything like that?"

"Everyone," Sonia said. She was being a ballerina that summer. At this point she rose up on her toes and pirouetted pretty badly, arcing her arms up over her head, a bower to tippy-toe under. She had short, plump arms.

"Men and women everywhere / In and out of doors / Morning noon and evening / Are doing intercause," she sang as she danced.

I was getting angry.

"My parents wouldn't do anything as dumb as that," I said.

"Ha, ha," she said darkly. "Your parents *especially.*"

I punched her in the mouth. She looked surprised, then burst into tears and turned and ran. I proceeded on down to the lake where I had been headed in the first place. I was meeting David there. We were going to fish off the dock. I had gone for the drop lines while he rounded up the bait.

"What took you so long?" he said when I got there. He was sitting on the end of the dock, his skinny legs dangling off it. Though we hadn't been at Zimmerman's Silver Birch Colony very long, we were already sunburned and David's nose was peeling.

"Nothing. That pest Sonia," I said.

He had a can of worms. I had never fished before and I didn't see how I was going to be able to thread a live worm onto the hook. I watched David do it and it made me sick.

"I don't think I can do that," I said.

"They don't feel anything," he said with contempt.

"How do you know? Look how it's squirming."

"I read it. See, it doesn't even bleed."

"Are you telling me that things that don't bleed have no feelings?"

"Very little," he said. "Don't you know that if you cut a worm in half both parts will grow new ends and you'll have two worms?"

He was a mine of information. I wondered if he knew anything about sex.

"You do it for me," I said.

"If you're going to fish you have to be able to bait your own hook."

I steeled myself and reached for a worm. Then, with my eyes closed, I hung it onto the hook through its middle. It was the best I could do and that was bad enough.

"You'll never catch a fish with that," David said. "He'll just take it right off the hook."

I lowered it anyway and sat there waiting.

"Sonia just told me a really dumb thing," I said.

"You're not supposed to talk when you're fishing. The fish will hear you. What did she tell you?"

"She's crazy, Sonia. She called it The Facts of Life."

"Oh, that."

I looked at David, stunned. "You know about it?" I said.

"Naturally."

"It's true?"

"How do you think babies get made?"

"But Sonia says people do it anyway, even when they're not making babies. She says they *like* it."

"Yeah."

"Why would they like something like that?"

"They have to like it. I mean, think about it. If they didn't like it, why would they ever do it? And if they didn't do it how would anybody ever get born? Actually, they love it. They even *call* it love."

"*That*'s not what love is," I said.

"It's one kind of love. It's carnal love."

"What's carnal?"

"Carnal means meat. Chili con carne. That's chili with meat."

"Oh, for Pete's sake, David!"

"Well, flesh, then. It's fleshy love."

At that moment something jerked my line, and I was so surprised I almost fell into the lake.

"I think I've got something," I screamed.

"Pull it up," David screamed. "Quick. Don't let it get away."

I pulled it up and threw it onto the dock. It was a fat little fish, all gold and silver in the sun. It looked like one of my mother's beaded evening bags flopping around there, except that it had an eye and that eye was staring at me. I looked away.

"I think I'll throw it back," I said.

"What do you want to do a dumb thing like that for?" David yelled. "When you're fishing and you catch a fish you're supposed to keep the fish, that's what it's all about."

"I don't care what it's all about. I'm going to throw it back. Take the hook out, will you?"

"Take it out yourself."

The fish was no longer flopping around. It was gasping. I knelt down warily and took hold of the line as near the fish's mouth as I dared. I couldn't see the hook anywhere. Tentatively, I tugged at the line and the fish gave a leap and so did I.

"It's stuck," I said.

"Naturally it's stuck. It's supposed to be stuck."

"Stop always telling me how things are supposed to be and come get this hook out of this fish," I hollered, very near hysteria. David came and held the fish with one hand and worked the line with the other.

"It won't come out," he said. "He swallowed the hook."

I looked at the fish and the fish looked at me. I don't know how long we looked at each other, but then I saw something I had never seen before. I saw the life go out of the fish's eye. One minute that eye had life in it and then it was gone. It was my first sight of death. I had seen dead things lots of times, in the fish market and the butcher shop, but this was my first encounter with actual dying.

I sat down on the dock and looked at the fish. As I looked, I could see the fish's scales gradually grow duller and duller. It went on happening. I looked at my hands that had done this thing. My own hands. Meanwhile, David's hands were tugging at the line and it was beginning to give. He had one sneakered foot on the fish's tail, pinning it to the dock. Suddenly the line came free, bringing with it not only the hook, but what must have been all that fish's insides, right through the fish's mouth. There was a lot of blood, too.

"That fish had blood," I said, and then I threw up my breakfast into the lake.

I left David and went to the swimming dock. Vic, the lifeguard, was alone there. He sat tilted back in a canvas chair, zinc ointment on his nose, his eyes hidden behind purple sunglasses.

"Hi," I said. When he didn't answer, I realized he was asleep. I sat down at the edge of the dock and looked at the brownish water, still feeling sick. The sun was strong on me and it felt good. I sat for a while, hoping it would burn away the poisons, and I looked at Vic. His skin was a good red-bronze color, and the hair on his muscled legs and forearms glinted gold in the sunlight. I looked at the flat planes of his chest and then at the enormous bulge in his swimming trunks. Then I saw Mrs. Paradise clumping towards the dock on flapping mules with heels about six inches high. I watched the way her hips and breasts swayed as she walked, thinking what a waste all that sideways motion was when you were going forward. Mrs. Paradise was about my mother's age, but my mother didn't like her. I had overheard snatches of conversation about her. Her husband had given her some money "to play with," whatever that meant, and she had run it up into "quite a little pile," and ever since then her husband had been afraid of her.

She came onto the dock and spread her towel next to the chair where Vic sat.

"Good morning, lover," she said. Vic came awake sluggishly, like a turtle.

"Oh, there you are," he said.

"Be a doll and rub some of this stuff on my back," Mrs. Paradise said, handing Vic a tube of suntan cream. She spread herself onto her towel, stomach down. There was a lot of her, most of it flesh, and most of that flesh concentrated in her chest and thighs and behind. She was carnal. I wondered how it felt, carrying all that around.

Vic hunkered down next to her and began to spread cream on her back, rubbing it in slow circles.

"Ooh, that feels good," Mrs. Paradise purred.

"Slept pretty late today for some reason, didn't you?" Vic said. "I didn't see you at breakfast."

"I wonder why," she said and then gave a funny laugh that wasn't a laugh. "Ooh, don't stop. You can do the backs of my legs now."

I was beginning to feel uncomfortable watching them, so I looked away. I looked down at my own body. I was wearing a pair of old green wool swimming shorts outgrown by David. Except at meals, they were practically all I had worn every day since we had gotten to Zimmerman's. I looked at the scab on my left knee and then I looked at my legs. They were perfectly straight legs, getting longer every minute. Arms, too. There were no hidden mysteries in my body. There were the bones, maybe an eighth of an inch of carne over that and then the skin. That was all. Functional, the way a body ought to be. Of course, there were the private parts, but there wasn't much to them, either, and besides I was sitting on those, which, except for going to the bathroom, was mainly what they were for. Whereas Vic's and Mrs. Paradise's private parts seemed much more public. I looked down at my chest. It was perfectly flat, no different from David's, and I meant to keep it that way.

Then, all at once, something in the day tilted, I don't know why, and I found that I was acutely aware of my nakedness and burning with shame, the feeling I'd had once or twice in dreams when I was at the Paramount Theater among thousands of people and I hadn't a stitch on except for my saddle shoes. Although Mrs. Paradise and Vic were the only people there, and they were as aware of me as they were of the dragonfly that swooped across my toes and began skimming the lake's surface in search of lunch, I felt so brazenly exposed that the only thing to do was to slide into the water and hide my nakedness. I paddled around for a while, treading water, watching the dragonfly and praying for an eclipse so that I could steal out in darkness back to our cabin and my clothes. A second dragonfly came along and settled on the back of the first one. The bottom dragonfly didn't seem to mind; it just went on about its business with the other one in tandem, their wings a lovely geometry of stained-glass windows.

I don't know how long I stayed in the water. The skin of my fingers had puckered to prune skin when I told myself that sooner or later I was going to have to come out of there and that the longer I waited the more people there were apt to be about. I swam around to the ladder furthest from Vic and Mrs. Paradise and, telling myself that I was a merchild and that they were ungifted with sight for fabled creatures and therefore blind to me, I came silently dripping up onto the dock, where I broke into a run. I ran all the way up the hill, past the dining hall and the social hall and around behind the tennis courts, and didn't stop until I was safely inside our cabin. I went straight into my mother's room. She was taking a nap. I stood at the foot of her bed for a while, looking at the soles of her feet. "Those are the soles of the feet of my own mother," I told myself, trying not to feel so angry with her.

I went to the mirror over her bureau and looked at my face. I had never thought much about my face, but now I wanted to see what sort of face it was and how much of a chance I was going to have in the world with it, and I couldn't see it. I could see this collection of eyes and nose and mouth and straight, tangled, wet hair, but I couldn't tell a thing about my face. It was so familiar to me that it had become the face of a stranger.

My mother stirred. In the mirror, I saw her eyes flutter open.

"What would you say my best feature was?" I said.

"Your eyes," she said, yawning.

"Why my eyes? Why not my nose or my mouth?"

"Because your eyes are so big and blue and they're what people see first. Bring me my cigarettes, puss."

I scooped them off the top of the bureau and brought them to her.

"I'm ordinary-looking though, aren't I?"

"You'll turn out all right," she said, humoring me. My anger came back then.

"You let me run around looking like this," I said.

"Looking like what?"

"Without even a real bathing suit with a top and a bottom."

"I thought you liked those drawers."

"I never even thought about them before," I yelled.

"Did you catch any fish?"

"I don't want to discuss that. What about this bathing suit, that's what I'm thinking about now."

"I'll go into town and buy you a bathing suit this afternoon. You want to go with me?"

"No. Just make sure it's a *real* bathing suit. I'm sick and tired of being the bottom rung of the ladder around here. All the guts came out of the fish through its mouth. I don't see why we have to have that pest Sonia here all summer ruining everything."

I stormed into my room and changed into a pair of regular shorts and a shirt and stormed on out, banging the screen door behind me. I felt like doing something difficult, so I headed for the tennis courts, thinking that if Herman, the tennis pro, were too busy to give me a lesson, I could just smash some balls around. There weren't many men at Zimmerman's during the week, as the fathers and husbands came out only for weekends. Just the staff and Mr. Rothman, a semi-invalid with a cane, and his son Jerry, a tall, sallow, seventeen-year-old on whose arm Mr. Rothman leaned when he had to navigate. I had to pass Mr. Rothman on my way to the tennis courts, as he was seated on a bench built around the trunk of a beech tree just off the path. Mr. Rothman was one of the few adults around who bothered to speak to children. He always had a pocket full of candy, and it was impossible to pass him without being offered some.

"Would you like some licorice, Allegra?" he asked. I don't like licorice but I did like Mr. Rothman. He had nice creases in his cheeks and a soft pleasant voice and a lot of dignity. I sat down next to him and thanked him for the licorice.

"Isn't it a beautiful day," he said. "I never cease to wonder at the sky here. I suppose that's because I never really get to see it on West Ninety-Third Street."

"Mr. Rothman," I said, "very few grownups ever bother to talk to children. Is it because they don't really think we're people?"

"Yes," he said.

I sucked on the long braid of licorice, tasting the black.

"Mr. Rothman," I said, "every day life gets harder and harder. Does that ever stop?"

"No," he said.

I took my leave. Herman was finishing a lesson with a pretty teenager named Dolores. I sat down and watched, still sucking the licorice. Herman was a wizard tennis player and my favorite of all the men on the staff. Before dinner most nights, and sometimes after it, too, a group of the staff men sat around with my mother and her cronies outside the social hall, talking and having cocktails. I could tell Herman was partial to my mother, even though she was thirty-two that summer, much older than Herman, who was still in graduate school studying to be a research physicist. Sometimes they even took walks together. I liked him anyway. Though not especially handsome, he had a vocabulary, and that interested me. I was beginning to realize that when you know a lot you need a larger and larger vocabulary so that you know that you know it.

"Greetings," Herman called. A ball had rolled to the side of the court where I was sitting and he came to get it. "You look in fine fettle today."

Fettle.

"I'm feeling a bit poorly today, Herman."

"I'm sorry to hear that. Perhaps we can find a remedy."

He went back to lob a few more balls to Dolores's backhand. For some reason I was glad to see that she missed most of them. She was pretty in her sparkling little white getup, but she was a lousy tennis player.

"Enough!" she cried, finally. "I'm worn out."

I watched them converge, winding up the lesson with a flurry of animated conversation. Dolores was one of those people who can't talk to anyone without touching them. I watched her hand dart back and forth, first to clutch one of Herman's hands, then a bicep, back to the hand, then a shoulder pat. She smiled radiantly all the while, her eyelashes flapping. I knew I would never in my life be able to act that way.

"Are you in love with Dolores?" I said when the latter had finally departed.

"Good lord, no," Herman said, laughing. "You want to play some tennis?"

"Are you in love with anyone?"

"Not at the moment. Why do you ask?"

"Were you ever in love with anyone?"

"Yes."

"How did it feel?"

He didn't answer right away. He had to think about it, I noticed.

"It feels like different things at different times," he said. "Why? Do you think you might be in love?"

"Don't be silly. If I were I'd know how it feels, wouldn't I?"

"Do you want to work on your serve?"

"When people love someone very much," I said, "why would they want to do intercause with them?"

Herman made a face. "Intercourse," he said. "That's a clinical term. When two people love each other they want to be very, very close. And that's something special and beautiful."

I looked hard at Herman to see if he was telling the truth. He was.

"But there's more to it than that, isn't there?" I said, thinking of Mrs. Paradise and Vic. "People do intercourse —"

"Have intercourse."

"— have intercourse even when they don't love each other, don't they?"

"Yes," Herman said after a pause. "In the way that people who enjoy food sometimes eat when they aren't particularly hungry. Making love when you aren't in love is different from making love when you are, but it can still be very nice."

The subject was more complicated than I had imagined. I was getting tired of it.

"Let's work on my serve," I said.

That night during dinner Mr. Rothman had some kind of fit on the dining room floor.

We had already finished the appetizer and the soup and were about midway through the stuffed breast of veal with mashed potatoes and carrots and peas when there was a strange loud wail, an animal sound, and everyone stopped what they were doing and saying and turned, in the sudden silence, toward where the sound had come from. And it was Mr. Rothman. He was on the floor, writhing and twitching and jerking, his tongue flapping around, and I never saw anything worse. His son Jerry jumped up and knelt beside him and stuffed a napkin into his mouth. I was sitting next to Sonia, who began to giggle. She always giggled when she didn't know what else to do. It never occurred to her that she could be silent and not do anything. I could have killed her, although I am sorry to say that instead of just feeling sorry for poor Mr. Rothman, I was frightened to death. I was so frightened that I had to get up and run out of the dining room. I ran all the way down to the lake where the sun was setting, huge and orange, all fire.

I sat down and watched the sun and thought about poor Mr. Rothman writhing there on the floor as though devils had gotten inside him. I had thought and asked a lot of questions that day, but the most important thing I learned had come in those moments of silence, for I knew then that people's bodies will do what they have to do without their owner's having anything to say about it, and that my own body would change, in spite of me, and get fleshier and fleshier, and I was going to have to grow up and be a woman. And I was even going to die. It was all there in my own body. I looked at the palm of my hand, my own hand, and saw the rotting that was written there, and the skeleton waiting inside. It was certain; only time stood between me and it. And there was nothing, absolutely nothing, that anyone in the world could tell me that would change it. I felt lonelier than I had ever felt in my life.

David came down to the lake, looking for me.

"Mom was worried about you," he said. "Are you okay?"

I started to cry. I felt too tired and confused to do anything else. David sat down next to me and waited, looking embarrassed.

"What are you crying for?" he said, finally.

"I don't know," I said. "Don't you ever cry?" It had been years since I remembered seeing him cry.

"Boys don't cry."

"What's so great about that?"

"Babies cry. Babies and girls."

"What's wrong with crying when you feel like it?" I said. "You laugh when you feel like it. David, if you really felt like crying, *could* you?"

"I doubt it," he said.

Maxine Hong Kingston

from *The Woman Warrior: Memoirs of a Girlhood Among Ghosts*

Maxine Hong Kingston was born in 1940 of Chinese immigrant parents, and grew up in the Chinatown of Stockton, California. She currently teaches at the University of California at Berkeley. Her books include The Woman Warrior: Memoirs of a Girlhood Among Ghosts *(1976),* China Men *(1980), and* Tripmaster Monkey: His Fake Book *(1989).*

WHEN WE CHINESE GIRLS LISTENED TO THE ADULTS TALK-STORY, WE learned that we failed if we grew up to be but wives or slaves. We could be heroines, swordswomen. Even if she had to rage across all China, a swordswoman got even with anybody who hurt her family. Perhaps women were once so dangerous that they had to have their feet bound. It was a woman who invented white crane boxing only two hundred years ago. She was already an expert pole fighter, daughter of a teacher trained at the Shao-lin temple, where there lived an order of fighting monks. She was combing her hair one morning when a white crane alighted outside her window. She teased it with her pole, which it pushed aside with a soft brush of its wing. Amazed, she dashed outside and tried to knock the crane off its perch. It snapped her pole in two. Recognizing the presence of great power, she asked the spirit of the white crane if it would teach her to fight. It answered with a cry that white crane boxers imitate today. Later the bird returned as an old man, and he guided her boxing for many years. Thus she gave the world a new martial art.

This was one of the tamer, more modern stories, mere introduction. My mother told others that followed swordswomen through woods and palaces for years. Night after night my mother would talk-story until we fell asleep. I couldn't tell where the stories left off and the dreams began, her voice the voice of the heroines in my sleep. And on Sundays, from noon to midnight, we went to the movies at the Confucius Church. We saw swordswomen jump over houses from a standstill; they didn't even need a running start.

At last I saw that I too had been in the presence of great power, my mother talking-story. After I grew up, I heard the chant of Fa Mu Lan, the girl who took her father's place in battle. Instantly I remembered that as a child I had followed my mother about the house, the two of us singing about how Fa Mu Lan fought gloriously and returned alive from war to settle in the village. I had forgotten this chant that was once mine, given me by my mother, who may not have known its power to remind. She said I would grow up a wife and a slave, but she taught me the song of the warrior woman, Fa Mu Lan. I would have to grow up a warrior woman

The call would come from a bird that flew over our roof. In the brush drawings it looks like the ideograph for "human," two black wings. The bird would cross the sun and lift into the mountains (which look like the ideograph "mountain"), there parting the mist briefly that swirled opaque again. I would be a little girl of seven the day I followed the bird away into the mountains. The brambles would tear off my shoes and the rocks cut my feet and fingers, but I would keep climbing, eyes upward to follow the bird. We would go around and around the tallest mountain, climbing ever upward. I would drink from the river, which I would meet again and again. We would go so high the plants would change, and the river that flows past the village would become a waterfall. At the height where the bird used to disappear, the clouds would gray the world like an ink wash.

Even when I got used to that gray, I would only see peaks as if shaded in pencil, rocks like charcoal rubbings, everything so murky. There would be just two black strokes – the bird. Inside the clouds – inside the dragon's breath – I would not know how many hours or days passed. Suddenly, without noise, I would break clear into a yellow, warm world. New trees would lean toward me at mountain angles, but when I looked for the village, it would have vanished under the clouds.

The bird, now gold so close to the sun, would come to rest on the thatch of a hut, which, until the bird's two feet touched it, was camouflaged as part of the mountainside.

The door opened, and an old man and an old woman came out carrying bowls of rice and soup and a leafy branch of peaches.

"Have you eaten rice today, little girl?" they greeted me.

"Yes, I have," I said out of politeness. "Thank you."

("No, I haven't," I would have said in real life, mad at the Chinese for lying so much. "I'm starved. Do you have any cookies? I like chocolate chip cookies.")

"We were about to sit down to another meal," the old woman said. "Why don't you eat with us?"

They just happened to be bringing three rice bowls and three pairs of silver chopsticks out to the plank table under the pines. They gave me an egg, as if it were my birthday, and tea, though they were older than I, but I poured for them. The teapot and the rice pot seemed bottomless, but perhaps not; the old couple ate very little except for peaches.

When the mountains and the pines turned into blue oxen, blue dogs, and blue people standing, the old couple asked me to spend the night in the hut. I thought about the long way down in the ghostly dark and decided yes. The inside of the hut seemed as large as the outdoors. Pine needles covered the floor in thick patterns; someone had carefully arranged the yellow, green, and brown pine needles according to age. When I stepped carelessly and mussed a line, my feet kicked up new blends of earth colors, but the old man and old woman walked so lightly that their feet never stirred the designs by a needle.

A rock grew in the middle of the house, and that was their table. The benches were fallen trees. Ferns and shade flowers grew out of one wall, the mountainside itself. The old couple tucked me into a bed just my width. "Breathe evenly, or you'll lose your balance and fall out," said the woman, covering me with a silk bag stuffed with feathers and herbs. "Opera singers, who begin their training at age five, sleep in beds like this." Then the two of them went outside, and through the window I could see them pull on a rope looped over a branch. The rope was tied to the roof, and the roof opened up like a basket lid. I would sleep with the moon and the stars. I did not see whether the old people slept, so quickly did I drop off, but they would be there waking me with food in the morning.

"Little girl, you have now spent almost a day and a night with us," the old woman said. In the morning light I could see her earlobes pierced with gold. "Do you think you can bear to stay with us for fifteen years? We can train you to become a warrior."

"What about my mother and father?" I asked.

The old man untied the drinking gourd slung across his back. He lifted the lid by its stem and looked for something in the water. "Ah, there," he said.

At first I saw only water so clear it magnified the fibers in the walls of the gourd. On the surface, I saw only my own round reflection. The old man encircled the neck of the gourd with his thumb and index finger and gave it a shake. As the water shook, then settled, the colors and lights shimmered into a picture, not reflecting anything I could see around me. There at the bottom of the gourd were my mother and father scanning the sky, which was where I was. "It has happened already, then," I could hear my mother say. "I didn't expect it so soon." "You knew from her birth that she would be taken," my father answered. "We'll have to harvest potatoes without her help this year," my mother said, and they turned away toward the fields, straw baskets in their arms. The water shook and became just water again. "Mama. Papa," I called, but they were in the valley and could not hear me.

"What do you want to do?" the old man asked. "You can go back right now if you like. You can go pull sweet potatoes, or you can stay with us and learn how to fight barbarians and bandits."

"You can avenge your village," said the old woman. "You can recapture the harvests the thieves have taken. You can be remembered by the Han people for your dutifulness."

"I'll stay with you," I said.

So the hut became my home, and I found out that the old woman did not arrange the pine needles by hand. She opened the roof; an autumn wind would come up, and the needles fell in braids – brown strands, green strands, yellow strands. The old woman waved her arms in conducting motions; she blew softly with her mouth. I thought, nature certainly works differently on mountains than in valleys.

"The first thing you have to learn," the old woman told me, "is how to be quiet." They left me by streams to watch for animals. "If you're noisy, you'll make the deer go without water."

When I could kneel all day without my legs cramping and my breathing became even, the squirrels would bury their hoardings at the hem of my shirt and then bend their tails in a celebration dance. At night, the mice and toads looked at me, their eyes quick stars and slow stars. Not once would I see a three-legged toad, though; you need strings of cash to bait them.

The two old people led me in exercises that began at dawn and ended at sunset so that I could watch our shadows grow and shrink and grow again, rooted to the earth. I learned to move my fingers, hands, feet, head, and entire body in circles. I walked putting heel down first, toes pointing outward thirty to forty degrees, making the ideograph "eight," making the ideograph "human." Knees bent, I would swing into the slow, measured "square step," the powerful walk into battle. After five years my body became so strong that I could control even the dilations of the pupils inside my irises. I could copy owls and bats, the words for "bat" and "blessing" homonyms. After six years the deer let me run beside them. I could jump twenty feet into the air from a standstill, leaping like a monkey over the hut. Every creature has a hiding skill and a fighting skill a warrior can use. When birds alighted on my palm, I could yield my muscles under their feet and give them no base from which to fly away.

But I could not fly like the bird that led me here, except in large, free dreams.

During the seventh year (I would be fourteen), the two old people led me blindfolded to the mountains of the white tigers. They held me by either elbow and shouted into my ears, "Run. Run. Run." I ran and, not stepping off a cliff at the edge of my toes and not hitting my forehead against a wall, ran faster. A wind buoyed me up over the roots, the rocks, the little hills. We reached the tiger place in no time – a mountain peak three feet three from the sky. We had to bend over.

The old people waved once, slid down the mountain, and disappeared around a tree. The old woman, good with the bow and arrow, took them with her; the old man took the water gourd. I would have to survive bare-handed. Snow lay on the ground, and snow fell in loose gusts – another way the dragon breathes. I walked in the direction from which we had come, and when I reached the timberline, I collected wood broken from the cherry tree, the peony, and the walnut, which is the tree of life. Fire, the old people had taught me, is stored in trees that grow red flowers or red berries in the spring or whose leaves turn red in the fall. I took the wood from the protected spots beneath the trees and wrapped it in my scarf to keep dry. I dug where squirrels might have come, stealing one or two nuts at each place. These I also wrapped in my scarf. It is possible, the old people said, for a human being to live for fifty days on water. I would save the roots and nuts for hard climbs, the places where nothing grew, the emergency should I not find the hut. This time there would be no bird to follow.

The first night I burned half of the wood and slept curled against the mountain. I heard the white tigers prowling on the other side of the fire, but I could not distinguish them from the snow patches. The morning rose perfectly. I hurried along, again collecting wood and edibles. I ate nothing and only drank the snow my fires made run.

The first two days were gifts, the fasting so easy to do, I so smug in my strength that on the third day, the hardest, I caught myself sitting on the ground, opening the scarf and staring at the nuts and dry roots. Instead of walking steadily on or even eating, I faded into dreams about the meat meals my mother used to cook, my monk's food forgotten. That night I burned up most of the wood I had collected, unable to sleep for facing my death – if not death here, then death someday. The moon animals that did not hibernate came out to hunt, but I had given up the habits of a carnivore since living with the old people. I would not trap the mice that danced so close or the owls that plunged just outside the fire.

On the fourth and fifth days, my eyesight sharp with hunger, I saw deer and used their trails when our ways coincided. Where the deer nibbled, I gathered the fungus, the fungus of immortality.

At noon on the tenth day I packed snow, white as rice, into the worn center of a rock pointed out to me by a finger of ice, and around the rock I built a fire. In the warming water I put roots, nuts, and the fungus of immortality. For variety I ate a quarter of the nuts and roots raw. Oh, green joyous rush inside my mouth, my head, my stomach, my toes, my soul – the best meal of my life.

One day I found that I was striding long distances without hindrance, my bundle light. Food had become so scarce that I was no longer stopping to collect it. I had walked into dead land. Here even the snow stopped. I did not go back to the richer areas, where I could not stay anyway, but, resolving to fast until I got halfway to the next woods, I started across the dry rocks. Heavily weighed down by the wood on my back, branches poking maddeningly, I had burned almost all of the fuel not to waste strength lugging it.

Somewhere in the dead land I lost count of the days. It seemed as if I had been walking forever; life had never been different from this. An old man and an old woman were help I had only wished for. I was fourteen years old and lost from my village. I was walking in circles. Hadn't I been already found by the old people? Or was that yet to come? I wanted my mother and father. The old man and old woman were only a part of this lostness and this hunger.

One nightfall I ate the last of my food but had enough sticks for a good fire. I stared into the flames, which reminded me about helping my mother with the cooking and made me cry. It was very strange looking through water into fire and seeing my mother again. I nodded, orange and warm.

A white rabbit hopped beside me, and for a moment I thought it was a blob of snow that had fallen out of the sky. The rabbit and I studied each other. Rabbits taste like chickens. My mother and father had taught me how to hit rabbits over the head with wine jugs, then skin them cleanly for fur vests. "It's a cold night to be an animal," I said. "So you want some fire too, do you? Let me put on another branch, then." I would not hit it with the branch. I had learned from rabbits to kick backward. Perhaps this one was sick because normally the animals did not like fire. The rabbit seemed alert enough, however, looking at me so acutely, bounding up to the fire. But it did not stop when it got to the edge. It turned its face once toward me, then jumped into the fire. The fire went down for a moment, as if crouching in surprise, then the flames shot up taller than before. When the fire became calm again, I saw the rabbit had turned into meat, browned just right. I ate it, knowing the rabbit had sacrificed itself for me. It had made me a gift of meat.

When you have been walking through trees hour after hour – and I finally reached trees after the dead land – branches cross out everything, no relief whichever way your head turns until your eyes start to invent new sights. Hunger also changes the world – when eating can't be a habit, then neither can seeing. I saw two people made of gold dancing the earth's dances. They turned so perfectly that together they were the axis of the earth's turning. They were light; they were molten, changing gold – Chinese lion dancers, African lion dancers in midstep. I heard high Javanese bells deepen in midring to Indian bells, Hindu Indian, American Indian. Before my eyes, gold bells shredded into gold tassels that fanned into two royal capes that softened into lions' fur. Manes grew tall into feathers that shone – become light rays. Then the dancers danced the future – a machine-future – in clothes I had never seen before. I am watching the centuries pass in moments because suddenly I understand time, which is spinning and fixed like the North Star. And I understand how working and hoeing are dancing; how peasant clothes are golden, as king's clothes are golden; how one of the dancers is always a man and the other a woman.

The man and the woman grow bigger and bigger, so bright. All light. They are tall angels in two rows. They have high white wings on their backs. Perhaps there are infinite angels; perhaps I see two angels in their consecutive moments. I cannot bear their brightness and cover my eyes, which hurt from opening so wide without a blink. When I put my hands down to look again, I recognize the old brown man and the old gray woman walking toward me out of the pine forest.

It would seem that this small crack in the mystery was opened, not so much by the old people's magic, as by hunger. Afterward, whenever I did not eat for long, as during famine or battle, I could stare at ordinary people and see their light and gold. I could see their dance. When I get hungry enough, then killing and falling are dancing too.

The old people fed me hot vegetable soup. Then they asked me to talk-story about what happened in the mountains of the white tigers. I told them that the white tigers had stalked me through the snow but that I had fought them off with burning branches, and my great-grandparents had come to lead me safely through the forests. I had met a rabbit who taught me about self-immolation and how to speed up transmigration: one does not have to become worms first but can change directly into a human being – as in our own humaneness we had just changed bowls of vegetable soup into people too. That made them laugh. "You tell good stories," they said. "Now go to sleep, and tomorrow we will begin your dragon lessons."

Nancy Brooks Brody

Lizzie Higgins

Nancy Brooks Brody was born in 1962 and spent her childhood in Manhattan. She is an artist, activist, and martial arts practitioner and instructor at the Wu-Tang Physical Culture Association. She now works as a forest firefighter in Washington State. "Lizzie Higgins" is her first published story.

LIZZIE HIGGINS HAD THE LONGEST THICKEST EYELASHES I'D EVER seen. The kind that curl up tight at the tips. And when wet with Bushy Hill Lake water they'd clump into stars above and below her big green eyes. I can still see her boyish face. Somewhere there is a beauty mark. I remember my mother commenting on her pretty face, saying how fresh and clean she always looked. And I'm not sure if she actually spoke out loud when she asked why didn't I look more like her, like that. But I answered by getting into the bath and scrubbing and scrubbing my olive face and dirty rough knees.

Lizzie is a little taller than me and can run just a little bit faster, hit the ball just a little further, climb, jump, sneak, swim, build, hide, throw and steal just a little bit better than me.

I like the way her jeans fade and how they hang down low on her hips. I like how her feet mark and shape and wear out her canvas sneakers. And I love the way she smells.

I can't remember her ever spending the night at my house, though I know it happened. We weren't ever really comfortable there. I don't know what it was, I don't know why. But I always felt nervous and unsure, like we weren't having enough fun. Like something was missing. It's a feeling I got alot, not just when she was there. A feeling like my family wasn't real, wasn't really happening. Like my family was a movie and I was a self-conscious little character in the film.

So by the time we were ten we spent all our time at her house. She lived on 85th Street. Me, I was on 86th. She was right off Central Park West. I was near Riverside Drive. Central Park is bigger, it's better. It's our country. We build go-carts, tree houses. We make out (but not with each other). We rescue animals, throw water balloons, stick fire-crackers in cigarettes for time bombs, shoot bee-bees, calling "Freeze! Hands up!" I'm Pepper, she's Christy Love.

When we smoke we like True Blues best, but a stick you can draw air through will always do in a pinch. At one point we steal a lot. Well, mostly I do look out and she steals. It's a good system, till we get caught.

She can stay out and play way past dark. So, by the time I climb onto her top bunk bed I'm so tired you'd think I'd drop right into sleep. But we won't, we'll laugh and talk and do Superman stunts all around, till we finally sleep, deep and long. And when it's morning, I'm usually up first, watching her, pretending I'm not trying to wake her. Listening, while her house fills with voices and music and the warm thick smell of sugary coffee cake fresh baked with crumbly cinnamon topping. Knowing that because it's the weekend maybe we'll even get to drink coffee.

You know how most buildings have lots of doors on every floor? Not hers. Her family's elevator door opens right onto their private vestibule, and for some reason that's cool. They never lock the apartment door, you just come in and out and in and out as you please. But if it is locked the key is hidden above the right side lamp next to the door. They have a little dog named Fritzy; Maggie, Lizzie's mom, can make her howl by howling too. Maggie loves Fritzy. I loved Maggie. Maggie was a real mom. With Maggie I always felt welcome. When I'd walk through that door, the first thing to meet me was the Higgins Family smell, sort of melting me, like coming in from the cold. The second would be Maggie saying my full name in a voice as though she hadn't seen me in a long long time, like she had really missed me. It sounded like, "Well, there she is, Miss Nancy Brooks Brody. If it isn't you. Where have you been and come right on in." Maggie was a large woman, a fat woman, she had to sew all her own clothes. I mean really really big. I don't know if Lizzie was embarrassed by her mom's size. I never mentioned it to her. No one did, not even to each other. I do remember my mother expressing concern for her health, for her heart. This scared me.

You'd know when Maggie hugged you, you felt good, you felt really hugged, but watch out when she caught you because she had a wooden spoon. My mom was so long and skinny, so beautiful. Everyone said so. But when she wanted me next to her, on her lap, I would squirm cause her knees were so bony. She didn't really have a lap so there wasn't much to sink into, nowhere to disappear.

I go to Lizzie's on Friday nights and come Saturday I'll call home to get permission to stay over until Sunday night. We're almost never inside. We're out running wild all day, sneaking through apartment windows that aren't our own, organizing the neighborhood into all kinds of mischief. Stopping in when we are hungry to make our famous cracker barrel sharp cheddar cheeses with mayo on Ritz. Those we'll take to the treehouse along with a jar of Skippy, and some cigarettes.

Lizzie has lots of pets, fish, guinea pigs, gerbils and a hamster she's named after me "PEE-WEE." She also has a dog, Alma – it's her very own dog. We let her off the leash, and when we want Alma back, she comes to Lizzie's four-tone call. Now, that's the same four tones I use to whistle my own dog back.

We go to P.S. 166 up until fifth grade. In fourth grade we're in the same class with Miss Durkin. And Miss Durkin is very strict. But when she's unlocking the door after lunch I can reach a finger and sometimes my whole hand under her skirt without her ever knowing. There's another girl in the class, Polly. Polly Edelson. I never liked Polly. Polly had bad breath. And she liked Lizzie too much. One time she came to school with her hair cut. Cut short like Lizzie's and mine. This made me mad. My anger drew me up and landed me right on top of her pounding my fists wherever I could. I lost a button on my J.C. Penney work shirt, got a scratch on my face and a phone call to my mom from the principal.

Her hair wasn't the only trouble. Polly had told a big lie about me and a hat. But it unfolded that it wasn't Polly who had lied. It was Lizzie. It was Lizzie's lies that had kept me and Polly at odds. It was crushing to find out Lizzie had tricked me and left me alone on the wrong side of a prank, feeling like a chump.

Just like that time a year earlier, when a bunch of really tough girls cornered me on top of the cobble stone and cement pyramid slides. They said they'd heard I was a tomboy. And was I a tomboy? When I proudly answered "yes" they shoved me around, circled me and said I'd have to fight Debbie Dominguez. Debbie was someone I was always a little scared of. She was so tough. Plus she had brothers. She got me down pretty quick and was dominating the fight when a teacher must of noticed the crowd and broke it up. They all said I'd get my ass kicked again at three o'clock. I told them I was going to the dentist after school, which was true. But they just said I should wait because after three I wouldn't have any teeth to need a dentist. All that really confused me because I had always thought being a tomboy was such a great thing, me and Lizzie would always say we were tomboys. We'd proclaim it like anything else would be terrible.

I never confronted Lizzie about her lies. And I never talked about being so scared in the school yard. It hurt too much and already by nine or ten I had a tremendous ego along with a strong pride. Too strong to allow anything soft to show so I just let it pass. Eventually, Debbie became my friend and even showed me the technique she had used to catch my foot and knock me down with such little effort.

Fifth grade graduation was the first and only time I ever saw Lizzie in a dress. And even then, she wore pants under the dress. So it was more of a long shirt than an actual dress. They were the white Danskin pants my mother had embarrassingly made me give to her one birthday. She never wore them before or after that but I remember their glaring presence on that one and only occasion.

I on the other hand repeatedly had huge long ugly fights with my mother over the dresses and skirts she'd planned for me to wear each day every day, and all the ribbons she wanted to tie into my hair. It made us both sick. Because my hair was straight and thin from time to time she would cut it very short, "a pixie" she'd say, to make it grow back thick. Almost everyone would think I was a boy, which both pleased and horrified me. Then I got my first pair of high tops. I loved them so much, the day I got them I refused to take them off and slept in them. This was when other girls would stuff their shirts for big fake busts. But at home alone I'd rummage the ashtrays for the longest Viceroy butts and stand in front of my parents' full-length mirror with a wadded up sock inside my jeans, or I'd poke my thumb out of the open zipper and hold it like a little dick. Sometimes, I'd ball up a sock inside the arms of a shirt to make bulging muscles. And I'd lay on the floor grinding into that sock, fantasizing that I was the hero rescuing some girl from a bad fate.

By complete and lucky coincidence, Lizzie and I got to Incarnation Camp together for many summers. In other words to really live together, to be in the real country, not just City Parks. Now we really are cowboys. We sleep in the same tent and share a set of bunk beds, her on bottom, me on top. The boys' tents have names like Cherokee, Cheyenne, and Iroquois, and the girls have names like Winds, Daisy, Dandelion, and Jasmine. At eight I rename our tent the Slick Chick Devils, taping a piece of construction paper over the flowery wooden sign. That year our counselor's name was April. We did not like April. We'd read her diary and hide her curiously stained panties.

The counselors we did like got all our attention. Bing, Joni, and Suki were our favorites. At night Bing would read to us. Books like *The Hobbit* or *The Lion, the Witch, and the Wardrobe*. That was OK, but mostly I'd just fall asleep, not keeping up with the stories. What I liked was when she'd sing to us and play her guitar. I never wanted her to stop. And it wasn't until years later when I heard those songs on the radio that I realized she hadn't written them. Songs like *Sounds of Silence, Suzanne the Plans*, the one about tea and oranges from China. And *Puff the Magic Dragon* whose ending always really hurt.

When we were a bit older, about twelve, we moved across Bushy Hill Lake to Pioneer Village. This was the summer after Lizzie was diagnosed with acute scoliosis. It didn't stop her from doing anything, but at night she had to wear a brace. It was a big plastic and metal contraption. It scared me a little at first and it made me sad to see Lizzie so obstructed and restrained. I think this was the first and only time she ever appeared vulnerable to me. The thing I liked was that she needed me to help her in and out of her brace. It was my job to assist her. First I'd hold it open. She'd face me and put her arms in, then wriggle the rest of her body, squeezing into the full molded torso. When she'd turn around, I'd cinch it and buckle it up tight. This was not something she could do alone and no one else in the tent ever did it for her. It was our routine, our ritual. It was a kind and quiet gesture that stood far apart from our rough and tumble ways.

I've always gotten weird cravings, mostly for sour things like pickles, olives, or sauerkraut. One night I woke from sleep with a wicked urge for tuna fish. I woke Lizzie up to let her know. "Help me with my brace," she said. Then we put on her navy blue hooded sweatshirts. This was our sneaking gear. I always felt protected in her sweatshirt, like a second story man or a spy. We didn't talk as we carefully made our way to the commissary. Lizzie had figured a way to break in. I took my tacit position as look-out guard. She went head first through the screen window she had climbed up to and pried open. Then out she came triumphantly through the front door holding a giant industrial-size can of tuna fish. We hustled away from the scene. I must of looked puzzled when she handed me the can because she grinned, and out from her pocket came a can opener. She didn't eat any of that tuna and a few bites satisfied me. So I chucked the can into the woods. Sometimes I picture that spot and a rusted-out can of tuna buried under a bunch of leaves and dirt. After that night it became kind of a thing. I'd do it too, sneak through the window, carting out boxes of Hershey bars and bags of marshmallows to hand out to the other kids on the sly.

One afternoon I was coming back to the tent from "Free Swim." There was Lizzie sitting on the tent platform. That was the summer that Lizzie had gotten her ears pierced, so she had a big bottle of alcohol to keep them from getting infected. "Watch this, Pee-Wee," as she doused a cotton ball with alcohol and put it onto the rim of the plastic bottle. She took a match and lit it. She said it was supposed to shoot straight up, but it just stuck there melting the bottle, ruining it. So she kicked it and the cotton ball shot under the tent. I guess there hadn't been a rain in a while because in seconds flames were raging, shooting out from all sides. We couldn't stop the fire. It's all a blur, but I know I ran for help. I remember a crowd of people flailing blankets and passing buckets of water. Lots of smoke and down feathers. We managed to get it out before the fire department arrived. I stood there in my bathing suit stunned and caught Lizzie's gaze. We knew no cute smiles were getting us out of this one. Ironically, none of our stuff got burnt but the other girls who we shared the tent with, who already didn't love us, lost a lot, a whole lot. They kept pulling burnt things from the rubble. I remember a really melted soap dish best.

I must of had a guilty face because everyone always assumed things were my fault. When the Camp Director questioned me separately on the picnic table in front of the commissary, I stuck to our lie that we were flicking matches. I guess we thought the alcohol part was worse. But it didn't matter, we didn't get kicked out. And it didn't change our ways. We'd still sneak out for illegal late-night skinny-dip swims, or take boats right out from under the sleeping noses of the Camp Director and his big dog, for some early misty morning mission of some navy blue hooded adventure.

Back home and at camp we always kept boyfriends. I loved to make out and organize whole groups into games that ended in massive kissing, be it Spin the Bottle, Run-Catch-Kiss, or Rescue; I didn't really like being alone with one boy. It was something I liked to do with Lizzie and watch her do. But it really bothered me when she went off alone with her boyfriend. I'd kind of wait around imagining how good I would treat her if I was him. I knew just what I'd do for her. I knew the store where I'd buy her the I.D. Bracelet with my name engraved on it. How I'd walk her home. Little things I could say to turn her mouth into a smile. I knew just how I'd hold her. One time she came back late. "Where were you?" I asked. She said she was at the lake. "What happened?" I asked, and my stomach cramped when she said she had let him finger her. I mean it was OK being with boys and having her be with boys as long as at the end of it, it was me and her leaving together, either back to our bunk beds in our tent, or back to our bunk beds in her room, where Lizzie Higgins is right there with me on top.

Horsegirl

Elizabeth Rose Campbell is a writer, videographer, and astrologer, who lives in Chapel Hill,
North Carolina, and Tivoli, New York. She was Assistant Editor of The Sun: A Magazine
of Ideas *from 1977 to 1981, and has had autobiographical essays published in* The Best of
the Sun *(1985 and 1986), and other anthologies. She is currently at work on a first novel,*
Horsegirl, *based on the following essay.*

THE WHITE HORSE

From infancy on, I dreamt every night about riding a white horse through a
desert. He picked his way around rocks, walking slowly and surely towards
some unknown destination, the night sky above us ablaze with the light of other
worlds.

As soon as I learned to talk, I began to beg my parents for a horse. Mama
and Daddy's answer was matter-of-fact. "You can have a horse when you earn
the money for it. By the time you save a hundred dollars, you'll be big enough
to take care of a horse."

It was as if they'd said, "You can have a horse when you're as old as Granny."
Still, I sensed it was fair, and in any case, non-negotiable. I got a very large
piggy-bank, and started saving, as did my older sister, Kack.

Kack was my mentor, coming home from kindergarten, teaching me to read
and write, to tie lasting knots in my shoelaces, and to draw a decent likeness of
a horse. She was also the leader of our pack – a group of children between the
ages of four and seven who roamed freely back and forth between backyards,
and off into the woods.

And it was in Kack's absence one day that I told my first lie. It was an
experiment, to see if what I wanted to be true would be true, if I said it loudly
enough. I went to the ball field, where I waved my hands wildly, and excitedly
announced, *"My horse has come! A white stallion! He's tied up in the garage!"*

Everyone followed me there, even the older children. But the garage was
empty, there was no horse there, and a burning shame washed over me.

FLYING

Meanwhile my dreams had shifted to flying dreams, short jaunts a few hundred feet above the ground, with take-offs from the roof of the little shed in the backyard that housed the well pump.

And then, at four, I shimmied up a ten-foot pole to see what the inside of one of Daddy's gourd birdhouses looked like. Clinging to the top, I saw for the first time from a height, over the back garden, beyond my tiny territorial boundaries, hanging there until I heard Mama's voice below me. "How did you get up there?" she asked, incredulous.

"I *clumb!*" I said, confessing to wings, and I remember the moment when Mama could have said, "You come down right now!" I waited for it with a kind of sinking dismay, but it never came.

"She climbs like a monkey," she announced to Daddy when he pulled up in his Chevy truck. And the two of them had me do it again, right away.

Not long after, Daddy put up a swing in the backyard, hung from the highest limb in the weeping willow tree. I remember I scrambled up at once, with Daddy gazing up at me from the ground, as if I were his own childhood come to life again. "Do you think I can fly?" I asked.

"No," he said, "You can climb, but you can't fly."

"Not ever?"

"Not ever," he said, sweetly sorry, but still firm.

I smiled back at him, with a burst of maternal love for this man, this father, certain that he was wrong, that one day I would fly.

DOLLY

The year I was nine, my parents built a new house on the edge of a great ravine, which my mother had played in as a child. The move meant two things: being closer to my mother's parents, and being closer to the possibility of horses, because there was a barn, just off our new property, on the opposite side of the ravine.

That summer, Kack and I pooled our piggybank savings and bought an older bay mare named Dolly. "She's gentle as they come, perfect for children," said the farmer who sold her to us.

But Dolly was a disappointment. Her personality was as flat as her coat was brown, she wanted nothing except to eat, uninterrupted. Her mood was a monotone except when exposed for the first time to horses she did not know which excited her into hysterics of squealing accompanied by staccato farts and a spray of urine. The other horses liked her behavior even less than I did, and retaliated by biting and kicking her, which aroused the only intense emotion I ever felt about her: the desire to defend her, have her not be hurt.

Though Dolly was dull, she was treated like a show horse in the three years we kept her between my ninth and twelfth birthdays, groomed excessively, and paraded out when company came.

She shared the horse pen with Tony, a gelding owned by Nancy, my regular riding companion. No one told us where we could and could not ride, though our mothers would trail us when we rode beyond our neighborhood, a polite distance behind the horses, so as not to interfere with our adventure.

BLAZE

The summer I was twelve, Dolly was loaded onto a trailer and sent off to my younger cousin's home to become their first horse. We replaced her with an eight-year-old American Saddle horse, known as Blaze. He was smart and spirited, beautiful in his blackness, the white blaze face broad, setting off enormous liquid eyes with long lashes. He had a perfectly rounded rump, and his tail and mane were long and thick.

I was confused by his perfection, so thrilled to have what I finally wanted. I shuffled my feet in their cowboy boots and stood back, not sure I could measure up, after all my complaining. After doddering Dolly, I was also a little afraid of this new horse. I loved to canter and gallop, but Blaze came to us with a ruined mouth, toughened by careless riders to the point where the language of bit and bridle had lost all subtlety, and his revenge was to move at his own speed, as unstoppable as a speeding train. Until I learned how agile he was in negotiating fallen tree limbs, low-hanging branches, quick turns in a path at high speed, I rode him white-knuckled with fear.

Blaze smelled that fear, and in our first six months together, he flaunted his power over mine whenever I entered the horse pen. His ears would go up, and he'd stare at me as if he'd never seen me before. Then he would begin to walk towards me, lightly alert, and hearing his steps behind me, I would quicken my pace without glancing back. If I looked, he'd flatten his ears and charge. The last hundred yards vanished in a blur of motion as I ran for the tackroom of the barn, a thousand pounds of horse at my heels. I would barely make it, slamming the door behind me before he slid to a neat halt inches from the threshold.

I'd peer out the window until I saw him meander back out in front, where he'd stand innocently, beautifully, shaking his head, as if he'd done nothing wrong. I'd sneak from the tackroom, bridle in hand, into the feedroom, get a small bucket of grain, and then slowly approach him. He would wait for me in the barnyard, watching, suddenly polite, then ate the grain with relish while I slipped the reins over his neck. After his snack, he demurely opened his mouth for the bit of the bridle when I held it up; the pleasure of leaving the pen was as great for him as for me.

I rode Blaze with a bareback saddle, which is a piece of foam rubber with fabric over it, and a girth, because I could never get the girth tight enough on the large Western saddle. At eighty pounds my body strength was limited and I liked riding bareback anyway, with just enough between his back and me that I didn't get soapy with his sweat.

The first month or two of riding included spells when he would take off in open spaces with a mixture of fury and daring. I learned early I couldn't stop him, and the best thing to do was just hang on and ride. With no opposition, he relaxed, became responsive to my voice in particular – whhhhooaaa, wwhhhhooaa big boy, bad boy, I crooned to him. He was mischievous, not mean-natured, I came to understand, and that was where he took up with me as partner.

Blaze rode well with other horses, and we would spend long summer days on rides through the paved streets in town, taking off up Cemetery Hill at a hard run, drawing up the horses at the high school, carefully crossing the busy road there, galloping across the baseball field, to leave Weldon proper, and enter South Weldon, parallel to the train tracks.

South Weldon was out of bounds to girls like me, a dilapidated stretch of rundown shacks and tiny houses, their yards crowded with junk vehicles, the occasional store selling little but Merita white bread, Coca-Colas, Sundrops, Moonpies, and chewing gum. People like Minnie Mae Dallas lived there, who ate raw hamburger as a snack, dropping red stringy clumps into her mouth. I used to see her on her porch, fat pasty white legs stretched out on a stool, straggly dogs biting at flies as they sat around her.

I was starting to look more like a gangly boy than a girl, short, but wiry and long-legged. If I was wearing my cowboy hat and boots, blue jeans, and black rain jacket, I put my hair under my hat and hoped to be mistaken for a mysterious male, Zorro's younger brother, never mind I had no mask. If my hair was plaited in braids, I was the Indian princess. Of course everybody in town knew who I was, but I rode Blaze as if through a town of strangers, eyes fixed on distant horizons.

I quickly outgrew the short neighborhood rides, and I began deliberately to look for places to ride Blaze where I could give him his head, not worry about pulling him in when what we both wanted was to run. There were two places to do that: South Weldon and Mush Island, on the river side of town, far from where my friends rode.

It was Minnie Mae who ultimately sent me to Mush Island. I'd pass her house every time I went through South Weldon, would see her, coming out of Wyche's Grocery with her Coca-Cola and her container of raw hamburger, as she waddled down the road towards her house. She'd look at me and yell the same thing every time she saw me, as I nudged Blaze to the right, away from her foreignness, the sheer blatancy of her, eager to make my turn off onto the dirt road.

"G'on get screwed! You g'on get screwed on that road you don't watch out!" she'd say.

Over the summer of 1963, I began to correlate her screeching with the looks on the faces of the men I'd encounter occasionally on that dirt road. They were all drinkers, both black and white, emerging from the bushes without warning, looking at me in a way I'd never been looked at before.

I remember one afternoon in particular, when I'd been riding with my friend, Sue. Two men stepped out of the bushes into the road ahead of us, and at once Sue said under her breath, "Let's get outta here!" Then she nudged her buck-skin, Ginger, into instant take-off, a hard run, as if released from a spring, and Blaze and I came thundering along after them.

We left the men behind in a cloud of dust, and I felt a wave of power I'd never felt on Dolly. She didn't have the youth or spirit — *to take off,* to inhabit that split-second of telepathic communication where the two of us merged into one superhuman/horse, transcendent and invulnerable.

At the end of the road, we brought the horses up, panting, all four of us breathless. "Minnie Mae is right," Sue said. "We *could* get screwed on this road."

Sue was my age, in the sixth grade too, but she had an older sister in high school, who had told her everything she needed to know about such things. Despite Kack, my knowledge was far more sketchy. Most of what I knew about sex was either private to me or was in the fourth grade health book that we'd read in school. I did find a *Playboy* magazine once, tossed casually on the shoulder of the highway, and I examined it carefully, knowing those big-breasted women wearing makeup and panties and no tops were supposed to be attractive to men. But it was anthropological to me – a drugstore sale item wrapped in brown paper I'd never seen anyone buy, mysteriously off the rack and tossed casually onto the shoulder of the highway. It must not be worth much. I left it there.

I'd seen Kack kissing Tom, her boyfriend, but they were both standing up and had on all their clothes. It was no different from seeing Mama and Daddy kissing, which they did all the time.

I'd never thought about kissing anybody – it seemed strange to me, that whole boy/girl thing, as Sue told me what *screwed* meant, that long afternoon, glancing back over our shoulders at the two stick figures far off, down the road, the men we'd left behind.

"Let's go home another way," I said, once she finished. Screwing was for Minnie Mae, as far as I was concerned. People who ate raw hamburger. Nobody I knew or loved had ever done such a thing, or would *want* to. It didn't sound very sanitary, or *romantic*.

It never occurred to me that what Sue had described was what I loved listening to Mama and Daddy do, the nights I crept halfway down the stairs, to just sit in the dark and eavesdrop on their pillow talk in the bedroom below, the door open, their words indistinguishable; soft laughter, silences, rustling of bed covers; one or other of them exhaling audibly in a way that didn't sound like tiredness, but something else entirely.

Blaze was well-behaved on highways, around cars, but cars and trucks were not always well-behaved around him, which was part of why it took us so long to get to Mush Island. In order to reach it, you had to cross a major bypass, where transfer trucks roared round the bend when they sighted us, blowing their horns, WAW WAW, as if we hadn't seen them. Once on the other side, the sounds of the highway fell away as we passed maintenance buildings for the farm that sprawled over the island, hundreds of acres of tobacco, cotton, soybeans, corn.

The horses always walked the first half mile, crossing the creek that funnelled into the Roanoke River on a rickety timber bridge. Otters hid when they saw us coming, dashing down the bank, their sleek black coats catching the sun. We reached the last few fishing shacks and the road forked.

To the right was a powdery dirt road that crossed the widest section of farmland, running for miles and miles without so much as a curve in it, nothing on either side but crops laid out in straight neat rows.

I'd been there before with Dolly, but she fell with me once, and I was never able to surrender to the run again. But this time it wasn't Dolly. This time it was Blaze.

"How far do you think they'll run?" Sue asked me, that first day, as we stood at the fork, the horses circling with impatience.

"I don't know," I answered. "I guess we'll find out." My voice quivered slightly with excitement, and I could see in Sue's quizzical glance a certain confusion about where I was and what I wanted. She was used to my dread of this ride, on Dolly.

We started at a slow canter, Blaze in front, Sue on her new horse Champ, behind, all four of us relaxing into the rocking motion of the ride, and the pleasure of the morning. Then Blaze began to accelerate, and I shifted into his body differently; as he flew, we flew. I could hear Champ and Sue behind us, heard Sue whoop. I whooped back.

We rode like that for fifteen minutes or more, passing field after field, the road unfurling ahead of us. And then suddenly I felt something shift in Blaze again, a kind of bliss in his body, a joy that surged through me too. All of the horses I'd ever held in my heart – the one that carried me as infant through the world of dreams, the white stallion in the garage – they all rushed into that moment. I buried my head in Blaze's mane, felt his body become long like a leopard's as his strides stretched further and further, my feet in the stirrups closer and closer to the ground, our rhythm so fluid, nothing mattered but this terrific sense of arrival.

Blaze slowed of his own accord, when we reached the woods at the far end of the farm, and when he did, I slid off of him, ran to his head, hugged him, cheeks wet with tears where the wind cut my eyes, both of us exhausted. We stood there trembling as the adrenalin left us, leaning against each other, panting. Sue and Champ galloped towards us and I smiled back at them, stunned. I had turned into someone else in the blink of an eye.

"Are you OK?" Sue asked.

"Yeah," I said breathlessly.

"I didn't know he could do that," she said, staring at Blaze.

I nodded, speechless.

"I didn't know *you* could do that," she added laughing. She dismounted, to get the water bottle, and handed it to me. And then she apologized. "Of course I knew you could. You just needed the right horse."

Blaze was definitely the right horse. And now that I knew I could, we could, and that there was a place to do it – to know: *I can fly*, to enter the full grace of physicality with another being, I wanted to do it all the time. I rode to Mush Island as often as possible the summer I was twelve, and on into the school year, through the fall, the winter, and on weekends.

Sometimes I went alone, and sometimes with other people – friends who loved it for the same reasons I did: that combination of safety – from cars, streets, roads, civilization – and unfettered wilderness.

At the far end of the island, there were trees so big that you could live in them. There was a jungle along the river bank, thickets of grasses and vines hid wild boar, wild pigs. And there were wild dogs as well, which lived off the boar.

Where the road finally looped back to the original fork, after four or five hours of riding, we used to pass a stable full of mules, whose delight at seeing Blaze and his rider made me laugh out loud. Their hee-haws and rolling eyes always gave us the opportunity to feel gallant, beautiful, royalty riding mysteriously out of the woods. I used to tip my hat to them, the mules, as they would squeal and pee in excitement, as Dolly had once done.

When I arrived home from these rides, I was always aware of entering another world: carpets and air-conditioning, the cheerful and somewhat pampered life waiting for me in the house above the ravine. I'd brush Blaze down, walk bowlegged up the hill, my thighs aching from gripping his back, smelling of my perspiration and his, to find Mama in the kitchen cooking dinner, Daddy working in the yard, Kack on the phone with her adolescent life. None of them asked that I be anything other than myself. "Just don't drop your wet towels on the floor," my mother reminded me over and over.

I'd eat dinner, kiss everybody goodnight, and go to bed early, my body happily exhausted from a long day's ride, and as often as not, those long summer days, I'd get up early the next morning, and do the same thing over again.

THE VIRGIN OATH

What changed everything overnight was the arrival of my menses the following summer. I was at Bible School when it happened, listening to the teacher say that God knew how many hairs were on everybody's head. I wondered if God knew why my stomach hurt. It started out like a warm moist fist in the bottom of my belly clenching and unclenching, and everytime it unclenched, I felt a warm wet release. Was I wetting my pants? Even though I'd heard about menstruation (*"Has she started yet?"* Nancy's mother asked mine) and knew it would happen to me sooner or later, I had never expected it would *hurt*.

I never said a word, just sat there and decided I was dying of appendicitis. Walking home later, I thought of my funeral, fantasized about eulogies. I instinctively knew something had changed forever.

In my own bathroom, I found the blood, was momentarily relieved, and then annoyed. I didn't want anybody to know what was going on between my legs, but this was an awful lot of blood.

I called Mama upstairs, whose response was so strange I didn't know what to think – she laughed, then became tender, hugged me, said, "No, no, you're OK, it's all right, this is it, you've *started.*"

"I'll be *right back,* "she said, almost gleeful, as I sat on the toilet, and she ran downstairs to get something. A camera? Was she going to take my picture? Her mood was so celebrative. I couldn't imagine her doing that to me, even though one of her deepest reflexes around major events was: take a picture.

I sat on the toilet, bleeding, sad with the birth of such an enormous unknowing, and wondering, "Who could ride a horse in this shape?"

I asked Mama that, when she returned with a funny-looking piece of circular elastic, with two pieces hanging down in the middle on either end.

"Oh you won't want to ride this week," she said, as she fumbled with the belt, and proceeded to explain, alternating between high humor and serious instruction, that I was now *a woman.*

"Your virginity and your name are your most precious possessions as a woman," Mama said. "A virgin takes to her marriage, to her husband, all of herself. She's saved herself for that, so she can build a family, which is why she only has intercourse with her husband."

Intercourse. All I could see in my mind's eye was the golf course. Green rolling lawns. Men with clubs putting. Mama and Daddy didn't play golf.

And this word *virgin* was so mixed up with church and Mary, mother of Jesus, I couldn't find a context for it that was human. *Keep your virginity.* Keep your Godliness? Out of your body? In your body? Away from other bodies?

Men were starting to change shape in my head, in a way they never had before. The men decided who they'd marry, who they wouldn't, based on this? Would I want to marry a man who wasn't a *virgin?*

"So," I said, "men can have intercourse before they get married, but women can't."

"Well," Mama answered, her pause carrying her discomfort, "some of them wait until they get married. But men are different from women. They need sex more, earlier. It's in their hormones. They can't help it."

I could tell she wasn't familiar with women who didn't wait and I could tell this was a dangerous conversation somehow, that Mama might not know what she was talking about. She might be talking "out of Granny's hat" – my phrase for old-fashioned rules. Granny wouldn't put a bottle of Coca-Cola to her lips because hard liquor came out of bottles.

But Mama clearly understood how to handle all this blood, and I got over my embarrassment quickly because she was so touched, so warmed by this oddity, kept hugging me, as if I'd performed a feat. I loved her like a sister, never daring to tell her I didn't believe everything she told me.

The morning after I got my period, when I went down to breakfast, I knew Mama had told Daddy because he kissed me shyly and his eyes were wet. "Congratulations," he said. "Now you're a woman." At first I just wanted to drop through the floor. Then my cheeks flamed bright red, and I was so sad that I couldn't even say "Thank you." I felt as if I'd lost my father, as if the friend I knew, with whom I'd buddied around as his boy, his brother, had suddenly disappeared. I didn't look at him for the rest of the meal, and I withdrew physically in a way I'd never done before, not wanting to touch or hug, and not sure why.

Kack and her boyfriend, Tom, were the only ones who could tease me about my new shyness, without risk of me running upstairs to my room.

"You have really nice eyes," Tom said out of the blue one afternoon in the middle of a poker game.

Kack looked at me carefully and said, "Maybe we should cut your hair this summer."

That was the summer my breasts got too big to ignore. I ignored them anyway, until I saw fresh photos of the family on the lawn, and there I stood in the front, my shoulders slightly hunched over, my breasts obviously outlined under a tight summer shirt, nipples little dark shadows. I was embarrassed by my own ignorance of how I looked. When Mama, Daddy, aunts, uncles saw the picture, I overheard their whispers of amused amazement: *time to get Bets a bra*.

I stopped riding Blaze as much that fall, distracted by all the changes, and suddenly a prisoner to the mirrors in the house – the full-length mirrors, the bathroom mirrors. I couldn't get enough of my own image.

Naked, my body was so sensual, so erotic. I stripped and stared, in the privacy of my bedroom. I was as confused by my own perfection and sleekness as I'd been by Blaze when he first arrived. I had my mother's small, strong frame, and her legs – the muscles like a dancer's. I had my father's facial features – dark brows and eyes, high cheekbones.

At school, I still dressed like a large child. And after school and on weekends

I wore farmer overalls, and Mickey Mouse t-shirts. I let my bangs grow out, happy to hide behind their ragged edges, anything to use as a screen for my bouts with unexpected shyness over nothing but the incredible embarrassment of being. I was a pendulum swinging wildly between the desire to be seen, as female in full bloom, and the desire to remain invisible, to fight what felt out of control, these changes from within and without.

For years, I had worn cut-off jeans and t-shirts under my choir robe which I wore every Sunday, even to Sunday school. The choir robe was my uniform of androgyny and a happy disguise for everything – loose and floppy. I resolved some indefinable tension that year, by suddenly deciding to wear nothing at all under it, not even underpants, stepping deliberately out of childhood, towards the sensual self, without anyone's knowledge or permission.

Meanwhile, bored by too much time alone in his pen, Blaze began to discover escape routes. He learned to open the latch on the gate with his mouth, and once a chain was installed as extra security, he tore himself a hole in the fence on the far side of the house. He never went to Mush Island, but he took to doing the town route I followed, all by himself, stopping at the stop signs, cantering where I'd canter, walking where I'd walk, and for a while we got phone calls from all over town. "I just saw your horse galloping up the hill towards South Weldon!"

Blaze was separating himself from me, as I was separating from him. I could still easily slip back into being tomboy, horsegirl, as well as the child who played with dolls. By then, however, Ken and Barbie had begun to make unfamiliar demands on me – that I lock the bedroom door, that I invent new dialogues for them. I remember one that culminated in taking off all their clothes and smushing their plastic bodies together – a scene I found vastly unsatisfying.

At other times, I would double-check the locked door, take all my clothes off except my bikini pants, and search for the peacock feather I'd won at the fair. Breathless with excitement, I slipped it inside the back of my panties, between the cheeks of my ass, and pranced back and forth before the mirror. I strutted self-consciously at first, heart pounding, then started to dance, hypnotized by the strong body sprouting pert breasts, by the sudden wildfire in the mischievous black eyes of the naked girl. I didn't stop until I was out of breath, perspiration rolling down my sides.

The heat of what had happened was so terrific, I expected the house to burst into flames. It did not. But the sound of a car pulling into the driveway sent me diving to the floor, yanking the feather out of my pants; *where are my clothes?*

Jeans and t-shirt back on, I took a deep breath before unlocking the door, and ran down to the horse pen to feed Blaze. I leaned against him while he chewed his grain, my cheek pressed against the velvet of his neck. I smelled the salty earth of him, the simplicity of our partnership, the silence and the thunder of it, still perfect, for a time.

Carson McCullers

from *The Member of the Wedding*

Carson McCullers was born in Columbus, Georgia, in 1917. She published her first novel,
The Heart Is a Lonely Hunter *(1940), when she was only twenty-three, and* The Member
of the Wedding *(1946) six years later. Both books center on independent-minded Southern
tomboys reminiscent of McCullers herself. Other books include* Reflections in a Golden Eye
(1941) and The Ballad of the Sad Café *(1951). McCullers died in 1967.*

IT HAPPENED THAT GREEN AND CRAZY SUMMER WHEN FRANKIE WAS
twelve years old. This was the summer when for a long time she had not been a
member. She belonged to no club and was a member of nothing in the world.
Frankie had become an unjoined person who hung around in doorways, and
she was afraid. In June the trees were bright dizzy green, but later the leaves
darkened, and the town turned black and shrunken under the glare of the sun.
At first Frankie walked around doing one thing and another. The sidewalks of
the town were gray in the early morning and at night, but the noon sun put a
glaze on them, so that the cement burned and glittered like glass. The sidewalks
finally became too hot for Frankie's feet, and also she got herself in trouble. She
was in so much secret trouble that she thought it was better to stay at home –
and at home there was only Berenice Sadie Brown and John Henry West. The
three of them sat at the kitchen table, saying the same things over and over, so
that by August the words began to rhyme with each other and sound strange.
The world seemed to die each afternoon and nothing moved any longer. At last
the summer was like a green sick dream, or like a silent crazy jungle under glass.
And then, on the last Friday of August, all this was changed; it was so sudden
that Frankie puzzled the whole blank afternoon, and still she did not understand.

"It is so very queer," she said. "The way it all just happened."

"Happened? Happened?" said Berenice.

John Henry listened and watched them quietly.

"I have never been so puzzled."

"But puzzled about what?"

"The whole thing," Frankie said.

And Berenice remarked: "I believe the sun has fried your brains."

"Me too," John Henry whispered.

Frankie herself almost admitted maybe so. It was four o'clock in the afternoon and the kitchen was square and gray and quiet. Frankie sat at the table with her eyes half closed, and she thought about a wedding. She saw a silent church, a strange snow slanting down against the colored windows. The groom in this wedding was her brother, and there was a brightness where his face should be. The bride was there in a long white train, and the bride also was faceless. There was something about this wedding that gave Frankie a feeling she could not name.

"Look here at me," said Berenice. "You jealous?"

"Jealous?"

"Jealous because your brother going to be married?"

"No," said Frankie. "I just never saw any two people like them. When they walked in the house today it was so queer."

"You jealous," said Berenice. "Go and behold yourself in the mirror. I can see from the color in your eye."

There was a watery kitchen mirror hanging above the sink. Frankie looked, but her eyes were gray as they always were. This summer she was grown so tall that she was almost a big freak, and her shoulders were narrow, her legs too long. She wore a pair of blue black shorts, a B.V.D. undervest, and she was barefooted. Her hair had been cut like a boy's, but it had not been cut for a long time and was now not even parted. The reflection in the glass was warped and crooked, but Frankie knew well what she looked like; she drew up her left shoulder and turned her head aside.

"Oh," she said. "They were the two prettiest people I ever saw. I just can't understand how it happened."

"But what, Foolish?" said Berenice. "Your brother come home with the girl he means to marry and took dinner today with you and your Daddy. They intend to marry at her home in Winter Hill this coming Sunday. You and your Daddy are going to the wedding. And that is the A and the Z of the matter. So whatever ails you?"

"I don't know," said Frankie. "I bet they have a good time every minute of the day."

"Less us have a good time," John Henry said.

"Us have a good time?" Frankie asked. "Us?"

The three of them sat at the table again and Berenice dealt the cards for three-handed bridge. Berenice had been the cook since Frankie could remember. She was very black and broad-shouldered and short. She always said that she was thirty-five years old, but she had been saying that at least three years. Her hair was parted, plaited, and greased close to the skull, and she had a flat and quiet face. There was only one thing wrong about Berenice – her left eye was bright blue glass. It stared out fixed and wild from her quiet, colored face, and why she had wanted a blue eye nobody human would ever know. Her right eye was dark and sad. Berenice dealt slowly, licking her thumb when the sweaty cards stuck together. John Henry watched each card as it was being dealt. His chest was white and wet and naked, and he wore around his neck a tiny lead donkey tied by a string. He was blood kin to Frankie, first cousin, and all summer he would eat dinner and spend the day with her, or eat supper and spend the night; and she could not make him go home. He was small to be six years old, but he had the largest knees that Frankie had ever seen, and on one of them there was always a scab or a bandage where he had fallen down and skinned himself. John Henry had a little screwed white face and he wore tiny gold-rimmed glasses. He watched all of the cards very carefully, because he was in debt; he owed Berenice more than five million dollars.

"I bid one heart," said Berenice.

"A spade," said Frankie.

"I want to bid spades," said John Henry. "That's what I was going to bid."

"Well, that's your tough luck. I bid them first."

"Oh, you fool jackass!" he said. "It's not fair!"

"Hush quarreling," said Berenice. "To tell the truth, I don't think either one of you got such a grand hand to fight over the bid about. I bid two hearts."

"I don't give a durn about it," Frankie said. "It is immaterial with me."

As a matter of fact this was so: she played bridge that afternoon like John Henry, just putting down any card that suddenly occurred to her. They sat together in the kitchen, and the kitchen was a sad and ugly room. John Henry had covered the walls with queer, child drawings, as far up as his arm would reach. This gave the kitchen a crazy look, like that of a room in the crazy-house. And now the old kitchen made Frankie sick. The name for what had happened to her Frankie did not know, but she could feel her squeezed heart beating against the table edge.

"The world is certainy a small place," she said.

"What makes you say that?"

"I mean sudden," said Frankie. "The world is certainy a sudden place."

"Well, I don't know," said Berenice. "Sometimes sudden and sometimes slow."

"Frankie's eyes were half closed, and to her own ears her voice sounded ragged, far away:

"To me it is sudden."

For only yesterday Frankie had never thought seriously about a wedding. She knew that her only brother, Jarvis, was to be married. He had become engaged to a girl in Winter Hill just before he went to Alaska. Jarvis was a corporal in the army and he had spent almost two years in Alaska. Frankie had not seen her brother for a long, long time, and his face had become masked and changing, like a face seen under water. But Alaska! Frankie had dreamed of it constantly, and especially this summer it was very real. She saw the snow and frozen sea and ice glaciers. Esquimau igloos and polar bears and the beautiful Northern lights. When Jarvis had first gone to Alaska, she had sent him a box of homemade fudge, packing it carefully and wrapping each piece separately in waxed paper. It had thrilled her to think that her fudge would be eaten in Alaska, and she had a vision of her brother passing it around to furry Esquimaux. Three months later, a thank-you letter had come from Jarvis with a five-dollar bill enclosed. For a while she mailed candy almost every week, sometimes divinity instead of fudge, but Jarvis did not send her another bill, except at Christmas time. Sometimes his short letters to her father disturbed her a little. For instance, this summer he mentioned once that he had been in swimming and that the mosquitoes were something fierce. This letter jarred upon her dream, but after a few days of bewilderment, she returned to her frozen seas and snow. When Jarvis had come back from Alaska, he had gone straight to Winter Hill. The bride was named Janice Evans and the plans for the wedding were like this: her brother had wired that he and the bride were coming this Friday to spend the day, then on the following Sunday there was to be the wedding at Winter Hill. Frankie and her father were going to the wedding, traveling nearly a hundred miles to Winter Hill, and Frankie had already packed a suitcase. She looked forward to the time her brother and the bride should come, but she did not picture them to herself, and did not think about the wedding. So on the day before the visit she only commented to Berenice:

"I think it's a curious coincidence that Jarvis would get to go to Alaska and that the very bride he picked to marry would come from a place called Winter Hill. Winter Hill," she repeated slowly, her eyes closed, and the name blended with dreams of Alaska and cold snow. "I wish tomorrow was Sunday instead of Friday. I wish I had already left town."

"Sunday will come," said Berenice.

"I doubt it," said Frankie. "I've been ready to leave this town so long. I wish I didn't have to come back here after the wedding. I wish I was going somewhere for good. I wish I had a hundred dollars and could just light out and never see this town again."

"It seems to me you wish for a lot of things," said Berenice.

"I wish I was somebody else except me."

So the afternoon before it happened was like the other August afternoons. Frankie had hung around the kitchen, then toward dark she had gone out into the yard. The scuppernong arbor behind the house was purple and dark in the twilight. She walked slowly. John Henry West was sitting beneath the August arbor in a wicker chair, his legs crossed and his hands in his pockets.

"What are you doing?" she asked.

"I'm thinking."

"About what?"

He did not answer.

Frankie was too tall this summer to walk beneath the arbor as she had always done before. Other twelve-year-old people could still walk around inside, give shows, and have a good time. Even small grown ladies could walk underneath the arbor. And already Frankie was too big; this year she had to hang around and pick from the edges like the grown people. She stared into the tangle of dark vines, and there was the smell of crushed scuppernongs and dust. Standing beside the arbor, with dark coming on, Frankie was afraid. She did not know what caused this fear, but she was afraid.

"I tell you what," she said. "Suppose you eat supper and spend the night with me."

John Henry took his dollar watch from his pocket and looked at it as though the time would decide whether or not he would come, but it was too dark under the arbor for him to read the numbers.

"Go on home and tell Aunt Pet. I'll meet you in the kitchen."

"All right."

She was afraid. The evening sky was pale and empty and the light from the kitchen window made a yellow square reflection in the darkening yard. She remembered that when she was a little girl she believed that three ghosts were living in the coal house, and one of the ghosts wore a silver ring.

She ran up the back steps and said: "I just now invited John Henry to eat supper and spend the night with me."

Berenice was kneading a lump of biscuit dough, and she dropped it on the flour-dusted table. "I thought you were sick and tired of him."

"I am sick and tired of him," said Frankie. "But it seemed to me he looked scared."

"Scared of what?"

Frankie shook her head. "Maybe I mean lonesome," she said finally.

"Well, I'll save him a scrap of dough."

After the darkening yard the kitchen was hot and bright and queer. The walls of the kitchen bothered Frankie – the queer drawings of Christmas trees, airplanes, freak soldiers, flowers. John Henry had started the first pictures one long afternoon in June, and having already ruined the wall, he went on and drew whenever he wished. Sometimes Frankie had drawn also. At first her father had been furious about the walls, but later he said for them to draw all the pictures out of their systems, and he would have the kitchen painted in the fall. But as the summer lasted, and would not end, the walls had begun to bother Frankie. That evening the kitchen looked strange to her, and she was afraid.

She stood in the doorway and said: "I just thought I might as well invite him."

So at dark John Henry came to the back door with a little week-end bag. He was dressed in his white recital suit and had put on shoes and socks. There was a dagger buckled to his belt. John Henry had seen snow. Although he was only six years old, he had gone to Birmingham last winter and there he had seen snow. Frankie had never seen snow.

"I'll take the week-end bag," said Frankie. "You can start right in making a biscuit man."

"O.K."

John Henry did not play with the dough; he worked on the biscuit man as though it were a very serious business. Now and then he stopped off, settled his glasses with his little hand, and studied what he had done. He was like a tiny watchmaker, and he drew up a chair and knelt on it so that he could get directly over the work. When Berenice gave him some raisins, he did not stick them all around as any other human child would do; he used only two for the eyes; but immediately he realized they were too large – so he divided one raisin carefully and put in eyes, two specks for the nose, and a little grinning raisin mouth. When he had finished, he wiped his hands on the seat of his shorts, and there was a little biscuit man with separate fingers, a hat on, and even a walking stick. John Henry had worked so hard that the dough was now gray and wet. But it was a perfect little biscuit man, and, as a matter of fact, it reminded Frankie of John Henry himself.

"I better entertain you now," she said.

They ate supper at the kitchen table with Berenice, since her father had telephoned that he was working late at his jewelry store. When Berenice brought the biscuit man from the oven, they saw that it looked exactly like any biscuit man ever made by a child – it had swelled so that all the work of John Henry had been cooked out, the fingers were run together, and the walking stick resembled a sort of tail. But John Henry just looked at it through his glasses, wiped it with his napkin, and buttered the left foot.

It was a dark, hot August night. The radio in the dining room was playing a mixture of many stations: a war voice crossed with the gabble of an advertiser, and underneath there was the sleazy music of a sweet band. The radio had stayed on all the summer long, so finally it was a sound that as a rule they did not notice. Sometimes, when the noise became so loud that they could not hear their own ears, Frankie would turn it down a little. Otherwise, music and voices came and went and crossed and twisted with each other, and by August they did not listen any more.

"What do you want to do?" asked Frankie. "Would you like for me to read to you out of Hans Brinker or would you rather do something else?"

"I rather do something else," he said.

"What?"

"Less play out."

"I don't want to," Frankie said.

"There's a big crowd going to play out tonight."

"You got ears," Frankie said. "You heard me."

John Henry stood with his big knees locked, then finally he said: "I think I better go home."

"Why, you haven't spent the night! You can't eat supper and just go on off like that."

"I know it," he said quietly. Along with the radio they could hear the voices of the children playing in the night. "But less go out, Frankie. They sound like they having a mighty good time."

"No they're not," she said. "Just a lot of ugly silly children. Running and hollering and running and hollering. Nothing to it. We'll go upstairs and unpack your week-end bag."

Frankie's room was an elevated sleeping porch which had been built onto the house, with a stairway leading up from the kitchen. The room was furnished with an iron bed, a bureau, and a desk. Also Frankie had a motor which could be turned on and off; the motor could sharpen knives, and, if they were long enough, it could be used for filing down your fingernails. Against the wall was the suitcase packed and ready for the trip to Winter Hill. On the desk there was a very old typewriter, and Frankie sat down before it, trying to think of any letters she could write: but there was nobody for her to write to, as every possible letter had already been answered, and answered even several times. So she covered the typewriter with a raincoat and pushed it aside.

"Honestly," John Henry said, "don't you think I better go home?"

"No," she answered, without looking around at him. "You sit there in the corner and play with the motor."

Before Frankie there were now two objects – a lavender seashell and a glass globe with snow inside that could be shaken into a snowstorm. When she held the seashell to her ear, she could hear the warm wash of the Gulf of Mexico, and think of a green palm island far away. And she could hold the snow globe to her narrowed eyes and watch the whirling white flakes fall until they blinded her. She dreamed of Alaska. She walked up a cold white hill and looked on a snowy wasteland far below. She watched the sun make colors in the ice, and heard dream voices, saw dream things. And everywhere there was the cold white gentle snow.

"Look," John Henry said, and he was staring out of the window. "I think those big girls are having a party in their clubhouse."

"Hush!" Frankie screamed suddenly. "Don't mention those crooks to me."

There was in the neighborhood a clubhouse, and Frankie was not a member. The members of the club were girls who were thirteen and fourteen and even fifteen years old. They had parties with boys on Saturday night. Frankie knew all of the club members, and until this summer she had been like a younger member of their crowd, but now they had this club and she was not a member. They had said she was too young and mean. On Saturday night she could hear the terrible music and see from far away their light. Sometimes she went around to the alley behind the clubhouse and stood near a honeysuckle fence. She stood in the alley and watched and listened. They were very long, those parties.

"Maybe they will change their mind and invite you," John Henry said.

"The son-of-a-bitches."

Frankie sniffled and wiped her nose in the crook of her arm. She sat down on the edge of the bed, her shoulders slumped and her elbows resting on her knees.

"I think they have been spreading it all over town that I smell bad," she said. "When I had those boils and that black bitter smelling ointment, old Helen Fletcher asked what was that funny smell I had. Oh, I could shoot every one of them with a pistol."

She heard John Henry walking up to the bed, and then she felt his hand patting her neck with tiny little pats. "I don't think you smell so bad," he said. "You smell sweet."

"The son-of-a-bitches," she said again. "And there was something else. They were talking nasty lies about married people. When I think of Aunt Pet and Uncle Ustace. And my own father! The nasty lies! I don't know what kind of fool they take me for."

"I can smell you the minute you walk in the house without even looking to see if it is you. Like a hundred flowers."

"I don't care," she said. "I just don't care."

"Like a thousand flowers," said John Henry, and still he was patting his sticky hand on the back of her bent neck.

Frankie sat up, licked the tears from around her mouth, and wiped off her face with her shirttail. She sat still, her nose widened, smelling herself. Then she went to her suitcase and took out a bottle of Sweet Serenade. She rubbed some on the top of her head and poured some more down inside the neck of her shirt.

"Want some on you?"

John Henry was squatting beside her open suitcase and he gave a little shiver when she poured the perfume over him. He wanted to meddle in her traveling suitcase and look carefully at every thing she owned. But Frankie only wanted him to get a general impression, and not count and know just what she had and what she did not have. So she strapped the suitcase and pushed it back against the wall. "Boy!" she said. "I bet I use more perfume than anybody in this town."

The house was quiet except for the low rumble of the radio in the dining room downstairs. Long ago her father had come home and Berenice had closed the back door and gone away. There was no longer the sound of children's voices in the summer night.

"I guess we ought to have a good time," said Frankie.

But there was nothing to do. John Henry stood, his knees locked and his hands clasped behind his back, in the middle of the room. There were moths at the window—pale green moths and yellow moths that fluttered and spread their wings against the screen.

"Those beautiful butterflies," he said. "They are trying to get in."

Frankie watched the soft moths tremble and press against the window screen. The moths came every evening when the lamp on her desk was lighted. They came from out of the August night and fluttered and clung against the screen.

"To me it is the irony of fate," she said. "The way they come here. Those moths could fly anywhere. Yet they keep hanging around the windows of this house."

John Henry touched the gold rim of his glasses to settle them on his nose and Frankie studied his flat little freckled face.

"Take off those glasses," she said suddenly.

John Henry took them off and blew on them. She looked through the glasses and the room was loose and crooked. Then she pushed back her chair and stared at John Henry. There were two damp white circles around his eyes.

"I bet you don't need those glasses," she said. She put her hand down on the typewriter, "What is this?"

"The typewriter," he said.

Frankie picked up the shell. "And this?"

"The shell from the Bay."

"What is that little thing crawling there on the floor?"

"Where?" he asked, looking around him.

"That little thing crawling along near your feet."

"Oh," he said. He squatted down. "Why, it's an ant. I wonder how it got up here."

Frankie tilted back in her chair and crossed her bare feet on her desk. "If I were you I'd just throw those glasses away," she said. "You can see good as anybody."

John Henry did not answer.

"They don't look becoming."

She handed the folded glasses to John Henry and he wiped them with his pink flannel glasses rag. He put them back on and did not answer.

"O.K." she said. "Suit yourself. I was only telling you for your own good."

They went to bed. They undressed with their backs turned to each other and then Frankie switched off the motor and the light. John Henry knelt down to say his prayers and he prayed for a long time, not saying the words aloud. Then he lay down beside her.

"Good night," she said.

"Good night."

Frankie stared up into the dark. "You know it is still hard for me to realize that the world turns around at the rate of about a thousand miles an hour."

"I know it," he said.

"And to understand why it is that when you jump up in the air you don't come down in Fairview or Selma or somewhere fifty miles away."

John Henry turned over and made a sleepy sound.

"Or Winter Hill," she said. "I wish I was starting for Winter Hill right now."

Already John Henry was asleep. She heard him breathe in the darkness, and now she had what she had wanted so many nights that summer; there was somebody sleeping in the bed with her. She lay in the dark and listened to him breathe, then after a while she raised herself on her elbow. He lay freckled and small in the moonlight, his chest white and naked, and one foot hanging from the edge of the bed. Carefully she put her hand on his stomach and moved closer; it felt as though a little clock was ticking inside him and he smelled of sweat and Sweet Serenade. He smelled like a sour little rose. Frankie leaned down and licked him behind the ear. Then she breathed deeply, settled herself with her chin on his sharp damp shoulder, and closed her eyes: for now, with somebody sleeping in the dark with her, she was not so much afraid.

The sun woke them early the next morning, the white August sun. Frankie could not make John Henry go home. He saw the ham Berenice was cooking, and that the special company dinner was going to be good. Frankie's father read the paper in the living room, then went downtown to wind the watches at his jewelry store.

"If that brother of mine don't bring me a present from Alaska, I will be seriously mad," said Frankie.

"Me too," agreed John Henry.

And what were they doing that August morning when her brother and the bride came home? They were sitting in the arbor shade and talking about Christmas. The glare was hard and bright, the sun-drunk bluejays screamed and murdered among themselves. They talked, and their voices tired down into a little tune and they said the same things over and over. They just drowsed in the dark shade of the arbor, and Frankie was a person who had never thought about a wedding. That was the way they were that August morning when her brother and the bride walked in the house.

"Oh, Jesus!" Frankie said. The cards on the table were greasy and the late sun slanted across the yard. "The world is certainy a sudden place."

"Well, stop commenting about it," said Berenice. "You don't have your mind on the game."

Frankie, however, had some of her mind on the game. She played the queen of spades, which were trumps, and John Henry threw off a little two of diamonds. She looked at him. He was staring at the back of her hand as though what he wanted and needed was angled eyesight that could cut around corners and read people's cards.

"You got a spade," said Frankie.

John Henry put his donkey necklace in his mouth and looked away.

"Cheater," she said.

"Go on and play your spade," said Berenice.

Then he argued: "It was hid behind the other card."

"Cheater."

But still he would not play. He sat there sad and holding up the game.

"Make haste," said Berenice.

"I can't," he said finally. "It's a jack. The only spade I got is a jack. I don't want to play my jack down under Frankie's queen. I'm not going to do it either."

Frankie threw her cards down on the table. "See!" she said to Berenice. "He don't even follow the first beginning laws! He's a child! It is hopeless! Hopeless! Hopeless!"

"Maybe so," said Berenice.

"Oh," Frankie said, "I am sick unto death."

She sat with her bare feet on the rungs of the chair, her eyes closed, and her chest against the table edge. The red greasy cards were messed together on the table, and the sight of them made Frankie sick. They had played cards after dinner every single afternoon; if you would eat those old cards, they would taste like a combination of all the dinners of that August, together with a sweaty-handed nasty taste. Frankie swept the cards from the table. The wedding was bright and beautiful as snow and the heart in her was mashed. She got up from the table.

"It is a known truth that gray-eyed people are jealous."

"I told you I wasn't jealous," Frankie said, and she was walking fast around the room. "I couldn't be jealous of one of them without being jealous of them both. I sociate the two of them together."

"Well, I were jealous when my foster brother married," said Berenice. "I admit that when John married Clorina I sent a warning I would tear the ears off her head. But you see I didn't. Clorina got ears like anybody else. And now I love her."

"J A," said Frankie. "Janice and Jarvis. Isn't that the strangest thing?"

"What?"

"J A," she said. "Both their names begin with J A."

"And? What about it?"

Frankie walked round and round the kitchen table. "If only my name was Jane," she said. "Jane or Jasmine."

"I don't follow your frame of mind," said Berenice.

"Jarvis and Janice and Jasmine. See?"

"No," said Berenice. "By the way, I heard this morning on the radio that the French people are chasing the Germans out of Paris."

"Paris," Frankie repeated in a hollow tone. "I wonder if it is against the law to change your name. Or to add to it."

"Naturally. It is against the law."

"Well, I don't care," she said. "F. Jasmine Addams."

On the staircase leading to her room there was a doll, and John Henry brought it to the table and sat rocking it in his arms. "You serious when you gave me this," he said. He pulled up the doll's dress and fingered the real panties and body-waist. "I will name her Belle."

Frankie stared at the doll for a minute. "I don't know what went on in Jarvis's mind when he brought me that doll. Imagine bringing me a doll! And Janice tried to explain that she had pictured me as a little girl. I had counted on Jarvis bringing me something from Alaska."

"Your face when you unwrapped the package was a study," said Berenice.

It was a large doll with red hair and china eyes that opened and closed, and yellow eyelashes. John Henry held her in a lying-down position, so that the eyes were shut, and he was now trying to open them by pulling up the eyelashes.

"Don't do that! It makes me nervous. In fact, take that doll somewhere out of my sight."

John Henry took it to the back porch where he could pick it up when he went home.

"Her name is Lily Belle," he said.

The clock ticked very slowly on the shelf above the stove, and it was only quarter to six. The glare outside the window was still hard and yellow and bright. In the back yard the shade beneath the arbor was black and solid. Nothing moved. From somewhere far away came the sound of whistling, and it was a grieving August song that did not end. The minutes were very long.

Frankie went again to the kitchen mirror and stared at her own face. "The big mistake I made was to get this close crew-cut. For the wedding I ought to have long bright yellow hair. Don't you think so?"

She stood before the mirror and she was afraid. It was the summer of fear, for Frankie, and there was one fear that could be figured in arithmetic with paper and a pencil at the table. This August she was twelve and five-sixths years old. She was five feet five and three quarter inches tall, and she wore a number seven shoe. In the past year she had grown four inches, or at least that was what she judged. Already the hateful little summer children hollered to her: "Is it cold up there?" And the comments of grown people make Frankie shrivel on her heels. If she reached her height on her eighteenth birthday, she had five and one-sixth growing years ahead of her. Therefore, according to mathematics and unless she could somehow stop herself, she would grow to be over nine feet tall. And what would be a lady who is over nine feet high? She would be a Freak.

In the early autumn of every year the Chattahoochee Exposition came to town. For a whole October week the fair went on down at the fairgrounds. There was the Ferris Wheel, the Flying Jinney, the Palace of Mirrors – and there, too, was the House of the Freaks. The House of the Freaks was a long pavilion which was lined on the inside with a row of booths. It cost a quarter to go into the general tent, and you could look at each Freak in his booth. Then there were special private exhibitions farther back in the tent which cost a dime apiece. Frankie had seen all of the members of the Freak House last October:

The Giant
The Fat Lady
The Midget
The Wild Nigger
The Pin Head
The Alligator Boy
The Half-Man Half-Woman

The Giant was more than eight feet high, with huge loose hands and a hang-jaw face. The Fat Lady sat in a chair, and the fat on her was like loose-powdered dough which she kept slapping and working with her hands – next was the squeezed Midget who minced around in little trick evening clothes. The Wild Nigger came from a savage island. He squatted in his booth among the dusty bones and palm leaves and he ate raw living rats. The fair gave a free admission to his show to all who brought rats of the right size, and so children carried them down in strong sacks and shoe boxes. The Wild Nigger knocked the rat's head over his squatted knee and ripped off the fur and crunched and gobbled and flashed his greedy Wild Nigger eyes. Some said that he was not a genuine Wild Nigger, but a crazy colored man from Selma. Anyway, Frankie did not like to watch him very long. She pushed through the crowd to the Pin Head booth, where John Henry had stood all afternoon. The little Pin Head skipped and giggled and sassed around, with a shrunken head no larger than an orange, which was shaved except for one lock tied with a pink bow at the top. The last booth was always very crowded, for it was the booth of the Half-Man Half-Woman, a morphidite and a miracle of science. This Freak was divided completely in half – the left side was a man and the right side a woman. The costume on the left was a leopard skin and on the right side a brassiere and a spangled skirt. Half the face was dark bearded and the other half bright glazed with paint. Both eyes were strange. Frankie had wandered around the tent and looked at every booth. She was afraid of all the Freaks, for it seemed to her that they had looked at her in a secret way and tried to connect their eyes with hers, as though to say: we know you. She was afraid of their long Freak eyes. And all the years she had remembered them, until this day.

"I doubt if they ever get married or go to a wedding," she said. "Those Freaks."

"What freaks you talking about?" said Berenice.

"At the fair," said Frankie. "The ones we saw there last October."

"Oh, those folks."

"I wonder if they make a big salary," she said.

And Berenice answered: "How would I know?"

John Henry held out an imaginary skirt and, touching his finger to the top of his big head, he skipped and danced like the Pin Head around the kitchen table.

Then he said: "She was the cutest little girl I ever saw. I never saw anything so cute in my whole life. Did you, Frankie?"

"No," she said. "I didn't think she was cute."

"Me and you both," said Berenice.

"Shoo!" John Henry argued. "She was, too."

"If you want my candy opinion," said Berenice, "that whole crowd of folks down yonder at the fair just give me the creeps. Ever last one of them."

Frankie watched Berenice through the mirror, and finally she asked in a slow voice. "Do *I* give you the creeps?"

"You?" asked Berenice.

"Do you think I will grow into a Freak?" Frankie whispered.

"You?" said Berenice again. "Why, certainy not, I trust Jesus."

Frankie felt better. She looked sidewise at herself in the mirror. The clock ticked six slow times, and then she said: "Well, do you think I will be pretty?"

"Maybe. If you file down them horns a inch or two."

Frankie stood with her weight resting on her left leg, and she slowly shuffled the ball of her right foot on the floor. She felt a splinter go beneath the skin. "Seriously," she said.

"I think when you fill out you will do very well. If you behave."

"But by Sunday," Frankie said. "I want to do something to improve myself before the wedding."

"Get clean for a change. Scrub your elbows and fix yourself nice. You will do very well."

Frankie looked for a last time at herself in the mirror, and then she turned away. She thought about her brother and the bride, and there was a tightness in her that would not break.

"I don't know what to do. I just wish I would die."

"Well, die then!" said Berenice.

And: "Die," John Henry echoed in a whisper.

The world stopped.

"Go home," said Frankie to John Henry.

He stood with his big knees locked, his dirty little hand on the edge of the white table, and he did not move.

"You heard me," Frankie said. She made a terrible face at him and grabbed the frying pan that hung above the stove. She chased him three times around the table, then up through the front hall and out of the door. She locked the front door and called again: "Go home."

"Now what makes you act like that?" said Berenice. "You are too mean to live."

Frankie opened the door to the stairway that led up to her room, and sat down on one of the lower steps. The kitchen was silent and crazy and sad.

"I know it," she said. "I intend to sit still by myself and think over everything for a while."

Cora Sandel

translated from the Norwegian by Barbara Wilson

The Child Who Loved Roads

Cora Sandel was born Sara Fabricius in 1880, the oldest daughter of a middle-class Norwegian family. As a young girl she wanted to become a painter, and at twenty-five left for Paris to continue her studies. She was strongly influenced by the French writer Colette, and particularly admired her book La Vagabonde. *She began to write at thirty-seven, after the birth of her son, Erik, and in subsequent years published several collections of short stories, among them* The Child Who Loved Roads *(1973). She also wrote a number of novels, and is best known for her* Alberta *trilogy (1926, 1931, and 1939). Cora Sandel died in 1974 at the age of ninety-three.*

MOST OF ALL SHE LOVED ROADS WITH THE SOLITARY TRACK OF A horse down the middle and with grass between the wheel ruts. Narrow old roads with lots of bends and nobody else around and here and there a piece of straw perhaps, fallen from a load of hay. The child turned springy and light as air on them, filled with happiness at breaking free, at existing. Behind each bend waited unknown possibilities, however many times you'd gone down the road. You could make them up yourself if nothing else.

Down the highway she walked, dragging her feet in dust and gravel. Dust and gravel were among the bad things in life. You got tired, hot, heavy, longed to be picked up and carried.

Then suddenly the narrow old road was there, and the child began to run, leaping high with happiness.

She hadn't been so tired after all, the grown-ups said. There's a lot grown-ups don't understand. You have to give up explaining anything to them and take them as they are, an inconvenience, for the most part. No one should grow up. No, children should stay children and rule the whole world. Everything would be more fun and a lot better then.

Early on the child learned that it was best to be alone on the road. A good ways in front of the others anyway. Only then did you come to know the road as it really was, with its marks of wheels and horses hooves, its small, stubborn stones sticking up, its shifting lights and shadows. Only then did you come to know the fringes of the road, warm from sun and greenness, plump and furry with wild chervil and lady's mantle – altogether a strange and wonderful world unto itself, where you could wander free as you pleased, and everything was good, safe, and just the way you wanted it.

At least it was in the summer. In winter the road was something else entirely. In the twilight of a snow-gray day your legs could turn to lead, everything was so sad. You never seemed to get any further; there was always a long ways to go. The middle of the road was brown and ugly, like rice pudding with cinnamon on it, a dish that grew in her mouth and that she couldn't stand. People and trees stood out black and sorrowful against the white. You did have the sledding hill, the field with deep snow for rolling on, the courtyard for building forts and caves, the skis without real bindings. For small children shouldn't have real bindings, the grown-ups said; they could fall and break their legs. In the twilight everything was merely sad, and nothing about it could compare to the roads in summer.

To be let loose on them, without a jacket, without a hat, *bare*, that was life the way it should be. Only one thing compared to it, the hills at the big farm, where she was often a guest.

There were paths bordered with heather and crowberry leading up to views over the blue fiord and to a light, never-still breeze that tickled your scalp. White stone protruded from the heather and the path. At the bottom of the hill you found wild strawberries, higher up blueberries, not just a few either, and bilberries. On top lay the crowberries in patches like large carpets.

The child could pass hours lying on her stomach near a bush, stuffing herself, and at the same time thinking of all sorts of things. She possessed an active imagination, seldom longed for company and could sometimes fly into a rage if she got it.

"You're so contrary," said the grown-ups. "Can't you be nice and sweet like the others, just a little? You should be thankful anyone wants to be with you," they said.

"It won't be easy for you when you're older," they also said.

The child forgot it as soon as it was said. She ran off to the road or the paths and remembered nothing so unreasonable, so completely ridiculous.

One road went from the house on the big farm, went along the garden where huge old red currant bushes hung over the picket fence, casually offering their magnificence; the road went across the fields, bordered by thin young trees, made a leap over a hill and swung two times like an S before it wandered out in the world and became one with the boring highway.

The child's own road, newly taken possession of summer after summer. Here no one came running after you, here you could wander without company. Nothing could happen but the right things. If anyone came driving or riding it was uncles, aunts or the farmboy. They saw you from a long distance away, they stopped; if they came by wagon you got a ride to the farm.

Here and on the hills were where the stories came into being, short ones and long ones. If they didn't look like they were living up to their promise, you just stopped and started a new one.

A place in life where freedom had no boundaries. Very different from what the grown-ups meant when they said, "in this life," or "in this world," and sighed. They also said, "in this difficult-life." As if to make things as nasty as possible.

Being together with someone – that was sometimes fun and sometimes not at all. You couldn't explain why or why not; it was part of everything you imagined and that you'd never dream of talking to grown-ups about. On the contrary, you held tightly to it, like someone insisting on something wrong they've done. Maybe it was "wrong"; maybe it was one of those things that ought to be "rooted out of you." Or at best to laugh about a little, to whisper over your head.

"Constructive" it wasn't, in any case. They were always talking about the necessity of doing "constructive things."

It could be fun, when Alette came, Letta. She was a redhead, freckled, full of laughter, easy to get along with. At her house, at the neighboring farm, was a chest in the loft, full of old-fashioned clothes. Dresses in wonderful light colors, flounce after flounce on the wide tarlatan skirts, a name that was far prettier than, for example, blue cotton cambric. A man's suit, yellow knee breeches and a green coat with gold buttons, an unbelievable costume that didn't look like anything the uncles wore. A folding parasol, a whole collection of odd hats. To dress up in all that, strut around in it, stumble in the long skirts, mimic the grown-ups and make them laugh where they sat on the garden steps, was fun enough for a while. But it was nothing to base a life on.

For that you could only use the roads, the paths and the hills.

Grown-up, well, you probably had to turn into one. Everyone did; you couldn't avoid it.

But like some of them? Definitely not.

In the first place the child was going to run her whole life, never do anything so boring as walk slowly and deliberately. In the second and third place . . .

The grown-ups didn't have much that was worthwhile. It was true they got everything they wanted, could buy themselves things they wanted and go to bed when they felt like it, eat things at the table that children didn't get – all the best things, in short. They could command and scold, give canings and presents. But they got long skirts or trousers to wear and then they *walked. Just* walked. You had to wonder if it had something to do with what was called Confirmation, if there wasn't something about it that injured their legs. There probably was, since they hid them and walked. They *couldn't* run any longer. Even though – you saw them dance; you saw them play "Widower Seeks A Mate" and "Last Pair Out."

Maybe it was their minds something was wrong with?

Everything truly fun disappeared from their lives, and they let it happen. None of them rebelled. On the contrary, they grew conceited about their sad transformation. Was there anything so conceited as the big girls when they got long skirts and put up their hair!

They walked, they sat and embroidered, sat and wrote, sat and chatted, knitted, crocheted. Walked and sat, sat and walked. Stupid, they were so stupid!

Trailing skirts were dangerous. She'd have to watch out, when the time came. Run away maybe.

At home, in the city street, were the mean boys.

Really big boys, the kind who were practically uncles, were often nice. They were the ones who organized the big circus in the empty lot, with trapeze artists, clowns and tickets that the grown-ups bought in complete seriousness: parquet circle, first class, second class. A ringmaster in a tuxedo went around the circus ring and cracked his long whip at the horses doing tricks. A true circus, so to speak, except that the horses consisted of two boys under a blanket that sometimes sagged in the middle. But that was easy to overlook.

The big boys arranged competition races in the winter, saw to it that you got new skis and real bindings; they were pillars of support. One of them once got up and lambasted his sister, who had tattled on him. A bunch of lies, made up, shameful, that you just had to sit there and take, for you didn't get anywhere saying it wasn't true.

They were pillars all the same.

But there was a half-grown kind, a mean kind, that made such a racket. They ran back and forth with wooden bats in their hands and the balls shot between them like bullets. In the winter they threw hard snowballs, and if anyone had put up an especially fine fort anywhere, they came rushing down in a crowd and stormed it, left it destroyed. Sometimes they threatened you with a beating. For no reason, just to threaten. The child was deathly afraid of them, took any roundabout way she could to avoid them; she would rather be too late for dinner.

Sometimes she *had* to come through enemy lines to get home. With her heart in her throat, with her head bowed as if in a storm, she sneaked sideways along the walls of the houses. The taunts rained down.

One day a boy of that sort came after the child, grabbed her arm, squeezed it hard and said, "You know what you are? Do you?"

No answer.

"You're just a girl. Go home where you belong."

Hard as a whip the words struck the child. Just a girl – *just*. From that moment she had a heavy burden to bear, one of the heaviest, the feeling of being something inferior, of being born that way, beyond help.

With such a burden on your back the world becomes a different place for you. Your sense of yourself begins to change.

But the roads remained an even bigger consolation than before. On them even "just a girl" felt easy, free and secure.

The child was one of those who feels sorry. For skinny horses and horses who got the whip, for cats who looked homeless, for children who were smaller than she was and who didn't have mittens in winter, for people who just generally looked poor, and for drunken men.

Why she was so sorry for drunken men was never clear. They'd drunk hard liquor; they could have left it alone. They were their own worst enemies, the grown-ups explained; if things went so badly for them it was their own fault.

In the child's eyes they were nothing but helpless. They tumbled here and there; sometimes they fell down and remained lying there – the policeman came and dragged them off roughly. Sorry for them, she was sorry for them; they couldn't help it, they couldn't help it for anything, however they'd come to be that way. They were like little children who can't walk on their own and do things wrong because they don't know any better.

The child cried herself to sleep at times on account of the drunkards. And on account of the horses, cats and poor people. Once you're like that, you don't have it easy. The cats she could have taken home if it hadn't been for the grown-ups. She wasn't allowed. As if one cat more or less mattered. You were powerless, in this as in everything.

On the summertime roads you forgot your troubles. If you met poorly clad people you usually knew who they were, where they lived, that they had nicer clothes at home that they saved for Sundays. The horses you met were rounded, comfortable, easy going. They waved their long tails up over thick haunches and grazed by the roadside as soon as they got a chance. The cats rubbed against your legs, purring loudly. Farm cats who belonged somewhere and were just out for a walk.

You hardly ever met anyone, though, whether people or animals. That was what was wonderful; it became more and more wonderful as the child grew older. She had a steadily stronger desire to keep making up stories in her head. There was no place that they came so readily as along a two-wheeled track with grass in between. Or up on the hill where the breeze brushed your scalp.

Time passed. The child ran, long braid flapping, on the roads.

If she was overtaken by the grown-ups, she heard, "You're too old now to be running like that. Soon you'll be wearing long skirts, remember. A young lady *walks*, she holds herself nicely, thinks about how she places her feet. Then she can't rush away like you do."

The child ran even faster than before. To get out of earshot, out of range as much as possible. Her legs had grown long; they were an advantage when she took to her heels. The braid swung, the lengthened skirt swung. The child thought – one day I won't turn around when they call, I won't wait for anyone. That might be sooner than they suspect. The roads lead much farther than I realized; they lead out into the world, away from all of them.

When she stopped, she looked around with new eyes, seeing no longer just the roadsides, but the horizons. Behind them lay what she longed for, craved. freedom.

But one of the big boys, the kind who were practically uncles, suddenly popped out of nowhere. He was Letta's cousin, had passed his high school exams, was a university student.

You didn't see much of him. Letta said he was stupid and conceited, a self-important fellow who kept to his room or with the grown-ups. He himself was definitely not all that grown up, said Letta, who remembered him in short pants, remembered that he stole apples at someone's and got a caning for it at home. That wasn't so very long ago; she'd been ten years old, on a visit to his parents. Now she was thirteen, almost fourteen.

He had a strange effect on the child; he upset her from the first moment in a way that was both painful and good. It was impossible to think of him when he was nearby and could turn up; you can't think when you're blushing in confusion. But out on the roads he crept into her thoughts to the extent that she couldn't get him out again; he took up residence there, inserted himself in the middle of an on-going story, which had to be completely changed. There was no other recourse.

The story came to be about him. He became the main character, along with herself. In spite of the fact that she didn't really know how he looked; she never quite risked looking at him. And in spite of the fact that he wore long trousers, *walked*, and consequently belonged to the poor fool category.

It was inexplicable, and she felt it as slightly shameful, a defeat. The child grew fiery red with embarrassment if he so much as made an appearance. As the misfortune was written on her face, it was necessary to avoid Letta and her family, to keep to the roads as never before.

You could go into Letta's garden without being seen.

Letta followed, full of suggestions; she wanted them to get dressed up like summers before, to make fun of the cousin, who was sitting on the steps with the grown-ups – to mimic him.

"He doesn't interest me."

"You think he interests me? That's why we can tease him a little, can't we?"

"I'm not interested in teasing such a disgusting person," explained the child, marveling at her own words.

"Come anyway, though."

"No."

"Why not?"

"Because I don't want to, that's why."

But it was a terribly empty feeling, when Letta gave up and walked away. Just to talk about him was a new and remarkable experience, was something she yearned for, wanted and had to do.

The child was beginning to *walk* on the roads. Slowly even. She stood still for long moments at a time. For no reason, to fuss with the tie on her braid, to curl the end of the braid around her fingers, to scrape her toe in the gravel, to stare out into space. She sat down in the grass by the roadside, trailed her hand searchingly around between the lady's mantle and water avens, did it over and over.

Finally her hand had found something, a four-leaf clover. Thoughtfully the child walked on with it, holding it carefully between two fingers.

"Well now, finally you're acting like a big girl," said one of the aunts, pleased. "Not a minute too soon. Good thing we don't have to nag you anymore. Good thing there's still a little hem to let out in your dress. Next week we'll get Joanna the seamstress."

Hardly was it said than the child set off at full speed, in defiance, in panic.

Without her having noticed it or understood it, she had allowed something to happen, something frightening, something detestable. Something that made *them* happy. But nothing should make them happy. For then they'd be getting you where they wanted you, a prisoner, some kind of invalid.

The child didn't hear the despairing sigh of a deeply worried grown-up. That would have made her relieved and calm. Instead she only felt torn by life's contradictions, bewildered and confused by them.

One day the cousin left; he was simply gone. Letta said, Who cares, he was conceited and engaged. Secretly naturally, but it had come out that he went around with a photograph and a pressed flower in his wallet, and that he used to meet the postman far down the highway. Letta's father had taken him into the office, talked with him for a long time, pointed out what a serious thing an engagement is, nothing for a green new graduate. Green, that was probably a good description of him. Anyway, his fiancée's father was nothing but a shoemaker, said Letta. She though the cousin's parents had been alerted.

"Imagine, engaged. Him!"

The child stood there and felt something strange in her face, felt herself grow pale. Not red at any rate, because then you got hot. This was a cold feeling.

"Well, good-bye," she said.

"Didn't you come to stay?"

The child was already gone, was out on the road, the good old road with the two curves like an S, with thin young trees along it and grass between the wheel tracks. Here was the same sense of escape as always; here you could run, not only in fantasy, but also free from all shame, everything deceitful that was out after you. And that was over now.

For it was over right away. In a short painful moment – as when a tooth is pulled out.

Follow the roads, never become what they call grown up, never what they call old, two degrading conditions that made people stupid, ugly, boring. Stay how you are now, light as a feather, never tired, never out of breath. It came down to being careful, not just for lengthened skirts, but also for anything like this.

For a moment the child stopped, fished out of her pocket a dried four-leaf clover, tore it in pieces and let the wind take the bits.

And then she ran on, over the farmyard, right up the path to the hill, where the fresh breeze blew.

PART FOUR

Out the Other Side

Alice Munro

from *Lives of Girls and Women*

Alice Munro was born in Ontario, Canada, in 1931, and attended the University of Western Ontario. She married, moved to Vancouver and Victoria, became the mother of three daughters, and, with her husband, opened the well-known bookstore Munro's Books. She has published seven collections of short stories, among them, Something I've Been Meaning to Tell You *(1974),* The Progress of Love *(1986), and* Open Secrets *(1994), as well as a novel,* Lives of Girls and Women *(1971). The following is set in a town in Canada, not long after the Second World War. The narrator's name is Del Jordan, and Frank Wales is a boy she once admired, passionately, from afar.*

THE SNOWBANKS ALONG THE MAIN STREET GOT TO BE SO HIGH THAT an archway was cut in one of them, between the street and the sidewalk, in front of the post office. A picture was taken of this and published in the Jubilee *Herald-Advance,* so that people could cut it out and send it to relatives and acquaintances living in less heroic climates, in England or Australia or Toronto. The red-brick clocktower of the post office was sticking up above the snow and two women were standing in the archway, to show it was no trick. Both these women worked in the post office, had put their coats on without buttoning them. One was Fern Dogherty, my mother's boarder.

My mother cut this picture out, because it had Fern in it, and because she said I should keep it, to show to my children.

"They will never see a thing like that," she said. "By then the snow will all be collected in machines and – dissipated. Or people will be living under transparent domes, with a controlled temperature. There will be no such thing as seasons anymore."

How did she collect all her unsettling information about the future? She looked forward to a time when towns like Jubilee would be replaced by domes and mushrooms of concrete, with moving skyways to carry you from one to the other, when the countryside would be bound and tamed forever under broad sweeping ribbons of pavement. Nothing would be the same as we knew it today,

[131

no frying pans or bobby pins or printed pages or fountain pens would remain. My mother would not miss a thing.

Her speaking of my children amazed me too, for I never meant to have any. It was glory I was after, walking the streets of Jubilee like an exile or a spy, not sure from which direction fame would strike, or when, only convinced from my bones out that it had to. In this conviction my mother had shared, she had been my ally, but now I would no longer discuss it with her; she was indiscreet, and her expectations took too blatant a form.

Fern Dogherty. There she was in the paper, both hands coquettishly holding up the full collar of her good winter coat, which through pure luck she had worn to work that day. "I look the size of a watermelon," she said. "In that coat."

Mr. Chamberlain, looking with her, pinched her arm above the bracelet wrinkle of the wrist.

"Tough rind, tough old watermelon."

"Don't get vicious," said Fern. "I mean it." Her voice was small for such a big woman, plaintive, put-upon, but in the end good-humored, yielding. All those qualities my mother had developed for her assault on life – sharpness, smartness, determination, selectiveness – seemed to have their opposites in Fern, with her diffuse complaints, lazy movements, indifferent agreeableness. She had a dark skin, not olive but dusty looking, dim, with brown-pigmented spots as large as coins; it was like the dappled ground under a tree on a sunny day. Her teeth were square, white, slightly protruding, with little spaces between them. These two characteristics, neither of which sounds particularly attractive in itself, did give her a roguish, sensual look.

She had a ruby-colored satin dressing gown, a gorgeous garment, fruitily molding, when she sat down, the bulges of her stomach and thighs. She wore it Sunday mornings, when she sat in our dining room smoking, drinking tea, until it was time to get ready for church. It parted at the knees to show some pale clinging rayon – a nightgown. Nightgowns were garments I could not bear, because of the way they twisted around and worked up on you while you slept and also because they left you uncovered between the legs. Naomi and I when we were younger used to draw pictures of men and women with startling gross genitals, the women's fat, bristling with needly hair, like a porcupine's back. Wearing a nightgown one could not help being aware of this vile bundle, which pajamas could decently shroud and contain. My mother at the same Sunday breakfast table wore large striped pajamas, a faded rust-colored kimono with a tasseled tie, the sort of slippers that are woolly socks, with a sole sewn in.

Fern Dogherty and my mother were friends in spite of differences. My mother valued in people experience of the world, contact with any life of learning or culture, and finally any suggestion of being dubiously received in Jubilee. And Fern had not always worked for the post office. No; at one time she had studied singing, she had studied at the Royal Conservatory of Music. Now she sang in the United Church choir, sang "I Know that My Redeemer Liveth" on Easter Sunday, and at weddings she sang "Because" and "O Promise Me" and "The Voice that Breathed O'er Eden." On Saturday afternoons, the post office being closed, she and my mother would listen to the broadcasts of the Metropolitan Opera. My mother had a book of operas. She would get it out and follow the story, identifying the arias, for which translations were provided. She had questions for Fern, but Fern did not know as much about operas as you would think she might; she would even get mixed up about which one it was they were listening to. But sometimes she would lean forward with her elbows on the table, not now relaxed, but alertly supported, and sing, scorning the foreign words. "*Do* – daa – do, da, *do*, da do-do –" The force, the seriousness of her singing voice always came as a surprise. It didn't embarrass her, letting loose those grand, inflated emotions she paid no attention to in life.

"Did you plan to be an opera singer?" I asked.

"No. I just planned to be the lady working in the post office. Well, I did and I didn't. The work, the *training*. I just didn't have the ambition for it, I guess that was my trouble. I always preferred having a good time." She wore slacks on Saturday afternoons, and sandals that showed her pudgy, painted toes. She was dropping ashes on her stomach, which, ungirdled, popped out in a pregnant curve. "Smoking is ruining my voice," she said meditatively.

Fern's style of singing, though admired, was regarded in Jubilee as being just a hair's breadth from showing off, and sometimes children did screech or warble after her, in the street. My mother could take this for persecution. She would construct such cases out of the flimsiest evidence, seeking out the Jewish couple who ran the Army Surplus store, or the shrunken silent Chinese in the laundry, with bewildering compassion, loud slow-spoken overtures of friendship. They did not know what to make of her. Fern was not persecuted, that I could see. Though my old aunts, my father's aunts, would say her name in a peculiar way, as if it had a stone in it, that they would have to suck, and spit out. And Naomi did tell me, "That Fern Dogherty had a baby."

"She never did," I said, automatically defensive.

"She did so. She had it when she was nineteen years old. That's why she got kicked out of the Conservatory."

"How do you know?"

"My mother knows."

Naomi's mother had spies everywhere, old childbed cases, deathbed companions, keeping her informed. In her nursing job, going from one house to another, she was able to operate like an underwater vacuum tube, sucking up what nobody else could get at. I felt I had to argue with Naomi about it because Fern was our boarder, and Naomi was always saying things about people in our house. ("Your mother's an atheist," she would say with black relish, and I would say, "No she isn't, she's an agnostic," and all through my reasoned hopeful explanation Naomi would chant *same difference, same difference.*) I was not able to retaliate, either out of delicacy or cowardice, though Naomi's own father belonged to some odd and discredited religious sect, and wandered all over town talking prophecies without putting his false teeth in.

I took to noticing pictures of babies in the paper, or in magazines, when Fern was around, saying, "Aw, isn't it *cute?*" and then watching her closely for a flicker of remorse, maternal longing, as if someday she might actually be persuaded to burst into tears, fling out her empty arms, struck to the heart by an ad for talcum powder or strained meat.

Furthermore, Naomi said Fern did everything with Mr. Chamberlain, just the same as if they were married.

It was Mr. Chamberlain who got Fern boarding with us in the first place. We rented the house from his mother, now in her third year, blind and bedridden, in the Wawanash County Hospital. Fern's mother was in the same place; it was there, in fact, on a visiting day, that they had met. She was working in the Blue River Post office at that time. Mr. Chamberlain worked at the Jubilee radio station and lived in a small apartment in the same building, not wanting the trouble of a house. My mother spoke of him as "Fern's friend," in a clarifying tone of voice, as if to insist that the word friend in this case meant no more than it was supposed to mean.

"They enjoy each other's company," she said. "They don't bother about any nonsense."

Nonsense meant romance; it meant vulgarity; it meant sex.

I tried out on my mother what Naomi said.

"Fern and Mr. Chamberlain might just as well be married."

"What? What do you mean? Who said that?"

"Everybody knows it."

"I don't. Everybody does not. Nobody ever said such a thing in my hearing. It's that Naomi said it, isn't it?"

Naomi was not popular in my house, nor I in hers. Each of us was suspected of carrying the seeds of contamination – in my case, of atheism, in Naomi's, of sexual preoccupation.

"It's dirty mindedness that is just rampant in this town, and will never let people alone."

"If Fern Dogherty was not a good woman," my mother concluded, with a specious air of logic, "do you think I would have her living in my house?"

This year, our first year in high school, Naomi and I held almost daily discussions on the subject of sex, but took one tone, so that there were degrees of candor we could never reach. This tone was ribald, scornful, fanatically curious. A year ago we had liked to imagine ourselves victims of passion; now we were established as onlookers, or at most cold and gleeful experimenters. We had a book Naomi had found in her mother's old hope chest, under the moth-balled best blankets.

Care should be taken during the initial connection, we read aloud, *particularly if the male organ is of an unusual size. Vaseline may prove a helpful lubricant.*

"I prefer butter myself. Tastier."

Intercourse between the thighs is often resorted to in the final stages of pregnancy.

"You mean they still do it *then?*"

The rear-entry position is sometimes indicated in cases where the female is considerably obese.

"Fern," Naomi said. "That's how he does it to Fern. She's considerably obese."

"Aggh! This book makes me sick."

The male sexual organ in erection, we read, had been known to reach a length of fourteen inches. Naomi spat out her chewing gum and rolled it between her palms, stretching it longer and longer, then picked it up by one end and dangled it in the air.

"Mr. Chamberlain, the record breaker!"

Thereafter whenever she came to my place, and Mr. Chamberlain was there, one of us, or both, if we were chewing gum, would take it out and roll it this way and dangle it innocently, till even the adults noticed and Mr. Chamberlain said, "That's quite a game you got there," and my mother said, "Stop that, it's filthy." (She meant the gum.) We watched Mr. Chamberlain and Fern for signs of passion, wantonness, lustful looks, or hands up the skirt. We were not rewarded, my defense of them turning out to be truer than I wished it to be. For I as much as Naomi liked to entertain myself with thoughts of their grunting indecencies, their wallowing in jingly beds (in tourist cabins, Naomi said, every time they drove to Tupperton *to have a look at the lake*). Disgust did not rule out enjoyment, in my thoughts; indeed they were inseparable.

Mr. Chamberlain, Art Chamberlain, read the news on the Jubilee radio. He also did all the more serious and careful announcing. He had a fine professional voice, welcome as dark chocolate flowing in and out of the organ music on the Sunday afternoon program *In Memoriam*, sponsored by a local funeral parlor. He sometimes got Fern singing on this program, sacred songs – "I Wonder as I Wander" – and nonsacred but mournful songs – "The End of a Perfect Day." It was not hard to get on the Jubilee radio; I myself had recited a comic poem, on the *Saturday Morning Young Folks Party*, and Naomi had played "The Bells of St. Mary's" on the piano. Every time you turned it on there was a good chance of hearing someone you knew, or at least of hearing the names of people you knew mentioned in the dedications. ("We are going to play this piece also for Mr. and Mrs. Carl Otis on the occasion of their twenty-eighth wedding anniversary, requested by their son George and wife Etta, and their three grandchildren, Lorraine, Mark and Lois, also by Mrs. Otis' sister Mrs. Bill Townley of the Porterfield Road.") I had phoned up myself and dedicated a song to Uncle Benny on his fortieth birthday; my mother would not have her name mentioned. She preferred listening to the Toronto station, which brought us the Metropolitan Opera, and news with no commercials, and a quiz program in which she competed with four gentlemen who, to judge from their voices, would all have little, pointed beards.

Mr. Chamberlain had to read commercials too, and he did it with ripe concern, recommending Vick's Nose Drops from Cross' Drugstore, and Sunday dinner at the Brunswick Hotel, and Lee Wickert and Sons for dead-livestock removal. "How's the dead livestock, soldier?" Fern would greet him, and he might slap her lightly on the rump. "I'll tell them you need their services!" "Looks to me more like you do," said Fern without much malice, and he would drop into a chair and smile at my mother for pouring him tea. His light blue-green eyes had no expression, just that color, so pretty you would want to make a dress out of it. He was always tired.

Mr. Chamberlain's white hands, his nails cut straight across, his graying, thinning, nicely-combed hair, his body that did not in any way disturb his clothes but seemed to be made of the same material as they were, so that he might have been shirt and tie and suit all the way through, were strange to me in a man. Even Uncle Benny, so skinny and narrow-chested, with his damaged bronchial tubes, had some look or way of moving that predicted chance or intended violence, something that would make disorder; my father had this too, though he was so moderate in his ways. Yet it was Mr. Chamberlain, tapping his ready-made cigarette in the ashtray, Mr. Chamberlain, who had been in the war, he had been in the Tank Corps. If my father was there when he came to see us – to see Fern, really, but he did not quickly make that apparent – my father would ask him questions about the war. But it was clear that they saw the war in different ways. My father saw it as an overall design, marked off in campaigns, which had a purpose, which failed or succeeded. Mr. Chamberlain saw it as a conglomeration of stories, leading nowhere in particular. He made his stories to be laughed at.

For instance he told us about the first time he went into action, what confusion there was. Some tanks had gone into a wood, got turned around, were coming out the wrong way, where they expected the Germans to come from. So the first shots they fired were at one of their own tanks.

"Blew it up!" said Mr. Chamberlain blithely, unapologetically.

"Were there soldiers in that tank?"

He looked at me in mocking surprise as he always did when I said anything; you would think I had just stood on my head for him. "Well, I wouldn't be too surprised if there were!"

"Were they – killed, then?"

"Something happened to them. I certainly never saw them around again. Poof!"

"Shot by their own side, what a terrible thing," said my mother, scandalized but less than ordinarily sure of herself.

"Things like that happen in a war," said my father quietly but with some severity, as if to object to any of this showed a certain female naiveté. Mr. Chamberlain just laughed. He went on to tell about what they did on the last day of the war. They blew up the cookhouse, turned all the guns on it in the last jolly blaze they would get.

"Sounds like a bunch of kids," said Fern. "Sounds like you weren't grown-up enough to fight a *war*. It just sounds like you had one big, idiotic, good time."

"What I always try to have, isn't it? A good time."

Once it came out that he had been in Florence, which was not surprising, since he had fought the war in Italy. But my mother sat up, she jumped a little in her chair, she quivered with attention.

"Were *you* in Florence?"

"Yes, ma'am," said Mr. Chamberlain without enthusiasm.

"In Florence, you were in Florence," repeated my mother, confused and joyful. I had an inkling of what she felt, but hoped she would not reveal too much. "I never thought," she said. "Well, of course I knew it was Italy but it seems so strange —" She meant that this Italy we had been talking about, where the war was fought, was the same place history happened, in the very place, where the old Popes were, and the Medici, and Leonardo. The Cenci. The cypresses. Dante Alighieri.

Rather oddly, in view of her enthusiasm for the future, she was excited by the past. She hurried into the front room and came back with the art-and-architecture supplement to the encyclopedia, full of statues, paintings, buildings, mostly photographed in a cloudy, cool, museum-gray light.

"There!" she opened it up on the table in front of him. "There's your Florence. Michelangelo's statue of David. Did you see that?"

A naked man. His marble thing hanging on him for everybody to look at; like a drooping lily petal. Who but my mother in her staunch and dreadful innocence would show a man, would show us all, a picture like that? Fern's mouth was swollen, with the effort to contain her smile.

"I never got to see it, no. That place is full of statues. Famous this and famous that. You can't turn around for them."

I could see he was not a person to talk to, about things like this. But my mother kept on.

"Well surely you saw the bronze doors? The magnificent bronze doors? It took the artist his whole life to do them. Look at them, they're here. What was his name — Ghiberti. Ghiberti. His whole life."

Some things Mr. Chamberlain admitted he had seen, some he had not. He looked at the book with a reasonable amount of patience, then said he had not cared for Italy.

"Well, Italy, maybe that was all right. It was the Italians."

"Did you think they were decadent?" said my mother regretfully.

"Decadent, I don't know. I don't know what they were. They don't care. On the streets in Italy I've had a man come up to me and offer to sell me his own daughter. It happened all the time."

"What would they want to sell a girl for?" I said, adopting as I easily could my bold and simple facade of innocence. "For a slave?"

"In a manner of speaking," said my mother, and she shut the book, relinquishing Michelangelo and the bronze doors.

"No older than Del here," said Mr. Chamberlain, with a disgust that in him seemed faintly fraudulent. "Not so old, some of them."

"They mature earlier," Fern said. "Those hot climates."

"Del. You take this book put it away." Alarm in my mother's voice was like the flap of rising wings.

Well, I had heard. I did not come back to the dining room but went upstairs and undressed. I put on my mother's black rayon dressing gown, splattered with bunches of pink and white flowers. Impractical gift she never wore. In her room I stared, goose-pimpled and challenging into the three-way mirror. I pulled the material off my shoulders and bunched it over my breasts, which were just about big enough to fit those wide, shallow cones of paper laid in sundae dishes. I had turned on the light beside the dressing table; it came meekly, warmly through a bracket of butterscotch glass, and laid a kind of glow on my skin. I looked at my high round forehead, pink freckled skin, my face as innocent as an egg, and my eyes managed to alter what was there, to make me sly and creamy, to change my hair, which was light brown, fine as a crackling bush, into rich waves more gold than muddy. Mr. Chamberlain's voice in my mind, saying *no older than Del here,* acted on me like the touch of rayon silk on my skin, surrounded me, made me feel endangered and desired. I thought of girls in Florence, girls in Rome, girls my age that a man could buy. Black Italian hair under their arms. Black down at the corners of their mouths. *They mature earlier in those hot climates.* Roman Catholics. A man paid you to let him do it. What did he say? Did he take your clothes off or did he expect you to do that yourself? Did he take down his pants or did he simply unzip himself and point his thing at you? It was the stage of transition, bridge between what was possible, known and normal behavior, and the magical bestial act, that I could not imagine. Nothing about that was in Naomi's mother's book.

There was a house in Jubilee with three prostitutes in it. That is, three if you counted Mrs. McQuade who ran it; she was at least sixty years old. The house was at the north end of the main street, in a yard all run to hollyhocks and dandelions, beside the B.A. service station. On sunny days the two younger women would sometimes come out and sit in canvas chairs. Naomi and I had made several trips past and had once seen them. They wore print dresses and slippers; their white legs were bare. One of them was reading the *Star Weekly.* Naomi said that this one's name was Peggy, and that one night in the men's toilet at the Gay-la dance hall she had been persuaded to serve a line-up, standing up. Was such a thing possible? (I heard this story another time, only now it was Mrs. McQuade herself who performed or endured this feat, and it was not at the Gay-la dance hall but against the back wall of the Blue Owl Cafe.) I wished I had seen more of this Peggy than the soft, mouse-brown nest

of curls above the paper; I wished I had seen her face. I did expect something –
a foul shimmer of corruption, some emanation, like marsh gas. I was surprised,
in a way, that she would read a paper, that the words in it would mean the same
things to her, presumably, as they did to the rest of us, that she ate and drank,
was human still. I thought of her as having gone right beyond human function-
ing into a condition of perfect depravity, at the opposite pole from sainthood
but similarly isolated, unknowable. What appeared to be ordinariness here –
the *Star Weekly,* dotted curtains looped back geraniums growing hopefully out
of tin cans in the whorehouse window, seemed to me deliberate and tantalizing
deception – the skin of everyday appearances stretched over such shame-
lessness, such consuming explosions of lust.

I rubbed my hipbones through the cool rayon. If I had been born in Italy my
flesh would already be used, bruised, knowing. It would not be my fault. The
thought of whoredom, not my fault, bore me outward for a moment; a restful,
alluring thought, because it was so final, and did away with ambition and
anxiety.

After this I constructed in several halting imperfect installments a daydream.
I imagined that Mr. Chamberlain saw me in my mother's black flowered dressing
gown, pulled down off the shoulders, as I had seen myself in the mirror. Then I
proposed to have the dressing gown come off, let him see me with nothing on
at all. How could it happen? Other people who would ordinarily be in the house
with us would have to be got rid of. My mother I sent out to sell encyclopedias;
my brother I banished to the farm. It would have to be in the summer holidays,
when I was home from school. Fern would not yet be home from the post office.
I would come downstairs in the heat of the late afternoon, a sulphurous still day,
wearing only this dressing gown. I would get a drink of water at the sink, not
seeing Mr. Chamberlain sitting quietly in the room, and then – what? A strange
dog, introduced into our house for this occasion only, might jump on me,
pulling the dressing gown off. I might turn and somehow catch the material on
the nail of a chair, and the whole thing would just slither to my feet. The thing
was that it had to be an accident; no effort on my part, and certainly none on
Mr. Chamberlain's. Beyond the moment of revelation my dream did not go. In
fact it often did not get that far, but lingered among the preliminary details,
solidifying them. The moment of being seen naked could not be solidified, it
was a stab of light. I never pictured Mr. Chamberlain's reaction, I never very
clearly pictured him. His presence was essential but blurred; in the corner of my
daydream he was featureless but powerful, humming away electrically like a
blue fluorescent light.

———

Naomi's father caught us, as we raced past his door on our way downstairs.

"You young ladies come in and visit me a minute, make yourselves comfortable."

It was spring by this time, windy yellow evening. Nevertheless he was burning garbage in a round tin stove in his room, it was hot and smelly. He had washed his socks and underwear and hung them on strings along the wall. Naomi and her mother treated him unceremoniously. When her mother was away, as now, Naomi would open a can of spaghetti and dump it on a plate, for his dinner. I would say, "Aren't you going to heat it?" and she would say, "Why bother? He wouldn't know the difference anyway."

In his room, on the floor, he had stacks of newsprint pamphlets which I supposed had to do with the religion he believed in. Naomi sometimes had to bring them from the post office. Taking her cue from her mother, she had great contempt for his beliefs. "It's all prophecies and prophecies," she said. "They have prophesied the end of the world three times now."

We sat on the edge of the bed, which had no spread on it, only a rough, rather dirty blanket, and he sat in his rocker opposite us. He was an old man. Naomi's mother had nursed him before she married him. Between his words there were usually large gaps, during which he would not forget about you, however, but fix his pale eyes on your forehead as if he expected to find the rest of his thought written out there.

"Reading from the Bible," he said genially and unnecessarily, and rather in the manner of one who chooses not to see objections he knows are there. He opened a large-print Bible with the place already marked and began to read in a piercing elderly voice, with some odd stops, and difficulties of phrasing.

> Then shall the kingdom of heaven be likened unto ten virgins, which took their lamps, and went forth to meet the bridegroom.
> And five of them were wise, and five were foolish.
> They that were foolish took their lamps, and took no oil with them:
> But the wise took oil in their vessels with their lamps.
> While the bridegroom tarried, they all slumbered and slept.
> And at midnight there was a cry made, Behold, the bridegroom cometh; go ye out to meet him.
> Then all those virgins arose, and trimmed their lamps.
> And the foolish said unto the wise, Give us of your oil; for our lamps are gone out.

Then it turned out of course – now I remembered hearing all this before – that the wise virgins would not give up any of their oil for fear they would not have enough, and the foolish virgins had to go out and buy some, and so missed the bridegroom coming and were shut out. I had always supposed this parable, which I did not like, had to do with prudence, preparedness, something like that. But I could see that Naomi's father believed it to be about sex. I looked sideways at Naomi to catch that slight sucking in of the corners of the mouth, the facial drollery with which she always recognized this subject, but she was looking obstinate and miserable, disgusted by the very thing that was my secret pleasure – poetic flow of words, archaic expressions. *Said unto; tarried, Behold the bridegroom cometh.* She was so offended by all this that she could not even enjoy the word *virgins.*

His toothless mouth shut. Sly and proper as a baby's.

"No more for now. Think about it when the time comes. There's a lesson for young girls."

"Stupid old bugger," said Naomi, on the stairs.

"I feel – sorry for him."

She jabbed me in the kidney.

"Hurry up, let's get out of here. He's liable to find something else. Reads the Bible till his eyes fall out. Serve him right."

We ran out outside, up Mason Street. These long light evenings we visited every part of town. We loitered past the Lyceum Theatre, the Blue Owl Cafe, the poolroom. We sat on the benches by the cenotaph, and if any car honked at us we waved. Dismayed by our greenness, our leggy foolishness, they drove on by; they laughed out their windows. We went into the ladies' toilet in the Town Hall – wet floor, sweating cement walls, harsh ammoniac smell – and there on the toilet door where only bad brainless girls wrote up their names, we wrote the names of the two reigning queens of our class – Marjory Coutts, Gwen Mundy. We wrote in lipstick and drew tiny obscene figures underneath. Why did we do this? Did we hate those girls, to whom we were unfailingly obsequiously pleasant? No. Yes. We hated their immunity, well-bred lack of curiosity, whatever kept them floating, charitable and pleased, on the surface of life in Jubilee, and would float them on to sororities, engagements, marriages to doctors or lawyers in more prosperous places far away. We hated them just because they could never be imagined entering the Town Hall toilets.

Having done this, we ran away, not sure whether or not we had committed a criminal act.

We dared each other. Walking under street lights still as pale as flowers cut out of tissue paper, walking past unlighted windows from which we hoped the world watched, we did dares.

"Be like you have cerebral palsy. *Dare.*"

At once I came unjointed, lolled my head, rolled my eyes, began to talk incomprehensibly, in a cross insistent babble.

"Do it for a block. Never mind who we meet. Don't stop. *Dare.*"

We met old Dr. Comber, spindly and stately, beautifully dressed. He stopped, and tapped his stick and objected.

"What is this performance?"

"A fit, sir," said Naomi plaintively. "She's always having these fits."

Making fun of poor, helpless, afflicted people. The bad taste, the heart-lessness, the joy of it.

We went to the park, which was neglected, deserted, a triangle of land made too gloomy, by its big cedar trees, for children's play, and not attracting people who went for walks. Why should anybody in Jubilee walk to see more grass and dirt and trees, the same thing that pushed in on the town from every side? They would walk downtown, to look at stores, meet on the double sidewalks, feel the hope of activity. Naomi and I all by ourselves climbed the big cedar trees, scraped our knees on the bark, screamed as we never needed to when we were younger, seeing the branches part, revealing the tilted earth. We hung from the branches by our locked hands, by our ankles; we pretended to be baboons, prattling and gibbering. We felt the whole town lying beneath us, gaping, ready to be astounded.

There were noises peculiar to the season. Children on the sidewalks, skipping and singing in their clear, devout voices.

> On the mountain stands a lady
> Who she is I do not know.
> All she wears is gold and silver.
> All she needs is a new pair of shoes!

And the peacocks crying. We dropped from the trees and set off to look at them, down past the park, down a poor unnamed street running to the river. The peacocks belonged to a man named Pork Childs who drove the town garbage truck. The street had no sidewalks. We walked around puddles, gleaming in the soft mud. Pork Childs had a barn behind his house for his fowl. Neither barn nor house was painted.

There were the peacocks, walking around under the bare oak trees. How could we forget them, from one spring to the next?

The hens were easily forgotten, the sullen colors of their yard. But the males were never disappointing. Their astonishing, essential color, blue of breasts and throats and necks, darker feathers showing there like ink blots, or soft vegetation under tropical water. One had his tail spread, to show the blind eyes, painted satin. The little kingly, idiotic heads. Glory in the cold spring, a wonder of Jubilee.

The noise beginning again did not come from any of them. It pulled eyes up to what it was hard to believe we had not seen immediately – the one white peacock up in a tree, his tail full out, falling down through the branches like water over rock. Pure white, pure blessing. And hidden up above, his head gave out these frantic and upbraiding and disorderly cries.

"It's sex makes them scream," said Naomi.

"Cats scream," I said, remembering something from the farm. "They will scream like anything when a tomcat is doing it to them."

"Wouldn't you?" said Naomi.

Then we had to go, because Pork Childs appeared among his peacocks, walking quickly, rocking forward. All his toes had been amputated, we knew, after being frozen when he lay in a ditch long ago, too drunk to get home, before he joined the Baptist Church. "Good evening, boys!" he hollered at us, his old greeting, his old joke. *Hello, boys! Hello girls!* yelled from the cab of the garbage truck, yelled down all streets bleak or summery, never getting any answer. We ran.

Mr. Chamberlain's car was parked in front of our house.

"Let's go in," said Naomi. "I want to see what he's doing to old Fern."

Nothing. In the dining room Fern was trying on the flowered chiffon dress my mother was helping her to make for Donna Carling's wedding, at which she would be the soloist. My mother was sitting sideways on the chair in front of the sewing machine, while Fern revolved, like a big half-opened parasol, in front of her.

Mr. Chamberlain was drinking a real drink, whisky and water. He drove to Porterfield to buy his whisky, Jubilee being dry. I was both proud and ashamed to have Naomi see the bottle on the sideboard, a thing that would never appear in her house. My mother excused his drinking, because he had been through the war.

"Here come these two lovely young ladies," said Mr. Chamberlain with great insincerity. "Full of springtime and grace. All fresh from the out-of-doors."

"Give us a drink," I said, showing off in front of Naomi. But he laughed and put a hand over his glass.

"Not until you tell us where you've been."

"We went down to Pork Childs' to look at the peacocks."

"Down to see the pea-cocks. To see the pretty pea-cocks," sang Mr. Chamberlain.

"Give us a drink."

"Del, behave yourself," said my mother with a mouth full of pins.

"All I want is to find out what it tastes like."

"Well I can't give you a drink for nothing. I don't see you doing any tricks for me. I don't see you sitting up and begging like a good doggie."

"I can be a seal. Do you want to see me be a seal?"

This was one thing I loved to do. I never felt worried that it might not be perfect, that I might not be able to manage it; I was never afraid that anybody would think me a fool. I had even done it at school, for the Junior Red Cross amateur hour, and everyone laughed; this marveling laughter was so comforting, so absolving that I could have gone on being a seal forever.

I went down on my knees and held my elbows at my sides and worked my hands like flippers, meanwhile barking, my wonderful braying bark. I had copied from an old Mary Martin movie where Mary Martin sings a song beside a turquoise pool and the seals bark in a chorus.

Mr. Chamberlain gradually lowered his glass and brought it close to my lips, withdrawing it, however, every time I stopped barking. I was kneeling by his chair. Fern had her back to me, her arms raised; my mother's head was hidden, as she pinned the material at Fern's waist. Naomi who had seen the seal often enough before and had an interest in dressmaking was looking at Fern and my mother. Mr. Chamberlain at last allowed my lips to touch the rim of the glass which he held in one hand. Then with the other hand he did something nobody could see. He rubbed against the damp underarm of my blouse and then inside the loose armhole of the jumper I was wearing. He rubbed quick, hard against the cotton over my breast. So hard he pushed the yielding flesh up, flattened it. And at once withdrew. It was like a slap, to leave me stung.

"Well, what does it taste like?" Naomi asked me afterwards.

"Like piss."

"You never tasted piss." She gave me a shrewd baffled look; she could always sense secrets.

I meant to tell her, but I did not, I held it back. If I told her, it would have to be re-enacted.

"How? How did he have his hand when he started? How did he get it under your jumper? Did he rub or squeeze, or both? With his fingers or his palm? Like *this?*"

There was a dentist in town, Dr. Phippen, brother of the deaf librarian, who was supposed to have put his hand up a girl's leg while looking at her back teeth. Naomi and I passing under his window would say loudly, "Don't you wish you had an appointment with Dr. Phippen? Dr. Feely Phippen. He's a thorough man!" It would be like that with Mr. Chamberlain; we would turn it into a joke, and hope for scandal, and make up schemes to entrap him, and that was not what I wanted.

"It was beautiful," said Naomi, sounding tired.

"What?"

"That peacock. In the tree."

I was surprised, and a little annoyed, to hear her use the word *beautiful,* about something like that, and to have her remember it, because I was used to have her act in a certain way, be aware of certain things, nothing else. I had already thought, running home, that I would write a poem about the peacock. To have her thinking about it too was almost like trespassing; I never let her or anyone in that part of my mind.

I did start writing my poem when I went upstairs to bed.

> *What in the trees is crying these veiled nights?*
> *The peacocks crying or the winter's ghost?*

That was the best part of it.

I also thought about Mr. Chamberlain, his hand which was different from anything he had previously shown about himself, in his eyes, his voice, his laugh, his stories. It was like a signal, given where it will be understood. Impertinent violation, so perfectly sure of itself, so authoritative, clean of sentiment.

Next time he came I made it easy for him to do something again, standing near him while he was getting his rubbers on in the dark hall. Every time, then, I waited for the signal, and got it. He did not bother with a pinch on the arm or a pat on the arm or a hug around the shoulders, fatherly or comradely. He went straight for the breasts, the buttocks, the upper thighs, brutal as lightning.

And this was what I expected sexual communication to be – a flash of insanity, a dreamlike, ruthless, contemptuous breakthrough in a world of decent appearances. I had discarded those ideas of love, consolation, and tenderness, nourished by my feelings for Frank Wales; all that now seemed pale and extraordinarily childish. In the secret violence of sex would be recognition, going away beyond kindness, beyond good will or persons.

Not that I was planning on sex. One stroke of lightning does not have to lead anywhere, but to the next stroke of lightning.

Nevertheless my knees weakened, when Mr. Chamberlain honked the horn at me. He was waiting half a block from the school. Naomi was not with me; she had tonsillitis.

"Where's your girl friend?"

"She's sick."

"That's a shame. Want a lift home?"

In the car I trembled. My tongue was dry, my whole mouth was dry so I could hardly speak. Was this what desire was? Wish to know, fear to know, amounting to anguish? Being alone with him, no protection of people or circumstances, made a difference. What could he want to do here, in broad daylight, on the seat of his car?

He did not make a move towards me. But he did not head for River Street; he drove sedately along various side streets, avoiding winter-made potholes.

"You think you're the girl to do me a favor, if I asked you?"

"All right."

"What do you think it might be?"

"I don't know."

He parked the car behind the creamery, under the chestnut trees with the leaves just out, bitter yellowy green. Here?

"You get into Fern's room? You could get into her room when everybody was out of the house?"

I brought my mind back, slowly, from expectations of rape.

"You could get in her room and do a little investigation for me on what she's got there. Something that might interest me. What do you think it would be, eh? What do you think interests me?"

"What?"

"Letters," said Mr. Chamberlain with a sudden drop in tone, becoming matter-of-fact, depressed by some reality he could look into and I couldn't. "See if she has got any old letters. They might be in her drawers. Might be in her closet. Probably keeps them in an old box of some kind. Tied up in bundles, that's what women do."

"Letters from who?"

"From me. Who do you think? You don't need to read them, just look at the signature. Written some time ago, the paper might be showing age. I don't know. Written in pen I recall so they're probably still legible. Here. I'll give you a sample of my handwriting, that'll help you out." He took an envelope out of the glove compartment and wrote on it: *Del is a bad girl.*

I put it in my Latin book.

"Don't let Fern see that, she'd recognize the writing. And not your Mama. She might wonder about what I wrote. Be a surprise to her, wouldn't it?"

He drove me home. I wanted to get out at the corner of River Street but he said no. "That just looks as if we've got something to hide. Now, how are you going to let me know? How about Sunday night, when I come around for supper, I'll ask you whether you've got your homework done! If you've found them, you'll say yes. If you've looked and you haven't found them, you'll say no. If for some reason you never got a chance to take a look, you say you forget whether you had any."

He made me repeat, "Yes means found them, no means didn't find them, forget means didn't get a chance to look." This drill insulted me; I was famous for my memory.

"All right. Cheers." Below the level that anybody could see, looking at the car, he bounced his fist off my leg, hard enough to hurt. I hauled myself and my books out, and once I was alone, my thigh still tingling, I took out the envelope and read what he had written. *Del is a bad girl.* Mr. Chamberlain assumed without any trouble at all that there was treachery in me, as well as criminal sensuality, waiting to be used. He had known I would not cry out when he flattened my breast, he had known I would not mention it to my mother; he knew now I would not report this conversation to Fern, but would spy on her as he had asked. Could he have hit upon my true self? It was true that in the dullness of school I had worked with my protractor and compass, I had written out Latin sentences [*having pitched camp and slaughtered the horses of the enemy by means of stealth, Vercingetorix prepared to give battle on the following day*] and all the time been conscious of my depravity vigorous as spring wheat, my body flowering with invisible bruises in those places where it had been touched. Wearing blue rompers, washing with soap that would nearly take your skin off, after a volleyball game, I had looked in the mirror of the girls' washroom and smiled secretly at my ruddy face, to think what lewdness I had been invited to, what deceits I was capable of.

I got into Fern's room on Saturday morning, when my mother had gone out to do some cleaning at the farm. I looked around at leisure, at the koala bear sitting on her pillow, powder spilled on the dresser, jars with a little bit of dried-up deodorant, salve, night cream, old lipstick and nail polish with the top stuck on. A picture of a lady in a dress of many dripping layers, like an arrangement of scarves, probably Fern's mother, holding a fat woollied baby, probably Fern. Fern for sure in soft focus with butterfly sleeves, holding a sheaf of roses, curls laid in layers on her head. And snapshots stuck around the mirror, their edges curling. Mr. Chamberlain in a sharp straw hat, white pants, looking at the camera as if he knew more than it did. Fern not so plump as now, but plump, wearing shorts, sitting on a log in some vacationtime woods. Mr. Chamberlain and Fern dressed up – she with a corsage – snapped by a street photographer in a strange city, walking under the marquee of a movie house where *Anchors Aweigh!* was showing. The post office employees' picnic in the park at Tupperton, a cloudy day, and Fern, jolly in slacks, holding a baseball bat.

I did not find any letters. I looked through her drawers, on her closet shelves, under her bed, even inside her suitcases. I did find three separate saved bundles of paper, with elastic bands around them.

One bundle contained a chain letter and a great many copies of the same verse, in pencil or ink, different handwritings, some typewritten or mimeographed.

> This prayer has already been around the world six times. It was originated in the Isle of Wight by a clairvoyant seer who saw it in a dream. Copy this letter out six times and mail it to six friends, then copy the attached prayer out and mail it to six names at the top of the attached list. Six days from the time you receive this letter you will begin to get copies of this prayer from all corners of the earth and they will bring you blessings and good luck IF YOU DO NOT BREAK THE CHAIN. If you break the chain you may expect something sad and unpleasant to happen to you six months to the day from the day when you receive this letter. DO NOT BREAK THE CHAIN. DO NOT OMIT THE SECRET WORD AT THE END. BY MEANS OF THIS PRAYER HAPPINESS AND GOOD LUCK ARE BEING SPREAD THROUGHOUT THE WORLD.
>
> *Peace and love, O Lord I pray*

Shower on this friend today.
Heal his(her) troubles, bless his(her) heart,
From the source of strength and love may he(she) never have to part.
— KARKAHMD

Another bundle was made up of several sheets of smudgy printing broken by blurred gray illustrations of what I thought at first were enema bags with tangled tubes, but which on reading the text I discovered to be cross sections of the male and female anatomy, with such things as pessaries, tampons, condoms (these proper terms were all new to me) being inserted or fitted on. I could not look at these illustrations without feeling alarm and a strong local discomfort, so I started reading. I read about a poor farmer's wife in North Carolina throwing herself under a wagon when she discovered she was going to have her ninth child, about women dying in tenements from complications of pregnancy or childbirth or terrible failed abortions which they performed with hatpins, knitting needles, bubbles of air. I read, or skipped, statistics about the increase in population, laws which had been passed in various countries for and against birth control, women who had gone to jail for advocating it. Then there were the instructions on using different devices. Naomi's mother's book had had a chapter about this too, but we never got around to reading it, being bogged down in "Case Histories and Varieties of Intercourse." All I read now about foam and jelly, even the use of the word "vagina," made the whole business seem laborious and domesticated, somehow connected with ointments and bandages and hospitals, and it gave me the same feeling of disgusted, ridiculous helplessness I had when it was necessary to undress at the doctor's.

In the third bundle were typewritten verses. Some had titles. "Homemade Lemon Squeeze." "The Lament of the Truck Driver's Wife."

Husband, dear husband, what am I to do?
I'm wanting some hard satisfaction from you.
You're never at home or you're never awake.
(A big cock in my pussy is all it would take!)

I was surprised that any adult would know, or still remember, these words. The greedy progression of verses, the short chunky words set in shameless type, fired up lust at a great rate, like squirts of kerosene on bonfires. But they were repetitive, elaborate; after awhile the mechanical effort needed to contrive them began to be felt, and made them heavy going; they grew bewilderingly dull. But the words themselves still gave off flashes of power, particularly *fuck*, which I had never been able to really look at on fences or sidewalks. I had never been able to contemplate before its thrust of brutality, hypnotic swagger.

I said no to Mr. Chamberlain, when he asked me if I had got my homework done. He did not touch me all evening. But when I came out of school on Monday, he was there.

"Girl friend still sick? That's too bad. Nice though. Isn't it nice?"

"What?"

"Birds are nice. Trees are nice. Nice you can come for a drive with me, do my little investigations for me." He said this in an infantile voice. Evil would never be grand, with him. His voice suggested that it would be possible to do anything, anything at all, and pass it off as a joke, a joke on all the solemn and guilty, all the moral and emotional people in the world, the people who "took themselves seriously." That was what he could not stand in people. His little smile was repulsive; self-satisfaction stretched over quite an abyss of irresponsibility, or worse. This did not give me second thoughts about going with him, and doing whatever it was he had in mind to do. His moral character was of no importance to me there; perhaps it was even necessary that it should be black.

Excitement owing something to Fern's dirty verses had got the upper hand of me, entirely.

"Did you get a good look?" he said in a normal voice.

"Yes."

"Didn't find a thing? Did you look in all her drawers? I mean her *dresser* drawers. Hatboxes, suitcases? Went through her closet?"

"I looked and looked everywhere," I said demurely.

"She must have got rid of them."

"I guess she isn't sentimental."

"Sentimental? I don't know what dose big words mean, little dirl."

We were driving out of town. We drove south on the No. 4 Highway and turned down the first side road. "Beautiful morning," said Mr. Chamberlain. "Pardon me – beautiful afternoon, beautiful day." I looked out the window; the countryside I knew was altered by his presence, his voice, overpowering foreknowledge of the errand we were going on together. For a year or two I had been looking at trees, fields, landscape with a secret, strong exaltation. In some moods, some days, I could feel for a clump of grass, a rail fence, a stone pile, such pure unbounded emotion as I used to hope for, and have inklings of, in connection with God. I could not do it when I was with anybody, of course, and now with Mr. Chamberlain I saw that the whole of nature became debased, maddeningly erotic. It was just now the richest, greenest time of year; ditches sprouted coarse daisies, toadflax, buttercups, hollows were full of nameless faintly golden bushes and the gleam of high creeks. I saw all this as a vast arrangement of hiding places, ploughed fields beyond rearing up like shameless mattresses. Little paths, opening in the bushes, crushed places in the grass, where no doubt a cow had lain, seemed to me specifically, urgently inviting as certain words or pressures.

"Hope we don't meet your mama, driving along here."

I did not think it possible. My mother inhabited a different layer of reality from the one I had got into now.

Mr. Chamberlain drove off the road, following a track that ended soon, in a field half gone to brush. The stopping of the car, cessation of that warm flow of sound and motion in which I had been suspended, jarred me a little. Events were becoming real.

"Let's take a little walk down to the creek."

He got out on his side, I got out on mine. I followed him, down a slope between some hawthorn trees, in bloom, yeasty smelling. This was a traveled route, with cigarette packages, a beer bottle, a Chicklet box lying on the grass. Little trees, bushes closed around us.

"Why don't we call a halt here?" said Mr. Chamberlain in a practical way. "It gets soggy down by the water."

Here in the half-shade above the creek I was cold, and so violently anxious to know what would be done to me that all the heat and dancing itch between my legs had gone dead, numb as if a piece of ice had been laid to it. Mr. Chamberlain opened his jacket and loosened his belt, then unzipped himself. He reached in to part some inner curtains, and "Boo!" he said.

Not at all like marble David's, it was sticking straight out in front of him, which I knew from my reading was what they did. It had a sort of head on it, like a mushroom, and its color was reddish purple. It looked blunt and stupid, compared, say, to fingers and toes with their intelligent expressiveness, or even to an elbow or a knee. It did not seem frightening to me, though I thought this might have been what Mr. Chamberlain intended, standing there with his tightly watching look, his hands holding his pants apart to display it. Raw and blunt, ugly-colored as a wound, it looked to me vulnerable, playful and naive, like some strong-snouted animal whose grotesque simple looks are some sort of guarantee of good will. (The opposite of what beauty usually is.) It did not bring back any of my excitement, though. It did not seem to have anything to do with me.

Still watching me, and smiling, Mr. Chamberlain placed his hand around this thing and began to pump up and down, not too hard, in a controlled efficient rhythm. His face softened; his eyes, still fixed on me, grew glassy. Gradually, almost experimentally, he increased the speed of his hand; the rhythm became less smooth. He crouched over, his smile opened out and drew the lips back from his teeth and his eyes rolled slightly upward. His breathing became loud and shaky, now he worked furiously with his hand, moaned, almost doubled over in spasmodic agony. The face he thrust out at me, from his crouch, was blind and wobbling like a mask on a stick, and those sounds coming out of his mouth, involuntary, last-ditch human noises, were at the same time theatrical, unlikely. In fact the whole performance, surrounded by calm flowering branches, seemed imposed, fantastically and predictably exaggerated, like an Indian dance. I had read about the body being in extremities of pleasure, possessed, but these expressions did not seem equal to the terrible benighted effort, deliberate frenzy, of what was going on here. If he did not soon get to where he wanted to be, I thought he would die. But then he let out a new kind of moan, the most desperate and the loudest yet; it quavered as if somebody was hitting him on the voice box. This died, miraculously, into a peaceful grateful whimper, as stuff shot out of him, the real whitish stuff, the seed, and caught the hem of my skirt. He straightened up, shaky, out of breath, and tucked himself quickly back inside his trousers. He got out a handkerchief and wiped first his hands then my skirt.

"Lucky for you? Eh?" He laughed at me, though he still had not altogether got his breath back.

After such a convulsion, such a revelation, how could a man just put his handkerchief in his pocket, check his fly, and start walking back – still somewhat flushed and bloodshot – the way we had come?

The only thing he said was in the car, when he sat for a moment composing himself before he turned the key.

"Quite a sight, eh?" was what he said.

The landscape was postcoital, distant and meaningless. Mr. Chamberlain may have felt some gloom too, or apprehension, for he made me get down on the floor of the car as we reentered town, and then he drove around and let me out in a lonely place, where the road dipped down near the CNR station. He felt enough like himself, however, to tap me in the crotch with his fist, as if testing a coconut for soundness.

That was a valedictory appearance for Mr. Chamberlain, as I ought to have guessed it might be. I came home at noon to find Fern sitting at the dining-room table, which was set for dinner, listening to my mother calling from the kitchen over the noise of the potato masher.

"Doesn't matter what anybody says. You weren't married. You weren't engaged. It's nobody's business. Your life is your own."

"Want to see my little love letter?" said Fern, and fluttered it under my nose.

> *Dear Fern, Owing to circumstances beyond my control, I am taking off this*
> *evening in my trusty Pontiac and heading for points west. There is a lot of the*
> *world I haven't seen yet and no sense getting fenced in. I may send you a postcard*
> *from California or Alaska, who knows? Be a good girl as you always were and*
> *keep licking those stamps and steaming open the mail, you may find a*
> *hundred-dollar-bill yet. When Mama dies I will probably come home, but not for*
> *long. Cheers, Art.*

The same hand that had written: *Del is a bad girl.*

"Tampering with the mails is a Federal offense," said my mother, coming in. "I don't think that is very witty, what he says."

She distributed canned carrots, mashed potatoes, meat loaf. No matter what the season, we ate a heavy meal in the middle of the day.

"Looks like it hasn't put me off my food, anyway," said Fern, sighing. She poured ketchup. "I could have had him. Long ago, if I'd wanted. He even wrote me letters mentioning marriage. I should have kept them, I could have breach-of-promised him."

"A good thing you didn't," said my mother spiritedly, "or where would you be today?"

"Didn't what? Breach-of-promised him or married him?"

"Married him. Breach-of-promise is a degradation to women."

"Oh, I wasn't in danger of marriage."

"You had your singing. You had your interest in life."

"I was just usually having too good a time. I knew enough about marriage to know that's when your good times stop."

When Fern talked about having a good time she meant going to dances at the Lakeshore Pavilion, going to the Regency Hotel in Tupperton for drinks and dinner, being driven from one roadhouse to another on Saturday night. My mother did try to understand such pleasures, but she could not, any more than she could understand why people go on rides at a fair, and will get off and throw up, then go on rides again.

Fern was not one to grieve, in spite of her acquaintance with opera. Her expressed feeling was that men always went, and better they did before you got sick of them. But she grew very talkative; she was never silent.

"As bad as Art was," she said to Owen, eating supper. "He wouldn't touch any yellow vegetable. His mother should have taken the paddle to him when he was little. That's what I used to tell him."

"You're built the opposite from Art," she told my father. "The trouble with getting his suits fitted was he was so long in the body, short in the leg. Ransom's in Tupperton was the only place that could fit him."

"Only one time I saw him lose his temper. At the Pavillion when we went to a dance there, and a fellow asked me to dance, and I got up with him because what can you do, and he put his face down, right away down on my neck. Guzzling me up like I was chocolate icing! Art said to him, if you have to slobber don't do it on my girl friend, I might want her myself! And he yanked him off. He did so!"

I would come into a room where she was talking to my mother and there would be an unnatural, waiting silence. My mother would be listening with a trapped, determinedly compassionate, miserable face. What could she do? Fern was her good, perhaps her only, friend. But there were things she never thought she would have to hear. She may have missed Mr. Chamberlain.

"He treated you shabbily," she said to Fern, against Fern's shrugs and ambiguous laugh. "He did. He did. My estimation of a person has never gone down so fast. But nevertheless I miss him when I hear them trying to read the radio news."

For the Jubilee station had not found anybody else who could read the news the way it was now, full of Russian names, without panicking, and they had let somebody call Bach *Batch* on *In Memoriam*, when they played "Jesu Joy of Man's Desiring." It made my mother wild.

I had meant to tell Naomi all about Mr. Chamberlain, now it was over. But Naomi came out of her illness fifteen pounds lighter, with a whole new outlook on life. Her forthrightness was gone with her chunky figure. Her language was purified. Her daring had collapsed. She had a new delicate regard for herself.

She sat under a tree with her skirt spread around her, watching the rest of us play volleyball, and kept feeling her forehead to see if she was feverish. She was not even interested in the fact that Mr. Chamberlain had gone, so preoccupied was she with herself and her illness. Her temperature had risen to over a hundred and five degrees. All the grosser aspects of sex had disappeared from her conversation and apparently from her mind although she talked a good deal about Dr. Wallis, and how he had sponged her legs himself, and she had been quite helplessly exposed to him, when she was sick.

So I had not the relief of making what Mr. Chamberlain had done into a funny, though horrifying, story. I did not know what to do with it. I could not get him back to his old role, I could not make him play the single-minded, simple-minded, vigorous, obliging lecher of my daydreams. My faith in simple depravity had weakened. Perhaps nowhere but in daydreams did the trap door open so sweetly and easily, plunging bodies altogether free of thought, free of personality, into self-indulgence, mad bad license. Instead of that, Mr. Chamberlain had shown me, people take along a good deal – flesh that is not overcome but has to be thumped into ecstasy, all the stubborn puzzle and dark turns of themselves.

In June there was the annual strawberry supper on the lawns behind the United Church. Fern went down to sing at it, wearing the flowered chiffon dress my mother had helped her make. It was now very tight at the waist. Since Mr. Chamberlain had gone Fern had put on weight, so that she was not now soft and bulgy but really fat, swollen up like a boiled pudding, her splotched skin not shady any more but stretched and shiny.

She patted herself around the midriff. "Anyway they won't be able to say I'm pining, will they? It'll be a scandal if I split the seams."

We heard her high heels going down the sidewalk. On leafy, cloudy, quiet evenings under the trees, sounds carried a long way. Sociable noise of the United Church affair washed as far as our steps. Did my mother wish she had a hat and a summer sheer dress on, and was going? Her agnosticism and sociability were often in conflict in Jubilee, where social and religious life were apt to be one and the same. Fern had told her to come ahead. "You're a member. Didn't you tell me you joined when you got married?"

"My ideas weren't formed then. Now I'd be a hypocrite. I'm not a believer."

"Think all of them are?"

I was on the veranda reading *Arch of Triumph*, a book I had got out of the library. The library had been left some money and had bought a supply of new books, mostly on the recommendation of Mrs. Wallis, the doctor's wife, who had a college degree but not perhaps the tastes the Council had been counting on. There had been complaints, people had said it should have been left up to Bella Phippen, but only one book – *The Hucksters* – had actually been removed from the shelves. I had read it first. My mother had picked it up and read a few pages and been saddened.

"I never expected to see such a use made of the printed word."

"It's about the advertising business, how corrupt it is."

"That's not the only thing is corrupt, I'm afraid. Next day they will be telling about how they go to the toilet, why do they leave that out? There isn't any of that in *Silas Marner*. There isn't in the classic writers. They were good writers, they didn't need it."

I had turned away from my old favorites, *Kristin Lavransdatter*, historical novels. I read modern books now. Somerset Maugham. Nancy Mitford. I read about rich and titled people who despised the very sort of people who in Jubilee were at the top of society – druggists, dentists, storekeepers. I learned names like Balenciaga, Schiaparelli. I knew about drinks. Whisky and soda. Gin and tonic. Cinzano, Benedictine, Grand Marnier. I knew the names of hotels, streets, restaurants, in London, Paris, Singapore. In these books people did go to bed together, they did it all the time, but the descriptions of what they were up to there were not thorough, in spite of what my mother thought. One book compared having sexual intercourse to going through a train tunnel (presumably if you were the whole train) and blasting out into a mountain meadow so high, so blest and beautiful, you felt as if you were in the sky. Books always compared it to something else, never told about it by itself.

"You can't read there," my mother said. "You can't read in that light. Come down on the steps."

So I came, but she did not want me to read at all. She wanted company.

"See, the lilacs are turning. Soon we'll be going out to the farm."

Along the front of our yard, by the sidewalk, were purple lilacs gone pale as soft, delicate scrub rags, rusty specked. Beyond them the road, already dusty, and banks of wild blackberry bushes growing in front of the boarded-up factory, on which we could still read the big, faded, vainglorious letters: MUNDY PIANOS.

"I'm sorry for Fern," my mother said. "I'm sorry for her life."

Her sad confidential tone warned me off.

"Maybe she'll find a new boy friend tonight."

"What do you mean? She's not after a new boy friend. She's had enough of all that. She's going to sing 'Where'er You Walk.' She's got a lovely voice, still."

"She's getting fat."

My mother spoke to me in her grave, hopeful, lecturing voice.

"There is a change coming I think in the lives of girls and women. Yes. But it is up to us to make it come. All women have had up till now has been their connection with men. All we have had. No more lives of our own, really, than domestic animals. *He shall hold thee, when his passion shall have spent its novel force, a little closer than his dog, a little dearer than his horse.* Tennyson wrote that. It's true. *Was* true. You will want to have children, though."

That was how much she knew me.

"But I hope you will – use your brains. Use your brains. Don't be distracted. Once you make that mistake, of being – distracted, over a man, your life will never be your own. You will get the burden, a woman always does."

"There is birth control nowadays," I reminded her, and she looked at me startled, though it was she herself who had publicly embarrassed our family, writing to the Jubilee *Herald-Advance* that "prophylactic devices should be distributed to all women on public relief in Wawanash County, to help than prevent any further increase in their families." Boys at school had yelled at me, "Hey, when is your momma giving out the proplastic devices?"

"That is not enough, though of course it is a great boon and religion is the enemy of it as it is of everything that might ease the pangs of life on earth. It is self-respect I am really speaking of. Self-respect."

I did not quite get the point of this, or if I did get the point I was set up to resist it. I would have had to resist anything she told me with such earnestness, such stubborn hopefulness. Her concern about my life, which I needed and took for granted, I could not bear to have expressed. Also I felt that it was not so different from all the other advice handed out to women, to girls, advice that assumed being female made you damageable, that a certain amount of care-fulness and solemn fuss and self-protection were called for, whereas men were supposed to be able to go out and take on all kinds of experiences and shuck off what they didn't want and come back proud. Without even thinking about it, I had decided to do the same.

Maria Hinojosa

from *Crews*

Maria Hinojosa is a correspondent for National Public Radio, and the host of NPR's Latino U.S.A. She lives in New York City. The following excerpt is from Crews: Gang Members Talk to Maria Hinojosa *(1995). The names of crew members have been changed to protect their privacy.*

I Trust the Crew More Than I Trust Any Guy

I don't know why we live for when no matter
what, you're gonna die. You do get tired after
a while of having to be always protecting yourself — watch that somebody's not gonna jump
you and watch that somebody's not gonna rob
or kill you. You get tired of it.

IN NEW YORK, GIRLS HAVE GOT TO HAVE A CREW, TOO. I HOOKED UP
with a girl crew from the Lower East Side of Manhattan. I had set up my meeting
for a day in late winter and I was getting ready to leave for it when I got a phone
call from my contact person. She told me the girls weren't going to be able to see
me. They were in a state of mourning. "Do you remember reading about a boy
who was stabbed in the heart over a pair of sunglasses?" my contact asked me.
"Well, that boy was a friend of the girls in the crew. They're very upset. I don't
think they'll be able to talk to you now. Give it a few days," my contact said.

The day we finally met, the girls made me wait for an hour. Then they
sauntered in. They were big girls, tall, with long hair, huge gold earrings, red
or brown lipstick, all surrounding a smaller girl who was pushing a big, black
leather baby carriage. Inside, a tiny little boy about three months old slept
soundly. At first they walked right by me. They had expected a little old lady
with gray hair and a tattered notebook. "We never thought that people like us,
Latinos, wrote books!" they said.

That first day I met most of the girls from the crew. Cindy was the leader. Sonya and Smooth B were seventeen-year-old twins, both pregnant. Chris was small and soft-spoken. Nicky was the one with the baby. The other girls took turns holding him, burping him, feeding him (with a bottle, because they all thought breastfeeding was kind of nasty). When the baby had to be changed, Nicky did it where none of us could see. She didn't want us to see his "thing." And there was Carmen: the one with the biggest smile who hardly spoke during the several hours we ended up meeting over the course of a couple of months. Everybody said Carmen was the smartest, the one who got the best grades in school, but she was also the shiest.

All of the girls were Puerto Rican and had grown up in housing projects on the Lower East Side. Their parents worked at blue-collar jobs. None of the girls spoke Spanish, but all of them except Smooth B understood it.

MH: Do you girls have a name?

SMOOTH B: Everybody always asks us that and we say no. When we walk down the street, we pass by people, and they all say "gangstas." But we don't pick a name 'cause we think it's stupid.

MH: Do most of the other girl crews have names?

SONYA: Yeah, like Ridge, DOF – Destroying Our Females. We used to have names, though.

They all laugh and smile and start calling out the names they used to use: DSG (Delancey Street Girls), GIC (Girls in Control).

CINDY: Like when we tag, we put LES to represent the Lower East Side.

SONYA: But we had that name GIC for a long time. We used to put it up on the walls. I was Starr.

SMOOTH B: I was always B. Now I'm Smooth B.

CINDY: I was always Dee. And Carmen always used to call herself Unique.

MH: So how long have you all been a crew?

CINDY: Since about third grade.

SMOOTH B: First it was just us 'cause we all lived in the same building, and you know how when you're young you can't leave the foot of your building, and you had nowhere to go except the front of your building 'cause your mother be calling you, "Come upstairs! Come home right now!"

MH: So how many girls are there now?

SMOOTH B: It's me, my sister, Carmen, Cindy, Chris, Marcy, Nicky, Cristina, Carmela – she's the youngest.

CARMEN: I'm the quietest.

SONYA: Carmela is the youngest, she's twelve, but she acts mature. She wants to be like us, to be older – you know, lipstick and stuff – but we hang out with her 'cause we don't want her to hang out with other girls, 'cause her friends, they all smoke. We do, too, but we don't influence her, we don't tell her, "Here, here, smoke this," and her friends do. So she just stays with us. We used to hang out with this other girl, Aisha, but she stole money from my mother, and if she steals money from me then she's not my friend. She's just a herb. A herb is what we call nerds, weaklings.

MH: Who can be part of your crew?

CINDY: People we can get along with – people we can trust. Who you can tell something to. Like if I say to Carmen I was with this guy, I know she won't go and tell someone – 'cause they a lot of girls who will do that.

MH: Do you have an initiation?

SONYA: No, we don't. Guys are different, they be like you have to prove yourself. With us, you don't have to prove yourself, but we'll test you. Like I'll tell her, "Oh, I slept with this guy," and if she goes and tells somebody else without asking if it's OK, then we know. So you could say we don't initiate, we just test you for your trustworthiness. There's one thing, though. If there's a new girl coming in, if anyone was to get jumped and the new girl don't jump in – then that's another thing. We're just gonna have to ban her because – well, maybe mess her up – because one of our girls got messed up, and she was there and didn't defend her.

SMOOTH B: If someone was to mess with one of us, the next day we'll find out who's the girl and mess them up.

CINDY: Yeah! We could pick on her, call her names. We could diss[1] you so low it's not even funny. Like with Aisha. We did her so good that when she walks by us now she lowers her head down. When she used to have problems with girls she always used to come to us and say "Let's go do something," but she's a liar. She lied to her mother saying I was a big-time drug dealer, that I smoke every day, that I light her up, that I always have money. She was lying. So one day I called her a bitch and when I was walking away she called me a bitch and I yelled out, "You got crabs! Go clean yourself." But she walked away with her boyfriend.

---

1. "Diss" means criticize, disrespect.

MH: You said those things to her with her boyfriend there? Weren't you afraid he was gonna hit you back?

CINDY: You crazy? No boy is gonna hit me!

SMOOTH B: Cindy is a guy-fighter!

CINDY: I don't care, you say something to me I'm gonna talk right back to you. You can be guy, girl, mother, father – if you gonna hit me, then I'm gonna have to hit you. If you try to hit me too hard then I'm gonna have to slice you. I'm not scared of nobody. If you gonna do something then you gotta do something good. You gotta beat the hell outta me like I won't remember, or kill me, 'cause, I'm sorry, if you don't kill me then I'm gonna come back and beat the hell out of you. [Pause] So, what, Maria, are you scared or something? [Laughs]

MH: No, but I'm thinking. You say you will beat up on anyone, right? How do you decide you are gonna mess someone up?

CINDY: I'm not gonna hit nobody first.

SMOOTH B: We don't start trouble!

CINDY: No, but if a girl gives us a dirty look –

SMOOTH B: She's gonna get one back –

CINDY: And we gonna say something.

SMOOTH B: Well, we do start trouble sometimes. Like, we'll walk by and see a girl we don't like and we'll be like, uugghhh. You know, we'll make her hear it so she can say something. Like when we used to get chopped,[2] we used to just bug out[3] and act real stupid. We act like, you know, like we don't care what happens, like the whole day is for us. One night we was all hanging out . . . Was I pregnant? Oh yeah, 'cause I remember everything that happened that night and usually when you get chopped you don't remember what happened.

CARMEN: We was hangin' out in the Village –

MH: You weren't making trouble that night?

SMOOTH B: Yes we were. Those people who hang out in the Village, they've got tight jeans with holes and they got those big heels, ugly shoes – white people. You know, some of them have purple hair and they got earrings everywhere. So sometimes we walk by and make fun of them or we'll bump people on purpose and stuff like that.

---

2. "Get chopped" means get high on marijuana.
3. "Bug out" means freak out, become upset.

CINDY: And we'll be like, *"Excuse you"* –

SMOOTH B: Most of the time when we did it we were high 'cause it's just a feeling like you in control. Nobody's in this world but you, and you have everything in the palm of your hands, so you push everybody and if they say something, you be like, yeeeaahh, what?

SONYA: It's like that one day – let's say your whole week was so messed up. Friday comes and we'll all get high and bug out and it's fun – the whole weekend. Everybody says that since we got pregnant that we didn't live our life to the fullest 'cause we're so young. But they don't know how much fun we had. To me I lived it to the fullest.

SMOOTH B: It's like the whole week you go to school, do what your mother says, do everything right, do your homework, clean, watch TV, and you know the next day you have to do it all over again. So Friday comes and there's no school on Saturday so we go and we used to hang out and act like there wasn't no law. Like we used to throw garbage cans or whatever – throw stuff at each other on the streets of the Village, throw ice when it snows, we used to chase guys. We used to beat up guys. We used to chase them and throw them on the floor – we had some good times.

CINDY: Acting like we didn't care about nothing. We didn't care if we got into trouble – if anybody would say something, if we got punished – that night was our night. Every Friday night was our night. But now it's mostly me and Chris who still smoke and stuff. The others can't 'cause they're pregnant.

SMOOTH B: You know what I like is, now that I don't smoke, when I see her get chopped I laugh 'cause I can't believe I used to do that and act that way – but if we were sober we wouldn't be doing that.

MH: But did you want to start something with people? What did you want?

CINDY: Well, sometimes I would like to fight somebody. It's just a feeling . . . to show you are big enough to fight anybody.

SMOOTH B: I learned a lot from my ex-boyfriend 'cause we used to fight like in the hallway of my old building or outside. I mean we used *fight;* we used to be outside, and he taught me this thing that when you fight you pull the guy's shirt over their face so you hit them underneath, and I used to do it to him. He would get mad and I threw him down on the sidewalk; he used to throw me. I used to have bruises and everybody used to think he was beating me up, but it was just fun 'cause I could take it. I loved it! It was so much fun. But the girls also protect each other. Like with Cindy, we all used to think her boyfriend was no good for her. Cindy was infatuated with this guy, Shore, and she was like calling him her husband, and I knew what he was all about 'cause I used to play around with him and he used to try to kiss me and hug me, and she used to see it and get mad, but she never did anything about it. And I felt wrong. I didn't mean to do it, but I wanted her to open her eyes and see what he was doing. We're a family. We don't want to see one of our sisters get hurt.

SONYA: So with the little girls in the crew we try to show them 'cause we been through it so we are like mothers to them. We don't let them smoke weed. Or they don't smoke in front of us.

CINDY: Like one night with Melody, I got her real chopped and made her smoke a lot, and I want her to do that with me so I can let her realize it's not good. The reason I smoke is 'cause I got too much problems. When I smoke weed, I just don't think about things and I am just like, yeeaah, cool. . . . I get scared, sometimes, I feel like . . . but I know weed doesn't do that . . . but sometimes I feel like I'm not gonna wake up and stuff like that. Like recently, I've been thinking like the life we live is not real and all this stuff is fake. 'Cause recently everything has been happening so fast. My mother found out I was having sex, she found out I was smoking cigarettes, she found a bag of weed, and two friends passed away. So much is happening, so you keep on smoking.

SMOOTH B: Teenagers these days have more problems than older people. Like, you know, how older people got problems, like money . . . we got money problems, too. We sixteen years old, we want things we can't have. We want everything. And we got boyfriend problems, and family. Mothers don't understand us. This is the nineties and they think it's like 1950. And mothers don't want to admit we're growing up.

MH: So, Sonya, what are the problems that you have that make you worried or upset?

SONYA: Well, I don't have problems now, but I used to have problems with boys. And also 'cause I want a lot of things I can't have. These days it's more how we look than how we are inside, Before, when you were little, you wear shorts and skirts and nothing ever mattered, But now, it's like your appearance. I want clothes, jewelry, things I never had before. Like last summer when I had a pair of sneakers that were supposed to be white and they were black so I asked my boyfriend for a pair. That was when he had a job and he had some money. Last summer, before my sweet sixteen, he was selling drugs. He would sell drugs when he wanted money fast. The problem is he got greedy with it until he got arrested.

MH: What'd you feel about him selling drugs?

SONYA: I didn't like it, All these guys want a fast way out instead of looking for

a job — but I was scared. That was all I needed, was to lose my boyfriend in jail,
But I really wanted things, you know, things I couldn't get from my mother.

SMOOTH B: No, you just wanted things from a boy.

SONYA: Because I never got anything from anybody! Like you feel special when
you get little heart things. It feels good. Like he loves you, like you mean
something to him, Getting something from a guy is like everything.

MH: [To Smooth B] You were also involved with a guy who was selling drugs?

SMOOTH B: All of us have been.

MH: Well, what you told me was that part of what your crew was all about was
to help each other out and keep each other going in the right direction, so how
is it that you all are going out with guys who sell drugs? [They all look at me
incredulously and laugh.]

SMOOTH B: OK, look. We are teenagers, right, and we want guys our age,
sixteen, seventeen, eighteen, nineteen years old. We don't go to business places
to look for guys, right? We walk down the street, they rap, we take, they rap,
and we find out later on that they sell. It's not like we are gonna run away and
tell them no, we don't want to talk to you guys 'cause you sell, because we grew
up around here and everybody we know sells. We're used to it. But it's something different if you use it. Because I know I wouldn't be with a guy who uses
all those drugs, sniffing, and all that.

MH: So the guys you know who sell don't use?

SMOOTH B: Well, yeah, but before I got together with my boyfriend, when he
was twelve or thirteen, he used every drug there was and he got sent upstate
cause of that; his mother sent him away. And so he stopped and all he does now
is smoke weed. And he sells. But now I'm not with him anymore.

MH: But you're gonna have his baby.

SMOOTH B: But we can't be together 'cause we fight all the time. The problem
is that he is the type that has gotten so much stuff done to him: He was abused
and everything. He is only sixteen years old and he feels like he is thirty because
he has been through so much. He feels like he is so old 'cause so much things
has happened to him during the years, and a lot of times he don't feel like he
wants to live. His cousin died, his father died. . . . It's a lot, and then to have me
on his back . . .

MH: Is he the kind of man you want to be with?

SMOOTH B: Forever? Well, I know I can get better, but I can't blame him for
doing the things he does. His mother loves him and everything, but she is on
his back, too, and then me acting like I was his mother . . . He needs space now.

MH: What about you, Cindy?

CINDY: Well, I didn't know that my boyfriend was doing these things. The day I met him he was all bopped up,[4] and I didn't know what that was like 'cause all I knew about was weed, drinking, and crack. I was fifteen when I met him. And then some people told me he was doing bop and I was like, What's that? And then they told me he was selling and getting himself into problems. Even though he doesn't look like the type. He dresses nice and I thought this guy was different, but I was wrong. He used to hit me when he was bopped. Then he stopped selling and then he started again, and then I started and then we had a fight 'cause he didn't want me doing that, and he hit me and I told him to go to hell. And then he said, "OK, do what you want to do," so I kept on selling, and then I ended up owing money to the guy I was selling for. I paid him back and then I just stopped.

MH: Why did you start selling?

CINDY: 'Cause I wasn't getting enough money even though I was working at an after-school program. It just isn't enough money to support me and the things I like to do. And my mother wasn't giving me enough money. But I didn't make that much money selling anyway.

MH: Have you all sold?

CINDY: No, just me.

SMOOTH B: But I used to hold material for the guys. You know, the cops know them but they got to get them, so the guys give it to us to hold and then the cops check them but they don't check us.

SONYA: That was the scary part. Like when I used to hold crills in my pocket, which is crack. I used to just walk through the park, just walk away from them, but it was scary, 'cause you know if you get caught you are doing at least a couple of months in jail. I used to hold guns, too. I did it like twice.

CINDY: I always hold a blade, but that's mine.

MH: But it's not like you need things really, not like you were hungry.

CINDY: Why? I don't know. The extra money in my pocket and money for my weed. And I want to start again. It's the thing to have money. You know, it's fast money. It's so fast. You sell one five-dollar bag and you're making two dollars.

SMOOTH B: But, you know, to me, when you sell weed, it's like it's not money.

---

4. "Bopped up" means high on angel dust.

It's like you sell a bag because you know you can get a bag for yourself for a dollar. You sell a couple bags and then you got money to buy some for yourself.

MH: All your friends who are supposed to be protecting you –

CINDY: They have told me to stop –

SMOOTH B: But we can't put a gun to her head and say, "Stop or I will pull the trigger." And with her, she won't get it even if you talk to her and talk to her. She won't get it through her head unless something happens to her.

MH: What will have to happen?

SMOOTH B: Maybe go to jail or get caught with stuff on her. But if the cops find weed on you all they do is open up the bags and throw the stuff on the floor and step on it. Out here that's what they do. Or if you get caught with a lot you get a misdemeanor.

CINDY: I never cared about getting caught. I don't care. I get in trouble in my house. I get screamed at and hit and I got so many problems it's not even funny. I don't want to get into that. I get in trouble and I don't care. I get in trouble for stupid things. I don't clean this or that.

SMOOTH B: No, you're lying, and I lecture her about this. She gets herself into problems. Her mother is paying three hundred dollars a month for her to go to Catholic school, and she is messing up the last year she is going to high school. And she swears she has so many problems, well, she brings it on. Her mother fights her and I tell her to just leave it. She fights with her mother, she curses her back, her mother hits her, and she tries to hit her mother back. And I will tell her to just leave it and shut up, that her mother will get tired and stop soon, but she don't listen. And her mother punishes her and won't let her have visitors 'cause she is messing up in school, and I tell her that she only has until June and then you leave! Done with high school. She don't want to listen. She still fights with her mother. And she wonders why she gets hit, why she gets punished and picked on, why they curse at her, but I know if she was my daughter and I was paying three hundred dollars a month for her to go to school I would kill her if she messed up!

CINDY: But I never asked for that! I never said to them, "Put me in this school and pay all this money –"

SMOOTH B: Her mother and her father, they want her to make something out of herself 'cause her sister died 'cause she was in the wrong track. And when her mom found the bag of weed in her house she hit her 'cause they think she's gonna smoke weed and go to crack and then go on to the harder stuff –

CINDY: It's not that I'm failing in school, I already got accepted to a local college. And I was student of the month. It's not that I'm doing badly, it's just that school got harder.

SMOOTH B: I lecture her all the time. Like, I used to fight with my mother all the time. I used to yell at her and hit her back. I used to make my mother cry. But I stopped all that 'cause that hurts her and she don't deserve it. Your mother and father, they don't give you all you want 'cause, boom, look what you do. In school. And if they tell you to come home at a certain time – she don't come home. If I had a mother and father that were so strict, I would do what I had to do. You know, clean up my room, do good in school, so they could see that I'm a good daughter. And then I'll get what I want. She got a phone and an answering machine, this makeup thing, her own room, a TV, her own VCR, stereo, a bedroom set.

CINDY: I got everything.

MH: But you still want to sell some weed?

CINDY: I've always got to have money. Even if it's just two dollars in my pocket. And I like to have things done my way. Like if I want to go out, you gonna have to let me go or else I'm gonna have a fight. You see, I'm the bad one: Cindy doesn't do this or that. They try to keep me in the house all the time. I have to do all the cleaning. Sometimes I say I'm gonna run away, but I can't 'cause I got no place to go. We argue a lot at the house. Not long ago they were arguing because some film from a camera got lost, and they were all yelling at me 'cause they thought I had lost it, like it was a big deal. And I said it seemed like the film was more important than me. And then they were saying that one of my friends took it. And meanwhile my sister had it, and I was crying and then my father started screaming at me for no reason. And then on Friday my father hit me 'cause I didn't clean my room. When they hit me I hit them back. Not like I want to, but to protect myself. You scream at me, I'm gonna scream right back, and they all know that. Violence is a way to live. That's the way you gotta live. You know, like even if a guy comes and he's twice your size and he says "Shut up" you have to say "No, you shut up."

SMOOTH B: Like if my boyfriend says, "I don't want you to be here while I'm selling," I would leave. But if he tells me to stay home all day or don't come outside, I'll be like OK, but then I'm right out the door after he leaves 'cause no way I'm gonna stay at home 'cause he says so. My mother doesn't tell me to stay at home so why should some guy? The guys think that once they got a girl they can say, like, "Stay home, stay home." Sometimes it's not to hurt them but to keep them. Like girls do the same thing. They say don't go there or do this 'cause they don't want to lose them.

CINDY: My ex-boyfriend used to do that. He would tell me what to do, to stay home and stuff –

SMOOTH B: And she used to do it. And I used to tell her, "Yo, he is taking over your life," but she wouldn't listen.

CINDY: Well, even so, he used to call me a lot. Sometimes he would call me at three in the morning. Anytime he called I was there.

SMOOTH B: You know what's funny? We're tough to everybody, to the world, with people we hang out with. But when it comes to a boyfriend-girlfriend relationship, we're weak. We're not as strong as everybody thinks we are.

SONYA: We are so eager to find somebody to tie down with –

SMOOTH B: To have somebody love us besides our mother and father and friends, to be sexual with somebody. To feel warmth and be loved by somebody. With our guys, we are weak. But with the guys we hang out with and the girls out there, we are tough.

from *Glimpses of Fifty Years:*
The Autobiography of an American Woman

Frances Willard (1839–1898) was born in Churchville, near Rochester, New York, and grew up on a farm in Wisconsin. As a child, she was a capable carpenter, who made sleds, whip-handles, and cross-guns, and spent many hours in her personal tree-house, known as "the Eagle's Nest."

Willard studied at North Western Female College, in Evanston, Illinois, and later became known as one of the leading woman educators of her day. She helped to found the Women's Christian Temperance Union and the International Council on Women, and published many works on temperance. She is best known for her autobiography, Glimpses of Fifty Years: The Autobiography of an American Woman *(1889). A selection of her journals was recently published, edited by Carolyn De Swarte Gifford; see* Writing Out My Heart: Selections from the Journals of Frances E. Willard *(1995).*

NO GIRL WENT THROUGH A HARDER EXPERIENCE THAN I, WHEN MY free, out-of-door life had to cease, and the long skirts and clubbed-up hair spiked with hair-pins had to be endured. The half of that down-heartedness has never been told and never can be. I always believed that if I had been left alone and allowed as a woman, what I had had as a girl, a free life in the country, where a human being might grow, body and soul, as a tree grows, I would have been "ten times more of a person," every way. Mine was a nature hard to tame, and I cried long and loud when I found I could never again race and range about with freedom. I had delighted in my short hair and nice round hat, or comfortable "Shaker bonnet," but now I was to be "choked with ribbons" when I went into the open air the rest of my days. Something like the following was the "state of mind" that I revealed to my journal about this time:

> This is my birthday and the date of my martyrdom. Mother insists that at last I *must* have my hair "done up woman-fashion." She says she can hardly forgive herself for letting me "run wild" so long. We've had a great time

over it all, and here I sit like another Samson "shorn of my strength." That figure won't do, though, for the greatest trouble with me is that I never shall be shorn again. My "back" hair is twisted up like a corkscrew; I carry eighteen hair-pins; my head aches miserably; my feet are entangled in the skirt of my hateful new gown. I can never jump over a fence again, so long as I live. As for chasing the sheep, down in the shady pasture, it's out of the question, and to climb to my "Eagle's-nest" seat in the big burr-oak would ruin this new frock beyond repair. Altogether, I recognize the fact that my "occupation's gone."

Something else that had already happened, helped to stir up my spirit into a mighty unrest. This is the story as I told it to my journal:

This is election day and my brother is twenty-one years old. How proud he seemed as he dressed up in his best Sunday clothes and drove off in the big wagon with father and the hired men to vote for John C. Frémont, like the sensible "Free-soiler" that he is. My sister and I stood at the window and looked out after them. Somehow, I felt a lump in my throat, and then I couldn't see their wagon any more, things got so blurred. I turned to Mary, and she, dear little innocent, seemed wonderfully sober, too. I said, "Wouldn't you like to vote as well as Oliver? Don't you and I love the country just as well as he, and doesn't the country need our ballots?" Then she looked scared, but answered, in a minute, " 'Course we do, and 'course we ought, – but don't you go ahead and say so; for then we would be called strong-minded."

These two great changes in my uneventful life made me so distressed in heart that I had half a mind to run away. But the trouble was, I hadn't the faintest idea where to run to. Across the river, near Colonel Burdick's, lived Silas Hayner and several of his brothers, on their nice prairie farms. Sometimes Emily Scoville, Hannah Hayner, or some other of the active young women, would come over to help mother when there was more work than usual; and with Hannah, especially, I had fellowship, because, like myself, she was venturesome in disposition; could row a boat, or fire a gun, and liked to be always out-of-doors. She was older than I, and entered into all my plans. So we two foolish creatures planned to borrow father's revolver and go off on a wild-goose chase, crossing the river in a canoe and launching out to seek our fortunes. But the best part of the story is that we were never so silly as to take a step beyond the old home roof, contenting ourselves with talking the matter over in girlish phrase, and very soon perceiving how mean and ungrateful such an act would be. Indeed, I told Mary and mother all about it, after a little while, and that ended the only really "wild" plan that I ever made, except another, not unlike it, in my first months at Evanston, which was also nothing but a plan.

"You must go to school, my child, and take a course of study; I wish it might be to Oberlin" – this was my mother's quiet comment on the confession. "Your mind is active; you are fond of books and thoughts, as well as of outdoors; we must provide them for you to make up for the loss of your girlish good times;" so, without any scolding, this Roman matron got her daughter's aspirations into another channel. To be busy doing something that is worthy to be done is the happiest thing in all this world for girl or boy, for old or young.

On the day I was eighteen, my mother made a birthday cake and I was in the highest possible glee. I even went so far as to write what Oliver called a "pome," which has passed into oblivion but of which these lines linger in memory's whispering-gallery:

I AM EIGHTEEN

The last year is passed:
The last month, week, day, hour and moment.
For eighteen years, quelling all thoughts
And wishes of my own,
I've been obedient to the powers that were
Not that the yoke was heavy to be borne
And grievous,
Do I glory that 'tis removed –
For lighter ne'er did parents fond
Impose on child.
It was a silver *chain:*
But the bright adjective
Takes not away the clanking *sound*
That follows it. . . .
The clock has struck!
O! heaven and earth, I'm free!
And here, beneath the watching stars, I feel
New inspiration. Breathing from afar

And resting on my spirit as it ne'er
Could rest before, comes joy profound.
And now I feel that I'm alone and free
To worship and obey Jehovah only. . . .

Toward evening, on this "freedom day," I took my seat quietly in mother's rocking-chair, and began to read Scott's *Ivanhoe*. Father was opposed to story books, and on coming in he scanned this while his brow grew cloudy.

"I thought I told you not to read novels, Frances," he remarked seriously.

"So you did, father, and in the main I've kept faith with you in this; but you forget what day it is."

"What day, indeed! I should like to know if the day has anything to do with the deed!"

"Indeed it has – I am eighteen – I am of age – I am now to do what *I* think right, and to read this fine historical story is, in my opinion, a right thing for me to do."

Tommy, the Unsentimental

Willa Cather (1876–1947) was born in Winchester, Virginia. When she was nine, her family moved to a ranch in Red Cloud, Nebraska, territory Cather afterwards made famous in such books as O Pioneers! *(1913) and* My Antonia *(1918). Other titles include the Pulitzer prizewinner* One of Ours *(1922),* A Lost Lady *(1923), and* Death Comes for the Archbishop *(1927).*

As a young woman Cather lived in Pittsburgh where she worked as a journalist. Later she moved to New York City to edit McClure's Magazine. *Her lifelong companion was Edith Lewis.*

"YOUR FATHER SAYS HE HAS NO BUSINESS TACT AT ALL, AND OF course that's dreadfully unfortunate."

"Business," replied Tommy, "he's a baby in business; he's good for nothing on earth but to keep his hair parted straight and wear that white carnation in his buttonhole. He has 'em sent down from Hastings twice a week as regularly as the mail comes, but the drafts he cashes lie in his safe until they are lost, or somebody finds them. I go up occasionally and send a package away for him myself. He'll answer your notes promptly enough, but his business letters – I believe he destroys them unopened to shake the responsibility of answering them."

"I am at a loss to see how you can have such patience with him, Tommy, in so many ways he is thoroughly reprehensible."

"Well, a man's likeableness don't depend at all on his virtues or acquirements, nor a woman's either, unfortunately. You like them or you don't like them, and that's all there is to it. For the why of it you must appeal to a higher oracle than I. Jay is a likeable fellow, and that's his only and sole acquirement, but after all it's a rather happy one."

"Yes, he certainly is that," replied Miss Jessica, as she deliberately turned off the gas jet and proceeded to arrange her toilet articles. Tommy watched her closely and then turned away with a baffled expression.

Needless to say, Tommy was not a boy, although her keen gray eyes and wide forehead were scarcely girlish, and she had the lank figure of an active half grown lad. Her real name was Theodosia, but during Thomas Shirley's frequent absences from the bank she had attended to his business and correspondence signing herself "T. Shirley," until everyone in Southdown called her "Tommy." That blunt sort of familiarity is not unfrequent in the West, and is meant well enough. People rather expect some business ability in a girl there, and they respect it immensely. That, Tommy undoubtedly had, and if she had not, things would have gone at sixes and sevens in the Southdown National. For Thomas Shirley had big land interests in Wyoming that called him constantly away from home, and his cashier, little Jay Ellington Harper, was, in the local phrase, a weak brother in the bank. He was the son of a friend of old Shirley's, whose papa had sent him West, because he had made a sad mess of his college career, and had spent too much money and gone at too giddy a pace down East. Conditions changed the young gentleman's life, for it was simply impossible to live either prodigally or rapidly in Southdown, but they could not materially affect his mental habits or inclinations. He was made cashier of Shirley's bank because his father bought in half the stock, but Tommy did his work for him.

The relation between these two young people was peculiar; Harper was, in his way, very grateful to her for keeping him out of disgrace with her father, and showed it by a hundred little attentions which were new to her and much more agreeable than the work she did for him was irksome. Tommy knew that she was immensely fond of him, and she knew at the same time that she was thoroughly foolish for being so. As she expressed it, she was not of his sort, and never would be. She did not often take pains to think, but when she did she saw matters pretty clearly, and she was of a peculiarly unfeminine mind that could not escape meeting and acknowledging a logical conclusion. But she went on liking Jay Ellington Harper, just the same. Now Harper was the only foolish man of Tommy's acquaintance. She knew plenty of active young business men and sturdy ranchers, such as one meets about live western towns, and took no particular interest in them, probably just because they were practical and sensible and thoroughly of her own kind. She knew almost no women, because in those days there were few women in Southdown who were in any sense interesting, or interested in anything but babies and salads. Her best friends were her father's old business friends, elderly men who had seen a good deal of the world, and who were very proud and fond of Tommy. They recognized a sort of squareness and honesty of spirit in the girl that Jay Ellington Harper never discovered, or, if he did, knew too little of its rareness to value highly. Those old speculators and men of business had always felt a sort of responsibility for Tom Shirley's little girl, and had rather taken her mother's place, and been her advisers on many points upon which men seldom feel at liberty to address a girl.

She was just one of them; she played whist and billiards with them, and made their cocktails for them, not scorning to take one herself occasionally. Indeed, Tommy's cocktails were things of fame in Southdown, and the professional compounders of drinks always bowed respectfully to her as though acknowledging a powerful rival.

Now all these things displeased and puzzled Jay Ellington Harper, and Tommy knew it full well, but clung to her old manner of living with a stubborn pertinacity, feeling somehow that to change would be both foolish and disloyal to the Old Boys. And as things went on, the seven Old Boys made greater demands upon her time than ever, for they were shrewd men, most of them, and had not lived fifty years in this world without learning a few things and unlearning many more. And while Tommy lived on in the blissful delusion that her role of indifference was perfectly played and without a flaw, they suspected how things were going and were perplexed as to the outcome. Still, their confidence was by no means shaken, and as Joe Elsworth said to Joe Sawyer one evening at billiards, "I think we can pretty nearly depend on Tommy's good sense."

They were too wise to say anything to Tommy, but they said just a word or two to Thomas Shirley, Sr., and combined to make things very unpleasant for Mr. Jay Ellington Harper.

At length their relations with Harper became so strained that the young man felt it would be better for him to leave town, so his father started him in a little bank of his own up in Red Willow. Red Willow, however, was scarcely a safe distance, being only some twenty-five miles north, upon the Divide, and Tommy occasionally found excuse to run up on her wheel to straighten out the young man's business for him. So when she suddenly decided to go East to school for a year, Thomas, Sr., drew a sigh of great relief. But the seven Old Boys shook their heads; they did not like to see her gravitating toward the East; it was a sign of weakening, they said, and showed an inclination to experiment with another kind of life, Jay Ellington Harper's kind.

But to school Tommy went, and from all reports conducted herself in a most seemly manner; made no more cocktails, played no more billiards. She took rather her own way with the curriculum, but she distinguished herself in athletics, which in Southdown counted for vastly more than erudition.

Her evident joy on getting back to Southdown was appreciated by everyone. She went about shaking hands with everybody, her shrewd face, that was so like a clever wholesome boy's, held high with happiness. As she said to old Joe Elsworth one morning, when they were driving behind his stud through a little thicket of cottonwood scattered along the sun-parched bluffs, "It's all very fine down East there, and the hills are great, but one gets mighty homesick for this sky, the old intense blue of it, you know. Down there the skies are all pale and smoky. And this wind, this hateful, dear, old everlasting wind that comes down like the sweep of cavalry and is never tamed or broken, O Joe, I used to get hungry for this wind! I couldn't sleep in that lifeless stillness down there."

"How about the people, Tom?"

"O, they are fine enough folk, but we're not their sort, Joe, and never can be."

"You realize that, do you, fully?"

"Quite fully enough, thank you, Joe." She laughed rather dismally and Joe cut his horse with the whip.

The only unsatisfactory thing about Tommy's return was that she brought with her a girl she had grown fond of at school, a dainty, white, languid bit of a thing, who used violet perfumes and carried a sunshade. The Old Boys said it was a bad sign when a rebellious girl like Tommy took to being sweet and gentle to one of her own sex, the worst sign in the world.

The new girl was no sooner in town than a new complication came about. There was no doubt of the impression she made on Jay Ellington Harper. She indisputably had all those little evidences of good breeding that were about the only things which could touch the timid, harassed young man who was so much out of his element. It was a very plain case on his part, and the souls of the seven were troubled within them. Said Joe Elsworth to the other Joe, "The heart of the cad is gone out to the little muff, as is right and proper and in accordance with the eternal fitness of things. But there's the other girl who has the blindness that may not be cured, and she gets all the rub of it. It's no use, I can't help her, and I am going to run down to Kansas City for awhile. I can't stay here and see the abominable suffering of it." He didn't go, however.

There was just one other person who understood the hopelessness of the situation quite as well as Joe, and that was Tommy. That is, she understood Harper's attitude. As to Miss Jessica's she was not quite so certain, for Miss Jessica, though pale and languid and addicted to sunshades, was a maiden most discreet. Conversations on the subject usually ended without any further information as to Miss Jessica's feelings, and Tommy sometimes wondered if she were capable of having any at all.

At last the calamity which Tommy had long foretold descended upon Jay Ellington Harper. One morning she received a telegram from him begging her to intercede with her father; there was a run on his bank and he must have help before noon. It was then ten thirty, and the one sleepy little train that ran up to Red Willow daily had crawled out of the station an hour before. Thomas Shirley, Sr., was not at home.

"And it's a good thing for Jay Ellington he's not, he might be more stony hearted than I," remarked Tommy, as she closed the ledger and turned to the terrified Miss Jessica." Of course we're his only chance, no one else would turn their hand over to help him. The train went an hour ago and he says it must be there by noon. It's the only bank in the town, so nothing can be done by telegraph. There is nothing left but to wheel for it. I may make it, and I may not. Jess, you scamper up to the house and get my wheel out, the tire may need a little attention. I will be along in a minute.

"O, Theodosia, can't I go with you? I must go!"

"You go! O, yes, of course, if you want to. You know what you are getting into, though. It's twenty-five miles uppish grade and hilly, and only an hour and a quarter to do it in."

"O, Theodosia, I can do anything now!" cried Miss Jessica, as she put up her sunshade and fled precipitately. Tommy smiled as she began cramming bank notes into a canvas bag. "May be you can, my dear, and may be you can't."

The road from Southdown to Red Willow is not by any means a favorite bicycle road; it is rough, hilly and climbs from the river bottoms up to the big Divide by a steady up grade, running white and hot through the scorched corn fields and grazing lands where the long-horned Texan cattle browse about in the old buffalo wallows. Miss Jessica soon found that with the pedaling that had to be done there was little time left for emotion of any sort, or little sensibility for anything but the throbbing, dazzling heat that had to be endured. Down there in the valley the distant bluffs were vibrating and dancing with the heat, the cattle, completely overcome by it, had hidden under the shelving banks of the "draws" and the prairie dogs had fled to the bottom of their holes that are said to reach to water. The whirr of the seventeen-year locust was the only thing that spoke of animation, and that ground on as if only animated and enlivened by the sickening, destroying heat. The sun was like hot brass, and the wind that blew up from the south was hotter still. But Tommy knew that wind was their only chance. Miss Jessica began to feel that unless she could stop and get some water she was not much longer for this vale of tears. She suggested this possibility to Tommy, but Tommy only shook her head, "Take too much time," and bent over her handle bars, never lifting her eyes from the road in front of her. It flashed upon Miss Jessica that Tommy was not only very unkind, but that she sat very badly on her wheel and looked aggressively masculine and professional when she bent her shoulders and pumped like that. But just then Miss Jessica found it harder than ever to breathe, and the bluffs across the river began doing serpentines and skirt dances, and more important and personal considerations occupied the young lady.

When they were fairly over the first half of the road, Tommy took out her watch." Have to hurry up, Jess, I can't wait for you."

"O, Tommy, I can't," panted Miss Jessica, dismounting and sitting down in a little heap by the roadside. "You go on, Tommy, and tell him – tell him I hope it won't fail, and I'd do anything to save him."

By this time the discreet Miss Jessica was reduced to tears, and Tommy nodded as she disappeared over the hill laughing to herself. "Poor Jess, anything but the one thing he needs. Well, your kind have the best of it generally, but in little affairs of this sort my kind come out rather strongly. We're rather better at them than at dancing. It's only fair, one side shouldn't have all."

Just at twelve o'clock, when Jay Ellington Harper, his collar crushed and wet about his throat, his eyeglass dimmed with perspiration, his hair hanging damp over his forehead, and even the ends of his moustache dripping with moisture, was attempting to reason with a score of angry Bohemians, Tommy came quietly through the door, grip in hand. She went straight behind the grating, and standing screened by the bookkeeper's desk, handed the bag to Harper and turned to the spokesman of the Bohemians.

"What's all this business mean, Anton? Do you all come to bank at once nowadays?"

"We want 'a money, want 'a our money, he no got it, no give it," bawled the big beery Bohemian.

"O, don't chaff 'em any longer, give 'em their money and get rid of 'em, I want to see you," said Tommy carelessly, as she went into the consulting room.

When Harper entered half an hour later, after the rush was over, all that was left of his usual immaculate appearance was his eyeglass and the white flower in his buttonhole.

"This has been terrible!" he gasped. "Miss Theodosia, I can never thank you."

"No," interrupted Tommy. "You never can, and I don't want any thanks. It was rather a tight place, though, wasn't it? You looked like a ghost when I came in. What started them?"

"How should I know? They just came down like the wolf on the fold. It sounded like the approach of a ghost dance."

"And of course you had no reserve? O, I always told you this would come, it was inevitable with your charming methods. By the way, Jess sends her regrets and says she would do anything to save you. She started out with me, but she has fallen by the wayside. O, don't be alarmed, she is not hurt, just winded. I left her all bunched up by the road like a little white rabbit. I think the lack of romance in the escapade did her up about as much as anything; she is essentially romantic. If we had been on fiery steeds bespattered with foam I think she would have made it, but a wheel hurt her dignity. I'll tend bank; you'd better get your wheel and go and look her up and comfort her. And as soon as it is convenient, Jay, I wish you'd marry her and be done with it, I want to get this thing off my mind.

Jay Ellington Harper dropped into a chair and turned a shade whiter.

"Theodosia, what do you mean? Don't you remember what I said to you last fall, the night before you went to school? Don't you remember what I wrote you – "

Tommy sat down on the table beside him and looked seriously and frankly into his eyes.

"Now, see here, Jay Ellington, we have been playing a nice little game, and now it's time to quit. One must grow up sometime. You are horribly wrought up over Jess, and why deny it? She's your kind, and clean daft about you, so there is only one thing to do. That's all."

Jay Ellington wiped his brow, and felt unequal to the situation. Perhaps he really came nearer to being moved down to his stolid little depths than he ever had before. His voice shook a good deal and was very low as he answered her.

"You have been very good to me, I didn't believe any woman could be at once so kind and clever. You almost made a man of even me."

"Well, I certainly didn't succeed. As to being good to you, that's rather a break, you know; I am amiable, but I am only flesh and blood after all. Since I have known you I have not been at all good, in any sense of the word, and I suspect I have been anything but clever. Now, take mercy upon Jess – and me –

and go. Go on, that ride is beginning to tell on me. Such things strain one's nerve. . . . Thank Heaven he's gone at last and had sense enough not to say anything more. It was growing rather critical. As I told him I am not at all superhuman."

After Jay Ellington Harper had bowed himself out, when Tommy sat alone in the darkened office, watching the flapping blinds, with the bank books before her, she noticed a white flower on the floor. It was the one Jay Ellington Harper had worn in his coat and had dropped in his nervous agitation. She picked it up and stood holding it a moment, biting her lip. Then she dropped it into the grate and turned away, shrugging her thin shoulders.

"They are awful idiots, half of them, and never think of anything beyond their dinner. But O, how we do like 'em!"

Bia Lowe

Drummer

Bia Lowe was born in 1950, and grew up in California. As a child she was a tomboy, a definition she enjoyed. "Tomboy meant I trusted the structure of tree limbs. Meant I knew the physics of flat stones against a taut skin of water." But as she grew older, Lowe began to struggle with a new definition. "Tomboy meant something sinister, what schoolmates in the city were beginning to call me, lez, Miss L, Miss H, Queer."

Bia Lowe's writing has appeared in a number of anthologies, including Sister and Brother: Lesbians and Gay Men Write About Their Lives Together *(1995). Her first book,* Wild Ride: Earthquakes, Sneezes and Other Thrills, *from which this memoir is taken, was published in 1995.*

IN A SIMPLE DRUM SET – THE KIND YOU SNUCK UP TO AT THE DANCE, the one you tapped furtively while the band was off guzzling punch at the break – there are cymbals, a kick drum and a snare.

The set, if you're right-handed, is laid out in a predictable arrangement. Cymbals are played with the right hand. The ride cymbal delineates the possible beats, pencils in all the corners, *sixty-six, sixty-six, sixty-six.* Each strike is a thin red second hand ticking each stand-and-be-counted moment, a field of brass filaments, a prairie. The crash cymbal serves as punctuation, an exclamation point at the end of a verse – with that *tisssss* we all cheer and catch the wave into the chorus. The *tak-tak-tak* is the snare, domain of the left hand, the verbal mind, the tongue, the mouth. The snare shouts declarations in the foreground, moves us through that prairie like a plow. Lastly, the kick drum *(tum-ta-tum)* is played by the right foot. The kick drum is the rhythm at the root of your being. It throbbed around you when you were only an exploding cell.

In utero, pulsation surrounded us, became us. At four weeks, our hearts took root within the curl of our bodies, and we managed a tintinnabulation of our own. We were both a part of and apart from the amniotic rhythm, a clacker inside a kettledrum.

———

All mammals breathe once for every four heartbeats. A measure of 4/4 time. We have a natural affinity for fours, our four limbs, the four seasons, the vortices of the compass, the sturdy, if sometimes stodgy, fixedness of a square. Don't forget the four chambers of the heart. Four is our ground, our anchor.

Rhythm expresses the heart's intent, no matter what melodic convolutions the cortex invents.

His drums were loud and shiny, commanded a presence like the snaps and pops of a bonfire. He was tall, dark, probably in his thirties, and wore a white sport coat. I was six, traveling with my family in Rome. I sucked spaghetti up through the tiny o of my lips, and marveled at the sheen of his hair. Night after night as my mouth made orange stains on my napkin, his band closed their set with "Arrivederci Roma."

On our last evening in Rome sobs stoppered up my nostrils. How could I bid *arrivederci* to my drummer? My mother consoled me with the drone of a hypnotist. "Tonight you feel your heart will break, but by morning your heart will have turned to stone." Sure enough, like the audience volunteer who wakes from her trance to find her lifelong passion for chocolate snuffed, by morning I was indifferent to the drummer in the white sport coat. My heart had turned to stone.

What was my heart anyway? Why had it thumped wildly inside my chest, and tricked me into thinking I could live the rest of my days in a Roman hotel? How could it choke me with tears at one moment, only to leave me blasé the next?

A friend recently saw a sonogram of her father's heart. Through the moonscape lens of sonography, on a small black and white TV, she peered at what looked like a rock in the ocean battered by waves. The crashing of the surf against the rock was, she realized, his heart's convulsion, the beat maintaining his life.

I've imagined the hollows of my heart like the interior of a red pepper, the walls of the chambers stippled and scarlet. The heart's musculature, of course, is less brittle, as taut as the flesh on an endurance swimmer. Atria and ventricles fill up like the locks of Suez. The pockets take turns bloating and squeezing until the blood and its cargo are dispatched back out into the body.

Our everyday image of the heart is the symmetrical bodice, the red satin bustier of valentines, but in reality it's the gory knot at the core of our circulation. A fist-size football, only tougher, it pounds out 100,000 beats a day, 365 days a year, and – knock on wood – eighty years, at least. The heart works like a horse.

By junior high I'd jerry-rigged my own method of drumming. I would tap one pencil against my homework. If hit just right, that small stack of binder papers rustled like the soft splash of a cymbal. Meanwhile the pencil in my other hand smacked the ream inside my textbook like the snap of a snare. I copied the riffs, the rolls, the crashes of the R&B songs I heard on my transistor radio.

During the day, the value of x may have occupied my mind, but by the evening, alone with the angst of my adolescence, the energy of R&B was a solace for my heart. Teen magazines worked their hard sell, but as far as I was concerned the hormonal wonderland they professed might as well have been science fiction. Teendom was a setup for failed assimilation. I was bullied into forfeiting the things I did best, to relinquish the feel of used muscles, to say good-bye to a view of the world one can only acquire from the loft of a tree. I despised nylons, girdles, dress shields, the works, and so slinked down the halls of my school with the hunched rebellion of James Dean. I was called a lez.

The music I tuned in to after school became my sanctuary, because within its confines, I could cope with, if not revel in, my solitude. I don't know what invisible force led me to the right end of the AM band, to KDAY, the one R&B station in the Bay Area, rather than to the bubble gum stations on the left end. But once I'd heard the alto voices of the Chiffons chiming "One Fine Day" I was hooked. Theirs was a madrigal beauty that ached a bit, a more interesting flavor than, say, just cream, more like chocolate which, because of its bitter-sweetness, won me, hands down. Then there was Smokey Robinson and the Miracles' "Shop Around," the Orlons' "Don't Hang Up," the Drifters' "Up on the Roof." I couldn't wait to return to my room so that I could isolate myself with the freshness of those rhythms, the glory of those harmonies, and the often hilarious stories of characters like Nadine and Johnny B. Goode. I was diving headfirst into insularity, but I was also learning about a larger world where the rules of gender were differently drawn.

No less masculine, only more intense, Smokey's voice soared in falsetto, so too, little Anthony's, Eddie Hendricks'. Dinah Washington's voice cut, abraded, teased. Her expression was large, not diminutive. Inside its breadth I recognized the timbre of authority, a summons to discover my own expression. I wasn't suited to the indignities of cinched waists, padded bras, gouging garters. Listening to Dinah's sass, Aretha's fire or Martha Reeves's brawn I was closer to being my own creature, a tiger burning in the night.

Remember the roll that begins "Dancing in the Street"? Calling for a revolution of global proportions, to let the spirit of celebration overtake the habit of repression. *Calling out around the world, are you ready for a brand new beat?* Under this anthem's spell we would disobey the laws of curfew or traffic. *Summer's here, and the time is right for dancin' in the street.* We would have no fear of crime or of the police. A call to arms of the Emma Goldman variety, the celebrative side of the civil rights movement, *All we need is music, sweet sweet music.*

Music is most certainly compulsion, the repetition that most assuredly will set things right. Percussion, then, is the architecture of compulsion. The temple in which instruments daven, genuflect, cadenza. The drummer is the vertebrae for a body of tonalities.

Drumming is a distillation not only of time, but of that organizing principle we call math. One may bring the language of mathematics to rhythm, translate double time into a series of fractions. Corral the zealous, tapping feet into a set of quarter notes. But one needn't be fluent in math to have a profound understanding of these thumps, tics and snaps. One can play by ear, by heart, by savancy. Percussion can play itself directly through the body without having to go through a scribe in the mind.

A drummer's genius is not narrative. The tonalities produced by drums do not approximate the human voice, or the cries of animals. There is no subject, no protagonist, no hero's journey. Whatever virtuosity a drummer might display, it's ultimately an embellishment on the rhythmic territory. On one level, a drummer's sensibility is like a mason's sensibility. Each brick is laid tight into the grid, a sure and solid thing. Today follows yesterday, as will tomorrow, today. In laying the bricks for this temple, drumming is an attempt to improve on that primeval chamber where Absolute Grace was comprehended in 4/4.

Sometimes the percussive genius veers off in defiance of the grid – a gap appears in the wall – a syncopation, a window. Our bodies respond to it. We ache for the safe enclosures of repetition, and are spellbound by a view. Syncopation withholds the teat, expectation is teased. The missing heartbeat resounds within the inner ear, tethers us to the hungers in our blood. The pulse is always amniotic, we remember the fish we were, we curl and thrust for immersion, just as exquisitely as we breach for an unknown.

———

In 1961 I met Kathy at summer camp. I don't know what invisible force led me to her, has led me, time and time again, to a sympathetic soul. She was an oddly joyous child, whose zeal and whose lack of WASPy virtues made her unpopular at an early age. Like me, she was an outsider. Too effusive, motherless since early childhood, she had orange kinky hair that spread itself out in every direction as though suspended, like sargassum, in water. The kids at her school taunted her and called her "steel wool."

Where someone else might have dumped me for not knowing the ropes at camp, Kathy hung out with me. Though she was already an accomplished trail rider, she accompanied me to the remedial corral, where the horse illiterate got their first taste of the saddle, and where a palomino pony lived his last senile days in a clockwise circle.

Astride Welsh Boy, the walk was a piece of cake. Getting to a canter was the hard part, not only because Welsh Boy had long since lost his joie de vivre, but because the intermediary gait, the trot, was impossibly bouncy, and usually ended with my being sprung from his back. While I waited on the sidelines for my next shot at equestrian glory, Kathy would sit with me and critique my style. "Grip with your knees," she'd advise, or "lean forward." "Try and relax your hips."

One day I forgot my rookie self-consciousness. I wanted nothing more than for Welsh Boy to canter and let him know my resolve. My body spoke an unmistakable idiom. We loped around the corral like Roy and Trigger, like The Lone Ranger and Silver, like Ginger and Fred, his back rocking me as smoothly as a hobbyhorse.

Kathy had given me the confidence to ride. I was no longer a nerd. I had, in fact, discovered a haven in this summer camp, a respite from the rigors of what I considered to be inane femininity. Throughout junior high we continued our summer camp alliance, sought refuge in that tomboy oasis, until we were finally reunited year-long in the same boarding school.

The Athenian School, like many progressive liberal arts schools of the sixties, was a safe haven for creeps like Kathy and me, rejects of the prep school industry. Both of us felt we could discover ourselves there without reproach. At weekend dances, Kathy pranced and spun with her whole heart, wailed, off-key, along with Otis Redding's "Try a Little Tenderness." Everyone loved to dance with her or at least near her. She gave herself to each song, moved with her elbows, shoulders and knees, like a hillbilly, like a chicken. Kathy blossomed, more popular than any prom queen might have been, had there been any.

I too left my old skin behind, and even my anal penmanship relaxed into a scrawl that is wholly my own. My old misery persisted only through the word *leẓ*. *Leẓ* lodged inside me like a burr. It had come to name me, to claim the longing I was supposed to outgrow. After classes I'd often seek out Kathy for solace, for her no-nonsense counsel. In the afternoon, orange light and neroli incense suffused her room, and the turntable whispered a scratchy version of Donovan's "Wear Your Love Like Heaven." "Lowe," she'd say, "whatever's in your heart is good." At the end of my senior year she wrote in my yearbook, "I wish I could stop you from worrying about being a lesbian. Since Henry D. Thoreau uses better words than me, here is a quote: *If a man does not keep pace with his companions, perhaps it is because he hears a different drummer. Let him step to the music which he hears, however measured or far away.* Have confidence in yourself because I do."

She had long since dismissed the values of assimilation that had been turned viciously upon her in childhood. Already on her own course, she embraced the realm of anomaly. Hers was a crackpot drum that marched her toward an adult life out of earshot of conventions. Even in her thirties, Kathy never straightened her hair. Her leg hair, too, remained staunchly natural, unshaven – a gutsy stand for a straight woman in posthippie, postfeminist times. Kathy, or Kit as she renamed herself, lived for two things: the children she worked with in her profession as a physical therapist, and kayaking. It's easy to picture her beaming from her kayak like a tomboy on a trail ride, rolling with the bucking water, her hair natural, kinky, on fire.

Many years after high school I stood on a balcony at the Circus Disco in Hollywood and surveyed a roomful of men moving in unison to "The Hustle." I realized, looking over that army of lovers, that my coming out was part of a larger social revolution.

Ours was a culture that felt a strong identification with other ethnic outsiders. Homos danced the pagan rhythms, spoke the outlaw's idiom. The mainstream feared our sexuality, so we got down and celebrated it. Disco was our call to arms. *Do a little dance. Make a little love. Get Down Tonight!*

Characterized by the open high hat on the strike before the down beat, a layering of rhythmic patterns, and a thundering bass beat, disco flaunted a Latin flavor, a pagan spice. It was a force to be reckoned with from the waist down. Like all African-derived music, disco – despite its co-option by Donny and Marie – was dance music, community music, an anthem for liberation.

———

I finally got to play the drums. I did, at last, hear the proper pop of a snare rather than the dull thud my history textbook once offered. The rustle of papers finally was realized as the sizzle of big brass cymbal.

I played in The Love Machine. Like any garage band we practiced weekly surrounded by old cans of paint and motor oil, the walls and ceiling sound-proofed by a few hundred egg cartons. I wasn't *terrible*, not as steady as Ringo, but better by far than Dennis Wilson. My biggest handicap was a sluggish left hand, and so I practiced the paradiddle, the drummer's dogged rosary, an exercise that promotes ambidexterity.

Like many garage bands we celebrated the sophomoric, but unlike most, we were all-girl, and lezzy at that. Our vulgarity had, we liked to think, a uniquely low-brow edge to it. We altered the lyrics of oldies to suit our "womyn loving womyn" sensibilities. "Woolly Bully," the sixties TexMex hit became Fluffy Muffy." The rocker "Born on the Bayou" transformed into "Born in a Test Tube," a paean for artificial insemination.

Though part of our shtick was irreverence, I was never without awe for the bright sounds produced from my drum set, sounds that riveted me to the present. I've never since experienced anything as joyful as playing with that group, being the backbone, supplying the beat. I'm only sorry Kit didn't see me play. I'm sure she would have cheered me on. As if, still sitting outside the corral, she'd urge me to go another round until I got it right.

Look, it's an autumn afternoon and the clear light has gone golden and the leaves on the trees as far as you can see in every direction are ablaze. But stretching even beyond what can be seen, is their collective bluster, like the seething of a gargantuan sea. These are the cymbal's strokes. And each tree your horse passes adds to the immensity.

The snare is the bronc carrying you through this landscape. You can't help but time your exhalation to his pace, can't keep your breath from falling with his hooves on the dust. Wherever your thoughts may take you this afternoon, you can't entirely leave his motion. His muscles roll beneath you, and his gait measures a rhythm that becomes, for the both of you, a joy.

And here with your heart beating fiercely with the knowledge of being alive at that moment is the steady kick drum. You, dear rider, are borne into this golden afternoon, as you were into the resounding sac of your mother's belly.

Kit died. Her kayak overturned and her head struck a rock. She was found in the bend of a river, an inverted Medusa, her hair like coils of magma cooling under water.

It's said that when a person has drowned the heart endures even after the brain's been strangled. What rhythms do hearts invent, what slow but ardent tempos can they keep, when no one's left to hear them?

And if, as some after-death experiences attest, the brain persists a while after the last heartbeat, what shape would our final thoughts take as they drift through our silent bodies, for the first time without accompaniment of a drum?

It's taken me several decades, but I've learned to listen to my heart. By this I mean I've learned to listen both to the emotional organ — the timpani who marched me toward a bed where a woman lies waiting, the drummer Kit advised me to follow — and to the biological heart, the gory pump, who toils ever faithfully on my behalf. At night when the anxious chatter of my thoughts makes Nod an impossible destination, I've learned to focus on the stalwart metronome inside me. My heart's spasms feel like a soft pat on my back, the body's show of support. I relax.

And as I pay more attention to my heart, it gradually evades me. The sly organ slows when I hush to it. It insists it is merely an accompanist, not a soloist. The quieter I become, the more it softens, until its seesaw is a lullaby.

In those few still moments when I'm alone with my own modest rhythm, before dreams waltz away with my attention, I'm filled with a love simply for being alive, for the invisible force that squeezes my ventricles, that locks and unlocks the rubine chambers, time after time, with a comforting, palpable *thump*.

Rose Tremain

from *Sacred Country*

Rose Tremain was born in London in 1943. She lives in Norwich, and teaches creative writing at the University of East Anglia. Her first two books, The Fight for Freedom of Women *(1973) and a life of Stalin (1975), were published only in the United States. Since 1976 she has written six novels and two volumes of short stories, among them* Sadler's Birthday *(1976),* The Swimming Pool Season *(1985), and* Sacred Country *(1992). The following excerpts are from* Sacred Country.

The series opens the moment Mary Ward, aged six, realizes with perfect clarity that she's not a girl after all, she is a boy. Over the course of the novel, Mary (renamed Martin) pursues this insistent identity, first in rural England, then in London, and finally in America.

Swaithey is the community in Suffolk, England, where Mary grows up. Cord is her grandfather; Miss McRae is her schoolteacher. Rob is a South African neighbor of hers in London and Edward Harker and Irene are trusted friends from Swaithey days.

1952

THE TWO-MINUTE SILENCE

On February 15th, 1952, at two o'clock in the afternoon, the nation fell silent for two minutes in honour of the dead king. It was the day of his burial.

Traffic halted. Telephones did not ring. Along the radio airwaves came only hushed white noise. In the street markets, the selling of nylons paused. In the Ritz, the serving of luncheon was temporarily suspended. The waiters stood to attention with napkins folded over their arms.

To some, caught on a stationary bus, at a loom gone suddenly still, or at a brass band rehearsal momentarily soundless, the silence was heavy with eternity. Many people wept and they wept not merely for the king but for themselves and for England: for the long, ghastly passing of time.

On the Suffolk farms, a light wet snow began to fall like salt.

The Ward family stood in a field close together. Sonny Ward had not known — because the minute hand had fallen off his watch — at what precise moment to begin the silence. His wife, Estelle, hadn't wanted them to stand round like this out in the grey cold. She'd suggested they stay indoors with a fire to cheer them and the wireless to tell them what to do, but Sonny had said no, they should be out under the sky, to give their prayers an easier route upwards. He said the people of England owed it to the wretched king to speak out for him so that at least he wouldn't stammer in Heaven.

So there they were, gathered round in a potato field: Sonny and Estelle, their daughter, Mary, and their little son, Tim. Pathetic, Sonny thought they looked, pathetic and poor. And the suspicion that his family's silence was not properly synchronised with that of the nation as a whole annoyed Sonny for a long time afterwards. He'd asked his neighbour, Ernie Loomis, to tell him when to begin it, but Loomis had forgotten. Sonny had wondered whether there wouldn't be some sign – a piece of sky writing or a siren from Lowestoft – to give him the order, but none came, so when the hour hand of his watch covered the two, he put down his hoe and said: "Right. We'll have the silence now."

They began it.

The salt snow fell on their shoulders.

It was a silence within a silence already there, but nobody except Mary knew that its memory would last a lifetime.

Mary Ward was six years old. She had small feet and hands and a flat, round face that reminded her mother of a sunflower. Her straight brown hair was held back from her forehead by a tortoiseshell slide. She wore round glasses to correct her faulty vision. The arms of these spectacles pinched the backs of her ears. On the day of the silence she was wearing a tweed coat too short for her, purple mittens, Wellingtons and a woollen head scarf patterned with windmills and blue Dutchmen. Her father, glancing at her blinking vacantly in the sleet, thought her a sad sight.

She had been told to think about King George and pray for him. All she could remember of the king was his head, cut off at the neck on the twopenny stamp, so she started to pray for the stamp, but these prayers got dull and flew away and she turned her head this way and that, wondering if she wasn't going to see, at the edge of her hopeless vision, her pet guineafowl, Marguerite, pecking her dainty way over the ploughed earth.

Estelle, that very morning, had inadvertently sewn a hunk of her thick black hair to some parachute silk with her sewing machine. She had screamed when she saw what she'd done. It was grotesque. It was like a crime against herself. And though now, in the silence, Estelle made herself be quiet, she could still hear her voice screaming somewhere far away. Her head was bowed, but she saw Sonny look up, first at Mary and then at her. And so instead of seeing the dead king lying smart in his naval uniform, she saw herself as she was at that precise moment, big in the flat landscape, beautiful in spite of her hacked hair, a mystery, a woman falling and falling through time and the fall endless and icy. She put her palms together, seeking calm. "At teatime," she whispered, "I shall do that new recipe for flapjacks." She believed her whispering was soundless, but it was not. Estelle's mind often had difficulty distinguishing between thoughts and words said aloud.

Sonny banged his worn flat cap against his thigh. He began to cough. "Shut you up, Estelle!" he said through the cough. "Or else we'll have to start the silence again."

Estelle put her hands against her lips and closed her eyes. When Sonny's cough subsided, he looked down at Tim. Tim, his treasure. Timmy, his boy. The child had sat down on a furrow and was trying to unlace his little boots. Sonny watched as one boot was tugged off, pulling with it a grey sock and revealing Timmy's foot. To Sonny, the soft foot looked boneless. Tim stuck it into the mud, throwing the boot away like a toy.

"Tim!" hissed Mary. "Don't be bad!"

"Shut you up, girl!" said Sonny.

"I can't hear any silence at all," said Estelle.

"Begin it again," ordered Sonny.

So Mary thought, how many minutes is it going to be? Will it get dark with us still standing here?

And then the idea of them waiting there in the field, the snow little by little settling on them and whitening them over, gave Mary a strange feeling of exaltation, as if something were about to happen to her that had never happened to anybody in the history of Suffolk or the world.

She tried another prayer for the king, but the words blew away like paper. She wiped the sleet from her glasses with the back of her mittened hand. She stared at her family, took them in, one, two, three of them, quiet at last but not as still as they were meant to be, not still like the plumed men guarding the king's coffin, not still like bulrushes in a lake. And then, hearing the familiar screech of her guineafowl coming from near the farmhouse, she thought, I have some news for you, Marguerite, I have a secret to tell you, dear, and this is it: I am not Mary. That is a mistake. I am not a girl. I'm a boy.

This was how and when it began, the long journey of Mary Ward.

It began in an unsynchronised silence the duration of which no one could determine, for just as Sonny hadn't known when to begin it, so he couldn't tell when to end it. He just let his family stand out there in the sleet, waiting, and the waiting felt like a long time.

MARY

I was the only boy at Weston Grammar.

There were ninety-seven girls and me.

On the first day, we had to announce our names to the class. The teacher said: "If any of you has a nickname by which you like to be called, then tell us what it is." She said: "My name is Miss Gaul, but I believe I am known as Gallus," and everybody laughed except me because I had never learned a word of Latin. I felt stupid and sad. I imagined Miss McRae saying: If you live in a lighthouse, Mary, there are certain things that may never reach you.

Almost every girl had a nickname. They blushed in turn as they said them. It was embarrassing. The girl next to me said: "My name is Belinda Mulholland, but I am quite often actually called Binky," and I saw her blush spread right up into the roots of her pale hair and down her scalp and into her neck and I thought, saying a thing you didn't really mean to say could be like poliomyelitis entering your veins and you could be crippled by it for ever.

When it came to my turn, I did not blush. I said: "My name is Mary Ward, but I've never been Mary, I have always been Martin, and I would like to be called Martin, please."

Miss Gaul wore her hair in a long plait, fastened around her head like a rope and when I said my name was Martin the rope sprang loose from its kirbygrip and unwound itself.

She said: "Marty? Very well, dear. We shall call you Marty."

And because of the jumping plait, I didn't feel able to contradict her.

The school was a large, grey building, built in Victorian times. When you opened your desk lid, you could breathe history. The inkwells were made of porcelain. In the corridors there were rows and rows of photographs of Old Girls wearing long skirts and the sweet smiles of the dead. At dinner time, the gravy tasted old, as though some mildewed wine had been poured into it. The kitchen staff were Portuguese, descendants of Vasco da Gama.

I liked the school uniform, especially the tie which was red and white and like a man's tie. I looked nicer in my uniform than I'd ever looked in any other clothes and the only bit of myself that I couldn't stand to see were my bare legs between my grey skirt and my grey socks. So I began to walk with my head held very high and my eyes behind my glasses looking out hungrily. And this new way of conducting myself (as Cord might have put it) was mistaken for an invitation to friendship. On the first morning, three girls came up to me at different times and offered to share their sweets with me. But I refused. I said: "No thanks. I don't like sweets," and I walked away. I didn't know how to be anybody's friend.

Then I saw Lindsey Stevens.

She was the tallest person in our class. She had long, heavy hair, tied back in a ribbon. Her eyes were sleepy and kind. You could tell that there had never been a moment in her life when she had not been beautiful. I stared at her until I was worn out and I remembered Miss McRae once saying that beauty can be tiring.

I closed my eyes. A teacher called Miss Whyte with a y was giving us our first physics lesson on earth. She was describing to us the principles of the thermos flask. She said: "The areas of contact between the inner and the outer wall are minimised to limit conduction of heat and the inner surfaces are silvered . . ." and I thought, I will get Lindsey Stevens to be my friend, or I will die.

1961

It was raining in Mary's room. When the lightning came, the rain had a shine on it.

Mary lay and stared at it. She thought, this is not meant to happen. Rain in a room is all wrong.

But it was of no vast significance. She was fifteen and she could see and feel damage all around. It had begun in her. Her flesh had refused to harden as she believed it would. It had disobeyed her mind. In her mind, she was Martin Ward, a lean boy.

She touched her breasts. The skin of them was very white, their texture indescribable, like no other part of her. They seemed like sacs enveloping the embryos of other things, as if something had laid two eggs under her skin and now these parasites were growing on her.

She always touched them when she woke, hoping vainly to find them shrunk or burst or sliced away. She touched them under the bedclothes in the dark, where she couldn't see them. She couldn't stand to look at them. In the day, she wound a crepe bandage round and round them seven times and fastened it with a safety pin. She was Martin in her mind and she hoped that, with the bandages on, it would be her mind that showed.

They were still there, hard yet squashy under her pyjamas. It was raining in her room but nothing else extraordinary had occurred, like the disappearance of her breasts. Mary had studied the monsoon in geography. Rain could bring change. There could be rivers where streets were, with dry goods and silk tassels floating on the water. Some people could be saved from starvation and others ruined. It might be the same in Swaithey, but nothing had happened to her.

Mary got up and went to the window. The next time the lightning came, she could see something large and metal lying on the grass. It was the television aerial. It had lost its original shape. Now, there would be nothing on the television screen for Estelle except a white storm. She would sit down in front of it and there would be no picture and no voices, so she would get up again and go looking for her pills that she carried round with her and put down anywhere and lost.

Mary listened for sounds of her family awake, but nobody seemed to be moving about and she thought this typical of them – a tempest comes and they all stay asleep in their own useless dreams and never hear it. Then, in the morning, they'll be amazed: Oh look, the roof's blown away, the cows have gone mad with fear and reared up in their stalls like stallions, the chickens are swimming! Sonny will swear and shout. Estelle will sit down with her pills and pull grey hairs from her head. Timmy will dry the chickens, one by one, in a teatowel and they will peck his knees.

Mary put on her dressing gown and fetched her torch from her night table. She liked her room. She didn't want it ruined by rain.

The house was silent. Mary tip-toed like a thief. In the kitchen she found Sonny asleep with his head on the table in a puddle of stout. The room smelled of his stout breath. Mary shone her torch on his face. There were bubbles like spittle in his coral ear. Since he'd bought his combine harvester and gone into debt for it, his drinking had got bad. Mary thought, one day, he will fall over on the earth and his ear will hit a stone – a stone that was never picked up and put into a starfish pail – and he will die.

She went to a cupboard and found some bowls. She decided she would set them out in a line under the eaves of her room and watch over them, like a person watching over saucers of spice in a Bombay market. The big monsoon drops would clank into them, making a peculiar kind of music.

1967

MARY:

My lover, Georgia Dickins, was thirty-nine. She worked for a weekly magazine called *Woman's Domain*. She ran the Problem Page. Her nom de plume on the Problem Page was D'Esté Defoe. She thought this a wonderful name, far superior to Georgia Dickins. And her readers liked it. Especially the barren readers. They sometimes put, as a kind of footnote to their Problem: "I hope you do not mind my saying that if God is good enough to give me a beautiful baby daughter I shall christen her D'Esté."

I thought it a ridiculous name. It sounded like a corrupted word, short for Destitute. But I didn't say this. I had to say enough hurtful things already. I had to say: "I don't know whether I love you, Georgia. I would like what I feel to be love, but I have a feeling that it isn't."

She would cry sometimes and her mascara tears would make her face stripy. And then she would catch sight of herself and say: "My God, I'm a wreck. I look like a badger. No wonder no one fucking loves me!"

She taught me to swear and to drink Campari. She showed me St. James's Park and Heal's department store. She tried to get me to love my breasts. She invited me to live with her in her flat in Notting Hill Gate, but I refused. I'd become fond of my building and my grey room. And I didn't want to wake up somewhere else, in a Heal's bed, lying with Georgia.

She was proud of the Problem Page. She said: "D'Esté Defoe is a woman with empathy. Her readers trust her. And she's a professional. She has a team of doctors and psychiatrists advising her. She offers genuine solutions." She talked like this, Georgia. As if she were always advertising something. She told me her flat was nicely situated. She said London was the toast of the world.

I was going to be twenty-one. I was still small. Sometimes I made myself hang from a door lintel, like in the old days. I wanted to reach 5 feet 4 inches. I hadn't given up on any possibility, not even on growing. And now I saw that a moment had arrived for action. I remembered Cord saying: "Without action, Martin, nothing can be begun, what!" He said this sitting beside me on the hearth rug making a paper chain. We were both of us drunk. Drunken words sometimes get remembered because they're unexpectedly wise.

I wrote a letter to the Problem Page. Every letter had to begin "Dear D'Esté Defoe." I made several drafts of my letter and then I typed it out in the *Liberty* offices, during a lull in rejections. This is how it went:

Dear D'Esté Defoe,

You may feel shocked by the contents of this letter. My problem is not one shared by any of your other readers, as far as I can tell.

I am a woman of twenty-one. Or rather, my body is a woman's body, but I have never felt like a woman or colluded with my body's deceit. In my mind, I am, and have been from childhood, male. This belief is an ineradicable thing. I am in the wrong gender.

I dress as a man. I loathe my breasts and all that is female about me. I have never been sexually attracted to a man. I do not even dream of Sean Connery.

Please help me. Please tell whether anyone else has ever felt this? Please tell me whether it could ever be possible to alter my body to fit my mind. Since the age of six, I have suffered very much and I want, at last, to take some action. I have no friends in whom I can confide.

I signed myself "Divided, Devon." I thought D'Esté Defoe would be attracted by the letter D. I had no faith in Georgia, but it was the team of doctors and counsellors she had mentioned that gave me hope.

The following evening I spent in the nicely situated flat. Georgia showed me a new kind of grapefruit she had discovered, with pink flesh. She loved new things. As she cut my half of the pink grapefruit she said: "D'Esté had an extraordinary letter today. From a transsexual."

I had never heard this word before. I thought, if there's a word for this, then it exists outside me, it exists in other people. I'm not alone.

Then I thought, is the time actually coming, is the date actually coming at last for the invention of Martin Ward?

It was difficult to concentrate on anything, on the grapefuit and then on Georgia's lips, tasting of Revlon. I wished I was in my grey room, sitting absolutely still.

Two weeks later, an answer to my letter appeared in *Woman's Domain:*

Dear Divided, Devon,

I have given a great deal of thought to your problem, and no, you are not unique. Others have suffered as you are suffering and have been helped by counselling and, in some cases, by surgery. The first male-to-female sex change operation was performed on an American GI, George Jorgensen, in 1952 and he/she is now living happily as Christine Jorgensen. In 1958 it was revealed that ship's doctor, Michael Dillon, had been born Laura Maude Dillon and had changed herself surgically.

But a word of warning, Divided, Devon. The route to surgery is long. And it is not a route that all can take. Your first step must be to see your GP and ask him to refer you to a psychiatrist specialising in sex counselling. Only he will be able to ascertain what path is the right one for you. Only he will be able to discover whether you could adapt to life as a member of the opposite sex. Put yourself in his hands and he will help you towards your future.

Good luck and *bon voyage!*

D'Esté Defoe

The person in whose hands I put myself was called Dr. Beales. The teams of experts at *Woman's Domain* found him for me.

I had thought all people like him had consulting rooms in Harley Street, but Dr. Beales did not. He had his consulting room in Twickenham and the journey there from Earl's Court took an hour and a half. Twickenham isn't really even in London, but in Middlesex. By the side of Dr. Beales's house flowed a slow bit of the Thames, brown as tea. The smell of it was rank. It reminded me of the smell of the Suffolk ditch where I'd found my green tennis ball. And after my first visit to Beales, I had a dream of my childhood on the old farm. I was picking stones and dusk was falling.

Dr. Beales had a face like a kitten, squashed and small but with bright eyes. He was about forty. His hair was black. He had a habit of pinching the slack skin under his chin. He dressed like a school teacher, in brown corduroy. He sat me down, within sight of the water, on a leather chair. He stared at me. He said: "You're very small. There aren't many men of your height."

I said: "Growing is something I've been trying to do for years and years."

He smiled. He had one of those smiles that vanishes the moment it's there, like English spring sunlight. He began to write notes on a pad. I imagined he was describing me to himself – the open-neck shirt I wore, my jeans and my jeans jacket, my heavy-frame glasses, my brown hair cut in a Beatles style by Rob, my look of dread.

He invited me to relax, to make myself comfortable in the chair, to look out at the water. I felt tired and far away from anywhere that I knew. The dirty river wasn't a consoling sight. I thought, if Rob were here he would say: "It's a bleddy cesspit, Mart. Nothing can stay alive in it."

Dr. Beales began asking me questions. He asked me whether I could mend an electric fuse and whether I knew the rules of cricket. He said: "Do you enjoy or repudiate domestic tasks, such as hoovering?" He said: "Are you jealous of men's superior strength?" He said: "Have you ever been train spotting?"

I kept one eye on the water, imagining shrimps and water snakes trying to have an existence there and drowning in sewage and floating to the surface, like feathers and like rope. I said that I had never possessed a Hoover. I said that I thought men used their strength to annihilate women, as my father had tried to annihilate me. I said: "If I'd let myself be a true girl in my childhood, I would have been destroyed."

Then Dr. Beales said: "I'd like you to tell me about your parents."

I turned from the river and stared at his kitten face. I was about to say that I still had dreams of being Sir Galahad and going to rescue my mother from Mountview and from Sonny when Dr. Beales gave me one of his fleeting smiles and said: "You know that they're going to have to be brought into this, don't you? Family support for what you're attempting to do is vital. Patients whose families are opposed have to fight an almost impossible battle."

So then I saw them arriving here: Sonny in his farm clothes, smelling of beer; Estelle in a polka-dot dress with her grey hair in a tangle.

I said: "They're dead."

"Ah," said Dr. Beales and he wrote this down – parents dead.

I was going to tell him that my father had been killed on the Rhine, but I realised in time that if he had died in the war I wouldn't have been born. So I thought then, I won't tell him about my life as it's been, but as it might have been. I'll tell him a story.

I said. "I was six years old when they died. They died in a plane going from Southampton to Cherbourg. The airline was called Silver City. You could put cars into those planes and fly them to France. My parents' car was a Humber Super Snipe and it died in the plane also."

Dr. Beales wrote this down, too – car dead.

"What happened to you then?" he asked.

I thought of Cord and Miss McRae and I knew that neither of them would want to come to Twickenham. I said: "I went to live with a family called Harker. They had been friends of my mother's. Edward Harker is a very wise person and he knows about my predicament and he would come and see you if this was necessary."

"And your adoptive mother?"

"Irene. I've never talked to Irene. Irene is very simple and good."

"If she's 'good,' then she might be in sympathy with you?"

"No. It'd be beyond her. Beyond her understanding."

"You can't be sure of this."

"Yes, I can."

"But she'll have to know, in the end."

"You mean, in the end when I'm a man?"

"You will never be a man. Not a true biological male. It's important that you understand this. Do you understand this?"

"Yes."

"You will — if you proceed, if I recommend that you proceed with hormone treatment and eventually surgery — be able to pass as a man in ninety-nine per cent of social situations. But you will not be a man. Nor will you any longer *be* a woman. Have you heard me? Are you keeping relaxed? Stay looking at the water while you answer."

I looked at the water. A barge was passing. Its cargo appeared to be stones. "What *will* I be?" I said.

Dr. Beales pinched and pulled his bit of neck skin. I imagined him old, looking like a turkey. "You will be a partially constructed male. The world will take you for a man and you will look like a man — to yourself. And so your internal conviction of your essential maleness will receive confirmation when you look in the mirror — and your anguish will cease, or so it is hoped."

The barge had gone by and was out of sight. The river banks were washed with the brown waves of its wake. I thought, by the time the water is quite still again, my fifty minutes here will be over.

I said: "Is this what has happened in the past?"

"What do you mean?"

"To other people like me — that their anguish ceased?"

"It is assumed," said Dr. Beales, "from what they told me. But we are running ahead of ourselves in any assumption about you. Because for all I know at the moment your idea of your maleness could be a delusion or you could be lying. I know nothing yet."

I said: "I lied about one thing."

"Yes?"

"About cricket. I do know its basic rules. My adoptive father, Edward Harker, makes cricket bats and he taught the rules to me and I used to practice bowling in his backyard."

"Oh yes?" said Beales. "What did you bowl, spinners or bouncers?"

"Spinners," I said. "I was a spinner and by the time I was twelve Edward was afraid to face me at the crease."

FORMS OF ADDRESS

Change didn't age Mary. It seemed to take her back in time.

This was the first thing she noticed – that she looked younger. Her body lost bulk. Small as she was, she began to look lanky, like a youth of thirteen or fourteen. And the hair that grew on her upper lip and in a little line around her jaw was like the hair of puberty, a faint brown fuzz.

She'd expected her breasts to shrivel. She'd imagined them looking like the breasts of an Indian woman of the Amazon forest she'd seen in a photograph at the Natural History Museum. The woman's age was thought to be ninety-nine. Instead, Mary's breasts got harder and smaller. They looked like the breasts of Lindsey Stevens three years before she had met Ranulf Morrit.

She felt light, almost weightless. She had a desire to run. The slowness of people in the street amazed her. She had dreams of her green tennis ball, how she used to hurl it away from her and run after it. In her lunch hours, she ran all the way to Hyde Park, then along the Serpentine to the boathouse. It was autumn in London. There were hardly any boaters.

One day, the boat attendant said to her "Want to take one out, lad?"

She went to see Sterns.

"Well?" he said.

She described her running, her feelings of weightlessness. She looked at the fish and saw them all flying and darting among their pieces of coral, as though her words had disturbed the water.

Sterns sat and smiled at her. "Good," he said. "This is working benevolently. Creatively, one could say."

"Will I grow?" said Mary. "Boys of fourteen grow."

Sterns tipped his head back and laughed. His voice was gentle, but his laugh was loud.

"No," he said, "but you may grow in spirit."

"What do you mean?" said Mary.

"I've seen this," said Sterns, "in most of those I've helped – usually males who wish to become female, but one other like yourself. It has to do with being always a little outside the world. When you are apart from something it is easier to be wise about it."

"I don't want to be 'apart from the world.' That's what I've felt all my life."

"Only because you have felt divided – apart from yourself, if you like. Now, soon, your two selves will be better integrated but your status in the world will still be a special status because you will have seen the world from two different perspectives. I needn't remind you that this isn't possible for most of us."

She told Sterns about the boat attendant. She said: "The word 'lad' stabbed me with pleasure."

Nadezhda Durova

translated from the Russian by Mary Fleming Zirin

from *The Cavalry Maiden*

Nadezhda Durova was born in Russia in 1783, the eldest child of a military family. From early on she was passionate about freedom and the military life, and extremely uninterested in such female accomplishments as sewing, knitting, and making lace.

In 1806, at the age of twenty-three (though she pretended to be younger), Durova cut off her hair, dressed herself in Cossack uniform, and ran off to join the Russian army. She experienced nine years of service in the war against Napoleon, and later wrote a series of books based on her adventures, among them, The Cavalry Maiden *(1836). In later life she continued to dress as a man. She wore a frock coat, smoked a pipe, and kept her hair close-cropped. Until the end of the First World War she was the only woman to win the St. George Cross. She died in 1866 and was buried with full military honors.*

MY CHILDHOOD YEARS

My mother, born Aleksandrovicheva, was one of the prettiest girls in Little Russia. At the end of her fifteenth year, throngs of suitors came to seek her hand. My mother's heart preferred hussar Captain Durov to all the many others, but unfortunately this was not the choice of her father, a proud, arbitrary Ukrainian *pan*.[1] He told my mother to put out of her head the fantastic idea of marrying a *Muscovite*, and a soldier at that. My grandfather ruled his family with an iron hand: any order of his was to be blindly obeyed, and there was no possibility of either placating him or changing any of his announced intentions. The consequence of this unreasonable severity was that one stormy autumn night my mother, who slept in the same room as her elder sister, stealthily rose

---

1. Ivan Il'ich Aleksandrovich (died c. 1789) was a provincial civil servant who had an estate near Pirjatin in the Poltava region. Durova's mother, Nadezhda, was born about 1765 and died, according to her daughter's account, in 1807. The huzzar was Andrej Vasil'evich Durov, born in Ufa province to the descendants of a Polish family (originally Turowski) who were resettled there from their native Smolensk-Polotsk region after Russia hegemony began in the 1650s.

from her bed, picked up her cloak and hood and, in stocking feet, crept with bated breath past her sister's bed, quietly opened the door into the drawing room, quietly closed it, dashed nimbly across the room and, opening the door into the garden, flew like an arrow down the long lane of chestnuts that led to a wicket gate. My mother hastily unlocked this little door and threw herself into the captain's arms. He was waiting for her with a carriage hitched to four strong horses who, like the wind then raging, rushed them down the Kiev road.

They were married in the first village and drove directly to Kiev, where Durov's regiment was quartered. Although my mother's act was excusable in light of her youth, love, and the virtues of my father, who was a very handsome man of gentle disposition and captivating manners, it was so contrary to the patriarchal customs of the Ukrainian land that in his first outbreak of rage my grandfather pronounced a curse on his daughter.

For two years my mother never stopped writing to her father to beg his forgiveness, but to no avail: he would hear none of it, and his rage grew in proportion to their attempts to mollify it. My parents finally gave up all hope of appeasing a man who considered obstinacy a mark of character. They ceased writing letters to her implacable father and would have resigned themselves to their lot, but my mother's pregnancy revived her flagging courage. She began to hope that the birth of her child would restore her to paternal favor.

My mother passionately desired a son, and she spent her entire pregnancy indulging in the most seductive daydreams. "I will give birth to a son as handsome as a cupid," she would say. "I'll name him Modest. I will nurse him myself, bring him up, teach him, and my son, my darling Modest, will be the joy of my life. . . ." So my mother dreamed but, as her time drew near, the pangs preceding my birth came as a most disagreeable surprise to her. They had had no place in her dreams and produced on her a first unfavorable impression of me. It became necessary to send for an *accoucheur*, who insisted on letting blood. The idea was extremely frightening to my mother, but there was nothing she could do about it; she had to yield to necessity. Soon after the bloodletting I came into the world, the poor creature whose arrival destroyed my mother's dreams and dashed all her hopes.

"Give me my child!" said my mother, as soon as she had recovered somewhat from her pain and fear. The child was brought and placed on her lap. But alas! this was no son as handsome as a cupid. This was a daughter – and a *bogatyr* of a daughter at that![2] I was unusually large, had thick black hair, and was bawling loudly. Mother pushed me off her lap and turned to the wall.

In a few days Mama recovered and, yielding to the advice of her friends, ladies of the regiment, decided to nurse me herself. They told her that a mother who nurses her child at the breast finds that the act alone is enough to make her begin loving it. I was brought; my mother took me from the maid's arms, put me to her breast, and gave me to suck. But I evidently sensed the lack of maternal love in that nourishment and therefore refused her every effort to make me nurse. Mama decided to exercise patience to overcome my obstinacy and went on holding me at the breast, but, bored by my continued refusal, she stopped watching me and began talking to a lady who was visiting her. At this point, evidently guided by the fate that intended me for a soldier's uniform, I suddenly gripped my mother's breast and squeezed it as hard as I could with my gums. My mother gave a piercing shriek, jerked me from her breast, threw me into the arms of her maid, and fell face down in the pillows. "Take her away; get that worthless child out of my sight, and never show her again," said Mama, waving her hand and burying her head in a pillow.

I was four months old when the regiment in which my father was serving received orders to go to Kherson. Since this was a domestic march, Papa took his family with him. I was entrusted to the supervision and care of my mother's chambermaid, a girl of her own age. During the day the maid sat with Mama in the carriage, holding me on her lap. She fed me cow's milk from a bottle and swaddled me so tightly that my face turned blue and my eyes were bloodshot. At our night's halts I rested, because I was handed over to a peasant woman brought in from the village who unswaddled me, put me to her breast, and slept with me all night. Thus after each day's march I had a new wetnurse.

Neither the changing wetnurses nor the agonizing swaddling impaired my health. I was very robust and vigorous, but incredibly vociferous as well. One day my mother was totally out of sorts; I had kept her awake all night. The march started at daybreak and Mama settled down to sleep in the carriage, but I began crying again and, despite all my nurses's attempts to comfort me, bawled louder by the hour. Vexed beyond measure, Mama flew into a rage and,

2. *Bogatyrs* were the warrior heroes of the Russian epic songs called *byliny*.

snatching me from the arms of the maid, threw me out the window! The hussars cried out in horror, jumped off their horses, and picked me up covered with blood and showing no sign of life. They would have returned me to the carriage, but Papa galloped up to them, took me from their arms and, in floods of tears, placed me on his saddle. Trembling and weeping, as pale as a corpse, he rode on without saying a word or turning his head in the direction where my mother rode. To the astonishment of everyone, I came back to life and, against all expectations, was not permanently maimed. The shock of the fall just left me bleeding from the nose and mouth. Papa raised his eyes to heaven with a joyful feeling of gratitude, and, clutching me to his breast, he went over to the carriage and said to my mother, "Give thanks to God that you are not a murderess! Our daughter is alive, but I will never return her to your power; I'll care for her myself." And with this he rode off and carried me with him until that night's halt without a word or glance toward my mother.

From that memorable day of my life my father entrusted me to God's providence and the care of flank hussar Astakhov, who was always at Papa's side in quarters as well as on the march.[3] I was in my mother's room only at night; as soon as Papa got up and went out, I was taken away, too. My tutor Astakhov carried me around all day, taking me into the squadron stables and sitting me on the horses, giving me a pistol to play with, and brandishing his saber while I clapped my hands and laughed out loud at the sight of the scattering sparks and glittering steel. In the evening he took me to hear the musicians who played various pieces at dusk, and I listened until I fell asleep. Only slumbering could I be brought back inside. If I were not sleeping, I became numb with fear and clung howling to Astakhov's neck at the mere sight of my mother's room. From the time of my aerial journey out the carriage window, Mama no longer interfered in any way in my life. She had another daughter to console her, this one really as handsome as a cupid and, as the saying goes, the apple of her eye.

Soon after my birth my grandfather forgave my mother and did so in the most solemn way: he went to Kiev, asked the archbishop to absolve him of his

---

3. Durova's biographer, Colonel Saks, says that the practice of using personal orderlies as nannies to officers' children was still common in the first decade of the twentieth century.

impetuous oath never to pardon his daughter, and, once he had obtained pastoral absolution, finally wrote to my mother that he forgave her and blessed her marriage and the child born of it. He asked her to come and see him both to accept the paternal blessing in person and to receive her dowry. My mother had no way of taking advantage of this invitation until Papa was forced to retire. I was four and a half when my father realized that he would have to leave the army. There were two cradles in his quarters in addition to my cot; such a family made life on the march impossible. He went to Moscow to seek a position in the civil service, and my mother took me and the other two children to live with her father until her husband's return.[4]

Once she took me from Astakhov's arms, my mother never knew a single calm or cheerful moment. Each day my strange sallies and knightly spirit angered her. I had memorized all the words of command and was wild about horses, and when my mother tried to make me knit shoelaces, I wept and begged her to give me a pistol, as I said, *to click*. In short, I was making the best possible use of the upbringing Astakhov had given me. Every day my martial propensities grew stronger, and every day my mother liked me less. I never forgot anything that I had learned in the constant company of the hussars; I ran and galloped around the room in all directions, shouting at the top of my voice "Squadron! To the right, face! From your places, charge – CHARGE!" My aunts laughed out loud and Mama, driven to desperation by it all, could not contain her vexation. She took me to her room, stood me in the corner, and drove me to bitter tears with abuse and threats.

My father obtained a post as mayor of a district capital and moved his entire family there.[5] My mother, who had come to dislike me wholeheartedly, seemed bent on doing everything she could to intensify and confirm my already invincible passion for freedom and the military life. She never allowed me to enjoy the fresh air of the garden, or even leave her side for half an hour. I had to sit in her room all day and weave lace. She herself taught me to sew and knit, and when

---

4. Children continued to be born to the Durovs regularly every two years or so until the turn of the century. Only four of them survived to adulthood: Nadezhda; Kleopatra, born in 1791; Vasilij, the first and only son, 1799; and Evgenija, 1801.

5. The city where Durova grew up was Sarapul, on the Kama river in the western foothills of the Urals.

she saw that I had neither inclination nor skill for those pursuits and that everything ripped and broke in my hands, she lost her temper, flew into a rage, and whipped those hands painfully.

I turned ten. My mother was careless enough to tell my father in my presence that she no longer had the strength to cope with Astakhov's ward, the hussar upbringing was deep-rooted, the fire in my eyes frightened her, and she would rather see me dead than with such propensities. Papa replied that I was still a child, and she should pay no attention to me. As the years went on, I would take on other propensities, and all this would pass. "Don't take these childish ways so much to heart, my friend," said Papa. But fate decreed that my mother would not believe or follow her husband's good advice. She continued to keep me in seclusion, denying me every youthful joy. I submitted in silence, but oppression matured my mind. I resolved firmly to shake off my heavy yoke and began in an adult way to work out plans for doing so. I decided to take every means to learn to ride horseback and shoot firearms and then, in disguise, to leave my father's house. In order to begin realizing the radical change in my life that I contemplated, I never missed a chance to slip away from my mother's supervision. These chances came whenever visitors arrived to see Mama. They kept her occupied and I, beside myself with joy, ran out into the garden to my arsenal – that is, the dark corner behind the shrubbery where I stored my bow and arrows, a saber, and a broken gun. Busy with my weapons, I was oblivious to everything else on earth, and only the shrill cries of the maids searching for me brought me running in alarm to meet them. They led me to the room where punishment was always waiting.

Thus passed the two years until I turned twelve. Just then Papa bought himself a saddlehorse, an almost untameable Circassian stallion. My father, who was an excellent rider, broke this handsome beast himself and named him Alcides. Now all my plans, intentions, and desires were concentrated on this steed. I decided to do all I could to accustom him to me – and I succeeded. I gave him bread, sugar, and salt; I took oats from the coachman on the sly and spread them in his manger; I stroked and caressed him, speaking to him as if he could understand me, until at last I had the haughty steed following me as meekly as a lamb.

Almost every day I got up at dawn, stealthily left my room, and ran to the stable. Alcides greeted me with a whinny. I gave him bread and sugar and led him out into the yard. Then I brought him over to the porch and mounted his back from the steps. His quick starts, frisks, and snorts did not alarm me in the least; I held onto his mane and let him run with me all around the yard. I had no fear that he would carry me outside the gates, because they were still locked. On one occasion this pastime was interrupted by the arrival of the groom who, with a shriek of fear and astonishment, rushed to stop Alcides as he galloped past with me. But the steed arched his head, reared, and broke into a run around the yard, frisking and kicking. It was fortunate for me that Efim was so numb with fear that he lost the use of his voice; otherwise his shout would have alarmed the household and drawn me harsh punishment. I quieted Alcides easily, caressing him with my voice and patting and stroking him. He slowed to a walk and, when I embraced his neck and pressed my face against it, he stopped at once because this was the way I always dismounted or, more accurately, slid down off him. Now Efim approached to take him, muttering through his teeth that he would tell my mother, but I promised to give him all my pocket money if he would say nothing and permit me to lead Alcides back to the stable. At this promise Efim's face cleared; he smiled wryly, stroked his beard, and said, "Well, so be it, if that rogue obeys you better than he does me!" Triumphantly I led Alcides into the stable and, to Efim's astonishment, the savage steed followed me meekly, arching his neck and bending his head to nibble lightly at my hair or shoulder.

With each passing day I grew more bold and enterprising, afraid of nothing on earth except my mother's wrath. It seemed quite odd to me that other girls of my age were frightened of being left alone in the dark; on the contrary, I was prepared in the dead of night to go into a graveyard, a forest, a deserted house, a cave, or a dungeon. In short, there was nowhere I would not have gone as boldly at night as in the daytime. Although I, like other children, had been told tales of ghosts, corpses, wood goblins, robbers, and water nymphs who tickled people to death, and although I believed this nonsense with all my heart, none of it frightened me. On the contrary, I thirsted for dangers and longed to be surrounded by them. If I had had the least freedom, I would have gone looking for them, but my mother's vigilant eye followed my every step and impulse.

One day Mama and some ladies went for an outing into the dense pine forest on the far side of the Kama. She took me with her, as she put it, to keep me from breaking my neck alone at home. This was the very first time in my life that I had been taken out into the open where I could see dense forest and vast fields and the wide river! I could barely catch my breath for joy, and we no sooner came into the forest than I, out of my mind with rapture, immediately ran off and kept running until the voices of the company were no longer audible. Then my joy was complete and perfect: I ran, frisked, picked flowers, and climbed to the tips of tall trees to see farther. I climbed slender birches and, holding tight to the crown, leaped off; the sapling set me down lightly on the ground.[6] Two hours flew like two minutes! In the meantime they were searching for me and calling me in chorus. I heard them, but how could I part with such captivating freedom? At last, completely exhausted, I returned to the company. I had no trouble locating them, because the voices had never stopped calling me. I found my mother and the other ladies in a terrible state of anxiety. They cried out in joy when they caught sight of me, but Mama, who guessed from my contented face that I had not strayed, but gone off of my own volition, flew into a violent rage. She poked my back and called me a damned pest of a girl, sworn to anger her always and everywhere!

We returned home. Mama pulled me by the ear all the way from the parlor to her bedroom. She took me over to the lace pillow and ordered me to get to work without straightening up or looking around. "Just you wait, you wretch, I'll tie you on a rope and give you nothing but bread to eat!" With these words she went to tell Papa about what she called my monstrous act, and I was left to sort bobbins, set pins, and think about the glories of nature which I had just seen for the first time in all their majesty and beauty. From that day, although my mother's supervision and strictness became even more unremitting, they could no longer either frighten or restrain me.

From morning to night I sat over work which, I must confess, was the vilest imaginable because, unlike other girls, I could not, would not, and did not want to acquire the skill, but ripped, ruined, and tangled it until before me lay a canvas ball with a repulsive, snarled strip stretching across it – my bobbin-lace. I sat patiently over it all day, patiently because my plan was prepared and my intentions resolute. At nightfall, when the house quieted down, the doors were locked, and the light in Mama's room went out, I got up, dressed stealthily,

6. . . . And climb back branches up a snow-white trunk
   Toward heaven, till the tree could bear no more,
   But dipped its top and set me down again. – ROBERT FROST, *"Birches"*

sneaked out across the back porch, and ran straight to the stable. There I took Alcides, led him through the garden to the cattleyard, mounted him, and rode out down a narrow lane straight to the riverbank and Startsev mountain. Then I dismounted again and led Alcides uphill, holding him by the halter because I didn't know how to bridle him and had no way of getting him to climb the mountain of his own volition. I led him by the halter across the precipitous slope until I reached a level spot, where I looked for a stump or hillock from which to remount. Then I slapped Alcides' neck and clicked my tongue until the good steed broke into a gallop, a run, and even a breakneck dash.

At the first hint of dawn I returned home, put the horse in the stable, and went to sleep without undressing. This was what led at last to the discovery of my nocturnal excursions. The maid who took care of me kept finding me fully clothed in bed every morning and told my mother, who undertook to find out how and why this came about. She herself saw me going out at midnight fully clothed and, to her inexpressible horror, leading the wicked stallion out of the stable! She thought I must be sleepwalking and did not dare stop me or call out for fear of alarming me. She ordered the manservant and Efim to keep an eye on me, and she herself went to Papa's room, roused him, and told him what had happened. My father, astonished, got up hastily to go and see this singular occurrence for himself. But it all ended sooner than they expected: Alcides and I were led back in triumph, each to his proper place. The servant whom Mother had ordered to follow me saw me trying to mount the horse and, unlike Mama, decided that I was no sleepwalker. He came out of ambush and asked me, "And where are you going, miss?"

After this affair my mother wanted without fail to rid herself of my presence at any cost and decided to take me to my old grandmother Aleksandrovicheva in Little Russia. I had entered my fourteenth year by then. I was tall, slim, and shapely, but my martial spirit was sketched on my features and, although I had white skin, bright rosy cheeks, sparkling eyes, and black brows, every day my mirror and Mama told me that I was very ugly. My face was pitted from smallpox, my features irregular, and Mother's continual repression of my freedom, her strict and at times even cruel treatment of me, had marked my countenance with an expression of fear and sadness. Perhaps I would at last have forgotten all my hussar mannerisms and become an ordinary girl like the rest if my mother had not kept depicting woman's lot in such a dismal way. In my presence she would describe the fate of that sex in the most prejudicial terms: woman, in her opinion, must be born, live, and die in slavery; eternal bondage, painful dependence, and repression of every sort were her destiny from the cradle to the grave; she was full of weaknesses, devoid of accomplishments, and capable of nothing. In short, woman was the most unhappy, worthless, and contemptible creature on earth! This description made my head reel. I resolved, even at the cost of my life, to part company from the sex I thought to be under God's curse. Papa, too, often said, "If I had a son instead of Nadezhda, I shouldn't have to worry about my old age; he would be my staff in the evening of my days." I would be ready to weep at these words from the father I loved so extravagantly. These two contradictory emotions – love for my father and aversion to my own sex – troubled my young soul with equal force. With a resolve and constancy rare in one so young I set about working out a plan to escape the sphere prescribed by nature and custom to the female sex.

[Editor's note: After the exploits described above, Durova lived for several months with her grandmother in Little Russia, and then with a religious-minded aunt. While she was gone, her father started an affair with the daughter of a local townsman. Her mother sent for Durova, hoping her presence would help restore family unity. But the plan did not succeed. Durova's father never returned to his wife, and her mother died young, aged only thirty-five, still mourning the husband she had lost.]

My mother, who no longer took any pleasure in society, led a reclusive life. I took advantage of this circumstance to win permission from my father to ride horseback. Papa ordered a Cossack *chekmen* tailored for me and gave me his Alcides.[7] From that time on I was always my father's companion on his excursions outside the city. He took pleasure in teaching me to ride handsomely, keeping a firm seat in the saddle and managing the horse skillfully. I was a quick student. Papa admired my ease, skill, and fearlessness. He said that I was the living image of him as a youth and that, had I been born a boy, I would have been the staff of his old age and an honor to his name. This set my head awhirl, and this time for good! I was no child; I had turned sixteen. The seductive

---

7. *Chekmen,* a long tunic with a fitted waist.

pleasures of society, life in Little Russia, and Kiriak's black eyes faded from my memory like a dream; brightly colored scenes of my childhood in camp among the hussars were sketched in my imagination instead. It all revived in my soul. I could not understand why I had not thought of my plan for nearly two years. My grief-stricken mother now described woman's lot in even more horrific colors. Martial ardor flared in my soul with incredible force; my mind swarmed with dreams, and I began searching actively for means to realize my previous intention: to become a warrior and a son to my father and to part company forever from the sex whose sad lot and eternal dependence had begun to terrify me.[8]

Before Mama went to Perm to seek treatment, a Cossack regiment arrived in our city to suppress the Tatars' incessant thievery and murder.[9] Papa often invited the colonel and his officers to dinner and went for rides with them outside the town, but I took the precaution never to take part in these excursions. I had to be sure that they never saw me in the *chekmen* and had no idea how I looked in men's clothing. I had a flash of inspiration when the Cossacks arrived in the city. Now I saw a sure way to carry out the plan I had undertaken so long ago. I saw the possibility of waiting for the Cossacks' departure and joining them for the journey to areas where regular army regiments were stationed.[10]

At last the decisive time came to act according to the plan as I had worked it out. The Cossacks received the order to move out, and they left on September 15, 1806. Their first full day's halt would be some fifty versts from the city. The seventeenth was my name-day, and the day on which, through fate, coincidence of circumstance, or invincible propensity, it was fixed for me to quit my father's

---

8. During the seven years missing from this account of her years at home, Durova married Visilij Chernov, a civil servant, on October 25, 1801. The birth of their son Ivan on January 7, 1803, was registered in Sarapul. After her husband was transferred to Irbit, Durova left him and returned to her father's house.

9. The Cossacks were people, mainly of Ukrainian and Russian stock, who had gradually been granted land on the frontiers and an autonomy unknown in Russia proper in exchange for service as auxiliary mounted police and cavalry.

10. By mid-1806 there was a strong probability that the Cossacks would be sent to Russia's western borders to reinforce the armies preparing to check the French in Prussia.

house and take up an entirely new way of life.[11] On September 17, I awoke before dawn and sat by my window to await its appearance; it might well be the last I ever saw in my own land. What awaited me in the turbulent world? Would not my mother's curse and my father's grief pursue me? Would they survive? Could they await the realization of my colossal scheme? How horrible it would be if their death took from me the goal of my actions! These thoughts now clustered and now passed one after another through my head. My heart constricted and tears glistened on my lashes. Just then dawn broke. Its scarlet glow quickly flooded the sky, and its beautiful light, flowing into my room, lit up the objects there: my father's saber, hanging on the wall directly opposite the window, seemed to catch fire. My spirits revived. I took the saber off the wall, unsheathed it, and looked at it, deep in thought. This saber had been my toy when I was still in swaddling-clothes, the comfort and exercise of my adolescent years; why should it not now be my defense and glory in the military sphere? "I will wear you with honor," I said, kissed the blade, and returned it to its scabbard. The sun rose. That day Mama presented me with a gold chain, and Papa, three hundred rubles; even my little brother gave me his gold watch. As I accepted my parents' gifts, I thought sorrowfully that they had no idea that they were outfitting me for a distant and dangerous road.

I spent the day with my girl friends. At eleven o'clock in the evening I came to say good-night to Mama as I usually did before going to bed. Unable to suppress my emotions, I kissed her hands several times and clasped them to my heart, something I had never done before nor dared to do. Although Mama didn't love me, she was moved by these extraordinary effusions of childlike affection and obedience; kissing me on the head, she said, *"Go with God!"* These words held a great significance for me, who had never before heard a single affectionate word from my mother. I took them as a blessing, kissed her hand for the last time, and left.

My rooms were in the garden. I occupied the ground floor of our little garden house, and Papa lived upstairs. He was in the habit of coming to see me for half an hour every evening. He enjoyed hearing me tell him where I had gone and what I had been doing or reading. Now, as I waited for my father's customary

11. The routine on long marches was two or three days on the road, bivouacking at night, for each full day of rest in a populated settlement. Thus Durova's plan was to reach the site of the Cossacks' September 17th halt before they moved on early the following morning.

visit, I laid my Cossack apparel on the bed behind the curtain, set an armchair by the stove, and stood beside it to wait for Papa to come to his rooms. Soon I heard the rustle of leaves under the footsteps of someone coming down the lane. My heart leaped! The door opened, and Papa came in. "Why are you so pale?" he asked, sitting down in the armchair. "Are you well?"

With an effort I suppressed the sigh that threatened to rend my breast. This was the last time that my father would come into my room with the assurance of finding his daughter there. Tomorrow he would pass it in grief, with a shudder. It would hold only a sepulchral void and silence!

Papa looked fixedly at me, "But what's wrong with you? You must be ill."

I said that I was only tired and chilled.

"Why don't you have them heat your room? It's getting damp and cold." After a short silence Papa asked, "Why don't you order Efim to run Alcides on a lunge? There's no getting near him. You yourself haven't ridden him for a long time, and you won't permit anyone else to do it. He's so restive that he rears up even in his stall; you really must exercise him."

I said that I would order it done and fell silent again.

"You seem melancholy, my friend. Goodnight; go to bed," said Papa, getting up and kissing my forehead. He put one arm around me and pressed me to his breast. I kissed both his hands, trying to hold back the tears which were already flooding my eyes. The quivering of my body betrayed the emotions in my heart. Alas! Papa ascribed it to the cold. "You see, you're chilled through," he said. I kissed his hands once more. "My sweet daughter!" said Papa, patting my cheek. He went out. I knelt beside the armchair he had sat in and bowed to the ground before it, kissing and washing with my tears the spot where his foot had rested.

Half an hour later, when my sorrow had abated somewhat, I got up to take off my female clothing. I went over to the mirror, cut off my curls, and put them away in a drawer. I took off my black satin dressing-gown and began putting on my Cossack uniform. After I had tied the black silk sash around my waist and put on the high cap with a crimson crown, I spent a quarter of an hour studying my transformed appearance. My cropped hair gave me a completely different countenance. I was certain that nobody would ever suspect my sex.[12]

---

12. Durova's service record (Nov. 6, 1807) describes her as about 5'5" tall and having a swarthy, pock-marked face, light brown hair, and hazel eyes.

A loud rustle of leaves and the snort of a horse told me that Efim was leading Alcides into the rear yard. For the last time I stretched my arms to the image of the Mother of God which had received my prayers for so many years and went out. The door of my father's house finally closed behind me, and – who knows? – perhaps it might never be open to me again!

I ordered Efim to take Alcides by the direct road to Startsev mountain and wait for me at the edge of the forest. I ran hastily to the bank of the Kama and dropped my dressing-gown there, leaving it on the sand with all the trappings of female dress. I was not so barbarous as to intend for my father to think that I had drowned, and I was convinced he would not do so. I only wanted to make it possible for him to answer without confusion any embarrassing questions from our short-witted acquaintances. After leaving the clothing on the bank, I took a goat track which led directly uphill. The night was cold and clear, and the moon was shining at its fullest. I stopped for one last look at the beautiful and majestic view that opened out from the mountain: beyond the river, Perm and Orenburg provinces were visible to a boundless distance. Vast, dark forests and mirror lakes were displayed as if in a painting. The city at the foot of the precipitous mountain slumbered in the midnight hush. The moon's rays played on and were reflected from the gilt domes of the cathedral and shone on the roof of the house where I grew up. . . . What were my father's thoughts now? Did his heart tell him that tomorrow his beloved daughter would no longer come to wish him good morning?

In the nocturnal silence Efim's shout and Alcides' powerful snort came distinctly to my hearing. I ran toward them, and I was just in time: Efim was shivering with cold and cursing Alcides, whom he could not manage, and me for my delay. I took my horse from his hands, mounted, gave him the fifty rubles I had promised him, and begged him not to say anything to Papa. Then I released Alcides' reins and disappeared in a flash from the dumbfounded Efim's view.

Alcides galloped at the same rapid pace for four versts but then, since I had to cover fifty versts that night to reach the hamlet where I knew the Cossack regiment had been assigned to halt, I reined in my steed's quick gallop and went at a walk. Soon I came into a dark pine forest some thirty versts across. Wishing to conserve Alcides' strength, I kept him walking and, surrounded by the deathly hush of the forest and the dark of the autumn night, I became absorbed in my own thoughts: And so I'm at liberty. Free! Independent! I have taken the freedom that is rightfully mine – the freedom that is a precious gift from heaven, the inalienable prerogative of every human being! I have found a way to take it and guard it from all future claims against it; from now to my grave, it will be my portion and my reward!

Storm clouds covered the sky. The forest became so dark that I could not see twenty feet ahead of me, and at last a cold north wind rose, forcing me to step up my pace. Alcides broke into a full trot, and at dawn I arrived in the hamlet where the Cossack regiment had spent their day of rest.

CHAPTER ONE

The colonel and his officers had long been awake and were all gathered in his quarters for breakfast when I came in. They were conversing noisily among themselves, but suddenly fell silent as they noticed me. The colonel approached me with a dumbfounded look, "Which troop are you in?"

I replied that I did not yet have the honor of being in any of them, but I had come to ask him for that favor. The colonel listened to me in astonishment, "I don't understand you. You are really not enrolled anywhere?"

"No, I'm not."

"Why not?"

"I haven't the right."

"What! What does that mean, a Cossack without the right to be enrolled in a Cossack regiment! What kind of nonsense is that?"

I said that I was not a Cossack.

"Well, who are you anyway?" asked the colonel, growing impatient. "Why are you in Cossack uniform, and what do you want?"

"I've already told you, Colonel, that I desire the honor of being enrolled in your regiment, although only until such time as we reach the regular army."

"But just the same I have to know who you are, young man, and, moreover, aren't you aware that nobody can serve with us except native Cossacks?"

"And I have no such intention; I am only asking you for permission to travel to the regular army in the rank and dress of a Cossack serving with you or your regiment. As to your question about who I am, I will say only what I can: I am a nobleman; I have left my father's house and am on my way to serve in the army without my parents' knowledge and volition. I cannot be happy in any calling except the military, and that is why I've decided in this instance to follow my own dictates. If you won't take me under your protection, I'll find some way to join the army on my own."

The captain watched me sympathetically as I spoke. "What shall I do?" he asked in a low voice, turning to a grizzled captain. "I haven't the heart to refuse him!"

"And why should you?" answered the captain indifferently. "Let him come with us."

"It might make trouble for us."

"How? On the contrary, his father and mother both will be grateful to you afterwards for giving him refuge. With his resolve and inexperience, he will come to grief if you send him away."

Throughout this brief exchange between the colonel and the captain, I stood leaning on my sword, firmly determined, if I were refused, to get on my mountain bred steed and ride alone to my intended goal.

"Very well then, young man," said the colonel, turning to me, "come with us, but I warn you that we are now on our way to the Don, and there are no regular troops there. Shchegrov! Give him a horse from our stables."

A tall Cossack, the colonel's orderly, started to carry out the command, but I made haste to take advantage of a chance to play the part of a soldier under orders and said, "I have a horse, your honor. I'll ride him, if you will permit it."

The colonel burst out laughing. "So much the better, so much the better! Ride your own horse. What's your first name anyway, my gallant lad?"

I said that I was called Aleksandr.

"And your patronymic?"

"My father's name is Vasily."

"So, Aleksandr Vasilevich, on the march you will ride always with the first troop, and dine and be quartered with me. Go to the regiment now; we are about to move out. Duty officer, order the men to mount."

Beside myself with joy, I ran to my Alcides and flew like a bird into the saddle. The spirited horse seemed to comprehend my rapture; he went proudly, arching his neck and flicking his ears rapidly. The Cossack officers admired Alcides' beauty and praised me, too, saying that I sat my horse well and had a fine Circassian waist. I had already begun to blush and become confused by the curious stares fixed on me from all sides, but this state could not be allowed to last for long. I quickly recovered and answered their questions courteously and plausibly in a firm, calm voice, seemingly quite oblivious to the general curiosity and talk aroused by my apparition among the Army of the Don.

At last the Cossacks had their fill of discussing and looking over my steed and me and formed ranks. The colonel came out, mounted his Circassian steed, and commanded, "To the right by threes." The regiment moved out. The first section, composed for the purpose of men with good voices, struck up the Cossacks' favorite song, "The Soul Is a Good Steed." Its melancholy tune plunged me into revery: how long had it been since I was at home? In the garb of my sex, surrounded by girl friends, loved by my father, and respected by everyone as the daughter of the town mayor? Now I am a Cossack, in uniform, wearing a saber. The heavy lance tires my arm, which has not yet reached full strength. Instead of girl friends, I am surrounded by Cossacks whose dialect, jokes, rough voices, and loud laughter all trouble me. An emotion like a desire to cry constricted my breast. I bent to the arched neck of my steed, hugged it, and pressed my face to it. This horse was a gift from my father. It alone was left to remind me of the days I had spent in his house. At last my conflicting emotions subsided. I sat up straight again and turned my attention to the sad autumn landscape, swearing with all my heart never to permit memories to sap my spirit, but to go my freely chosen way with firmness and constancy.

The march lasted over a month. I was delighted with my new situation. I learned to saddle and unsaddle my horse and led him to water just like the others. On the march the Cossack officers often raced their horses and invited me to test the speed of my Alcides against them also, but I love him too much to agree to that. Besides, my good steed is no longer in the first bloom of youth; he is already nine years old, and, although I am convinced that there is no horse in the entire Cossack regiment who can equal Alcides in speed as well as beauty, I am not so inhumanly vain as to exhaust my comrade for the hollow satisfaction of prevailing over the scraggy chargers of the Don.[13]

At last the regiment reached the boundary of its lands and set up camp to await review, after which the men would be dismissed to their homes. The waiting and the review lasted three days. During that time I roamed the boundless Don steppe on foot with a gun or went riding. After the review, groups of Cossacks went their separate ways. It was a picturesque sight: a few

---

13. Durova has taken seven years off Alcides' age as well as her own.

hundred Cossacks, dispersing across the broad steppe, rode away from the site of the review in all directions. The scene reminded me of the scattered flight of ants when I chanced to fire a blank charge from a pistol into their hill.

Shchegrov called me to the colonel. "Well now, young man, our wanderings are at an end. And what about yours? What do you intend to do?"

"Go on to the army," I answered boldly.

"And of course you know where it is located? You know which road to take, and you have means for the journey?" asked the colonel with a wry smile.

His irony made me blush. "I will inquire about the place and the road, Colonel, and as to means, I have money and a horse."

"Your means are good only for the want of better. I pity you, Aleksandr Vasilevich! From your actions more than your words I've become convinced of your noble origins. I don't know the reasons which have compelled you to quit your father's house at such a young age but, if it is really a desire to serve in the army, then only your inexperience can conceal from you the endless difficulties you will have to overcome before you attain your goal. Think it over."

The colonel fell silent. I was silent also, and what could I say? Threatening me with difficulties! Advising me to think it over! Perhaps that might have been useful to hear at home, but since I have already gone two thousand versts, I can only continue and, whatever the difficulties, conquer them with a firm will. So I thought, but I kept my silence.

The colonel began again. "I see that you don't want to speak frankly with me. Perhaps you have your reasons, but I haven't the heart to let you go to certain destruction. Take my advice, remain here with me on the Don for now. The protection of a man of experience is indispensable to you. For the time being I offer you my home; live there until we set out on the next march. You won't be bored. I have a family, our climate, as you see, is very warm, there is no snow until December, and you can ride for pleasure as much as you like – my stable is at your service. Now we will go to my house, and I'll turn you over to my wife before I go on to join Platov in Cherkassk.[14] I'll be stay-

---

14. Matvej Platov was *ataman* (commander) of the Don Cossacks from 1801 until his death in 1818.

ing there until the next march, which won't be long in coming. Then you can travel with us as far as the regular army. Will you agree to follow my advice?"

I said that I accepted his proposal with sincere gratitude. It didn't take much wit to see how advantageous it would be for me to reach the regular army without attracting attention or arousing anyone's suspicion.

The colonel and I got into an open carriage and set out for Razdorskaja stanitsa, which was his home. His wife was greatly overjoyed by her husband's arrival. She was a middle-aged, comely, tall, plump woman with black eyes, brows, and hair, and the swarthy complexion common to the entire Cossack tribe. Her fresh lips smiled agreeably as she spoke. She took a great liking to me and was very kind to me, marveling that my parents let me, as she put it, "gad about the world" at such an extraordinarily young age. "You can't be more than fourteen, and here you are, alone in foreign parts. My son is eighteen, and I let him go to foreign lands only with his father, but alone! Oh, God! What might not happen to such a fledgling? Stay with us a while, you'll grow at least a little, you'll mature, and when our Cossacks are off on the march again, you'll go with them, and my husband will be like a father to you." As she talked, the colonel's good lady was setting the table with various treats – honey, grapes, cream, and sweet, newly pressed, wine. "Drink, young man," said my benevolent hostess. "What are you afraid of? Even we women drink it, by the glassful, and our three-year-old children drink it like water."

I had never tasted wine before, and so I drank the nectar of the Don with great pleasure. My hostess kept her eyes fixed on me. "How little you resemble a Cossack! You're so pale, so slender, so shapely – like a young lady. That's what my women think; they've already told me you're a girl in disguise!" And with this, the colonel's wife burst out laughing artlessly, without in any way suspecting how well her women had guessed, and what a faint heart her words gave the young guest whom she was so cordially plying with treats.

From that day I took no pleasure in staying with the colonel's family, but roamed the fields and vineyards from morning to night. I would have liked to leave for Cherkassk, but I feared new questions. It was not hard to see how badly the Cossack uniform concealed my striking difference from the native Cossacks; they all shared a distinctive countenance, and therefore my appearance, manners, and even my way of expressing myself were the object of their curiosity and speculation. Moreover, as I found myself continually remarked, I often became confused, blushed, avoided conversation, and went off into the fields all day even in bad weather.[15]

The colonel had not been home for a long time; his duties kept him in Cherkassk. My monotonous and idle life was becoming unbearable. I decided to leave and search out the army, although my heart quivered at the idea that I could expect the same questions and the same curiosity everywhere. But at least, I thought, they would be somewhat incidental, unlike here, where I served as the continual object of remark and speculation.

I decided to leave the next day at dawn and went home before nightfall to inform my hostess of my departure and prepare my horse and gear. As I came into the yard, I noticed an unusual bustle and scurry among the colonel's servants; I noticed a great number of carriages and saddle horses. I entered the parlor, and the first person I met was the newly returned colonel. A crowd of officers surrounded him; none of them, however, was among those with whom I had come to the Don.

"Hello, Aleksandr Vasilevich," said the colonel in response to my bow. "Have you gotten bored here in our land? Gentlemen, permit me: this is a Russian nobleman; he will accompany us to our destination." The officers bowed slightly to me and went on talking about their march. "Well now, how have you passed your time, Aleksandr Vasilevich? Have you come to love our Don, and isn't there anything on the Don you've come to love as well?" The colonel accompanied this with a sly, ironic smile.

I blushed as I caught the sense of the last question, but I replied politely in

---

15. In the 1839 *Notes* (48–49), Durova recorded her impression of the Don Cossacks' way of life: "Of the pure patriarchal customs of the Army of the Don in its native land, I found the most noble to be that all their lieutenants, captains, and even colonels did not disdain to work in the fields! It was with great respect that I watched these valiant warriors, who had grown gray in martial exploits, whose bravery made their weapons dreaded, upheld the government which they served, and did honor to the land where they were born – it was with great respect, I say, that I watched them cultivating that land: they themselves mow the grass of their fields, they themselves rake it into stacks. How nobly they make use of the time when they are at rest from warriors' occupations! How can one not honor people whose entire life, from childhood to the grave, is dedicated to the good either of their country or their family? How can one not prefer them to those who pass the best years of their lives tormenting defenseless hares and giving their children's bread to packs of borzoj hounds?"

the spirit of the joke that I had done my best to avoid becoming so attached to their beautiful land that I would pay for it with later regrets.

"You did very well," said the colonel, "because tomorrow at first light both we and you must bid farewell to our quiet Don! The Ataman regiment has been entrusted to me, and we have orders to march to Grodno province. There you will have a chance to join any regular regiment that suits you; there are lots of them there." [16]

At three in the morning I saddled Alcides and led him to the Cossack ranks. But since the colonel wasn't there yet, I tied up my horse and went into the parlor where the officers were all assembled. A great number of young Cossack women had come to see their husbands off. I witnessed a moving scene. Shchegrov, who was always at the colonel's side on the march, was with him on the Don also; his father, mother, wife, and three lovely grown daughters had come to see him off and once more bid him farewell. It was affecting to see the forty-year-old Cossack bowing to the ground to kiss the feet of his father and mother and receive their blessing, and afterwards himself blessing in exactly the same way the daughters who fell to his feet. This parting ritual was completely new to me and made a most mournful impression on my soul! "This," I thought, "is how children should part from their father and mother. But I ran away! Instead of a blessing, reproaches of aggrieved parents have pursued me, and perhaps. . . ." Horrible thought!

Absorbed in these sad reflections, I didn't hear them all go out, leaving the parlor empty. A rustling noise behind me caught my attention and wrenched me from my mournful reveries most disagreeably. One of the colonel's women was creeping up behind me, "And why are you still standing here alone, young lady? Your friends are mounted, and Alcides is running around the yard," she said with the look and ironic smile of a true satan. My heart shuddered and suffused with blood. I made haste to get away from this *Meguera!*

The Cossacks were already in formation. Nearby my Alcides was pawing the ground with impatience. As I rushed to catch him, I met the colonel's stern gaze: "In your situation you should always be first; for you it's imperative,

---

16. The officer who commanded the Ataman regiment during the 1807 Prussian campaign was Stepan Balabin.

Aleksandr Vasilevich," he said, riding out before the ranks. At last the traditional "To the right by threes" set the regiment moving. Soon "The Heart Is a Good Steed" rang out again, and the scenes of our earlier life on the march were renewed, but I am no longer the same girl. Having aged a few months, I have grown bolder, and I am no longer thrown into confusion at every question. The officers of the Ataman regiment, better educated than the others, remarking in my deportment the courtesy that serves as a mark of good upbringing, treat me with respect and seek out my company.

[Editor's note: In the months that followed, Durova abandoned the Cossacks and joined the Polish Horse, under the command of a Captain Kazimirski.]

Every day I get up at dawn and head for the muster-room; from there we all go together to the stables. My uhlan mentor praises my quick comprehension and constant readiness to practice evolutions, if need be from morning to night. He says that I'll be a gallant lad. I must confess, however, that brandishing the heavy lance – especially the completely worthless maneuver of swinging it over my head – makes me deathly tired, and I have already hit myself on the head several times. I am also ill-at-ease with the saber; it always seems to me that I will cut myself. I would more readily suffer a wound, however, than display the slightest timidity.

I spend all morning in training and then go to dine with Kazimirski who quizzes me with paternal indulgence, asking me whether I like my present pursuits and what I think of the military craft. I replied that I have loved the military craft from the day of my birth; that martial pursuits have been and will be my sole exercise; that I consider the warrior's calling the noblest of them all and the only one in which it is impossible to admit any vices whatsoever because fearlessness is the primary and indispensable quality of the warrior. Fearlessness is inseparable from greatness of soul, and the combination of these two great virtues leaves no room for vice and low passions.

"Do you really think, young man," asked the captain, "that it is impossible to have qualities meriting respect without being fearless? There are many people who are timid by nature and have outstanding qualities."

"I can well believe it, Captain. But I also think that a fearless man must surely be virtuous."

"Perhaps you're right," said the captain with a smile. "But," he added, patting me on the shoulder and twirling his mustaches, "let's wait for ten years or so, and also for your first battle. experience can be rather disillusioning."

After dinner Kazimirski lay down for a nap, and I went to the stable to give my horse his midday portion of oats. After this I was free to do whatever I wanted until six in the evening.

However exhausted I get from brandishing all morning that sister to the saber, the heavy lance, and from riding in formation and jumping obstacles, my fatigue passes after half an hour of rest, and from two to six I roam the fields, mountains, and forests on foot, fearlessly, tirelessly, and without a care. Freedom, a precious gift from heaven, has at last become my portion forever! I respire it, revel in it, feel it in my heart and soul. It penetrates and animates my existence. You, young women of my own age, only you can comprehend my rapture, only you can value my happiness! You, who must account for every step, who cannot go fifteen feet without supervision and protection, who from the cradle to the grave are eternally dependent and eternally guarded, God knows from whom and from what – I repeat, only you can comprehend the joyous sensations that fill my heart at the sight of vast forests, immense fields, mountains, valleys, and streams and at the thought that I can roam them all with no one to answer to and no fear of anyone's prohibition. I jump for joy as I realize that I will never again in my entire life hear the words: *You, girl, sit still! It's not proper for you to go wandering about alone.* Alas, how many fine clear days began and ended which I could watch only with tear stained eyes through the window where my mother had ordered me to weave lace. This mournful recollection of the oppression in which my childhood years were passed puts a quick end to my cheerful capers. I remain downcast for an hour or so as I recall life at home, but fortunately I recollect it less and less each day, and just the mere thought that my liberty is as boundless as the horizon makes me giddy with joy.

Virginia Woolf

from *Orlando*

Virginia Woolf (1882–1941) was born in London. In her memoir Moments of Being *(1976) she notes that she and her sister, Vanessa, "were both what was called tomboys: that is, we played cricket, scrambled over rocks, climbed trees, were said not to care for clothes and so on."*

In 1912 Woolf married the political theorist Leonard Woolf, with whom she later established the Hogarth Press. Among her many novels, Mrs. Dalloway *(1925),* To the Lighthouse *(1927),* Orlando *(1928), and* The Waves *(1931) are perhaps the best known.*

The following takes place only a few weeks after Orlando has been transformed ("painlessly and completely") from a man into a woman. As a man, Orlando was a swashbuckling nobleman and poet, who served as the British Ambassador at the Sultan's Court in Constantinople. As a woman, travelling incognito with a band of gypsies and (now) en route back to England, she is still struggling to make sense of her new life.

Sasha is a Russian sweetheart from long ago.

WITH SOME OF THE GUINEAS LEFT FROM THE SALE OF THE TENTH pearl of her string, Orlando had bought herself a complete outfit of such clothes as women then wore, and it was in the dress of a young Englishwoman of rank that she now sat on the deck of the *Enamoured Lady*. It is a strange fact, but a true one that up to this moment she had scarcely given her sex a thought. Perhaps the Turkish trousers, which she had hitherto worn had done something to distract her thoughts; and the gipsy women, except in one or two important particulars, differ very little from the gipsy men. At any rate, it was not until she felt the coil of skirts about her legs and the Captain offered, with the greatest politeness, to have an awning spread for her on deck that she realised, with a start the penalties and the privileges of her position. But that start was not of the kind that might have been expected.

It was not caused, that is to say, simply and solely by the thought of her chastity and how she could preserve it. In normal circumstances a lovely young woman alone would have thought of nothing else; the whole edifice of female government is based on that foundation stone; chastity is their jewel, their centre piece, which they run mad to protect, and die when ravished of. But if one has been a man for thirty years or so, and an Ambassador into the bargain, if one has held a Queen in one's arms and one or two other ladies, if report be true, of less exalted rank, if one has married a Rosina Pepita, and so on, one does not perhaps give such a very great start about that. Orlando's start was of a very complicated kind, and not to be summed up in a trice. Nobody, indeed, ever accused her of being one of those quick wits, who run to the end of things in a minute. It took her the entire length of the voyage to moralise out the meaning of her start, and so, at her own pace, we will follow her.

"Lord," she thought, when she had recovered from her start, stretching herself out at length under her awning, "this is a pleasant, lazy way of life, to be sure. But," she thought, giving her legs a kick, "these skirts are plaguey things to have about one's heels. Yet the stuff (flowered paduasoy) is the loveliest in the world. Never have I seen my own skin (here she laid her hand on her knee) look to such advantage as now. Could I, however, leap overboard and swim in clothes like these? No! Therefore, I should have to trust to the protection of a blue-jacket. Do I object to that? Now do I?" she wondered, here encountering the first knot in the smooth skein of her argument.

Dinner came before she had untied it, and then it was the Captain himself — Captain Nicholas Benedict Bartolus, a sea-captain of distinguished aspect, who did it for her as he helped her to a slice of corned beef.

"A little of the fat, Ma'am?" he asked. "Let me cut you just the tiniest little slice the size of your finger nail." At those words, a delicious tremor ran through her frame. Birds sang; the torrents rushed. It recalled the feeling of indescribable pleasure with which she had first seen Sasha, hundreds of years ago. Then she had pursued, now she fled. Which is the greater ecstasy? The man's or the woman's? And are they not perhaps the same? No, she thought, this is the most delicious (thanking the Captain but refusing) to refuse, and see him frown. Well, she would, if he wished it, have the very thinnest, smallest shiver in the world. This was the most delicious, to yield and see him smile. "For nothing," she thought, regaining her couch on deck, and continuing the argument, "is more heavenly than to resist and to yield; to yield and to resist. Surely it throws the spirit into such a rapture that nothing else can. So that I'm not sure," she continued, "that I won't throw myself overboard, for the mere pleasure of being rescued by a blue-jacket after all."

(It must be remembered that she was like a child, entering into possession of a pleasaunce or toy cupboard; her arguments would not commend themselves to mature women, who have had the run of it all their lives.)

"But what used we young fellows in the cockpit of the *Marie Rose* to say about a woman who threw herself overboard for the pleasure of being rescued by a blue-jacket?" she said. "We had a word for them. Ah! I have it. . . ." (But we must omit that word; it was disrespectful in the extreme and passing strange on a lady's lips.) "Lord! Lord!" she cried again at the conclusion of her thoughts, "must I then begin to respect the opinion of the other sex, however monstrous I think it? If I wear skirts, if I can swim, if I have to be rescued by a blue-jacket, by God!" she cried, "I must!" Upon which, a gloom fell over her. Candid by nature, and averse to all kinds of equivocation, to tell lies bored her. It seemed to her a roundabout way of going to work. Yet, she reflected, the flowered paduasoy – the pleasure of being rescued by a blue-jacket – if these were only to be obtained by roundabout ways, roundabout one must go, she supposed. She remembered how, as a young man, she had insisted that women must be obedient, chaste, scented, and exquisitely apparelled. "Now I shall have to pay in my own person for those desires," she reflected; "for women are not (judging by my own short experience of the sex) obedient, chaste, scented, and exquisitely apparelled by nature. They can only attain these graces, without which they may enjoy none of the delights of life, by the most tedious discipline. There's the hair-dressing," she thought, "that alone will take an hour of my morning; there's looking in the looking-glass, another hour; there's staying and lacing; there's washing and powdering; there's changing from silk to lace and from lace to paduasoy; and there's being chaste year in year out. . . . ." Here she tossed her foot impatiently, and showed an inch or two of calf. A sailor on the mast, who happened to look down at the moment, started so violently that he missed his footing and only saved himself by the skin of his teeth. "If the sight of my ankles means death to an honest fellow who, no doubt, has a wife and family to support, I must, in all humanity, keep them covered," Orlando thought. Yet her legs were among her chiefest beauties. And she fell to thinking what an odd pass we have come to when all a woman's beauty has to be kept covered, lest a sailor may fall from a mast-head. "A pox on them!" she said, realising for the first time, what, in other circumstances, she would have been taught as a child, that is to say, the sacred responsibilities of womanhood.

"And that's the last oath I shall ever be able to swear," she thought; "once I set foot on English soil. And I shall never be able to crack a man over the head, or tell him he lies in his teeth, or draw my sword and run him through the body, or sit among my peers, or wear a coronet, or walk in procession, or sentence a man to death, or lead an army, or prance down Whitehall on a charger, or wear seventy-two different medals on my breast. All I can do, once I set foot on English soil, is to pour out tea, and ask my lords how they like it. "D'you take sugar? D'you take cream?" And mincing out the words, she was horrified to perceive how low an opinion she was forming of the other sex, the manly, to which it had once been her pride to belong. "To fall from a mast-head," she thought, "because you see a woman's ankles; to dress up like a Guy Fawkes and parade the streets, so that women may praise you; to deny a woman teaching lest she may laugh at you; to be the slave of the frailest chit in petticoats, and yet to go about as if you were the Lords of creation. – Heavens!" she thought, "what fools they make of us – what fools we are!" And here it would seem from some ambiguity in her terms that she was censuring both sexes equally, as if she belong to neither; and indeed, for the time being she seemed to vacillate; she was man; she was woman; she knew the secrets, shared the weaknesses of each. It was a most bewildering and whirligig state of mind to be in. The comforts of ignorance seemed utterly denied her. She was a feather blown on the gale. Thus it is no great wonder if, as she pitted one sex against the other, and found each alternately full of the most deplorable infirmities, and was not sure to which she belonged – it was no great wonder that she was about to cry out that she would return to Turkey and become a gipsy again when the anchor fell with a great splash into the sea; the sails came tumbling on deck, and she perceived (so sunk had she been in thought, that she had seen nothing for several days) that the ship was anchored off the coast of Italy. The Captain at once sent to ask the honour of her company ashore with him in the long boat.

When she returned the next morning, she stretched herself on her couch under the awning and arranged her draperies with the greatest decorum about her ankles.

"Ignorant and poor as we are compared with the other sex," she thought, continuing the sentence which she had left unfinished the other day, "armoured with every weapon as they are, while they debar us even from a knowledge of the alphabet" (and from these opening words it is plain that something had happened during the night to give her a push towards the female sex, for she was speaking more as a woman speaks than as a man, yet with a sort of content after all) "still – they fall from the mast-head – " Here she gave a great yawn and fell asleep. When she woke, the ship was sailing before a fair breeze so near the shore that towns on the cliffs' edge seemed only kept from slipping into the water by the interposition of some great rock or the twisted roots of some ancient olive tree. The scent of oranges wafted from a million trees, heavy with the fruit, reached her on deck. A score of blue dolphins, twisting their tails, leapt high now and again into the air. Stretching her arms out (arms, she had learnt already, have no such fatal effects as legs) she thanked Heaven that she was not prancing down Whitehall on a war-horse, not even sentencing a man to death. "Better is it," she thought, "to be clothed with poverty and ignorance, which are the dark garments of the female sex; better to leave the rule and discipline of the world to others; better to be quit of martial ambition, the love of power, and all the other manly desires if so one can more fully enjoy the most exalted raptures known to the human spirit, which are," she said aloud, as her habit was when deeply moved, "contemplation, solitude, love."

"Praise God that I'm a woman!" she cried, and was about to run into the extreme folly – than which none is more distressing in woman or man either – of being proud of her sex, when she paused over the singular word, which, for all we can do to put it in its place, has crept in at the end of the last sentence; Love. "Love," said Orlando. Instantly – such is its impetuosity – love took a human shape – such is its pride. For where other thoughts are content to remain abstract nothing will satisfy this one but to put on flesh and blood, mantilla and petticoats, hose and jerkin. And as all Orlando's loves had been women, now, through the culpable laggardry of the human frame to adapt itself to convention, though she herself was a woman, it was still a woman she loved; and if the consciousness of being of the same sex had any effect at all, it was to quicken and deepen those feelings which she had had as a man. For now a thousand hints and mysteries became plain to her that were then dark. Now, the obscurity, which divides the sexes and lets linger innumerable impurities in its gloom, was removed, and if there is anything in what the poet says about truth and beauty, this affection gained in beauty what it lost in falsity. At last, she cried, she knew Sasha as she was, and in the ardour of this discovery, and in the pursuit of all those treasures which were now revealed, she was so rapt and enchanted that it was as if a cannon ball had exploded at her ear when a man's voice said, "Permit me, Madam," a man's hand raised her to her feet; and the fingers of a man with a three-masted sailing ship tattooed on the middle finger pointed to the horizon.

"The cliffs of England, Ma'am," said the Captain, and he raised the hand which had pointed at the sky to the salute. Orlando now gave a second start, even more violent than the first.

"Christ Jesus!" she cried.

Happily, the sight of her native land after long absence excused both start and exclamation, or she would have been hard put to it to explain to Captain Bartolus the raging and conflicting emotions which now boiled within her. How tell him that she, who now trembled on his arm, had been a Duke and an Ambassador? How explain to him that she, who had been lapped like a lily in folds of paduasoy, had hacked heads off, and lain with loose women among treasure sacks in the holds of pirate ships on summer nights when the tulips were abloom and the bees buzzing off Wapping Old Stairs? Not even to herself could she explain the giant start she gave, as the resolute right hand of the sea-captain indicated the cliffs of the British Islands.

"To refuse and to yield," she murmured, "how delightful; to pursue and to conquer, how august; to perceive and to reason, how sublime." Not one of these words so coupled together seemed to her wrong; nevertheless, as the chalky cliffs loomed nearer, she felt culpable; dishonoured; unchaste; which, for one who had never given the matter a thought, was strange. Closer and closer they drew, till the samphire gatherers, hanging half-way down the cliff, were plain to the naked eye. And watching them, she felt, scampering up and down within her, like some derisive ghost who, in another instant will pick up her skirts and flaunt out of sight, Sasha the lost, Sasha the memory, whose reality she had proved just now so surprisingly – Sasha, she felt, mopping and mowing and making all sorts of disrespectful gestures towards the cliffs and the samphire gatherers; and when the sailors began chanting, "So good-bye and adieu to you, Ladies of Spain," the words echoed in Orlando's sad heart, and she felt that however much landing there meant comfort, meant opulence, meant conse-quence and state (for she would doubtless pick up some noble Prince and reign, his consort over half Yorkshire), still, if it meant conventionality, meant slavery, meant deceit, meant denying her love, fettering her limbs, pursing her lips, and restraining her tongue, then she would turn about with the ship and set sail once more for the gipsies.

from *Stone Butch Blues*

Leslie Feinberg was born in 1949. S/he came of age as a young butch lesbian in the factories and gay bars of Buffalo, New York, and is now nationally known in the lesbian/gay/bi and transgender movements. In 1994 s/he opened the Stonewall 25 Rally in New York City, which drew one million people from across the country and around the world.

Feinberg is a journalist, a grass-roots activist, and a typesetter by trade. Her first book was Stone Butch Blues *(1993). The narrator is a "stone he/she" named Jess Goldberg (that is, a full-time butch lesbian, as compared to a Saturday-night butch, who might pass as straight all week.) Theresa is a former lover.*

Feinberg's latest book is Transgender Warriors: Making History from Joan of Arc to Dennis Rodman *(1997).*

I'M LYING IN MY BED TONIGHT MISSING YOU, MY EYES ALL SWOLLEN, hot tears running down my face. I don't think I've ever felt so all alone. There's a fierce summer lightning storm raging outside.

Tonight I walked down streets looking for you in every woman's face, as I have each night of this lonely exile. I'm afraid I'll never see your laughing, teasing eyes again.

Earlier, I was walking in this big city with a woman. A mutual friend had fixed us up, sure we'd have a lot in common, since we're both into "politics."

Well, we sat in a coffee shop and she talked about Democratic politics and seminars and photography and problems with her co-op and how she's opposed to rent control. Small wonder. Daddy is a real estate developer.

I couldn't understand what she was talking about most of the time. I'm looking at her while she's talking, thinking to myself that I'm a stranger in this woman's eyes. She's looking at me, but she doesn't see me.

Then she finally says she hates this society for what it's done to "women like me" who hate themselves so much that they have to look and act like men.

I feel myself getting flushed and my face twitches a little and I start telling her all cool and calm about how women like me have existed since the dawn of time, before there was oppression, and how their societies respected them, and she's got her very interested expression on, and besides it's time to leave.

So we walk by a corner where these cops are laying into a homeless man and I stop and mouth off to the cops and they start coming at me with their clubs raised and she tugs my belt to pull me back. And I just look at her, and suddenly I'm feeling things well up in me that I thought I had buried. I'm standing there remembering you like I don't see the cops about to hit me, like I'm falling back into another world, a place I want to go to again.

And suddenly my heart hurts and I realize how long it's been since my heart has felt anything.

I need to go home to you tonight. I can't. So I'm writing you this letter.

I remember years ago, the day I started working at the plant and you had already been there a few months, and how your eyes caught mine and played with me before you set me free. I was supposed to be following the foreman to fill out some forms, but I was too busy wondering what color your hair was under that white paper net and how it would look and feel in my fingers, down loose and free. And I remember how you laughed gently when the foreman came back and said, "You comin' or not?"

All of us he-she's were mad as hell when we heard you got fired the next week because you wouldn't let the superintendent touch your breasts. I still unloaded on the docks for another couple of weeks, but I was mopey. It just wasn't the same when your light went out.

I couldn't believe it the night I went to that new club on the West Side (a new bar almost every other week). There you were, leaning up against the bar, your jeans too tight for words and your hair, your hair all loose and free.

And I remember that look in your eyes again. You didn't just know me; you liked what you saw. And this time, ooh, woman, we were on our own turf. I could move the way you wanted me to, and I was glad I'd gotten all dressed up.

Our own turf . . . "Would you dance with me?"

You didn't say yes or no, just teased me with your eyes, straightened my tie and smoothed my collar, and took me by the hand.

You had my heart before you moved against me like you did. Tammy was singing "Stand by Your Man," and we were changing all the "he's" to "she's" inside our heads to make it fit right. After you moved that way, you had more than my heart. You made me ache and you liked that. So did I.

The older butches always warned me, if you want to keep your marriage, don't go to the bars. But I've always been a one-woman butch. Besides, this was our community, the only one we belonged to, so we went every weekend.

There were two kinds of fights in the bars. Most weekends had one kind or the other, some weekends both.

There were the fist fights between the butch women – full of booze, shame, jealous insecurity. Sometimes the fights were awful and spread like a web to trap everyone in the bar, like the night you-know-who lost her eye when she got hit upside the head with a bar stool.

I was real proud that in all those years I never hit another butch woman. See, I loved them too, and I understood their pain and their shame, because I was so much like them. I loved the lines etched in their faces and hands and the curves of their work-weary shoulders. Sometimes I looked in the mirror and wondered what I would look like when I was their age. Now I know!

In their own way, they loved me too. They protected me, because they knew I wasn't a "Saturday-night butch." (The weekend butches were scared of me, because I was a stone he-she If only they had known how powerless I really felt inside!) But the older butches, they knew the whole road that lay ahead of me, and they wished I didn't have to go down it, because it hurt so much.

When I came into the bar in drag, kind of hunched over, they told me, "Be proud of what you are," and then they adjusted my tie sort of like you did.

I was like them. They knew I didn't have a choice. So I never fought them with my fists. We clapped one another on the back in the bars and watched one another's back at the factory

But then there were the times that our real enemies came in the front door – drunken gangs of sailors, Klan-type thugs, psychopaths, cops. You always knew when they came in, because someone had the foresight to pull the plug on the jukebox. No matter how many times it happened, we all still went, "Aw . . ." when the music stopped, and then we got down to business.

When the bigots came in, it was time to fight, and fight we did. We fought hard, butch and femme, men and women together.

When the music stopped and it was the cops at the door, someone plugged the music back in and we switched dance partners. We in our suits and ties paired off with our drag queen sisters in their dresses and pumps. It's hard to remember that it was illegal then for two women or two men to sway to music together. When the music ended, the butches bowed, our femme partners curtsied, and we returned to our seats, our lovers, and our drinks to await our fates.

That's when I remember your hand on my belt, up under my suit jacket. That's where your hand stayed the whole time the cops were there. "Take it easy, honey. Stay with me, baby, cool off," you'd be cooing in my ear as if singing a lover's song sung to warriors who needed to pick and choose their battles to survive.

We learned fast that the cops always pulled the police van right up to the bar door and left snarling dogs inside so that we couldn't get out. We were trapped, all right.

Remember that night you stayed home with me after I got my hand caught in the machine at the factory? That was the night . . . you remember. The cops picked out the most stone butch of them all to destroy with humiliation, a woman everyone said "wore a raincoat in the shower." We heard they stripped her, slow, in front of everyone in the bar, and laughed at her trying to cover up her nakedness. Later she went mad, they said. Later she hung herself.

What would I have done if I had been there that night?

I'm remembering the busts in the bars in Canada. Packed in the police vans, all the Saturday-night butches giggled and tried to fluff up their hair and switch clothing so that they could get thrown in the tank with the femme women – said it would be like "dyin' and goin' to heaven."

We never switched clothing. Neither did our drag queen sisters. We knew, and so did you, what was coming. We needed our sleeves rolled up, our hair slicked back, to live through it. Our hands were cuffed tight behind our backs. Yours were cuffed in front. You loosened my tie, unbuttoned my collar, and touched my face. I saw the pain and fear for me in your face, and I whispered it would be all right. We knew it wouldn't be.

I never told you what they did to us down there – queens in one tank, stone butches in the next – but you knew. One at a time they would drag our brothers out of the cells, slapping and punching them, locking the bars behind them fast in case we lost control and tried to stop them – as if we could.

They'd handcuff a brother's wrists to his ankles or chain him, face against the bars. They made us watch.

Sometimes we'd catch the eyes of the terrorized victim, or the soon-to-be, caught in the vise of torture, and we'd say gently, "I'm with you, honey, look at me, stay with me, we'll take you home."

We never cried in front of the cops. We knew we were next.

The next time the cell door opens it will be me they drag out and chain spread-eagled to the bars.

Did I survive? I guess I did. But only because I knew I might get home to you.

They let us out last, one at a time on Monday morning. No charges: Too late to call in sick to work, no money, hitchhiking, crossing the border on foot, in rumpled clothes, bloody, needing a shower, hurt, scared.

I knew you'd be home if I could get there.

You ran a bath for me with sweet-smelling bubbles. You always laid out a fresh pair of white BVDs and a t-shirt for me and left me alone to wash off the first layer of shame.

I remember, it was always the same. I would put on the briefs, and then I'd just get the t-shirt over my head and you would find some reason to come into the bathroom, to get something or put something away. In a glance you would memorize the wounds on my body like a road map – the gashes, bruises, ciga-rette burns.

Later, in bed, you held me gently, touching me everywhere, the tenderest touches reserved for the places I was hurt, knowing each and every sore place – inside and out.

You didn't flirt with me right away, knowing I wasn't feeling confident enough to be sexy. But later you coaxed my pride back out again, showing me how much you wanted me. You knew melting the stone again would take you weeks.

Lately I've read these stories by women who are angry with stone lovers, even mocking their passion when they finally give way to trusting, to being touched.

And I'm wondering: did it hurt you, the times I couldn't let you touch me? I hope it didn't. You never showed it if it did. You knew it wasn't you I was keeping myself safe from. You treated my stone self as a wound that needed loving healing. Thank you. No one's ever done that since. If you were here tonight – well, it's hypothetical, isn't it?

I never said these things to you.

Tonight I remember the night I got busted alone, on strange turf. You're probably wincing already, but I have to say this to you out loud.

That night, we drove ninety miles to a bar to meet friends who never showed up. (Later we found out they were at home drinking and fighting.)

That night, when the cops raided the club, I was the only he-she in the place, and that one cop with gold bars on his uniform came right over to me and told me to stand up.

He put his hands all over me, pulled up the band of my jockeys, and told his men to cuff me: I didn't have on three pieces of women's clothing. I wanted to fight right then and there because I knew that chance would be lost in a moment.

But I also knew that everyone would be beaten that night if I fought back, so I just stood there. I saw that they had pinned your arms behind your back and cuffed your hands. One cop had his arm across your throat. I remember the look in your eyes. It hurts me even now.

They cuffed my hands so tight behind my back that I almost cried out.

· Then the cop unzipped his pants real slow with a smirk on his face and ordered me down on my knees.

At first I thought to myself, "I can't!" Then I said out loud to myself and to you and to him, "I won't!" I never told you this before, but something changed inside of me in that moment. I learned the difference between what I can't do and what I refuse to do.

I paid the price for that lesson. Do I have to tell you every detail? Thank you.

When I got out of the tank the next morning, you were there; you bailed me out. No charges – they just kept the money. You had waited all night long in that police station. Only I know how hard that was for you to withstand their leers, their taunts, their threats. I knew you cringed with every sound you strained to hear from back in the cells. You prayed you wouldn't hear me scream. I didn't.

When we got outside into the parking lot, you stopped and put your hands lightly on my shoulders and avoided my eyes. You gently rubbed the bloody places on my shirt and said, "I'll never get these stains out."

Damn anyone who thinks that means you were relegated in life to worrying about my ring-around-the-collar.

I knew exactly what you meant. It was such an oddly sweet way of saying, or not saying, what you were feeling. Sort of the way I shut down emotionally when I feel scared and hurt and helpless and say little funny things that seem so out of context.

You drove us home with my head in your lap all the way, caressing my face. You ran the bath. Set out my fresh underwear. Put me to bed. Stroked me carefully. Held me gently.

That night I woke up and found myself alone in bed. You were drinking alone at the kitchen table, head in your hands. You were sobbing.

I took you firmly in my arms and held you, and you struggled and beat against my chest with your fists, because the enemy wasn't there to hit. Moments later you recalled the bruises on my chest and cried even harder, sobbing, "It's my fault, I couldn't stop them."

I've always wanted to tell you this: in that one moment I knew you really did understand how I felt in life. Choking on anger, feeling so powerless, unable to protect myself or those I loved most, yet fighting back again and again, unwilling to give up. I didn't have the words to tell you this then. I just said, "It'll be okay, it'll be all right."

And then we smiled ironically at what I'd said, and I took you back to our bed and made the best love to you I could, considering the shape I was in. You knew not to try to touch me that night. You just stroked my hair and cried and cried.

When did we get separated in life, sweet warrior woman? We thought we'd won the war of liberation when we embraced the word *gay*. Then, suddenly, there were professors and doctors and lawyers coming out of the woodwork telling us that meetings should be run by Robert's Rules of Order. (Who died and left Robert god?)

We dressed up after work for the new meetings on campus, but they drove us out, made us feel ashamed of how we looked. They said we were male chauvinist pigs: the enemy. It was women's hearts they broke. We were not hard to send away. We went quietly.

The plants closed, something we never could have imagined.

That's when I was sent into exile and began passing as a man. Strange to be exiled from your own gender to borders that will never be home.

You were banished too, to another land, with your own gender, and yet forced apart from the women you loved as much as you tried to love yourself.

For more than twenty years I have lived on this lonely shore, wondering what became of you. Did you wash off your Saturday-night makeup in shame? Did you burn in anger when women said, "If I wanted a man, I'd be with a real one"?

Are you turning tricks today? Are you waiting tables or learning WordPerfect?

Are you in a lesbian bar looking out of the corner of your eye for the butchest woman in the room? Do the women there talk about Democratic politics and photography and co-ops? Are you with women who bleed only monthly on their cycles?

Or are you in another blue-collar town, lying with an unemployed auto worker who is much more like me than they are, listening for the even breathing of your sleeping children? Do you bind his emotional wounds the way you tried to heal mine?

Do you ever think of me in the cool night?

I've been writing this letter to you for hours. My ribs hurt bad from a beating two weeks ago. You know.

I never could have survived this long if I'd never known your love. Yet still I ache with missing you. I need you so.

Only you could melt this stone. Are you ever coming back?

The storm has passed now. There is a pink glow at the horizon outside my window. I am remembering the nights I fucked you deep and slow until the sky was just this color.

I can't think about you anymore; the pain is swallowing me up. I have to put your memory away, like a precious sepia photograph. There are still so many things I want to tell you, to share with you.

Since I can't mail you this letter, I'll send it to a place where they keep women's memories safe. Maybe someday, passing through this big city, you will stop and read it. Maybe you won't.

Good night, my love.

PART FIVE

Tomboys Resurgent

Grace Paley

Ruthy and Edie

Grace Paley was born in the Bronx in 1922. As a girl she was a tomboy, tough and lively and rambunctious. "When I was a little girl I was a boy. . . . I could hardly wait to continue being a boy so that I could go to war and do all the other exciting boyish things."

In later years, Paley's tomboy spirit reemerged in her work as a feminist, peace activist, and teacher. Her first book of stories, The Little Disturbances of Man: Stories of Men and Women at Love, *appeared in 1959. Since then she has published two more collections of stories:* Extraordinary Changes at the Last Minute *(1974) and* Later the Same Day *(1985), from which this story is taken, as well as a book of poems,* Leaning Forward *(1985). She divides her time between New York City and Thetford, Vermont.*

ONE DAY IN THE BRONX TWO SMALL GIRLS NAMED EDIE AND RUTHY were sitting on the stoop steps. They were talking about the real world of boys. Because of this, they kept their skirts pulled tight around their knees. A gang of boys who lived across the street spent at least one hour of every Saturday afternoon pulling up girls' dresses. They needed to see the color of a girl's underpants in order to scream outside the candy store, Edie wears pink panties.

Ruthy said, anyway, she liked to play with those boys. They did more things. Edie said she hated to play with them. They hit and picked up her skirt. Ruthy agreed. It *was* wrong of them to do this. But, she said, they ran around the block a lot, had races, and played war on the corner. Edie said it wasn't *that* good.

Ruthy said, Another thing, Edie, you could be a soldier if you're a boy.

So? What's so good about that?

Well, you could fight for your country.

Edie said, I don't want to.

What? Edie! Ruthy was a big reader and most interesting reading was about bravery – for instance Roland's Horn at Roncevaux. Her father had been brave and there was often a lot of discussion about this at suppertime. In fact, he sometimes modestly said, Yes, I suppose I was brave in those days. And so was your mother, he added. Then Ruthy's mother put his boiled egg in front of him

[243

where he could see it. Reading about Roland, Ruthy learned that if a country wanted to last, it would require a great deal of bravery. She nearly cried with pity when she thought of Edie and the United States of America.

You don't want to? she asked.

No.

Why, Edie, why?

I don't feel like.

Why, Edie? How come?

You always start hollering if I don't do what you tell me. I don't always have to say what you tell me. I can say whatever I like.

Yeah, but if you love your country you have to go fight for it. How come you don't want to? Even if you get killed, it's worth it.

Edie said, I don't want to leave my mother.

Your mother? You must be a baby. Your mother?

Edie pulled her skirt very tight over her knees. I don't like it when I don't see her a long time. Like when she went to Springfield to my uncle. I don't like it.

Oh boy! said Ruthy. Oh boy! What a baby! She stood up. She wanted to go away. She just wanted to jump from the top step, run down to the corner, and wrestle with someone. She said, You know, Edie, this is *my* stoop.

Edie didn't budge. She leaned her chin on her knees and felt sad. She was a big reader too, but she liked *The Bobbsey Twins* or *Honey Bunch at the Seashore*. She loved that nice family life. She tried to live it in the three rooms on the fourth floor. Sometimes she called her father Dad, or even Father, which surprised him. Who? he asked.

I have to go home now, she said. My cousin Alfred's coming. She looked to see if Ruthy was still mad. Suddenly she saw a dog. Ruthy, she said, getting to her feet. There's a dog coming. Ruthy turned. There *was* a dog about three-quarters of the way down the block between the candy store and the grocer's. It was an ordinary middle-sized dog. But it *was* coming. It didn't stop to sniff at curbs or pee on the house fronts. It just trotted steadily along the middle of the sidewalk.

Ruthy watched him. Her heart began to thump and take up too much space inside her ribs. She thought speedily, Oh, a dog has teeth! It's large, hairy, strange. Nobody can say what a dog is thinking. A dog is an animal. You could talk to a dog, but a dog couldn't talk to you. If you said to a dog, STOP! a dog would just keep going. If it's angry and bites you, you might get rabies. It will take you about six weeks to die and you will die screaming in agony. Your stomach will turn into a rock and you will have lockjaw. When they find you, your mouth will be paralyzed wide open in your dying scream.

Ruthy said, I'm going right now. She turned as though she'd been directed by some far-off switch. She pushed the hall door open and got safely inside. With one hand she pressed the apartment bell. With the other she held the door shut. She leaned against the glass door as Edie started to bang on it. Let me in, Ruthy, let me in, please. Oh, Ruthy!

I can't. Please, Edie, I just can't.

Edie's eyes rolled fearfully toward the walking dog. It's coming. Oh, Ruthy, please, please.

No! No! said Ruthy.

The dog stopped right in front of the stoop to hear the screaming and banging. Edie's heart stopped too. But in a minute he decided to go on. He passed. He continued his easy steady pace.

When Ruthy's big sister came down to call them for lunch, the two girls were crying. They were hugging each other and their hair was a mess. You two are nuts, she said. If I was Mama, I wouldn't let you play together so much every single day. I mean it.

Many years later in Manhattan it was Ruthy's fiftieth birthday. She had invited three friends. They waited for her at the round kitchen table. She had been constructing several pies so that this birthday could be celebrated in her kitchen during the day by any gathered group without too much trouble. Now and then one of the friends would say, Will you sit down, for godsakes! She would sit immediately. But in the middle of someone's sentence or even one of her own, she'd jump up with a look of worry beyond household affairs to wash a cooking utensil or wipe crumbs of flour off the Formica counter.

Edie was one of the women at the table. She was sewing, by neat hand, a new zipper into an old dress. She said, Ruthy, it wasn't like that. We both ran in and out a lot.

No, said Ruth. You would never have locked me out. You were an awful sissy, sweetie, but you would never, never have locked me out. Just look at yourself. Look at your life!

Edie glanced, as people will, when told to do that. She saw a chubby dark-haired woman who looked like a nice short teacher, someone who stood at the front of the schoolroom and said, History is a wonderful subject. It's all stories.

It's where we come from, who we are. For instance, where do you come from, Juan? Where do your parents and grandparents come from?

You know that, Mizz Seiden. Porto Rico. You know that a long-o time-o, Juan said, probably in order to mock both languages. Edie thought, Oh, to whom would he speak?

For Christsakes, this is a party, isn't it? said Ann. She was patting a couple of small cases and a projector on the floor next to her chair. Was she about to offer a slide show? No, she had already been prevented from doing this by Faith, who'd looked at the clock two or three times and said, I don't have the time, Jack is coming tonight. Ruth had looked at the clock too. Next week, Ann? Ann said O.K. O.K. But Ruthy, I want to say you have to quit knocking yourself. I've seen you do a million good things. If you were such a dud, why'd I write it down in my will that if anything happened to me, you and Joe were the ones who'd raise my kids.

You were just plain wrong. I couldn't even raise my own right.

Ruthy, really, they're pretty much raised. Anyway, how can you say an awful thing like that? Edie asked. They're wonderful beautiful brilliant girls. Edie knew this because she had held them in her arms the third or fourth day of life. Naturally, she became the friend called aunt.

That's true, I don't have to worry about Sara anymore, I guess.

Why? Because she's a married mommy? Faith asked. What an insult to Edie!

No, that's O.K., said Edie.

Well, I do worry about Rachel. I just can't help myself. I never know where she is. She was supposed to be here last night. She does usually call. Where the hell is she?

Oh, probably in jail for some stupid little sit-in or something, Ann said. She'll get out in five minutes. Why she thinks that kind of thing works is a mystery to me. You brought her up like that and now you're surprised. Besides which, I don't want to talk about the goddamn kids, said Ann. Here I've gone around half of most of the nearly socialist world and nobody asks me a single question. I have been a witness of events! she shouted.

I do want to hear everything, said Ruth. Then she changed her mind. Well, I don't mean everything. Just say one good thing and one bad thing about every place you've been. We only have a couple of hours. (It was four o'clock. At six, Sara and Tomas with Letty, the first grandchild, standing between them would be at the door. Letty would probably think it was her own birthday party. Someone would say, What curly hair! They would all love her new shoes and her newest sentence, which was Remember dat? Because for such a long time there had been only the present full of milk and looking. Then one day, trying to dream into an afternoon nap, she sat up and said, Gramma, I boke your cup. Remember dat? In this simple way the lifelong past is invented, which, as we know, thickens the present and gives all kinds of advice to the future.) So, Ann, I mean just a couple of things about each country.

That's not much of a discussion, for Christsake.

It's a party, Ann, you said it yourself.

Well, change your face, then.

Oh. Ruth touched her mouth, the corners of her eyes. You're right. Birthday! she said.

Well, let's go, then, said Ann. She stated two good things and one bad thing about Chile (an earlier visit), Rhodesia, the Soviet Union, and Portugal.

You forgot about China. Why don't you tell them about our trip to China?

I don't think I will, Ruthy; you'd only contradict every word I say.

Edie, the oldest friend, stripped a nice freckled banana she'd been watching during Ann's talk. The thing is, Ruth, you never simply say yes. I've told you so many times, *I* would have slammed the door on you, admit it, but it was your house, and that slowed me down.

Property, Ann said. Even among poor people, it begins early.

Poor? asked Edie. It was the Depression.

Two questions – Faith believed she'd listened patiently long enough. I love that story, but I've heard it before. Whenever you're down in the dumps, Ruthy. Right?

I haven't, Ann said. How come, Ruthy? Also, will you please sit with us.

The second question: What about this city? I mean, I'm kind of sick of these big international reports. Look at this place, looks like a toxic waste dump. A war. Nine million people.

Oh, that's true, Edie said, but Faith, the whole thing *is* hopeless. Top to bottom, the streets, those kids, dumped, plain dumped. That's the correct word, "dumped." She began to cry.

Cut it out, Ann shouted. No tears, Edie! No! Stop this minute! I swear, Faith said, you'd better stop that! (They were all, even Edie, ideologically, spiritually, and on puritanical principle against despair.)

Faith was sorry to have mentioned the city in Edie's presence. If you said the word "city" to Edie, or even the cool adjective "municipal," specific children usually sitting at the back of the room appeared before her eyes and refused to answer when she called on them. So Faith said, O.K. New subject: What do you women think of the grand juries they're calling up all over the place?

All over what place? Edie asked. Oh, Faith, forget it, they're going through something. You know you three lead such adversarial lives. I hate it. What good does it do? Anyway, those juries will pass.

Edie, sometimes I think you're half asleep. You know that woman in New Haven who was called? I know her personally. She wouldn't say a word. She's in jail. They're not kidding.

I'd never open my mouth either, said Ann. Never. She clamped her mouth shut then and there.

I believe you, Ann. But sometimes, Ruth said, I think, Suppose I was in Argentina and they had my kid. God, if they had our Sara's Letty, I'd maybe say anything.

Oh, Ruth, you've held up pretty well, once or twice, Faith said.

Yes, Ann said, in fact we were all pretty good that day, we were sitting right up against the horses' knees at the draft board – were you there, Edie? And then the goddamn horses started to rear and the cops were knocking people on their backs and heads – remember? And, Ruthy, I was watching you. You just suddenly plowed in and out of those monsters. You should have been trampled to death. And you grabbed the captain by his gold buttons and you hollered, You bastard! Get your goddamn cavalry out of here. You shook him and shook him.

He ordered them, Ruth said. She set one of her birthday cakes, which was an apple plum pie, on the table. I saw him. He was the responsible person. I saw the whole damn operation. I'd begun to run – the horses – but I turned because I was the one supposed to be in front and I saw him give the order. I've never honestly been so angry.

Ann smiled. Anger, she said. That's really good.

You think so? Ruth asked. You sure?

Buzz off, said Ann.

Ruth lit the candles. Come on, Ann, we've got to blow this out together. And make a wish. I don't have the wind I used to have.

But you're still full of hot air, Edie said. And kissed her hard. What did you wish, Ruthy? she asked.

Well, a wish, some wish, Ruth said. Well, I wished that this world wouldn't end. This world, this world, Ruth said softly.

Me too, I wished exactly the same. Taking action, Ann hoisted herself up onto a kitchen chair, saying, ugh my back, ouch my knee. Then: Let us go forth with fear and courage and rage to save the world.

Bravo, Edie said softly.

Wait a minute, said Faith . . .

Ann said, Oh, you . . . you . . .

But it was six o'clock and the doorbell rang. Sara and Tomas stood on either side of Letty, who was hopping or wiggling with excitement, hiding behind her mother's long skirt or grabbing her father's thigh. The door had barely opened when Letty jumped forward to hug Ruth's knees. I'm gonna sleep in your house, Gramma.

I know, darling, I know.

Gramma, I slept in your bed with you. Remember dat?

Oh sure, darling, I remember. We woke up around five and it was still dark and I looked at you and you looked at me and you had a great big Letty smile and we just burst out laughing and you laughed and I laughed.

I remember dat, Gramma. Letty looked at her parents with shyness and pride. She was still happy to have found the word "remember," which could name so many pictures in her head.

And then we went right back to sleep, Ruth said, kneeling now to Letty's height to kiss her little face.

Where's my Aunt Rachel? Letty asked, hunting among the crowd of unfamiliar legs in the hallway.

I don't know.

She's supposed to be here, Letty said. Mommy, you promised. She's really supposed.

Yes, said Ruth, picking Letty up to hug her and then hug her again. Letty, she said as lightly as she could, She *is* supposed to be here. But where can she be? She certainly is supposed.

Letty began to squirm out of Ruth's arms. Mommy, she called, Gramma is squeezing. But it seemed to Ruth that she'd better hold her even closer, because, though no one else seemed to notice – Letty, rosy and soft-checked as ever, was falling, already falling, falling out of her brand-new hammock of world-inventing words onto the hard floor of man-made time.

Barbara Nimri Aziz

Al-Dawwára

Barbara Nimri Aziz was born in Canada, where she was educated at Queen's University and spent her growing-up years among the Rideau lakes. An anthropologist by training, she now works as a freelance journalist, undertaking regular assignments to the Middle East. She is the co-founder and director of RAWI (Radius of Arab American Writers) and lives in New York City.

WHEN I WAS SEVEN YEARS OLD, I LONGED TO BE A BOY. ONLY AFTER I had passed forty did it occur to me that what I really wanted was to please my father. An Arab immigrant man, he was brought up to feel it was essential for him to have a son. So much did I love him that I myself wanted to be that son. Of course it never worked. Moreover, I was forfeiting the opportunity to be my father's ideal daughter: the traditional "nice girl" (American or Arab, it hardly mattered) – the kind of girl who adorns herself, who is trained to serve and entertain and become a mother, one who seeks the protection of a man.

But in some ways I was lucky. After all, my father still loved me even if I did not fit those dreams. Umma too (my mom) loved and accepted me just the way I was.

Already at the age of eight, I was in possession of the values and drive that Americans call tomboyish. My family learned the word "tomboy" and agreed that it applied to me, but at home they called me *"dawwára"* – wanderer, explorer. (*Dawahr* is the masculine.) To be *al-dawwára* was to be someone who was always on the move: restless, searching, a person who defies the norm, an adventurer. In Arab terms, it is unequivocally positive.

I liked being called a dawwára. I also liked being known as a "tomboy." The two identities worked together to help me flourish, focusing my drive and dreams, quietly shaping the foundations of my career, first as a field anthropologist, then as an overseas correspondent, and now in my early middle age, as a freelance journalist.

I was the second of two daughters. My sister was a year older than me, but we were very different. I was versatile and adventurous by nature, bold and at the same time contemplative, tolerant with others but frugal with myself. I chose action over talk, durability over style. My sister studied cooking and designed dolls' dresses. I remember her huddled into corners with her friends, all of them giggling and gossiping, and fondling each other's clothes and hair. I myself disliked this endless talk: talk about ugly girls, talk about other girls who did not strive to make themselves pretty. The more I listened, the more separate I became. I told my sister they were silly, and I wore my shirts loose and sloppy to emphasize my difference from them all. They could have that little social world for themselves.

Not surprisingly, as a child, I had few friends.

None of this meant that I was in any way like a stereotypical boy. Far from it. I did not play with trucks and guns. I did not punch other children, even in play; nor did I collect baseball cards or go in for team sports. (Although I remember that I did collect stones!) At the time, I was attracted to boys since they had access to outdoor things like climbing trees and cycling. But either they were unavailable, or they too seemed somehow silly.

I think it was Umma who reassured me that my lack of playmates was not a character defect. "It's true," she said, "you don't have friends like your sister does; she's different from you."

From the age of six to about eleven, I stayed close to Umma. She was a quiet woman, not demonstrative. From being with her so much I came to feel that solitude was something natural, something smooth. I associated her quietness with her silky, olive oil hands. She worked all the time, it seemed; she painted the house and she ran the store; she plucked chickens in the yard and repaired the clothesline and the fence. Yet her hands always remained soft. I used to study her hands as they tossed thin flat discs of Arabic bread onto a huge baking sheet, as they sorted through dried herbs or lentils, mixed cans of paint, or turned the pages of a magazine I knew she wished she could read.

Like most other Asian mothers, Umma never said she was too busy for me. I was welcome beside her anytime. If I was quiet and did not demand verbal interaction, I could remain there, whatever she was doing and whomever she was with.

But as much as I loved her, Umma could not offer the companionship I really needed. I wanted answers to all the questions I had about the world: how machines worked and why the stock market crashed, and why the Jews were treated that way, and where was Korea, and who were Gamal Abdal Nasser and De Gaulle. I wanted to visit zoos and galleries and museums. I wanted someone to take me on an airplane, or even on a train. I wanted someone who could pitch baseballs to me.

Umma could not help me with those things. She was an immigrant who worked long hours in our small fruit store with my father. She could not even read to me, either in Arabic or English, since, unlike her own mother in the old country, my Umma had never gone to school. And she was still dreaming for herself, I think.

Children who find themselves alone often become absorbed in books. I did not. First, books were never presented to me for answers or solutions. I found books in the library, almost by chance. Once there, I gravitated to illustrated adventure stories. *National Geographic* expeditions, Tarzans, and anthropomorphic tigers absorbed me (Nimri, my middle name, from my mother, means tigress), as did wild elephants and canoeing Indians, and mounted horsemen traversing the plains of Mongolia or Montana. All those protagonists were on the move. All were male – except perhaps the elephant and the tiger. In any case, none so absorbed my imagination that it was enough simply to read about them. These heroes inspired me to action.

But where is a solitary girl to go? Before I had a bike, I walked, and walked. I was always on my own, so I had to look out for myself, which meant I became a good observer. I noted landmarks along the way in order to make sure I found my way back. I learned to measure time and distances. Strangers interested me, and I paid close attention to the new faces around me, learning to observe them at a distance, by their behavior. They call this street language today. It's also the basis of fieldwork in anthropology and journalism.

Meanwhile I was developing my own body awareness. In the absence of competitors or teammates, I judged my strength by the size of my biceps, the number of push-ups and chin-ups I could do, the height of the trees I could scale. I remember feeling it was crucial that I could defend myself. In the fifties, we knew nothing of kung fu or Mace. And I didn't have a dog. I simply wanted to be strong in order to get where I wanted to go.

Then my parents bought me a bicycle, a red and silver machine with a basket and a rack. I was barely twelve at the time, the only girl in the town with a bicycle of her own. Silently encouraged by Umma, I would take off on solitary expeditions far beyond the town limits, often staying out late into the evening with my steel companion. I know she told my grandmother and father, "Barbara's all right; she'll take care of herself." Umma stood up for me like that; she cleared a path for me to run.

My expeditions with that bike proved to be a wonderful way to learn about myself as a physical being. On a trail or a roadway, I learned how to assess danger, and how much I could risk, crossing a highway or river, ascending a mountain, confronting strangers. When friends today tell me I am brave because I work alone in the Himalayas, or in Iraq, I do not understand them. Nothing is that simple. Bravery is made up of skills we accumulate, skills like self-reliance, assessing risk, endurance, and so forth. As a child, I was not naive about my risk-taking. I simply felt that if something happened, I would have to figure out what best to do.

Umma, I now realize, was my model. To me, she was a totally self-sufficient woman. My earliest memory is of her foraging along the roadside beyond the city limits, picking ripe red seedcones from sycamore trees. Later, we took them home and dried them, ready to mix with other herbs. We made *"za'tar,"* an aromatic Arabic paste for our breakfast toast. *Za'tar* could not be bought in any store and it could not be translated either. Umma was its only source.

Umma also dug up dandelion shoots and gathered grape leaves off roadside bushes, all for our table. It was not a matter of poverty, but of taste. This was a woman willing to forage for what she wanted, despite the frowns of passersby. "Poor immigrants," they may have thought. Or, "Why don't these people just go back to where they came from?" I suspect no one ever called Umma a tomboy.

I foraged at her side, learning how to choose the most tender leaves. I also had my own child agenda, hammering together a birdhouse, or scaling a tree or digging up worms and anthills.

Involuntarily I began to grow in other directions. After I turned fifteen, I had a series of crushes on boys my age. People stopped calling me a tomboy (Shouldn't tomboys fall in love?), but I was still dawwára in my family. That teenage "normalcy" did not supplant my earlier interests, in any case. By then my tomboy habits had built something enduring in me. Dawwára was embedded in my character.

Because I was more proficient now, I enjoyed hiking, cycling, and fishing and other tomboy explorations even more. I was not about to let go of the few skills that gave me some real confidence. I was comfortable in my loose shirt and sneakers. And there was no boy I loved enough to pursuade me to discard my walking boots for a pair of slippers, or my sturdy bike for a passenger seat in his car.

This was the fifties, and boys did not invite a girl on a cycling or camping date. This was the era of the automobile. And with the automobile came sex: or at least new sexual possibilities. I was not a prude. I was ready to try out certain things with my dates, but since I was not in the driver's seat, I felt pinned down, awkward, and confused. I missed my bicycle.

I graduated from bicycle to car with the help of Sheila, the first real friend I ever had. Sheila was only two years older than me but she seemed years ahead as a dawwára. She'd been a horse-riding champion at the age of eleven and by the time I met her she already knew how to drive a car, a skill she gladly shared with me. At that time, we both wanted to be transport truck drivers.

In contrast to me, Sheila was a good talker; I remember that she found ways for us to meet truck drivers at local carnivals and horse shows. Later on, when I began to hitchhike, I never turned down a lift in a truck. Truck drivers seemed sturdy and self-sufficient, seated up in that cabin, hands on the wheel, alone for days and nights on the road.

In college I became part of an international world of foreign students: women and men from Britain and Kenya and India, as well as Canadians from farms or big cities. This felt completely natural to me. At first, I studied marine biology, and this gave me lot of pleasure: a microscopic world as vast as oceans in which my eye could travel. But once I took a course in sociology and met John Meisel, I knew I wanted to explore world histories and cultures. John was an eminent political scientist, but he was an unusual character, even for a professor, and he recognized some similar qualities in me. Because of this, I think, he did not simply urge me to pursue sociology. He suggested when I graduated that I might work in India with Tibetan refugees.

I graduated with a degree in biology. Immediately afterwards, I sold my bike and a radio, withdrew my summer savings, and headed for England. From there I made my way to India, not by bike this time, but overland in a Landrover with two Australian women. That was 1963 and I was twenty-two.

The three years I worked in the Indian Himalayas and travelled around the subcontinent drew on every cell of my tomboyhood: the wanderer and explorer in me, my silence and curiosity, my ability to take risks, and my ease in the company of strangers. I found that Indian and Arab cultures are alike in many ways. Our music and languages and family traditions, our habit of sitting for many moments in silence, and then our sudden overwhelming intensity – these things overlap and interconnect.

Anthropological fieldwork came easy to me, just as overseas assignments as a journalist were always what I preferred. I did well at the University of London, but I eschewed theoretical social commentaries for what we call ethnography: the art of the description of cultures.

This would become my forte. By then I was a superb observer of human behavior, and I was willing to venture into the least known, most physically challenging places. I chose the border of Nepal and Tibet, in sight of Mt. Sagarmatha, and I stayed there for more than a year. I did not live among nomads, but in a settlement with a Tibetan monastery nearby, where I became close friends with the nuns.

Sometimes I walked through the mountains alone, at other times with porters or villagers returning from the weekly market in the valley. There were those who thought I should be a nun, because nuns were contemplative and independent. Others concluded that this is what odd Americans do; others again said I was a new breed of wanderer.

As a child, I often walked several hundred meters onto the frozen lake near our house, stepping over the ice, exhilarated by the feeling that I was on my own. In the biting winter, I became absorbed by the delicacy of patterns on the thick surface of the ice. Part of that beauty was its secrecy: even then I felt I was a privileged witness.

I was happy in Nepal, doing fieldwork in Sherpa or Tibetan homes, crowded around a fire with a score of others, all drunk and cozy in the smoke together. I was alone in that I often had to make decisions alone; and the solitude was hard at times. Yet the truth is I was never really alone. I lived in a busy village of nine hundred people and I was immersed in a complex web of personalities and history. I learned to use my anthropological writing to challenge others' stereotypes and open these worlds to distant Westerners. When I saw a chance to reach a wider public through journalism, I was spurred towards a new career.

Around 1980, my politics began to change. I wanted to know more about my own Arab people who were either invisible or miscast as villains both in news and in fiction. I also wanted to write for a larger readership than a handful of experts around the world.

In 1988 I took the greatest risk of my life. I left the academy and the meticulously drawn conclusions of anthropology and set myself down (unannounced and uninvited) among strangers in the Middle East to write articles from there for what I would find to be a hostile American public. Once again I was the tomboy, daring to go it alone.

Now, however, I had a lifetime of analytical skills behind me; I was a master interviewer; I could write; and I could still jump on a lorry or a bike to get to my destination.

Today, I travel on assignment in Iraq, Gaza, and Lebanon. I have to be physically fit, ready to work at 5:00 A.M., even after a gruelling fourteen-hour bus trip, or a long flight. In the evening I may take supper with a schoolgirl and her parents, and afterwards, drink and talk with Arab writer friends until dawn. On assignment, company is a matter of chance, not design.

Yes, on occasion, I've been followed or interrogated. But these are small risks, risks I know that I must take. I do not let them stop me. I have my assignment, my passport, my return ticket; and I count on these. Even so, there is always some danger. I accept it as part of any life. I feel prepared. As a young anthropologist in Tibet or Nepal, I dared a lot. Today, almost twenty years later, working as an overseas correspondent and freelance journalist, I'm still at it.

Even now, I can hear my Umma, watching her dawwára at work or play. "It's all right," she says. "Barbara can take care of herself."

Gail B. Griffin

Into the Woods

Gail B. Griffin was born in Detroit in 1950. She has taught English and women's studies at Kalamazoo College in Michigan since 1977. She is the author of two books of autobiographical essays: Calling: Essays on Teaching in the Mother Tongue *(1992) and* Season of the Witch: Border Lines, Marginal Notes *(1995), from which this memoir is taken. Her poetry has appeared in several journals and in* Contemporary Michigan Poetry: Poems from the Third Coast *(1987). She lives in Kalamazoo, but goes "Up North" whenever possible.*

> Land of the silver birch, home of the beaver,
> I will return to thee, hills of the north;
> Blue lake and rocky shore,
> I will return once more. . . .
>
> — A CAMP SONG

JULY, 1989

I am Up North. Ask a Michigander where Up North begins and you will get an array of answers, but we are no less sure of where it *is* or of when we are there. We also agree that the capital of Up North is T. C., Traverse City, huddled at the foot of the Mission Peninsula, which bisects Grand Traverse Bay. The particular corner of Up North where I find myself is southeast of Traverse City on the Boardman River, a cold, clear, fast stream that runs through dense forest. I'm sharing with my buddy Marigene a spacious A-frame cabin owned by a mutual friend. Marigene climbs trees and saws off dead limbs; I sit in the sun and read. She plays with her dog, Rigby (as in Eleanor); I sit in the shade and read. Iridescent turquoise dragonflies circle and land, veer away, coupling in air. The afternoons buzz. The sun drips down through the trees.

One day, bored with tree surgery, Marigene suddenly pipes up, "Wanna go look for your camp?" I have told her that I navigated the Boardman on a raft during my years at Camp Arbutus, a camp for girls on one of a chain of five small, pristine lakes southeast of T.C.

I attended Camp Arbutus every summer from 1960, when I turned ten, through 1965, when I got too old. For the first two years I did month-long sessions; thereafter, nothing but the whole eight weeks. I remember those months very simply. Endless depths of mottled green sunlight, clear blue water, the smell of dry pine needles and tar in the heat, and the sounds of girls' voices. With effort I can dredge up tears, anger, fear, jealousy, illness, rain. But, I recognize with a slight shock, those summers were the most entirely happy time in my life.

Yet they weren't a time. They were a series of times, six times, brief timeless times between the ordered real-time of the school year. Camp lay at the margins of my real life, where my real friends didn't go, where my parents played no part after they dropped me off. Perhaps this partially explains why my recollections of camp seem somewhat dreamlike. Camp had its distinct culture, its rituals, heroes, values, standards, lore. Camp was down the rabbit hole, through the looking glass, over the rainbow. And one day late in each June, I crossed over.

Literally, physically, Camp was something of a secret, hidden place. As Marigene and I drive off in search of it, I remember only the feeling of turning in off the main road (what road? what road was it?), parking in a small lot to the left, and walking down a long, dusty drive until the woods closed behind me and the sounds of the outside world died away. Then, suddenly, Camp opened up before me, with the Lodge on a rise to the right, the road down to the directors' cabins straight ahead, and the trail to Happy Hollow, for the littlest campers, to the left. Throughout the rolling woods behind the lodge were the cabins, idiosyncratically named. And further ahead, beyond it all, the hill sloped steeply down to the shore of small, tranquil Lake Arbutus, ringed with jagged, green-black evergreens.

I have been down this road so often in my dreams; it was my enchanted place, my somehow primal place. And when I wake from dreams in which I've gone back, I always yearn for a while, like one in exile who has dreamed of home.

I have told Marigene that I have no idea how to get there. Her road map gives us only the location of the lake. "That's all we need," she says confidently. "We'll find it." We drive around the general area between Mayfield and the lake for a while. Somehow it all looks far too civilized; I remember a darker, more mysterious landscape. We've been at this for only about fifteen minutes when suddenly, coming around a curve of blacktop, there it is: a sign, the one I used to crane my neck in the back seat of my mother's car to see, announcing in letters made of rope: "CAMP ARBUTUS."

I yelp. Marigene laughs and turns into the entry way. As we park in the lot on the left, I announce that I'm a little scared.

"Why?" Marigene asks, loving this.

"I have no idea."

Because it's the Twilight Zone, that's why. Because I don't know what lies down that road.

Or who.

By the third or fourth summer, coming back here was as close as my suburban white post-fifties life got to mystical. The place waited for me, always the same, and that continuity was at least half its value, as my life between ten and fifteen erupted with disorienting, profound changes. My Happy Hollow month was July of 1960, when I turned ten; the preceding December my father had died. After my third summer, in 1962, my mother remarried. For me this meant a new house in a different suburb, a new school just as I entered junior high, a new stepbrother and stepsister and extended family, new people everywhere in my life. Between my fourth and fifth summers, 1963 and 64, my only brother married and moved to Oregon, and my stepfather died suddenly. And in May of 1965, a month before my last Arbutus summer commenced, my mother married again, and so we moved again – another new stepbrother and stepsister, new city, new house, new school, this time just as I entered high school.

When I map it out like this, my own life looks so dramatic that I hardly recognize it. And on top of it all – or rather, beneath it – came puberty. My first summer at camp, I was a tall-for-my-age ten-year-old with a pixie haircut whose chief joys in life were playing the piano and watching "Bonanza." By the time I left Arbutus for the last time, weeping profusely, I had turned fifteen, had breasts and periods and long bleached hair and had discovered, via Paul McCartney, rock and roll and the meaning of passion. Those years, from ten to fifteen, form an arduous, perilous passage in any girl's life. For girls like I was, they are the Danger Zone defined by Carol Gilligan and others, the time of loss of voice, both literally and metaphorically. The tough, limber, confident little girl falls silent, weakens, looks away, forgets how to say "I want," "I know," "I see." Her self-expressions become corrupt, convoluted, self-destructive. In my life, family events had made these years positively tumultuous. But as a kid, in the midst of such experience, you normalize it. It's the only life you know, so it can't be extraordinary to you. I see myself at twelve or fourteen, raised to be cooperative, helpful, a trooper, mature-for-my-age, and I find myself hanging on to the saddlehorn of a runaway, bucking life. But when I walked down this entry road each summer, a promise was reconfirmed: something remained unchanged, something waited – the dark pines reflected in the lake, the same faces calling, the same songs and rituals. This was a place where my belonging deepened with every turn of the seasons, unlike the rest of my life, where family was repeatedly reconfigured, where home didn't exist either as a temporal or spatial concept, and where everyone and everything was new, awkward, without past. Here I was met at the end of the road not only by old friends but by a familiar self. I stepped up to her and ran off into the woods.

That was half the mystery and wonder of Camp – that it endured. But the other half was that it didn't. It was transitory, ephemeral. Though I never saw it disappear, I knew it did. I tried to imagine it in winter, snowbound and silent, the lake frozen gray, doors and gates locked, horses transported south, boats in drydock. It scared me and I stopped. It was easier to imagine that Camp simply vanished into a wrinkle in time, reappearing with the summer. My own private Brigadoon.

By the time Marigene and I reach the point where I know Camp is about to appear around the next bend in the dirt road, I am breathless with eagerness and anxiety. Maybe I don't even want to see it again.

But there it is.

The first thing I notice is a long wooden table at the bottom of the rise to the Lodge. A bunch of pubescent girls and younger boys seems to be lounging around, in chairs or on top of the table. Don't they have a schedule to follow? And –

Wait a minute: *BOYS?*

There are *boys* at Camp Arbutus?

Marigene is smiling into the sun, looking around, taking it all in. One of the girls, about twelve, long honey-colored hair in a thick ponytail, saunters over and says in a distinct English accent, "Can I help you?" Who ARE these children? I stammer that I used to go to camp here, that I just want to walk around if it's all right. "Sure it is," she shrugs. "But Mac's here, if you want to see her. She'd probably remember you."

Mac is here? Twenty-five years after I left my last sneaker print in the pine-needled dust, Grace MacDonald still exists, here? Well, of course. This is Never Never Land.

Mac was the Assistant Director. The directors, a somewhat regal older couple (regality being a relative quality in pedal pushers), were the Elizabeth-and-

Philip figureheads; Mac was the prime minister. She did gruff-with-a-heart-of-gold to perfection. There she'd be, on the margins of any camp activity, standing silent, cross-armed, a small ironic smile. We feared her a little, and I desperately wanted her approval.

Well, there's a little gray in the dark, wavy, thick modified D.A. But Mac remembers me. "Griffin," she repeats several times, narrowing her eyes to see me at eleven or twelve. And then to my amazement she reels off the names of counselors and fellow campers of my era. "What about Sam?" I ask. "Have you heard anything about her?"

She nods deeply, then shakes her head. "Born again."

"No! Sam?" Wild, profane, tomboy Sam?

"Yep, born-again Christian."

As long as we're into heresies, I ask about the boys. The answer is depressing: insurance has become so formidable that they've had to expand. "But we only take the younger ones," she assures me. "Pre-teenage." Small comfort.

Mac owns the camp now, I'm gratified to hear – bought it when Elizabeth and Philip abdicated south. But she fears she can't hold it long. The costs are staggering. She shakes her head. I think of the very worldly, obviously privileged girl who met us. At the table with her were a couple brown Indian faces. Of course: the camp has been internationalized by the influx of business and professional families from overseas, who send their kids to private schools and private camps. I picture the faces gathered in the Lodge in 1962: not one non-white face among them. Nearly all of us were from Michigan and northern Ohio, suburbs like Bloomfield Hills or Upper Arlington. The depth of my innocence then, coming back here for six summers and never knowing that this was an absolute luxury.

With Mac's blessing, Marigene and I head off on a walking tour of Camp. It occurs to me that I might be in one of my dreams. I put my feet down softly, quietly, afraid it will all crumble. We range up over "the Hill" beyond the Lodge, dotted with the cabins of middle-aged campers, twelve to fourteen; and down into "the Hollow," a cluster of cabins for younger girls. I am ransacking my memory for the names of the cabins I was in; I know they're wedged somewhere in a fold of my brain. They float back: Cedar, West Wind. . . . As we move to higher ground, scraps of the blue lake appear and vanish through the trees just as they used to.

The ache in my shoulders is like a low hum in the background. I have learned to stroke through it, on and on, turning my wrists forward at the end to put a tail on the J. If I hold it just a fleet second, the bow will swing to the left. But I don't, and the canoe surges gently across the water. One day I am standing up in the stern of a huge war canoe, feet apart, calling out "Stroke! Stroke!" to the eight girls sitting in front of me, feeling like something out of "Ben Hur." What does coxing a war canoe have in common with the nineteen-sixties, with Swinging London, the dead Kennedys, we shall overcome? What does it have to do with Capezios, white eyeliner, strawberry vanilla lipstick? Nothing. Not a blessed thing. I stand there timeless, ridiculous, mythic, in command of my boat.

We stand still and breathe. The warm smell of dry pine needles mingles with the other woodscents. Small rushes of wind bend the tops of the pines. It is quiet, deserted, but I hear muffled sounds – shots from the riflery range, arrows thwopping into straw-stuffed targets. "I was really good at archery," I tell Marigene.

"Yeah?" she says.

"I still have the certificates and medals someplace."

I get so that I can find almost by feel the particular spot in the air where my arrow tip belongs: just to the right of the bullseye and up slightly. The feathers hiss over my fingers and the metal tip buries itself in the red vinyl, the shaft quivering in the air. My right bicep throbs quietly, it's a heavy bow. Last summer I couldn't draw the string back far enough, to the place alongside my right cheek, so tight that sometimes when I straighten my three fingers the string burns my skin as it shoots forward.

Beyond the archery range, I begin to lose my bearing. Paths converge and separate, heading off into the woods. I know that at some point my feet will know, my body will know which one to take, the one that led toward the horses. You had riding three days a week, MWF or TTS. Those were the best days. It was an uphill trek, maybe a quarter mile, and then the green pine smell would give way to warm brown horse smell.

It's a peculiar, difficult gesture, holding him back and urging him forward at once, so that he breaks from a walk straight into a canter without slipping into a trot. It's especially hard bareback. But so is sitting a trot. He's a big bay, sixteen hands, black mane and tail, with those huge, lucid, intelligent brown eyes that only horses have, and only some of them. His name is Toy, for his bigness. You

rotate to a different horse every class, with some allowances made for size and
temperament — of horse and of rider, that is. But the days I know I have Toy
waiting for me are days of swallowed anticipation. To swing my right leg over
and settle onto his solidity, to feel his muscles shift, the forward lurch of him, the
steady gait. The moment he breaks into a canter, the fear followed by something
like ecstasy. Pelvis moving to his rhythm, hands quiet and close to his withers,
trying to keep still from the waist up, the slight lean into a turn, hugging his
round sides with my thighs, trying to remember to sit tall, not to lean down toward
his beautiful neck. The sun rushing by through the blurry trees. Don't stop. Don't
ever stop. Stop time here, right here.

For a fleet moment I wonder if Toy is still here, and then I realize it's been
twenty-three years. And I have not been on a horse since the last summer I was
here. I am thirty-nine years old. When I was here, I could not imagine thirty-
nine. Mac was probably not yet thirty-nine then. For me, the depth of sophistica-
tion, wisdom, and general coolness was seventeen, the age of most of the CIT's,
Counselors-in-Training. They laughed at things we didn't understand, went to
T.C. on Saturday nights and wouldn't tell us about it on Sunday, had breasts
and great haircuts, boyfriends at home and stories to tell. They sang suggestive
songs, winked at us, implied always that although they had to enforce the rules,
things would be different if they ran the place.

I am running from the softball diamond, up the hill toward my cabin. I am
crying, desperately, passionately. I have hurt Sam somehow, thrown or swung
wild and watched the ball connect with her shoulder or back. Am I running away
from her? After her? Away from my shame, from proffered solace, from and into
my conviction that I am a Jonah, an awkward, graceless loser? Sam the
invincible, the freckled, grinning everybody's-favorite, the born winner: wounded,
bruised by my stupidity. Sam was a camper at age eight, making her now the elect
of the elect, the one who knows all the lore, the secrets, the precedents, the songs
and stories, the drill, the program, the style. She is the camp's child; I can't
imagine her having a regular home, and parents. The mischief shining in her eyes
is barely held in check by her CIT responsibilities and loyalty to Arbutus, and no
authority figure can stay angry at her. She is the androgyne, solidly built,
muscular, with short, slick black hair. Completely unselfconscious, always in
motion. To see her throw her head back and laugh stops my heart. I would die to

please her, get her attention, impress her, make her laugh. I would die to be born again as Sam.

There is no feeling like the crush of a pubescent girl on an older one, none on this earth.

What did it mean to be a girl at Camp? It seems, in memory, that all the lines were redrawn, all the Outside World rules, categories, labels, requirements were irrelevant. Neither femininity nor ladylikeness raised her tiresome head all summer. Prissy, fastidious, or vain girls were ridiculed: they had come to the wrong place. We ran and sweated and yelled and laughed, we made alliances and fought, we wore no make-up and outfits that didn't match, we let our hair dry in the sun after swimming and washed it once a week if we remembered; we were always on our way into or out of the lake so it was wet most of the time anyway. We giggled at the two males in our world, the dour, decrepit busdriver and the teenaged handyman, and went back to being completely satisfied with ourselves and each other.

Heading back toward the Lodge, I can't resist running down to Slide-Inn, the cabin in which I spent my third summer. The origin of its name is obvious from its situation, perched halfway down the bluff to the lake. Coming down the path from the Lodge on a rainy day, you often did literally slide in.

I am running down from the Lodge on a hot afternoon, sneakers slapping the path. If my toe catches on a root, I'm gone. The momentum carries me up the steps and through the cabin door, which slams behind me. Probably I have dashed back to get something I forgot before I lope off to riflery.

Inside, it seems unbearably close, hot. It couldn't have been this small, but it must have been, because the walls are covered, completely covered, in names and dates: in ink, pencil, marker, calcified toothpaste. And one of them is mine. Marigene spots it first, on a rafter above a top bunk. In the middle of the wood floor, I stand, sweating, looking up at it. GAIL GRIFFIN '62 in pale green — probably Crest, then a new brand.

I always try to grab the top bunk. You can hide there, if you need to. And at night you can lie on your side at the inside edge of the metal frame, your face close to

the screen, watching the darkness settle down. Taps blow, sometimes sweetly, at 9
p.m., when dark is just gathering at the western edge of the Eastern Time Zone on
daylight savings in July and August. When dark comes it is absolute. The cabins
have no electricity, so if someone goes out to the bathroom, a flashlight's bright
circle bounces along a path. I feel the edge of the air turn chill, I hear a zillion
crickets. I hear the footsteps of two counselors along a path, their soft laughter.
And one night, with a cold jolt to the stomach, I hear a wild, utterly clear, utterly
insane laugh from across the still lake.

We are teenaged girls, or nearly, and we know about dangers in the dark. We
tell stories about The Hook, The Babysitter. "The call's coming from inside the
house!" "And hanging on the door handle is a HOOK!" The maniacal laugh
came from inside the woods, our woods. it's like the animal skull we found on
South Manitou Island — the vacant eyes, the memento mori at the center of
paradise.

The next day our counselor tells me about loons.

Something wants to stay forever, something wants to go. Our last stop is the
Lodge itself, and this is a small shock: again, of course, smaller than the vast,
woody shrine I remember, but also clearly in disrepair, dusty, almost seedy. The
wonderful smell is the same: decades of woodsmoke coating the walls, ceiling,
windows. Down the lake side of the central living room, with the big stone
fireplace, runs the long porch lined with tables where we gathered three times a
day, sang a grace ("Oh, the Lord is good to me, / And so I thank the Lord /
For giving me the things I need, / The sun and the rain and the appleseed. . . .")
ate, sang again, a funny song this time, and went on to the next phase of a day
organized by the clanging Lodge bell.

At the opposite end of the central room from the fireplace, the birchbark
canoe still hangs. Not *a* but *the* birchbark canoe. Supposedly the genuine article,
Indian-made. And at the end of every summer, in the holiest, most secret-
shrouded ritual of all, the CITs carefully took it from the log where it hung,
bore it down to the lake, and held it by the gunwales as, out of the woods,
emerged the one camper chosen worthiest to paddle it out across the glassy
waters of Lake Arbutus at sunset.

It was always an older girl, a long-time camper, resident of Donut or Nejee.
In 1965, August — my last days at Camp, though I didn't know it — daily life
became a prayer. Back in the World, I would never get the honors that counted
among girls. This is my world, I prayed, let it be me.

But wasn't me. It was Annie, a sunny, warm, wonderful girl whom everybody, including me, adored. I was given the first-runner-up honor: that of writing Camper's Diary, the long narrative poem that would be read at the final ceremonies. I was, if you will, that summer's Camp Arbutus Homer. So that I would have time to compose this epic, I was told far in advance, sworn to secrecy. Unable to share my sorrow, I went away to my top bunk and sobbed. A counselor found me there and asked why I wasn't wherever I was supposed to be. I lied and said I didn't feel well, had cramps. She insisted on taking me to Pill Hill, the infirmary, where I lay on a cot all afternoon feeling miserable and ashamed.

Ingrate that I was, little shit. Second place in the whole camp wasn't good enough? Didn't I know how appropriate this honor was for me? Well, yes, I did. That was why I didn't want it. I didn't want to be me, articulate and literary. I wanted to be the other thing, the one everybody loved, chosen to kneel in that canoe and pull the water past its swelling white flanks with a perfect J-stroke, no waves, no wake. I wanted to strike out toward sunset, across the cool lake, a silhouette against the peachy sky, with the entire camp population on shore, silently watching me.

Instead, I wrote the poem, which everybody said was the best one anybody had ever written. And for the rest of my life I have written the poem and yearned to paddle the birchbark canoe.

On the way out, I notice a huge wooden sign hanging outside the Lodge. CAMP ARBUTUS 25th BIRTHDAY 1962. Below are a dozen or so squares of shellacked wood, attached to each other like quilt pieces, each made by one cabin in the summer of 1962. Quickly my eyes find "Slide Inn," woodburned sloppily into the pine. And a list of our names – me, Annie, Lisa, Mary Ann. . . . "There you are again!" Marigene hoots, delighted. "Do you remember doing this?"

I do.

There we are, twenty-seven years later, for these new-age campers to peruse and wonder about and probably sneer at. These girls who probably like Madonna and do drugs and lose their virginities at eleven – and these BOYS. What do they know? We were mighty. "Campers, campers, hats off to you," went one of our songs. It had been a time, hadn't it, a vintage time. And we had left our marks, hadn't we? Burned in wood. Looped in toothpaste.

"Arbutus moon," went a song sung at the end of campfires, just before we crept back to our cabins to sleep, "I'd like to be as lovely as you are, Arbutus moon."

It is not until we are back at our outpost on the Boardman that I know what I have understood in going back, the subliminal discovery that has been whispering in me all day.

Camp was a holy place for me always, for many reasons. If you are vulnerable to the particular blue-and-green, pine-smelling, deep-souled beauty of Up North, it is haunting. It was also a place of belonging in years when I felt transient. It was a place where, in the very years when girls weaken toward womanhood, I became strong, had certificates and ribbons and biceps and hard thighs to show for it. In the time when the power born in us seeps out of us into things and people around us, and we begin our lifelong search to find it again, I found it here, in wind and water and the muscular back of a bay horse.

But above all, it was a female place, a girl place. In the very years when we begin that long, complicated slide into the world of men, this was a world of women, little and big. A place out of time, stretching from little-girlhood across the great divide into womanhood. It was a place where girls could be strong and weak, stupid and smart, silly and serious, plain and pretty, could learn and take chances and fail and triumph, all of it apart from the gender police, the sexual strait-jacketing of Real World adolescence. It was the only place where a girl like me could approach something that felt like freedom.

Was it the first time in my life I felt free?

It was certainly the last.

Teresa Jordan

The Conceit of Girls

Teresa Jordan was born and grew up on a ranch in the Iron Mountain Country of southeastern Wyoming, the fourth generation of her family to work that land. As a young girl, her proudest possessions were her great-grandmother's silver-inlaid spurs, which she used daily, in the "horse and cow work which made up [her] childhood."

These days, Teresa Jordan lives in Nevada with her husband, Hal Cannon. She is the author of Cowgirls: Women of the American West *(1982) and* Riding the White Horse Home: A Western Family Album *(1993), and writes frequently about the West and its rural culture.*

BACK WHEN I WAS VERY SMALL AND MY FATHER WAS A GIANT AND AL- ways in a hurry, I remember trotting along at his side, trying to keep up with his long-legged stride. I have come across such scenes in fiction, and I have also heard friends describe similar experiences out of their own lives. Often, the father is not only a giant but a bad guy, oblivious to his little girl's needs, or consciously insensitive, or downright cruel. But in my own memory, the sun shines on a slant and the grass is still wet with dew. The day vibrates with purpose and I feel a strength in my legs, a capacity in my lungs, a competence that, looking back now, I realize was completely at odds with my age. My father is going to work, and he has asked me to come along.

Perhaps we are heading for the shop, where my little hands will be able to fit the grease gun to a nozzle deep in the bowels of the baler, a task that had left my father in a sputtering rage the night before. Or maybe we are heading to the pickup to take salt and mineral to the cattle. I'll "ride shotgun" to get the gates and I'll use my own pocketknife to open the sacks of supplement. Or perhaps I am a little older and we saddle up and head out for the high country to find a bull missing from the roundup. The critter isn't in the first pasture we check, or the second, or the third. By the time we find him, sick with footrot and on the fight, my father's colt has played out and is no longer useful. He stands to the side as I do the hard and dangerous work of getting the bull headed home. The bull tries to take me, sometimes feinting and other times charging, time and again. If the bull becomes *too* angry, my father will suggest we leave him for another day, but my horse works well, and we pivot out of the way and come back at the bull until finally he turns down the trail and limps off like it was his own idea all along. We arrive at a neighbor's corral at dark, after having ridden forty miles or more. We put the bull in a pen and call my mother to pick us up. A cloudburst explodes just as she arrives, and we slip-slide the gumbo road home through thunder and lightning and blinding rain as my father tells her how he couldn't have gotten the bull out of the hills without me. It's true. If I hadn't been along, he would have come home empty-handed. We both know this, and it makes us feel good. I am ten years old, or maybe twelve.

I must have been a wild one as a child. For the first two or three years I attended our rural neighborhood's one-room school; I was the only girl. Even before that, I hung out with my older brother, Blade, and his friends. I learned to ride, to fight, to shoot, to swear. I remember wanting to be a boy, and I remember thinking it unfair that the boys tried to keep me out of things simply because I was a girl. But I also remember feeling special because I *was* a girl and I got in anyway. I was certainly aware of the differences between us, and I remember noting with some pride, though probably only to myself, that I had seen every boy in the neighborhood pee, but they hadn't seen me. I'm not talking about being a peeping Tommi here, sneaking around in the bushes, trying to cop a view. Because I was "one of the boys," they answered the call of nature unselfconsciously. I was not enough one of the boys to do the same. The fact that I kept score indicates that I wasn't really one of the boys at all.

A few moments of epiphany from those years:

We were moving cattle and I was riding along behind the herd, swearing effusively. I was using words I had learned from the boys, who had learned them from the men, and I was using words I'd learned from the men directly, since I worked with them almost as much as the boys did. I was having a great time, chirping and ki-yipping and cussing as cowboys are wont to do when they ride behind cows, when suddenly I broke off mid-syllable. What stopped me? As I look back now, I simply don't know. It's as if I suddenly heard myself and was shocked, which means that I must have caught some clue wafting on the wind from the men around me, or even from the universe at large, that my behavior was inappropriate. It's not that I quit swearing from that moment on

(I still swear more than, say, my husband), but I changed from being truly foul-mouthed to indulging in only an occasional "shit" or "damn."

A second memory: I was with my family at a party at our neighbors', the Hirsigs. It might have been Christmas or perhaps the gathering after a day of branding. The whole neighborhood was there, as well as several families from town. I jumped at the chance to play with the Hirsigs' two daughters, both younger than I, and the half-dozen town girls of various ages. We ran in a pack. Buddy, the Hirsigs' father, was younger than my own, and more playful. He had infinite patience with kids and we were all crazy about him. At one point, we swarmed around, begging him to pick us up. When my turn came, I crawled up into his lap, as I had seen several other girls do, and I snuggled up against him. I remember distinctly stroking his cheek. And then suddenly I grew hot with shame and slunk down, only to be replaced by another girl. Again, what happened? I know for a fact that Buddy did nothing wrong, nothing lascivious. But where did I learn my own seductive behavior? What made me suddenly conscious of it? Why did I feel such shame? And why did I seem to be the only one perplexed? It was as if I suddenly became aware of the difference between being a tomboy, an identity of which I was passionately proud, and being a daddy's girl, *any* daddy's girl. At some level I must have recognized that I could cuss (mildly) or I could coo, but I couldn't do both.

And a third recollection: One day in school, Blade and I got into a terrible fight. This must have been during the years when I was still the only girl. At any rate, we were both young enough that I held a slight advantage of strength, something I would soon lose forever. I had him pinned to the floor and I brandished a ruler with which I intended to strike him. The sun glinted off its metal edge, and in my memory, it loomed as lethal as a saber. I suddenly became aware of my own violence, and let the ruler clatter to the floor. I don't know how the fight ended, but neither of us was mortally wounded. And I don't remember for sure if that was the last time I ever fought a boy, but I rather suspect that it was.

These memories are united by an underlying current of eroticism, and also by my growing awareness of the threat of exile. I realize now that I was learning not to garner too much attention. More than anything else, I wanted access to the world of men, which is to say, in my particular circumstance, to the world of nature and animals and physical work. If I were too wild or too sexy, access could be denied or could become dangerous, facts that served to smooth my rough edges.

Where was my mother in all this? The short answer is, in the house. She was not a tomboy, horses frightened her, and she did not particularly enjoy hard physical labor. But neither was she a typical housewife (whatever that is). She was a good-enough housekeeper and an excellent cook. She also kept the books and made out the payroll, did much of the hiring, drove to town for parts. She belonged to service clubs and lobbied for the Stockgrower's Association. When I was in fifth grade, she started teaching our one-room school.

In retrospect, she was a remarkably self-contained woman. She was never frightened to stay alone in our house fifty miles from town when my father was away on business; whatever worry she felt when he or one of us kids were late home from riding, she managed to conceal. If she were to describe the partnership she felt with my father in business terms, she would probably have given herself the title of Executive Secretary; for her, he was absolutely first in command, but she knew she was essential. She also kept a certain part of her life for herself, through friendships and reading. She loved both conversation and ideas; she subscribed to a variety of magazines and a book club, and I remember once she took a correspondence course in Art History from the Metropolitan Museum.

Though my mother was not herself an outdoorsy woman, she supported my tomboy ambitions. Since both Blade and I worked outside, she divided the domestic chores evenly between us, and she never tried to make me into a little lady. (Though I do remember her once sinking down in exhaustion in a Montgomery Ward's dressing room when we were shopping for school clothes and I was being particularly obnoxious about not wanting to wear any damn dresses.) She greeted my advances in cowboy craft and daring with the same enthusiasm she did those of my brother.

As much as I loved participating in the world of men, I also loved my mother's world which was softer and gentler and much more intimate. We could talk about anything – work, men, sex, poetry, mathematics, baking – and we spent hours together in the kitchen cooking or in the car driving the long road to town. But my mother's world was distinct in my mind from the more generalized world of women, something I imagined as much more boring, filled as it was reputed to be with babble about babies and recipes and other uninteresting stuff. My mother disparaged this world, as did most ranch women I knew. I thought this was particular to ranch culture until I left it and found that many women – including those who would never have thought of themselves as tomboys – professed a similar superiority to mundane feminine concerns. It was as if we could believe in our own value, and that of a few hand-picked friends, only in contrast to "women" who, as a group, didn't interest us much.

In her short stories and memoirs, Mary Clearman Blew, herself ranch-raised in Montana, often describes a certain sort of rancher's daughter who shadows her father and is his "boy." These girls are usually slim-hipped, quiet, competent, sexless. I recognize them; if I was never as quiet as some instinct told me I should be, androgyny still bought me safe passage. I started out working with my father but I soon began working with the other men, something that was possible – and comfortable – because the possibility of sparks between us simply never existed.

For the most part, it worked. In my entire working life, I have had only two uncomfortable encounters with men. One was with a young man my father had fired earlier in the day. I didn't know about his dismissal, and was working with a colt in the round corral when he approached me. We made small talk for a while and then he followed me when I took the horse back to the barn. I grained the colt and turned him out. When I hung up the halter and turned around, the young man cornered me. I was scared but also excited; we had never worked together, but I found him incredibly handsome. He took off my glasses and said, "You aren't so bad looking without these things," a line that didn't exactly meet my young adolescent imaginings of romance. Then he took off his hat and placed it on my head, saying, "Where I hang my hat is my home." I gave his hat back to him – I'd like to think without hesitation – and said, "This house doesn't take boarders," or some such line, not bad for a rank beginner. Then I hightailed it out of the barn.

The memory still gives me the creeps. Even before I learned that my father had fired him, I must have recognized that his advance had less to do with attraction for me than it did with some simmering hostility. The moment radiated with a potential for ugliness. I escaped unscathed but the experience left me aroused and confused; at a deeper level, it also warned me of the dangers that lurked around the slightest departure from androgyny.

The second experience came during my junior year of college when I returned to school after my mother's sudden death. Her loss had shattered me and I suppose a certain vulnerability leaked through my careful armor. A professor made a pass at me. I still remember how shocked I was, and how upset. I fled his office and from that point on, I avoided him. He had been a mentor and important advisor. Now I dropped out of his class and changed my major. This last step I had planned to do anyway, but the experience reminded me of what was at stake when sex got mixed up with things.

It was not, in my particular world view, that sensuality was not allowed. *Flirting* was the problem, not romance itself. From ninth grade on, I almost always had a boyfriend; those times I did not and was "available" were excruciatingly uncomfortable. How I connected with boyfriends in the first place is somewhat of a mystery. We almost always met within the context of shared interest or work – through the high school speech program, for instance, or in college seminars, or later, at professional conferences – but I followed unwritten rules. Our involvement could not threaten my ability to continue my interest. In other words, we had to be peers; I could never have gotten involved with someone I worked *for* rather than with. The move from collegiality to kissing was always painful for me, and I was terrifically relieved when that period of limbo came to an end. Once in a relationship, I was at ease with my own physicality. And outside that relationship, I was "taken" and therefore sexless – which meant it was once again safe to work with men. A primary relationship, in other words, let me move freely in the rest of my life; based on such utilitarian concerns, it's not surprising that they didn't last. I was in my mid-thirties before I felt secure enough to spend a couple of years alone and learned to fully function on my own. Only then could I meet the partner with whom I could imagine spending the rest of my life.

I was not the only tomboy I knew throughout my girlhood. In time, the Hirsigs started school, and Jennie Mai Bonham moved with her family to a community nearby. The four of us formed our own small gaggle of gutsy girls, and, as my world expanded, I met others. We had our conceits. We could move comfortably in the world of men, and we knew what secrets we needed to keep in order to get along. We claimed our places among women, too, often with a certain sense of superiority that we learned from our mothers. And many of us insisted on an authority unavailable to the generation that preceded us. If we couldn't have marriages based on true equality, we wouldn't marry at all. Few of us could be comfortable as "executive secretaries"; we wanted offices of our own.

As the years have passed and I look back on us from some distance, I realize that many of us had something else in common that denied our conceits, a certain discomfort with ourselves as women at all, something that manifested itself in our bodies as we matured. Some of us became anorexic, melting off our breasts and hips and even eliminating our periods; others gained weight, sometimes a lot of it. Our bodies became war zones of irony as we sought to starve or gorge the very strength and competence that gave us identity and joy in the world.

For those of us who grew up on ranches, the West was a canvas against which we played out our lives, and it provided historical precedent for our own activities through figures such as Annie Oakley and Calamity Jane. Oakley was born in Ohio, but gained worldwide recognition riding with Buffalo Bill's Wild West. She was tiny and demure, and her reputation as a proper lady meant as much to her as her place among the best marksmen in the world. She valued femininity yet was ultimately androgynous, safe within a sense of propriety so strong it occasionally made her seem something of a prig, and unavailable sexually because of her business partnership and marriage to Frank Butler. Calamity Jane occupied the other end of the spectrum. Large and mannish, she drank and brawled and wore men's clothes. She bragged about working as a freight driver and uniformed scout, claimed a love affair with Wild Bill Hickok (which seems to have been a fabrication), and died as a prostitute and alcoholic.

I suspect that many tomboys teeter, to greater or lesser degree, between these two poles of propriety and wildness, femininity and mannishness. For some of us, real comfort with ourselves as women – strong, competent, *and* sexual – has become possible only as we mature into middle age.

Three or four summers ago, when I lived in Salt Lake City, a dear friend came to visit. We sat outside on the stoop in the heat of the day catching up, and in time the conversation meandered to our childhoods." I don't remember a single time in all my growing up," she told me, "that my father, or any man for that matter, took me seriously – or even really saw me." And then she started to weep.

We had been close for many years, this friend and I, and we knew much about the hurts and joys of each other's lives. Still, I had never known her to express such naked pain before, and I reached out to her in that hot noon sun. Her childhood in an Eastern suburb could not have been more different than mine on a Wyoming ranch. She perceived herself as small and invisible, on the edges looking in; I worried that if I were too noticeable, too large or loud or rowdy, I would be expelled from what I perceived as the center. But we were sisters under the skin. Both of us measured our worth as girls by how we were seen by men.

The ranch where I was raised was sold the year I graduated from college. For twenty years, I have led an urban life. Recently, my husband and I bought a small ranch in Nevada, and as I struggle to remember what I have forgotten, and realize how terribly much I never knew, I wonder if my memories of competence are an illusion. But if I didn't have the chance to bring the skills I was learning into full maturity, the chance I was given to participate, and to be taken seriously, gave me confidence to do other things such as travel tens of thousands of miles alone right out of college and to renovate a house on my own.

As I write, Shannon Faulkner, the first female to enter the famed Citadel Military Academy, has withdrawn due to illness and hazing. A woman of my mother's generation probably could never have imagined a girl being allowed to attend; few women of my own could imagine a girl wanting to. Faulkner is my stepdaughter's age; I hope that their daughters, should they have them, will find that particular path, and many others, open to them without question. If such a course interests them, I hope that they can follow it without being set apart – or setting themselves apart – from other women, and without having to ravage the part of themselves that makes them women. I hope that we can mature into the sort of society that insists that all girls (and all boys, too), no matter what their interests, will have the chance to be seen and heard and taught and respected.

Anne LaBastille

Tomboy

Anne LaBastille was born in New York City and grew up in Montclair, New Jersey. As a teenager she took a job at a resort in the Adirondacks, and later went on to study conservation of natural resources at Cornell University and wildlife management at Colorado State. Her Ph.D. is in wildlife ecology. LaBastille's first book, Woodswoman, *appeared to great acclaim in 1976. Since then she has published* Assignment Wildlife *(1978),* Women and Wilderness *(1980),* Beyond Black Bear Lake *(1987),* The Wilderness World of Anne LaBastille *(1992), and* Birds of the Mayas *(1994). She travels widely, or spends her time at home in her Adirondack cabin, "West of the Wind," with her two German shepherds.*

> I found nature my most reliable companion. In the beginning nature
> provided adventure; later it was the source of much deeper emotional and
> aesthetic pleasure. — *from an interview with* E. O. WILSON,
> *Entomologist Extraordinaire*

"YOU *CAN'T* GO HIKING IN THE WOODS," PRONOUNCED MY MOTHER, her 200-pound frame pulsing with Teutonic authority. "And you *can't* go camping."

I was ten years old and I was stunned. Meanwhile my head was thrumming with outdoor visions from the books I'd been reading under the bedcovers, page by flashlit page, each night. Books like *Boy with a Pack* and *Jonathan Goes West* by Stephen W. Meader, *The Yearling* by Marjorie Kinnan Rawlings, and *Bruce* and *Wolf* by Albert Payson Terhune, the great writer of dog stories.

"Why not?" I wailed.

"Girls don't *do* that!" was her emphatic reply.

Even then her reasoning seemed wrong. Call it my French genes; the French love of "Equality, Liberty, and Fraternity"; or my French ancestors storming the Bastille. I was old enough to sense I had to defy this unjust dictate.

My lifelong rebellion against convention has made it possible to hike the 130-mile Northville – Lake Placid Trail in the Adirondack Mountains by myself. To spend three months on a solo writing assignment exploring the Amazon

Basin via cruise ship, dugout canoe, small plane, helicopter, jeep, and on foot through the jungle. To conduct an ecological field survey on one of the wildest peninsulas in the Dominican Republic. And, in daily life, to live alone with two loyal German shepherds, in a log cabin I built myself, with no road, electricity, or indoor plumbing.

Perhaps my tomboy quest for freedom began halfway up a huge white pine, at our modest home in the New Jersey suburbs. I spent hours in a hand-made tree-house, swaying in the wind, reading, whittling, and calling to crows. They came to learn my voice and cawed right back. Sometimes I'd climb up at night and gaze east towards the glittering fringe of light that was New York City. I never wanted to go *there*. Instead I'd turn west where a low range of hills bulked dark and compelling (no condos then). I yearned to roam in *those* haunts.

My tree-house was a refuge from the many lessons in "How to Become a Young Lady" which my mother inflicted upon me. She herself had been trained as a concert pianist and was eager that I follow in her footsteps. She arranged for art, ballet, drama, piano, cello, and ballroom dancing classes during my years at elementary school. One of the worst fights we ever had occurred over ballroom dancing. Even now I remember her voice as she ordered me down from the pine tree, and demanded that I don silk stockings and dab on nail polish before she rushed me off (screeching) to waltz with equally miserable little boys. Later, she enrolled me (at age fourteen) in a private girls' day high school and bought me a pink cashmere sweater and matching plaid skirt to wear my first day there! I protested, but to no avail. My mother's mind was made up. Variations on the "can't" theme became more adamant as I approached fifteen. "You *can't* get a job working out-of-doors." Followed by, "No, of course you *can't* drive a car across the United States. You're staying right here in New Jersey." Everything I wanted to do seemed wrong.

Even so, life remained tolerable as long as I could come home from school, change into old pants and shirt, and scale my pine tree. Here I felt calm, happy, and at peace.

Even at Christmas, when I begged for boots, a backpack, and a rifle, my mother presented me with more sheet music, more silk stockings, and more goop to smear on my straight brown hair and set into curls. Eventually her *"can'ts"* embraced dating boys, wearing lipstick, and anything that had to do with sex. She needn't have worried. I was far too ugly.

Perhaps I should tell the reader how I looked then: skinny and pale, with big buck teeth (later amplified by steel braces), pipestem legs, mousy hair, and big hands. Even at fifteen, I hadn't a hint of breasts. Looking back, I realize how discouraging it must have been for my mother. Here she was, slavishly obeying society's rules in order to bring up a "nice young girl," hoping perhaps, to marry me to a "Henry Ford." And I thwarted her at every step. Meanwhile, the poor woman was struggling in a bitter marriage. My father was seldom home as he worked long hours in New York City as a college language professor, seemed to ignore me when he came home, and slept in the attic. I barely knew my father. Yet, even now it's clear how he could have shaped my life by taking time to take me camping, fishing, and climbing hills. Or, just talking to me about animals and teaching me French. But, he, too, was obeying the social mores of the late 1940s and early 1950s.

Steadfastly I refused to cooperate in this grand plan. I roamed vacant lots, golf courses, and pond shores late afternoons and weekends. I scaled fences, crawled on my belly to filch daffodils and peonies, caught polliwogs and lightning bugs for my room, and slunk through the woods like an Indian. My parents gave me a big chow dog and I named him "Wolf." He went everywhere with me. How delighted we were with each other. How we loved to race across those precious golf greens.

There were times, in the long, yellow twilights of spring, when I'd play ball with neighborhood boys in the street. But I often fell, skinning my knees horribly, while watching the frothy chartreuse flowers of budding maples spin to the ground instead of fly balls.

It wasn't easy being a tomboy then. For one thing, I had to sneak around a lot. Getting out of the house was an adventure in itself. I would cross the upstairs hall, tiptoe through my mother's bedroom, creep into the sunporch, slide open a window, and shinny down a tall cedar without the slightest sound. The glory of it was that no fifty-year-old, fatty-pie mother would ever be able to track me down. In short, I was a fierce little tomboy outdoors, and a meek, quiet girl inside. For years I was a real double agent. At puberty, I was still playing cowboys and Indians in the woods. This made me something of an oddity among my rather well developed schoolmates. Theirs was a world of surreptitious cigarettes, liquor, boyfriends, borrowing their parents' cars, and petting . . . all banned by the conservative high school. So they had to be double agents of a sort, as well. If this was expected of me, it was not forthcoming. Boy-girl flirtations and cosmetics were not the center of my existence. Nature and animals gave me much more pleasure, even though less socially acceptable. I can't remember having any playmates to share the outdoors with. Only books bolstered my choice, and a deep yearning to be twenty-one and on my own.

Despite my ongoing dissension with my mother, I see in all truthfulness, she did give me two valuable gifts. One was her genes for writing. She was a *good writer*, and managed to earn all my high school tuition with articles and publicity blurbs. She also knew how to encourage me in my own writing process and short pieces. From roughly seven years of age, I "published" tiny books with crayoned drawings and hand-blocked "texts," bound at the back with colorful ribbons. Vague memories linger of my mother's pride when I won a poetry contest at age sixteen; and again, when my very first article appeared in the then-popular *Nature* magazine (not the current scientific journal *Nature*).

Writing led me further into the world of real books. There were no girl role models or heroes unfortunately. Most stories seemed to be about boys, horses, and big dogs. Yet I knew from reading that *somewhere* lay a place with green forests, clear lakes, bears, and Bambis. And that *someday* I would find that place. But, it certainly wasn't in New Jersey.

Abruptly, when I was seventeen, my mother and father divorced. Mom maneuvered me down to Florida, insisting I would love a career in marine biology at the University of Miami. (At least the biology part was right.) What her motives were I never found out. Suddenly I was living in a dorm at a large university with three roommates. It meant a lot more freedom. But it was still difficult to be a tomboy.

Mother said I should join a girls' sorority. She whispered to be careful with boys. She called every evening to be sure I was in my dorm room at the mandatory 9:00 P.M. She even cultivated the dorm "mother" and recruited her to watch me. My dreams of adventure: to drive, buy a car, shoot a rifle, were still flatly forbidden. Worst of all, dogs were not allowed in campus dorms. My beloved Wolf languished as a guard dog on the hot and distant Florida Keys.

So I continued to be a double agent. I asked various boys in my classes to teach me to drive. Then I got my license. Next I bought a beat-up old Model T Ford and hid it near campus. Soon I had joined the University Rifle and Pistol Club and was learning how to shoot. One shining afternoon I took a bus downtown and entered a gun shop. With shaking hands, I selected a cheap .22 rifle and paid for it out of my meager $25/month allowance. I carried it proudly down the main drag, Flagler Street (inside a case). By law a firearm had to be carried in a case, yet I was sure everyone could see I was carrying a gun, my *very own gun*. How proud and cocky I felt. But back at the dorm I made sure to hide it lest the dorm mother found it and reported back to my mother.

Evenings I'd sign into the dorm register, then jump back over the fence where a Melaleuca tree threw dark shadows and provided climbing branches. I wasn't going to meet a boy; the tryst was with myself at my special place. Next to a turquoise canal cut in white limestone and edged with frilly Australian pines, I'd lie on my back listening to the tropical breeze and watching the enormous sparkling stars. By next afternoon, I'd be back stalking the canal edge, gigging silvery mullet which swam in from Biscayne Bay.

Once I got a ride down to the Keys and brought Wolf back to my room. It was a mistake to believe my roommates would help me hide him. Three days later, my big loveable chow with the purple tongue and bushy tail was removed by mother and taken back to her friend's property on Key Largo. I was "court-marshalled" to a month at the dorm with no free evenings.

Because my mother's alimony barely covered college tuition, room and board, I went to work during my sophomore year at the National Audubon Society's Miami office. For the first time, I was really introduced to the natural wilds through field guides, topographic maps, wildlife tours – and to my first serious boyfriend. Hank was an Audubon Society tour leader and led wildlife excursions into the Everglades National Park, Florida Keys, and Lake Okeechobee country. He took me out there whenever possible. It was a new world of snowy egrets, mangrove mazes, sheet water shining in the saw grass, rosette spoonbills against crimson sunsets – and – kissing. The tropical tip of Florida began to compete with my northern mountain dream world.

One day Dr. Roger Tory Peterson came to visit our Miami office. It was the mid-fifties and he was already acclaimed for his *A Field Guide to Birds* (East of the Rockies). We were all very excited to meet him. My boss, Charlie Brookfield, his secretary, all the tour leaders, and this lowly assistant were on hand. I was too shy to approach the distinguished ornithologist, even though I had purchased a copy of his book, so I asked Charlie if he'd get an autograph for me.

Instead my boss pushed me to the front of the staff and introduced me to Dr. Peterson. I was tongue-tied. But the tall, blond bird artist shook hands graciously. He kindly spent several minutes chatting with me, autographed the guide, and advised me to continue in the natural history field. He made a tremendous impression. That night I penned these words in my new book: "May this book bring me closer to becoming an Audubon wildlife tour leader."

It did. Three years later, after graduating from college, I was hired to guide birding trips into the Florida wilderness – the first woman ever at any of the Audubon offices.

Years later, in 1994, Dr. Peterson presented me with the Roger Tory Peterson Award – National Nature Communicator. Being a lot less bashful by then, I took the opportunity to remind Roger of our meeting almost forty years before. "You helped start me in my career as an ecologist. You were and are an inspiration to me." It was a delight to close the circle in this way.

During that sophomore year in Miami, I also discovered my first female role model: Dr. Eugenie Clark. Her book, *Lady with a Spear*, described the great obstacles she encountered in becoming a professional marine biologist. For years she had wanted to do research on poisonous sea life in the South Pacific. But the only ships penetrating this remote area were Navy destroyers and patrol boats. Women were completely banned. Then, Dr. Clark had to move heaven and earth to get permission even to visit her study area. Only when the Navy realized her studies would have direct impact on saving ship-wrecked sailors (for example, by helping them avoid the fatal sting of a scorpion fish) did they agree to take her along. Once there, she established friendships with two Polynesian fishermen. They became her hired assistants and paddled her in an outrigger canoe among uncounted, uninhabited islands and reefs for over a year.

Dr. Clark's research *did* have great importance to anyone trying to survive in the South Pacific. It was also crucial in providing me, and who knows how many other young women readers, with the courage we needed to persist. Dr. Clark was young and single, just like me, I told myself. "If *she* could make a life studying marine animals, then so can *I*, studying wildlife."

Years later, while conducting interviews for my fourth book, *Women and Wilderness*, I was able to say all this to the shark scientist and finally thank her. Another circle closed beautifully.

Towards the end of my second year at the University of Miami, a tall, tanned classmate, by the *un*likely name of Lowell Thomas (not the real radio news announcer), became my best buddy. He thought nothing of meeting me at the dorm with a bagful of rattlesnakes. He searched the pine woods for reptiles to sell for meat to a canning factory, thus helping pay his tuition. One day Lowell gave me a glass snake (really an elongated lizard whose tail breaks off like glass if roughly handled). I named her "Clementine" and promptly put her in my roommate's bed. The shrieks and bedlam that ensued almost got me thrown out of college – along with the snake.

Lowell's snake increased my reputation as a nature freak. But this no longer mattered, for by now I had the comraderie of other students who loved the outdoors as much as I.

Despite my Audubon job, Hank, Lowell, and the bewitching Everglades, I decided to transfer to Cornell University for my junior and senior years. In part this was a move away from my mother's smothering domination. But it was also true that Cornell was the first land-grant college to accept women in America, and has a tradition of independence for students. I valued these things. Also, the Department of Natural Resources offered excellent courses, and by now I knew that I wanted a career in wildlife and conservation. *This* college would refute all my mother's *"can'ts."*

That first year at Cornell, I leaped, mesmerized, into all the scientific "olo-gies": ornithology, herpetology, geology, mammalogy, entomology, ecology, not to forget forestry and big game management. My professors were kind, helpful, and seemingly charmed by the first energetic tomboy they had seen in their classes for years. Occasionally the Dean of the Agriculture College would call one of them to inquire why a twenty-year-old girl was going to class in patched jeans and a red-and-black lumberjack shirt with bare feet (until snow flew) and dirty, calloused hands. "It's not becoming to the campus," he would fuss.

"Listen," retorted one forestry professor, defending my eccentricities, "she's making all A's and she loves her course work. She's learned to run a chain saw and goes timber cruising on snowshoes. I don't care how dirty her hands are [it was probably pine pitch]. Send me a few more high-spirited kids like Anne."

There were many negatives still operating in college. Some professors had the attitude, "What the hell does she think she's doing majoring in Natural Resources? She should be taking Home Economics."

There were other institutionalized difficulties with being a female student. Women at Cornell still had dorm curfew hours and surveillance, while men did not. Nor could they play football, baseball, or ice hockey as the men did. The Veterinary School, Law School, Architecture School, and Engineering School simply did not admit women in the mid-1950s (as was also true of hundreds of other colleges).

When the wildlife curriculum listed a Wildlife Diseases course as required, I had to get special permission, as a woman, to enter the Vet School. Stares from the all-male staff and students almost drove me out that first day. Despite the equality which Ezra Cornell had promised men and women alike, the basic fact was that women were still expected to take conventional courses that would lead to nursing, teaching, or library science. And/or get married, have kids, and become homemakers.

I did not want to do any of these things, so I learned to scuba dive, did a winter deer study alone, and went goose hunting with local male acquaintances. (Once only – I could not bear killing these regal birds which fly so elegantly.)

Upon graduation (second woman who ever graduated with a B.S. in that Department of Natural Resources), I canvassed all forty-eight continental states for a job in a state wildlife or conservation department. At that time many outdoor professions were closed to women (for example, timber cruiser, wildlife manager, forest ranger, conservation officer, and national park superintendent). Every state but Wyoming wrote back "No." And Wyoming offered only an *un*paid post as assistant wildlife technician! How could I afford to *go* there, much less *work* there? After the encouragement I'd gotten in my studies, I was totally unprepared for the prejudice and unfairness towards women in America's job market. I didn't know where to turn to use my profession, and I raged at the injustice of all this.

Then one of my professors happened to mention a German woman, an ethologist, who had spent years studying elk behavior in Europe and Wyoming. "Write her," he counselled. "See if she needs an assistant."

I did. She did. And, in this way, I met my second female role model . . . a real live one. Dr. Margaret Altmann was well along in years, frumpy, stern, intelligent, tough, and by then a world authority on the behavior of hoofed mammals. She invited me to drive with her to Jackson Hole, Wyoming. Well, it wasn't quite across the USA, but it was two-thirds of the way, so I said yes. We camped in Grand Teton National Park. I had my very own tent and horse; things I'd dreamed about for years. I accompanied Margaret into the high meadows where cow elk were calving. I took copious notes for her, received frequent instructions and scoldings, and began to understand what a woman could do in the field. I also fell in love with the West.

When my month's apprenticeship was up, I had to go back to upstate New York for a summer job in the Adirondacks. I splurged my remaining savings on cowboy boots and a black Stetson. All that was left was my pay check – $35 and change. Just enough for a one-way bus ticket to Newark, N.J. By then, my dad had remarried and lived nearby. I wanted to see him again. Stuffing my clothes, bread, cheese, and canteen in a duffle bag, I boarded the bus looking like a wrangler. As I took a last look at that magnificent saw-toothed range of mountains, I vowed to return next summer and become a cowgirl.

This dream never came true. For one thing my dad and I finally got to know each other as we never had before. I came to love him and my stepmother deeply. For another, while I was teaching riding and waterskiing at the rustic

Adirondack Inn, I fell in love with my boss. He was much older than me. I idolized his strength, decisiveness, independence, and rugged good looks. (Yes, dear reader, I know a psychiatrist would have something to say.) He didn't seem to mind my patched jeans and dirty hands any more than my professors had. In fact, he approved heartily of my hard work and taught me many new skills. The following spring, after my short stint as an Audubon wildlife tour leader, we got married.

Our union, which lasted seven years, helped make his hotel a better place. Together we cut forty cords of firewood each fall, driving our own skid truck and bulldozer. We ran chain saws, did rough carpentry, and cesspool maintenance. We designed nature trails and operated ski boats. I learned to shoe our horses and take guests for nature walks through the woods. I even stitched colorful Mexican serapes as curtains for the paneled birch dining room and lounge. Little did I realize that these aspects of hotel life would eventually enable me to build my log cabin and live as a woodswoman.

My husband's motto was, "If you want something done, do it yourself." It was a motto born of necessity for we lived seventy-five miles from the nearest city, twenty-five miles from a village. In time, it became my motto, too. "LaBastille, You Can Handle Anything."

Hotel life was a demanding eighteen-hour-day workout, with no privacy and little creativity. I secretly longed to write, research, and study again. Eventually, I set up a small desk in a corner of our bedroom, and started writing wildlife columns for a local weekly newspaper (subscription about 200). They paid $5 for a ten-inch piece. I'd spend all day Sunday reading and writing about my subject, loving every minute. My by-line was "Woman of the Woods."

Yet this insignificant baby step towards being a professional writer apparently made my husband jealous. My writing did not help his hotel. It meant I spent fewer hours working there. It did not seem to please him that I'd found a satisfying occupation; instead, he began wanting children. I didn't. Our marriage became as shaky as a hemlock that's stood too long.

Another small step towards independence came when I announced my desire to explore the local trails leading to fifty-odd lakes in our area. I wanted to know them all, and eventually, become an Adirondack guide. (This was an old and respected tradition, though it rarely included women.) In order to prepare myself, I went off hiking, every Tuesday or Thursday, with an old-time guide, Bob Burkhardt. Bob was a wise and knowledgeable man who always showed the greatest respect and caring. He knew the forest intimately, trapped furbearers each winter, and shared all his woods-lore. Yet eyes were surely raised in that tiny, conservative hamlet when two people, both married to someone else, were spending long hours together alone in the woods! It didn't matter that Bob was thirty-five years older than me.

After Bob died, I continued my explorations with another, older, more famous guide, Rodney Ainsworth. He was even more knowledgeable and attentive than Bob had been. I nicknamed him the "Iron Butterfly." Tough as a birch burl on the outside, inside Rodney had a heart as delicate as a swallowtail's wing. He'd often show up with his big, sweat-stained packbasket, bearing red rambling roses for me and a pack of hot dogs for my German shepherds.

In their ways, both Bob and Rodney became my make-believe grandfathers – the ones I'd never had. They shared what they loved most with me, I loved what they had to teach, and so they loved me. It was the first unconditional love I'd known. Their tutelage *did* help me become a licensed New York State guide in the early 70s – one of a handful of women since the late 1800s. Today, in New York State, however, there are dozens of females among the two thousand (approximately) licensed guides.

Meanwhile, my taking off into the woods once or twice a week caused yet more friction between my husband and me. He might have saved our marriage by going hiking and camping with me, taking time to canoe and climb as a break from endless hotel duties. But he was always too busy. In 1965, we divorced.

At that point, my father died, and I was still estranged from my mother. So, I really had no family. I was free to follow my dream. Like Thoreau, I decided to build my own log cabin on a wild lake with no road, electricity, phones, or indoor plumbing. Like Thoreau, I decided to devote my time to writing and wildlife. Coincidentally, I moved into my 12-by-24-foot abode on Black Bear Lake the very same day Henry moved into his 10-by-15-foot cabin on Walden Pond, 120 years before . . . July 4th: Independence Day!

It took me years to build up a reputation as a reliable free-lance writer and consultant. During part of that time, I went back to Cornell for a Ph.D. in wildlife ecology. Surprise! This time the freakish freshman, the barefoot rebel, was no longer found so charming by her mentors. She was serious and determined. She knew what she wanted and was prepared to work for it. Professors reacted in various manners. Some were as pleasant and helpful as before. But others seemed convinced that my quest was a waste of time. One actually refused to let me audit his course. And one went out of his way to say that if I pursued my studies in wildlife, I'd probably end up a neurotic old maid like ————(a renowned bird ethologist).

Perseverance was worth more than good grades in those years. I plodded through to receive my doctorate. Two days later I was hired as an Assistant Professor in the Department of Natural Resources – the first woman on a staff of about twenty men. (At least by then there were dozens of women students taking this curriculum.)

At last I was on equal footing. But now I noted an edge of competition, envy, and aggression among my former mentors. One or two refused to talk to me, even to say "Good Morning" in the halls. I felt angry and cheated. After all, I'd paid my dues. Why couldn't they accept a woman who'd entered an all-male profession the correct way, the hard way?

Eventually, all long-term tomboys have to rebel. The accumulation of injustices is just too much. My first and most dramatic rebellion had been in running away from my mother and Miami. The second was in divorcing my husband, leaving that hated hotel, and building my very own private place. After two years, I resigned from academia to become an independent author and consultant, working out of my Adirondack log cabin.

I had finally formalized my youthful behavior and made a lifelong commitment to being a tomboy, which in turn served to make my career both more productive and more professional. The integration of that rebel girl into daily grown-up life brought a pride and self-esteem previously missing. It also gave me certain skills and freed me to take important risks. For example, when I visited *National Geographic* in hopes of an assignment, the editor asked me to write about the six-million-acre Adirondack Park – the largest park in the continental USA, albeit a state park containing private lands. "We've had four other writers try and fail," he said cheerfully. "How do *you* plan to tackle it?"

Barely pausing to think I answered, "I'll backpack alone with my German shepherd across the Park, from south to north, on the Northville – Lake Placid Trail. I'll describe the wildlife and the forests. Tell what it's like to live in a cabin at the edge of wilderness." The story ran May 1975 as "The Adirondacks – My Backyard."

This adventurous approach, plus not being afraid of snakes and bugs, worked well on another, even bigger assignment. *Audubon*'s legendary editor, Les Line, told me, "Why don't you go down to the Amazon Basin and poke around. Tell us about the ravages to the environment; about the conservation efforts. Can you do it?"

"Sure," I said, my heart racing with excitement. So I travelled 4,000 miles up and down the Amazon River. Drove 500 miles along the new, dirt Transamazonica Highway. Flew into minuscule airports where wild animal pelts, gold nuggets, live macaws, monkeys, and orchids were the main exports. Took a forty-foot dugout canoe with a conservation team deep into Peru's Manu National Park (then the largest park in South America). One night my tent stood 100 miles from the nearest inhabited settlement, and headhunters were rumored to roam nearby. The jig-saw piece came together under the title, "Amazonia – Heaven or Hell?"

Those teenage years of racing around with Wolf and noticing every wild thing also made me into an observant field ecologist. Later, the prime consulting job of my life was making an ecological survey for a proposed national park in the Dominican Republic. My plan was to backpack 50 miles around the isolated, sun-blasted, waterless peninsula where no one lived. To photograph the superb seascapes and man-of-war bird rookeries, whales swimming past, the old Indian shell middens, and an abandoned historic lighthouse. And then to lay out a proposed nature trail, swimming and snorkeling beaches, and camping areas. In short, to create a park master plan.

My assistants were two black fishermen, Ramon, aged forty-five, and Louis, seventy-five. We took along a donkey to carry our gear. Every three days a huge helicopter flew in to bring us drinking water. In the evenings, we'd bring water from the sea to take a cooling rinse. One evening, I stood on the brink of a sea cliff and dropped a bucket on a rope into the boiling surf forty feet below. The tug from the waves almost pulled me in. I teetered a moment, then stepped back. Ramon and Louis raced towards me and hugged me wildly. "Señorita, señorita," they moaned.

"What's this for?" I asked in astonishment.

Ramon dropped his arms and said piteously, "Señorita, if you had fallen in and drowned, we would have been arrested and probably accused of murdering a white American lady. Maybe put to death . . ."

Thereafter, I was much more cautious. I hadn't realized how my tomboy ways could be inappropriate in a Third World country where race, poverty, and ironclad conservatism towards women were still the norm. We came through the ten-day endurance hike in good health and as firm friends.

Throughout my consulting career, I've made it a point to keep fit. No one would hire a fat, flabby woman for the kind of work I do. *My* image of the perfect tomboy, then, is a woman who stays lean, tan, muscular; who dresses in clean attractive outdoor clothing and footwear which allow her to move freely; who wears her hair long (pig-tails and chignons are great to work in), and this still spells femininity. She goes barefoot whenever possible (for strong soles and arches) and cuts her nails short. This is how I like to see myself in a mirror and what I strive for. Obviously I've known many other grown-up tomboys in all sizes, shapes, haircuts, and clothing. They have their own mental images and standards to follow.

In the mid-1970s I committed an audacious act which was quite dependent on being in good physical shape. The New York State Department of Environmental Conservation had finally opened the positions of environmental conservation officer and forest ranger to women. Two exams were being given – one on written knowledge, the other physical fitness. The tests were open to anyone regardless of sex, religion, color, creed. But you had to have a bachelor's degree from college and you had to be under forty.

I determined to pass those exams just to prove a woman could do it, and do it as well as a man. However, I was a little bit older than forty. So I adjusted my age by sort of squiggling up one number. The paperwork went through, the test dates were mailed out, and I began spending every spare moment jogging, jumping, swimming, and lifting weights. I passed both tests in spite of being only 5′ 4″ and 120 pounds. Soon, however, I knew that I'd be caught. The last requirement was to produce a birth certificate. I didn't dare squiggle that up! End of my career as a game warden or forest ranger . . .

Yet the point had been made. The door had been pushed open a crack further. And things continue to improve. Today there are female officers routinely working in state conservation departments, state police troops, state forestry agencies, and so on, not to mention federal ones. At times it seems impossible that such old prohibitions against women ever existed!

Fortunately, the feminist movement and the environmental movement came into fashion at about the same time – around 1970. It was easy for me to move from tomboy to eco-feminist. I felt great relief, a sense of camaraderie, and a justification for my life after being alone in my double quest for so long. Furthermore, seeing thousands of independent women caring for Planet Earth further legitimizes our tomboy roles.

Nowadays I lecture a lot about my book, *Women and Wilderness*, with slides of super women professionals. I find my life has changed from having had *no* female role models and struggling to find a way, to knowing two or three, to *being* a role model for countless young girls and female college students. Even older married women contemplating divorce write me for advice. The mail keeps coming . . .

The outpouring of feminist literature has also brought encouragement to women and helped establish a "good old girls" network. It has helped promote *my* books – *Woodswoman, Beyond Black Bear Lake* (sequel), *Women and Wilderness, Mama Poc,* and *The Wilderness World of Anne LaBastille.* Sometimes I smile and wonder how many girl children are hiding under their bed covers, reading with a flashlight about girls with packs, big dogs, and rifles. Girls with scuba tanks, cameras, and light planes.

My mother would no doubt be proud of my publications and conservation awards if she were still alive. My father would glow quietly if he heard of my memberships in formerly all-male groups like the Explorers Club, the Cosmos Club, and the Outdoor Writers of America Association. As a university professor, he'd certainly approve of the Woodswoman Scholarship Fund I've set up in my will for needy graduate women students in the field of wildlife ecology at Cornell. It's my way of saying "Thank you!" . . . another well-closed circle. Nevertheless, something tells me that my parents might not have changed so much. They might still be trying to slip a pair of silk stockings under the Christmas tree.

New Year's Eve, Lunch, Housework, and Stripped

Minnie Bruce Pratt was born in Alabama in 1946. She is the author of We Say We Love Each Other *(1992),* Rebellion: Essays 1980-1991 *(1991), and* Crime Against Nature *(1990), the 1989 Lamont Poetry Selection of the Academy of American Poets. The following stories are from her latest book,* S/He *(pronounced "See"), which was published in 1995. The "you" to whom they are addressed is Pratt's lover, transgender warrior Leslie Feinberg.*

NEW YEAR'S EVE

On the subway platform, you lean me against a pillar and kiss me. We talk idly, waiting for the next train; we've already exited one that was unmovably crowded. After a drunk man behind us began to mutter and elbow, you said, "Let's get off this ride from hell," and we rushed out at Christopher Street. You say you've learned to obey your instinct for trouble, the feeling that on nights like this a fistfight could break out at any moment, and there we would be, startlingly *there,* so obvious, but obviously *what?* You in your sports jacket, white shirt and tie; me in a silk skirt, flimsy blouse, sparkling glass jewelry at my neck and ears. In the crowded car when I put my head on your shoulder, with your arm around me, people stared at us. Curious to be so conventional in dress and to draw so much attention. Something too intimate and queer about how we do maleness and femaleness together in public. Perhaps it's easier for you to slip through if you're not with me. One glance and you're a gay man to them, or a slightly ambiguous boy. But when you're with me, I see their eyes flicker: If he's gay, why is he with her? Why is she with him? If they are two women, why do they look so much like a woman and a man? What are they up to?

A crowd of young women, with one or two men, come through the turnstiles, down from the Village. They are young enough to be my children. One has a long waterfall of brown hair, and a pale face bright with red lipstick. She wears a blue pinstripe man's suit, with a tie. I say to you, suddenly and meanly, "You know what makes me angry? Heterosexual women who dress up as men, playing at being butch, not knowing what it's like, unconscious." You look at the young woman, say mildly, "I'm not sure she's straight. In any case, you're for freedom of gender expression, right?" Smiling patiently at me, you lean against a steel beam, your shirt unbuttoned half-way open, your white T-shirt stretched tight over your chest. "And I don't think it's possible to cross-dress even once in this culture and not think about it. But people are uncomfortable with the bringing together of opposites." You tell me that in the old bars there were femmes who often dressed exactly like this woman, and some butches hadn't liked it either. I wince and agree that yes, I'm uncomfortable with her combination of masculinity and femininity.

I look up and see her laughing on the platform, getting away with it, playing. No one near her on the platform has raised a hand to punish her for defying *man* and *woman*. I look up and see myself fifteen years earlier, sitting in my classroom on the edge of my desk – short hair, jeans, flannel shirt, a gold hoop in each pierced ear. In the hall the other women teachers walked by in neat print dresses, in beige skirt suits. My students eyed me, a woman dressed more like a man, who therefore looked like a lesbian to them. One day when we were discussing the women's movement, a student actually risked the request: Could we talk about lesbians? But I said nothing, too scared because other women at the school, in positions more powerful than I, were being fired with this accusation. No words to tell my students about that, or the children taken away, or the threats of violence. No way to say, *Any woman who steps outside the confines of womanhood will be called a lesbian.* Some days I taught my class wearing 82nd Airborne parachute pants, a thin pink blouse, an orange ribbon threaded around my collar. One way to express the puzzle of how to be a woman who had broken out and was clothing herself as she fell into the future, pulling on pieces of maleness and femaleness as she whirled through the air. One day my department chair called me in for a conference. She had gotten complaints about how I dressed.

You tug on my hand and say, "Get ready to jump in." The train arrives with the shriek of sharpening knives. I leave behind on the platform the young woman who flaunts herself in extremes of man and woman, defiantly standing between opposites that would grind her to nothing. I take my anger and step into the car. The doors snap together, and eyes immediately follow you and me.

The other passengers begin to wonder about what kind of woman, what kind of man we are. Are we getting away with some illicit pleasure, some forbidden game that they will never get to play?

LUNCH

I am sitting in on lunch at the deli where you are meeting with a new acquaintance, and I am struggling with my pronouns. She is a big woman, over six feet, with a pulled-back ponytail and a sweet face. She is a woman with a spouse of fifteen years and four children and a life that started out as male and is now being lived as female. "At least," she says, "I am more that than I am a man." The inadequacy of the words. The duality of pronouns. She is talking to me about you, a narration of a moment on the phone with you, "So I said to *him* . . ."

This is not a man passing on the street who sees you as a man, arm in arm with me, a woman. This is not a lesbian who watches us dancing at a party, and sees you as either a butch lesbian or a woman trying to be a man, and me as femme or deluded. This is someone who lives in a world where gender and sex are fluid. Not an academic exercise, but what she tells the kids about who she was as their father. The shock to me of *you* sitting here as *him,* at this ordinary formica table, though of course that is the pronoun that suits your masculine spirit, short hair, oxford shirt, men's slacks. The word spoken about you not in hostility or misperception, but because, for you both, that is how flexible gender is.

Meeting you for the first time over curried chicken and *masala dosa,* she is socially appropriate to refer to you as *him.* Meanwhile, you are saying that you are a woman and transgendered, that your masculinity is a range of gender expression that should be available to all women, as femininity should be to men. You insist that you are *him* and also *her.* When I enter the conversation, I call you both by your given names to be respectful. The either/or pronouns suddenly are the jaws of a steel trap snapping shut on infinities that exist where body, self, sex, gender, the world, and lunch intersect.

The fluorescent light brightens in the little deli, as if a cloud has shifted from the sun. Your words become sharper and more distinct, someone turning up the volume on a radio. I see and hear the bothness, the severalness of this moment, a chaotic heightening of sense very akin to my first look at who really lives under the rigid grid of *black* and *white*. In a long-ago meeting of first-grade parents, every person was a woman of color except me, except some of them were almost as light-skinned as me, sitting there worrying about their children like me, and like the women who were darker-skinned than us. Then later, in the city, I met proper Black ladies walking home, gloved and hatted, from church. Their profiles, lips pursed, were exactly those of my aunts. And even later I learned how the laws of race and property had been laid over us, the bodies of some white men had lain on us, reproducing *white* and *black*, producing *owner* and *owned*, to divide our lives.

Over the clatter of the lunch-time rush, she says that she did "the femme thing" for a while to prove she was a woman, but now she believes in not denying her past. In the past I have denied I was a woman. The pronoun *she* was a trap set by others to catch me. I watch her talk, cheeks flushed pink, eyes gleaming silver and green. I imagine wrapping womanhood around me like a length of shimmering metallic cloth. She looks at me frequently as she talks, careful to divide her attention between you and me. How my aunts talked to me as a little girl, curly-headed and new in my mother's arms. No words from them to me without sex or gender.

Suddenly I see you and me and her on the edge of town, a place out of my view when I was growing up, like the Quarters or the Milltown, but this another kind of gathering. It is a world of those the world casts out, calls freaks, the women-men of the sideshow at the circus, seen as tawdry, pitiful, hidden, wasted, walking their path of reeking sawdust between the tents. Except the people there have lovers, marriages, children, poor-paying jobs. They have marigolds in pots, they play the harmonica, they write books. You live there, and now I live there too, with those who know they are both *man* and *woman*, those who have transmuted one to the other, those who insist they are neither. Outside the pegged tents people stand and peer in at us, no words for us, though just by stepping over the ropes they could join us. I could cross back into that staring crowd and be without question a woman amusing herself, Sunday afternoon at the carnival. But I would rather stay here and talk to you in this in-between place, sitting with a friend, our food spread out, savory, spicy, on the table before us.

HOUSEWORK

My ninety-year-old aunt leans back in her recliner and demands with friendly curiosity, "But tell me, which one of you does the cooking?" She herself hates to cook. When she was in her own home, she preferred to mow the lawn in bermuda shorts her husband disapproved of. Since she was widowed, she's shared a home with another aunt, her younger sister, who fixes the cornbread, field peas, squash casserole, for our dinner. I have introduced you as *she*. After years of rumors, I am bringing you home, without apology. You joke that you are my dead father's every fear: a working-class Jew, a Communist, an antiracist political organizer – who is also a stone butch transgendered lesbian. You are the one he feared was taking over the world, and you've ended up married to his daughter.

But my aunt is more interested in what happens to household work when two women share it. She doesn't assume I cook and you don't or that you can use a screwdriver and I can't. She doesn't assume there is a connection between *masculine*, *feminine*, and who does certain kinds of work in our home. She just asks her question. Sometimes she slips and calls you "he," just like I occasionally do. There was the time, at the beginning of our life together, when you and I debated about the laundry. I wanted you to sort by fabric and colors, and you said you couldn't, you'd tried in the past and made a big mess, and I began to get mad. You said, "I'm not a man because I have laundry dyslexia." There was the earlier time we were discussing the complex politics of genital mutilation, imperialism, and race. You said, "You are talking to me as if I don't have a clitoris."

There was the time we went to the Bureau of Motor Vehicles to get your driver's license. They demanded your birth certificate, which you couldn't show them. It said *she*, and you needed a license with *he*, a piece of plastic with the pronoun that matched your looks so a policeman on a lonely road at night would not say, "You – get out of the car." The only ID you had were bills with your name and address, and, from the hospital you were born in, a frayed piece of paper with your name and the genderless inkprint of your baby feet. The BMV clerks would accept none of it. I leaned against the counter, playing your bored girlfriend, while you fought through the bureaucratic layers.

———

Meanwhile, the people who had stood in line behind us took their test. First, the nervous sixteen-year-old white boy who'd waited with this father; then the middle-aged white man in a suit who'd stared at us until I stared back and made him look away; then a Latino with his name sewn on his overalls; then a Latina with a baby in a stroller. Each had to convince the authorities that he or she belonged within these borders. Those with white skin had almost enough proof without a single piece of paper. For those with dark skin, often no number of documents was sufficient. I got my driver's license on my sixteenth birthday; it was so easy. The examiners saw *white* and *woman,* and I fit myself without question into one of the boxes. Either *M* or *F,* either *W* or *N.* After all, the state demanded I live in one or the other. In my billfold was the document, the piece of plastic that proved I passed the test.

Finally you were handed your test, officially stamped, by a uniformed butch woman who seemed like a dyke. With an angry "Sir," she passed you through, a man making trouble, not someone who could almost be her. No room in that line for questions about what is *man,* what is *woman.* The State has a compelling interest in matters of ownership, to know which is which, a fact that has nothing to do with how we share chores in our house. But before we sit down to dinner with her, my aunt asks again, "And who does the cooking?"

STRIPPED

The *Times* story is a few inches of words hidden in the back pages of the newspaper I've spread out on our kitchen table. I only notice it because of the headline, the sudden fear that this could almost be you and me: "Woman Who Posed As a Man Is Found Slain With 2 Others." On New Year's Day, Brandon Teena, born a female, living as a man in a small Nebraska town, was murdered, shot in a farmhouse along with the white woman friend he was staying with and a visiting African-American man. Brandon was the only one mutilated with a knife. The week before he had been raped by the two men eventually arrested for his murder. But first, determined to prove he was "really" a woman, they had stripped him at a party, in front of a woman he had dated. Some days earlier the police had decided that his life was a menacing deception. When they'd picked him up on some minor charge and his identification didn't match, the police made sure the town knew he was lying about who he was. But he was clear to his friends: He felt like a man inside; he didn't feel like a woman or a lesbian. He didn't have the money for the operation, yet. Within a month he was dead.

———

When I was a girl, I had a nightmare that still comes back sometimes: *I am standing naked at the center of a circle of people. They laugh at me or point or yell ugly foul words or stare silently. They are clothed. I am stripped down to nothing but my girl's body, and I am ashamed. There is something wrong with me.* I used to think that only women had this nightmare. Now I think everyone dreams of being stripped, but the pointing fingers accuse us of different crimes. People stretch out their hands to show that they know the truth of us better than we do. They strip away our clothes, our words, our skin, our flesh, until we are nothing but a pile of butcher's bones, and then they point and say that is who we are.

I sit in our kitchen and read a *Village Voice* article about the murders. The writer, a lesbian, gleefully gossips with Brandon's ex-girlfriends and repeats salacious details: how "she" fooled them with a dildo, how "she" wouldn't allow touch at breast, thigh, genitals. The writer admits Brandon lived as a man, but she strips him down to prove that he was not. For her, everything has to match – genitals, clothes, pronouns. Besides, how could he be such a good lover of women unless he were a woman? She decides he is a confused lesbian – her kind of lesbian, she writes, a butch woman who turns her on, who gets her hot. The sheriff, who had refused to arrest the rapists when Brandon reported their crime, said, "So far as I'm concerned, you can call it *it.*" Throughout the article, the writer calls him *her:* "She was shot execution-style." The writer never mentions he died when he insisted he would choose his own pronoun.

Susan Moon

The Tomboy Returns!

Susan Moon is the author of a book of fiction, The Life and Letters of Tofu Roshi *(1988). She is the editor of* Turning Wheel, *the quarterly journal of the Buddhist Peace Fellowship, and co-editor, with Lenore Friedman, of* Being Bodies: Buddhist Women Writing About Embodiment *(1997).*

Moon lives in Berkeley, California, and is the mother of two grown sons. She says she still wears blue or black jeans most days — better than a skirt for sitting with her legs splayed out, putting her feet on the desk, or riding a bicycle.

I'VE LEARNED HOW TO PASS FOR A WOMAN. I LEARNED TO BRUSH MY long blonde hair every day, and I wear contact lenses when I'm trying to look pretty. From time to time, I even put on a dress without being bribed. I got married, gave birth to two children, nursed them, raised them. But there's a nine-year-old inside of me who still remembers all the good climbing trees in the faraway neighborhood where I grew up, and which shrubs have the straightest twigs to make arrows out of. I've been missing her lately, needing her help, and wanting to make amends to her for the betrayals she suffered.

I'm divorced, my children have flown, and I've got nobody to make breakfast for. Menopause, that old crone, is knocking at the door. At fifty, flushed and sweating after my morning tea, I need my tomboy self again: her adventurous spirit, her brave refusal to be limited by social expectations. If I honor her, I hope she'll come forward.

In third grade at school, I was the only girl in Joel's Gang. In order to get in, you had to have a wrestling match with everybody who was already a member, but fortunately you didn't have to win. We ran around pretending to be fierce, charging through the middle of the sissy girls' hopscotch games. We practiced wrestling holds on each other and played mumbledy-peg in the forsythia bushes, where the teachers wouldn't see our jackknives.

In those days my mother used to pay me a quarter to put on a dress, on the occasions when a dress was called for — like the visit of a relative. Otherwise I wore dungarees with a cowboy belt.

With the boys in my neighborhood – Robert and Skipper, Evan and Sammy – I played cops and robbers, and cowboys and Indians: racist, violent games which, years later, I righteously tried to keep my own children from playing. We climbed trees and rode *no hands* on our bicycles. I had cap pistols hanging on hooks on my bedroom wall. I traded baseball cards, memorized the batting averages of all the players on the Boston Braves, and played catch by the hour. I read the Hardy Boys Mysteries and *Lou Gehrig, Boy of the Sand Lots.* I started the Robin Hood Club, the Pirate Club, and the Cowboy Comic Collectors Club.

I wore boys' bathing trunks every summer, until I was eight or nine years old. I put on a girls' bathing suit, with all that frilly and deceptive packaging that poked its bones into my flat chest, only after another girl taunted me: *You think you're a boy! You think you're a boy!* I was so mad I got out of the swimming pool and hid her clothes in a closet. She went home in a wet bathing suit and I pretended I didn't know anything about it.

But why was I in Joel's Gang, instead of playing hopscotch? It was my way of refusing to submit.

I think of my parents' body language. My mother didn't seem happy inside her skin. She moved as if trying to hide her body with her body. Other women, too, seemed to move in shuffle and shadow. But in my father's body there was elasticity and readiness. He used to walk a lot, and ride a bicycle. When my mother wanted to go somewhere, she drove a car.

Everywhere I looked, men were running the show, and women were just the helpers: the president and his wife, the school principal and his secretary, the dentist and his hygienist, the pilot and the stewardess. Though I couldn't have stated it consciously, I breathed in the knowledge that a woman's body was not a powerful place to live.

As for me, I wanted to run and jump and climb over fences, even if it meant tearing my clothes. I didn't try to pretend I was a boy, I just wanted to be ungendered, and therefore unlimited. I hated getting my hair cut, for example, and had a wild bush of hair, like a feral child. I didn't want to have to look pretty, but I liked the way I looked in my classy felt cowboy hat – a "real" one like "real" cowboys wore. Far from being a denial of my sexuality, I think my tomboyhood gave me good practice at living in my body and finding pleasure there.

My parents never objected to my bathing trunks or cowboyphilia, and my mother patiently quizzed me on baseball statistics when I asked her to. But I think it wasn't quite okay for me to be a tomboy. I looked up *tomboy* in Doctor

Spock, by whose lights I was raised, but he says nothing on the subject. I think my parents must have been at a loss. Perhaps they feared that I would never agree to brush my hair my whole life long, and, by logical extension, that I would never become a wife-and-mother.

I think so because in the fourth grade, I was sent to dancing school – ballroom dancing! – years before my schoolmates had to undergo this horrible humiliation. I was taught to sit with my ankles crossed until a boy, in parallel agony no doubt, asked me to dance. I learned to do the "box step," an apt name for a spiritless movement that had nothing whatever to do with dancing. ("Step-step-right-together-step-step-left-together.")

For a brief period, I was sent on Sunday afternoons to the home of an elderly Jewish refugee from Vienna who gave me sewing lessons, an activity in which I had no interest whatever. Because I suffered from night terrors and frequent nightmares, I was taken to a child psychiatrist. He asked me mortifying questions like, "Have any of the girls in your class at school begun to menstruate?" It was rumored that one particular girl had already gotten 'the curse," but I didn't see that it was any of his business, and so I answered numbly, "I don't know." For Christmas he gave me a perfume-making kit, which I poured down the toilet in disgust.

But there were contradictory messages in my own family. On the one hand, my grandmother told me that I should brush my hair 100 strokes a day to make it shine. "On doit souffrir pour etre belle," she said, with a hint of irony in her voice. One must suffer to be beautiful. On the other hand, a photograph in a family album shows me and my two younger sisters marching around on the lawn at my grandparents' house, pretending to be soldiers, drilling, with sticks over our shoulders for rifles, wearing three-cornered newspaper hats. Grandpa, who came from a military family, was our drill sergeant. We're obviously having a great time, puffing out our childish chests.

But I always knew I wasn't a boy. One day I went into the nearby vacant lot which we kids called "the woods." I was carrying my precious hand-made bow, and I was looking for arrows. I pushed my way through a tangled arch of bushes, and there was the neighborhood bully, sitting on a stump. He was an archetypal figure, like Butch, the leader of the West Side Gang, in the *Little Lulu* comics I read so avidly. "Give me that bow or pull down your pants," he demanded. Girl that I was, trained to obedience, it never occurred to me that there were any other choices. I handed him the bow.

Not long after, the neighborhood kids gathered in my friend Sammy's backyard for a wrestling tournament. My turn came to wrestle the dreaded bully. I got him to the ground and held him down for the count of ten. I had won! Fair and square. But when I released him and we stood up, I saw that he wanted to kill me for defeating him in public. Terrified, I turned and ran, and he ran after me. I remember the rush of adrenaline which put wings on my heels. I made it safely home, locked the door behind me, and collapsed in fright. The fact that I had just wrestled him to the ground had no transfer value. As soon as the structured contest was over, I went back to being a girl who was scared of a bully.

Another time, Skipper and Evan and I were riding our bicycles around the neighborhood, and stumbled on an old Victorian carriage house. Upstairs, in the unlocked attic, we searched through boxes, and found a huge purple jewel, which we stole and buried in Skipper's backyard, ten paces from the maple tree and fifteen paces from the corner of his garage. We solemnly promised each other we'd leave it buried there forever, or at least until we grew up. Then, if one of us was in trouble, we'd dig it up, sell it and use the money to help that person.

That night I couldn't go to sleep for feeling guilty, and finally I gave in and told my mother about the stolen jewel. The next day, she made us dig it up and take it back and apologize. Luckily, the lady who lived in the Victorian house was not too mad. She explained that the jewel was a glass doorknob. She told us to stay out of her carriage house and she gave us some cookies. Skipper and Evan were not pleased with me, cookies notwithstanding. Why did I tell? Because I was the only girl? Is that why you shouldn't let women into men's clubs?

Already, by the fifth grade, things had begun to change in ominous ways. Starting that year, girls had to wear skirts or dresses to our school. There was no rule *against* dungarees, however, so I wore both: the dress on top, the blue denim sticking out the bottom. From then on, I had to wear a dress to school. (It's hard to believe now, but when I went to Radcliffe in the sixties, we weren't allowed to wear pants to class unless it was snowing.)

In sixth grade, the ground continued to shift under my feet. I made friends with girls, some of whom, to my surprise, turned out to have things in common with me. At recess, I sometimes played jacks instead of dodge ball.

By seventh grade, my former playmates in Joel's Gang had lost interest in me. They began dating the very girls whose hopscotch games we had disrupted a few years before – girls who whispered and giggled in the bathroom, girls who wore, to my disgust, tight skirts. Try to climb a tree in a tight skirt!

And then puberty hit, like a curtain coming down. I grew breasts: tender objects which weren't there before, bodies on top of my body. They came like strangers, and I was supposed to welcome them as part of myself, even though I'd lived all thirteen years of my life without them. The left one started first, and I remember examining myself in the mirror and worrying that the right one would never catch up.

Then, when I was thirteen, I woke up one morning with dried blood on my pajama bottoms. I had imagined "the curse" would come in a red flood that would run out from under my desk and along the classroom floor. My mother gave me a pad, and explained how to attach it. Remember those horrible elastic belts with hooks in front and back? She was pleased and supportive. But I felt ashamed – I had been claimed by my tribe, marked irrevocably as a second-class citizen. I would be one of them after all. My tree-climbing days were over.

I certainly couldn't buck biology, and it never occurred to me (until much later) that I could buck the social definitions that went with it. And so I began to behave accordingly. I tried to please my teachers, to look pretty, to act polite. I grew my hair, and brushed it. At school dances I waited in silent terror that I wouldn't be asked to dance. If asked, I danced in an agony of shyness, unable to think of anything to say. In high school, by a strange twist of fate, I was invited to a formal prep school dance by Joel, of Joel's Gang. We had barely spoken to each other since the third grade. We fox-trotted together, speechless and miserable, no longer able to practice wrestling holds on each other.

All during college and into my twenties, I spurned athletic pursuits as being somehow for stupid people, especially if those people were female. Enthusiasm for physical activity had come to mean the opposite of smart, hip, and sexy. Physical exuberance was gone. I wore constricting undergarments. I hoped I wouldn't sweat, and that the wind wouldn't muss my hair. I now see *this* as my betrayal of my sex – this nice resignation, this alienation from the body called "femininity."

These days, I go to a gym, and I lift weights. I want muscles – muscles that show. I like the way they look. I like to feel strong. I like to do the bench press, to shove that big heavy bar up off my chest. If I was wrestling with the bully, I probably couldn't push him off me, but I'd sure try.

Now that I'm looking menopause in the face, I wonder if I'm coming around full circle, back to where I was before puberty. I may not wear a boy's bathing suit again, but I hope that the older I get the more I'll be able to ignore what's considered appropriate. When my body is no longer limber enough to climb trees, I hope I'll still have a limber and unladylike mind.

I've spent the last thirty-five years or so trying to look attractive, and more or less succeeding. The habit dies hard. But now, as a middle-aged woman, I find I am acquiring a certain transparency. Some people seem to be able to see right through me. (Can you guess which ones?) Granted, I'd rather be pretty than ugly, but the whole matter of physical beauty is becoming irrelevant – just as it was when I was nine – and in this there is some measure of relief.

For years, one of my noticeable features has been a great mass of thick blonde hair. But just a few months ago, wanting, as Yeats said, to be "loved for myself alone and not my yellow hair," I cut my hair very short, and now I own neither hairbrush nor comb. This cutting off has been both liberating and terrifying.

And it's not just a question of how I look. There's the more important matter of behavior. When I was a tomboy I started a Robin Hood club and organized cudgel tournaments. Now my creative projects may be less athletic than when I was nine, but I hope I can rediscover that brave spirit, that determination to follow my heart. When I was nine I didn't waste my time being nice. I didn't do other people's laundry, or read the manuscripts of people I hardly knew, just as a favor. My nine-year-old self thinks it would be a good idea for me to join a friend in Maine in October to photograph the blueberry barrens. Or go on retreat to a Benedictine monastery in northern California, where I can stay in a cottage made of a wine barrel and read about saints.

I'm grateful for my tomboy time, because, as my grandmother used to say, "old age is not for sissies." If I hadn't had all that practice climbing forbidden trees, I think I would more easily slip into loneliness and fear as I grow old.

The crone who's knocking at my front door is not a stranger – she's the nine-year-old girl in dungarees, her hair a glad tangle, come to guide me back to my bravest, freest self. She says I never have to brush my hair again, unless I want to. She says it's not too late to learn to play the drums.

J. California Cooper

A Jewel for a Friend

J. California Cooper was born in San Francisco, California, and now lives in rural Texas. She has published a number of books, including A Piece of Mine *(1984), from which this story is taken,* Homemade Love *(1986),* In Search of Satisfaction *(1994), and* Some Love, Some Pain, Sometime *(1995).*

I HAVE MY SON BRING ME DOWN HERE TO THIS HOMEGROWN GRAVEYARD two or three times a week so I can clean it and sweep it and sit here among my friends in my rocking chair under this Sycamore tree, where I will be buried one day, soon now, I hope. I'm 90 years old and I am tired . . . and I miss all my friends too. I come back to visit them because ain't nobody left in town but a few old doddering fools I didn't bother with when I was younger so why go bother now just cause we all hangin on? Its peaceful here. The wind is soft, the sun is gentle even in the deep summer. Maybe its the cold that comes from under the ground that keeps it cool. I don't know. I only know that I like to rest here in my final restin place and know how its gonna be a thousand years after I am put here under that stone I have bought and paid for long ago . . . long ago.

After I eat my lunch and rest a bit, I gets down to my real work here in this graveyard! I pack a hammer and chisel in my bags and when I's alone, I take them and go over to Tommy Jones' beautiful tombstone his fancy daughter bought for him and chip, grind and break away little pieces of it! Been doin it for eleven years now and its most half gone. I ain't gonna die til its all gone! Then I be at peace! I ain't got to tell a wise one that I hate Tommy Jones, you must know that yourself now! . . If I am killin his tombstone! I hate him. See, his wife, my friend, Pearl, used to lay next to him, but I had her moved, kinda secret like, least without tellin anyone. I hired two mens to dig her coffin up and move her over here next to where I'm going to be and they didn't know nobody and ain't told nobody. It don't matter none noway cause who gon pay somebody to dig her up again? And put her back? Who cares bout her? . . . and where she lay for eternity? Nobody! But me . . . I do.

See, we growed up together. I am Ruby and she is Pearl and we was jewels.

We use to always say that. We use to act out how these jewels would act. I was always strong, deep red and solid deep. She was brown but she was all lightness and frail and innocent, smooth and weak and later on I realized, made out of pain.

I grew up in a big sprawling family and my sons take after them, while Pearl growed up in a little puny one. Her mama kissed her daddy's ass til he kicked hers on way from here! That's her grave way over there . . . Way, way over there in the corner. That's his with that cement marker, from when he died two years later from six bullets in his face by another woman what didn't take that kickin stuff! Well, they say what goes around . . . But "they" says all kinda things . . . can't be sure bout nothing "they" says. Just watch your Bible . . . that's the best thing I ever seen and I'm 90! Now!

Anyway, Pearl and me grew up round here, went to school and all. A two room school with a hall down the middle. Pearl nice and everybody should of liked her, but they didn't. Them girls was always pickin on her, til I get in it. See, I was not so nice and everybody did like me! Just loved me sometime! I pertected her. I wouldn't let nobody hurt her! Some of em got mad at me, but what could they do? I rather fight than eat! Use to eat a'plenty too! I was a big strong, long-armed and long-legged girl. Big head, short hair. I loved my eyes tho! Oh, they was pretty. They still strong! And I had pretty hands, even with all that field work, they still was pretty! My great grandchildren takes care of em for me now . . . rubs em and all. So I can get out here two or three times a week and hammer Tommy Jones' gravestone. Its almost half gone now . . . so am I.

When we got to marryin time . . . everybody got to that, some in love and some just tryin to get away from a home what was full of house work and field work and baby sister and brother work. I don't know how we was all too dumb to know, even when we got married and in a place of our own, it was all headin down to the same road we thought we was gettin away from! Well, I went after Gee Cee! He was the biggest boy out there and suited me just fine! I use to run that man with rocks and sticks and beat him up even. He wouldn't hurt me, you know, just play. But I finally got him to thinkin he loved me and one night, over there by the creek behind the church, way behind the church, I gave him somethin he musta not forgot . . . and we was soon gettin married. I didn't forget it . . . I named it George, Jr. That was my first son.

In the meantime the boys all seem to like Pearl and she grinned at all of em! She seem to be kinda extra stuck on that skinny rail, Tommy Jones, with the bare spot on the side of his head! He liked everybody! A girl couldn't pass by him without his hand on em, quick and fast and gone. I didn't like him! Too shifty for me . . . a liar! I can't stand a liar! His family had a little money and he always looked nice but he still wasn't nothin but a nice lookin liar what was shifty! Still and all, when I had done pushed Pearl around a few times tryin to make her not like him, he began to press on her and every way she turned, he was there! He just wouldn't let up when he saw I didn't like him for her! He gave her little trinkets and little cakes, flowers, home picked. Finally she let him in her deepest life and soon she was pregnant and then he got mad cause he had to marry her! I fought against that and when he found out it made him grin all the way through the little ceremony. I was her best lady or whatever you call it, cause I was her best friend.

Then everything was over and we was all married and havin children and life got a roll on and we had to roll with it and that took all our energies to survive and soon we was back in the same picture we had run away from cept the faces had changed. Stead of mama's faces, they was ours. And daddy's was the men we had married. Lots of times the stove and sink was the same and the plow was the same. In time, the mules changed.

Well, in time, everything happened. I had three sons and two daughters, big ones! Liked to kill me even gettin here! Pearl had one son and one daughter. Son was just like his daddy and daughter was frail and sickly. I think love makes you healthy and I think that child was sickly cause wasn't much love in that house of Pearl's, not much laughter. Tommy Jones, after the second child, never made love to Pearl again regular, maybe a year or two or three apart. She stayed faithful, but hell, faithful to what? He had done inherited some money and was burnin these roads up! He'd be a hundred miles away for a week or two, whole lotta times. Pearl worked, takin them children with her when I could'n keep em. But I had to rest sometimes, hell! I had five of my own and I had done told her bout that Tommy Jones anyway! But I still looked out for her and fed em when she couldn't. Yet and still, when he came home he just fall in the bed and sleep and sleep til time to get up and bathe and dress in the clothes he bought hisself and leave them again! If she cry and complain he just laugh and leave. I guess that's what you call leavin them laughin or somethin!

One day he slapped her and when he saw she wasn't gonna do nothin but just cry and take it, that came to be a regular thing! For years, I mean years, I never went over her house to take food when she didn't have some beatin up marks on her! I mean it! That's when she started comin over to the cemetery to clean it up and find her place. She also began savin a nickle here and a dime there to pay for her gravestone. That's what she dreamed about! Can you imagine that?!! A young, sposed to be healthy woman daydreamin bout dyin!!? Well, she did! And carried that money faithfully to the white man sells them things and paid on a neat little ruby colored stone, what he was puttin her name on, just leavin the dates out! Now!

My sons was gettin married, havin babies, strong like they mama and papa, when her son got killed, trying to be like his daddy! He had done screwed the wrong man's daughter! They put what was left of him in that grave over there, behind that bush of roses Pearl planted years ago to remember him by. Well, what can I say? I'm a mother, she was a mother, you love them no matter what! The daughter had strengthened up and was goin on to school somewhere with the help of her father's people. And you know, she didn't give her mother no concern, no respect? Treated her like the house dog in a manger. I just don't blieve you can have any luck like that! It takes time, sometime, to get the payback, but time is always rollin on and one day, it will roll over you! Anyway even when the daughter had made it up to a young lady and was schoolin with the sons and daughters of black business people, she almost forgot her daddy too! She was gonna marry a man with SOMETHIN and she didn't want them at the weddin! Now! And tole em! Her daddy went anyway, so she dressed him cause he was broke now, and after the weddin, got his drunk ass out of town quick as lightnin cross the sky and he came home and taunted Pearl that her own daughter didn't love her! Now!

Well, time went on, I had troubles with such a big family, grandchildren comin and all. Love, love, love everywhere, cause I didn't low nothin else! Pretty faces, pretty smiles, round, fat stomachs, and pigtails flying everywhere and pretty nappy-headed boys growin up to be president someday even if they never were .. they was my presidents and congressmen! I could chew em up and swollow em sometimes even today grown as they are! We could take care of our problems, they was just livin problems . . . everyday kinds.

Pearl just seem to get quiet way back in her mind an heart. She went on but she was workin harder to pay for that tombstone. The name was complete, only the last date was open and finally it was paid for. With blood, sweat and tears for true . . . seem like that's too much to pay for dyin!

One night I had bathed and smelled myself up for that old hard head of mine, Gee Cee, when a neighbor of Pearl's came runnin over screamin that Tommy Jones was really beatin up on Pearl. I threw my clothes on fast as I could and ran all the way and I was comin into some age then, runnin was not what I planned to do much of! When I got there, he had done seen me comin and he was gone, long gone, on them long, narrow, quick to run to mischief feet of his! I had got there in time to keep him from accidently killin her, but she was pretty well beat! He had wanted her rent and food money, she said, but she would not give it to him, so he beat her. She cried and held on to me, she was so frail, so little, but she was still pretty to me, little grey hairs and all. She thanked me as I washed her and changed the bed and combed her hair and fed her some warm soup and milk. She cried a little as she was tellin me all she ever wanted was a little love like I had. I cried too and told her that's all anybody wants.

When I was through fixin her and she was restin nice and easy, I sat by the bed and pulled the covers up and she said, "Hold my hand I'm so cold." Well I grabbed her hand and held, then I rubbed her arms tryin to keep her warm and alive. Then, I don't know, life just kept rollin and I began to rub her whole little beautiful sore body . . . all over . . . and when I got to them bruised places I kissed them and licked them too and placed my body beside her body in her bed and the love for her just flowed and flowed. One minute I loved her like a child, the next like a mother, then she was the mother, then I was the child, then as a woman friend, then as a man. Ohhhhh, I loved her. I didn't know exactly what to do but my body did it for me and I did everything I could to make her feel loved and make her feel like Gee Cee makes me feel, so I did everything I could that he had ever done to me to make me feel good, but I forgot Gee Cee . . . and I cried. Not sad crying, happy cryin, and my tears and my love were all over her and she was holding me. She was holding me . . . so close, so close. Then we slept and when I wakened up, I went home . . . and I felt good, not bad. I know you don't need nothin "forever," just so you get close to love sometime.

Well Pearl got better. When we saw each other, we weren't embarrassed or shamed. She hit me on my shoulder and I thumped her on her head as we had done all our lives anyway. We never did it again, we didn't have to!

Pearl wasn't made, I guess, for the kind of life she had somehow chosen, so a few years later she died and Tommy Jones picked her plot, right over there where she used to be; and put her there and the tombstone man put that old-brand-new ruby colored gravestone on her grave. The preacher said a few words cause there wasn't much to pay him with and we all went home to our own lifes, of course.

Soon, I commence to comin over here and sweepin and cleanin up and plantin plants around and this ole Sycamore tree, Pearl had planted at her house, was moved over here before Tommy Jones got put out for not payin rent. I planted it right here over where Gee Cee, me and Pearl gonna be. I likes shade. Anyway I was out here so much that's how I was able to notice the day Pearl's tombstone disappeared. Well, I like to died! I knew what that tombstone had gone through to get there! Right away I had my sons get out and find out what had happened and they found out that Tommy Jones was livin mighty hard and was mighty broke and had stole that tombstone and took it way off and sold it for a few dollars! You can chisel the name off, you know? But I can't understand what anyone would want a used tombstone for! I mean, for God's sake, get your own!! At least die first-class even if you couldn't live that way! Well, we couldn't find how to get it back so that's when I started payin on another one for her, and yes, for me and Gee Cee too. They's paid for now.

In the meantime, liquor and hard livin and a knife put Tommy Jones to rest, and imagine this, that daughter of theirs came down here and bought ONE gravestone for her DADDY!!! To hold up her name I guess, but that's all she did, then she left! Ain't been back!

Well, life goes on, don't it! Whew!

Now I come here over the years and chip away and chisel and hammer away cause he don't deserve no stone since he stole Pearl's. He never give her nothin but them two babies what was just like him and then he stole the last most important thing she wanted! So me, I'm gonna see that he don't have one either! When it's through, I'm gonna be through, then the gravestone man can bring them two stones over here, they bought and paid for! And he can place them here beside each other, for the rest of thousands of years. I'm in the middle, between Gee Cee and Pearl, like I'm sposed to be. They don't say much, but Ruby and the dates and Pearl's on hers, and the dates. Then my husband's name and the children on mine and her children's on hers. And that's all. I mean, how much can a gravestone say anyway?

AFTERWORD

After Ruby died at 91 years of age, Gee Cee was still living at 90 years of age and he had a marker laid across the two graves saying, "Friends, all the way to the End." It's still there.

translated from the French by Una Vincenzo Trowbridge and Enid McCleod

My Mother and the Forbidden Fruit

Sidonie Gabrielle Colette was born in Burgundy, France, in 1873. She was not the sort of child who grew up wanting to write. Instead, she "knew how to climb, how to whistle and run – gifts useful to a squirrel or bird or doe." It is easy to imagine her pale, pointed face gleaming among the leaves of a walnut tree, or rushing off, her sabots clattering, the "eager cabin boy of the family vessel."

Years later, Colette would describe this idyllic childhood in a wide range of books, among them, La Maison de Claudine (1922), Naissance du Jour (1928), and Sido (1929). Her autobiography, Earthly Paradise (1966), was edited by Robert Phelps from the writings of a lifetime. For the harsher, more complex side of her life, compare La Vagabonde (1911), Chéri (1920), and Le Blé en herbe (1923).

Colette wrote more than seventy books in the course of her writing career, and is still one of the few women granted a place in the French literary canon. She died in Paris in 1954.

THE TIME CAME WHEN ALL HER STRENGTH LEFT HER. SHE WAS AMAZED beyond measure and would not believe it. Whenever I arrived from Paris to see her, as soon as we were alone in the afternoon in her little house, she had always some sin to confess to me. On one occasion she turned up the hem of her dress, rolled her stocking down over her shin, and displayed a purple bruise, the skin nearly broken.

"Just look at that!"

"What on earth have you done to yourself this time, Mother?"

She opened wide eyes, full of innocence and embarrassment.

"You wouldn't believe it, but I fell downstairs!"

"How do you mean –'fell'?"

"Just what I said. I fell, for no reason. I was going downstairs and I fell. I can't understand it."

"Were you going down too quickly?"

"Too quickly? What do you call too quickly? I was going down quickly. Have I time to go downstairs majestically like the Sun King? And if that were all . . . But look at this!"

On her pretty arm, still so young above the faded hand, was a scald forming a large blister.

"Oh goodness! Whatever's that!"

"My footwarmer."

"The old copper footwarmer? The one that holds five quarts?"

"That's the one. Can I trust anything, when that footwarmer has known me for forty years? I can't imagine what possessed it, it was boiling fast, I went to take it off the fire, and crack, something gave in my wrist. I was lucky to get nothing worse than the blister. But what a thing to happen! After that I let the cupboard alone. . . ."

She broke off, blushing furiously.

"What cupboard?" I demanded severely.

My mother fenced, tossing her head as though I were trying to put her on a lead.

"Oh, nothing! No cupboard at all!"

"Mother! I shall get cross!"

"Since I've said, 'I let the cupboard alone,' can't you do the same for my sake? The cupboard hasn't moved from its place, has it? So, shut up about it!"

The cupboard was a massive object of old walnut, almost as broad as it was high, with no carving save the circular hole made by a Prussian bullet that had entered by the right-hand door and passed out through the back panel.

"Do you want it moved from the landing, Mother?"

An expression like that of a young she-cat, false and glittery, appeared on her wrinkled face.

"I? No, it seems to me all right there – let it stay where it is!"

All the same, my doctor brother and I agreed that we must be on the watch. He saw my mother every day, since she had followed him and lived in the same village, and he looked after her with a passionate devotion which he hid. She fought against all her ills with amazing elasticity, forgot them, baffled them, inflicted on them signal if temporary defeats, recovered, during entire days, her vanished strength; and the sound of her battles, whenever I spent a few days with her, could be heard all over the house till I was irresistibly reminded of a terrier tackling a rat.

At five o'clock in the morning I would be awakened by the clank of a full bucket being set down in the kitchen sink immediately opposite my room.

"What are you doing with that bucket, Mother? Couldn't you wait until Josephine arrives?"

And out I hurried. But the fire was already blazing, fed with dry wood. The milk was boiling on the blue-tiled charcoal stove. Nearby, a bar of chocolate was melting in a little water for my breakfast, and, seated squarely in her cane armchair, my mother was grinding the fragrant coffee which she roasted herself. The morning hours were always kind to her. She wore their rosy colors in her cheeks. Flushed with a brief return to health, she would gaze at the rising sun, while the church bell rang for early Mass, and rejoice at having tasted, while we still slept, so many forbidden fruits.

The forbidden fruits were the overheavy bucket drawn up from the well, the firewood split with a billhook on an oaken block, the spade, the mattock, and above all the double steps propped against the gable window of the woodhouse. There were the climbing vine whose shoots she trained up to the gable windows of the attic, the flowery spikes of the too-tall lilacs, the dizzy cat that had to be rescued from the ridge of the roof. All the accomplices of her old existence as a plump and sturdy little woman, all the minor rustic divinities who once obeyed her and made her so proud of doing without servants, now assumed the appearance and position of adversaries. But they reckoned without that love of combat which my mother was to keep till the end of her life. At seventy-one, dawn still found her undaunted, if not always undamaged. Burnt by the fire, cut with the pruning knife, soaked by melting snow or spilled water, she had always managed to enjoy her best moments of independence before the earliest risers had opened their shutters. She was able to tell us of the cats' awakening, of what was going on in the nests, of news gleaned, together with the morning's milk and the warm loaf, from the milkmaid and the baker's girl, the record in fact of the birth of a new day.

It was not until one morning when I found the kitchen unwarmed, and the blue enamel saucepan hanging on the wall, that I felt my mother's end to be near. Her illness knew many respites, during which the fire flared up again on the hearth, and the smell of fresh bread and melting chocolate stole under the door together with the cat's impatient paw. These respites were periods of unexpected alarms. My mother and the big walnut cupboard were discovered together in a heap at the foot of the stairs, she having determined to transport it in secret from the upper landing to the ground floor. Whereupon my elder brother insisted that my mother should keep still and that an old servant should sleep in the little house. But how could an old servant prevail against a vital energy so youthful and mischievous that it contrived to tempt and lead astray a body already half fettered by death? My brother, returning before sunrise from attending a distant patient, one day caught my mother red-handed in the most wanton of crimes. Dressed in her nightgown, but wearing heavy gardening sabots, her little gray septuagenarian's plait of hair turning up like a scorpion's tail on the nape of her neck, one foot firmly planted on the crosspiece of the beech trestle, her back bent in the attitude of the expert jobber, my mother, rejuvenated by an indescribable expression of guilty enjoyment, in defiance of all her promises and of the freezing morning dew, was sawing logs in her own yard.

Selected Bibliography

CHILDREN'S BOOKS

Louisa May Alcott. *Jack and Jill: A Village Story.* (1880). Garden City, N.Y.: Nelson Doubleday, 1956.

Louisa May Alcott. *Little Women.* (1868). Edited and with an introduction by Elaine Showalter. New York: Penguin, 1989.

Carol Ryrie Brink. *Caddie Woodlawn.* (1935). New York: Collier Books, 1970.

Elizabeth Burleson. *Middl'un.* Chicago: Follett Publishing Co., 1968.

Susan Coolidge. *What Katy Did.* (1872). Boston: Little, Brown & Co., 1938.

Beaulah Marie Dix. *Merrylips.* London: Macmillan Publishers, 1906.

Elizabeth Enright. *Thimble Summer. (1938). New York: Dell Publishing Co., 1966.*

Louise Fitzhugh. Harriet the Spy. New York: Harper & Row, Publishers, 1964.

Norma Klein. *Tomboy.* New York: Simon & Schuster, 1978.

Jane Langton. *The Boyhood of Grace Jones.* New York: Harper & Row, Publishers, 1972.

Lois Lenski. *Texas Tomboy.* Philadelphia: J. B. Lippincott Co., 1950.

Astrid Lindgren. *Pippi Longstocking.* (1950). New York: Viking Penguin, 1978.

Elizabeth Stuart Phelps. *Gypsy Breynton.* (1866). New York: Dodd, Mead & Co., 1894.

Elizabeth Stuart Phelps. *Gypsy's Cousin Joy.* (1866). New York: Dodd, Mead & Co., 1876.

Elizabeth Stuart Phelps. *Gypsy's Sowing and Reaping.* (1866). New York: Dodd, Mead & Co., 1876.

Elizabeth Stuart Phelps. *Gypsy's Year at the Golden Crescent.* (1867). New York: Dodd, Mead & Co., 1876.

Ruth Sawyer. *Roller Skates.* (1936). New York: Puffin, 1986.

Ruth Sawyer. *The Year of Jubilo.* New York: Viking Press, 1940.

Kate Seredy. *The Good Master.* (1935). New York: Puffin, 1986.

T. H. White. *Mistress Masham's Repose.* (1946). New York: Capricorn Books, 1960.

Laura Ingalls Wilder. *Little House on the Prairie.* (1935). New York: Harper, 1953.

ADULT FICTION

Becky Birtha. *Lovers' Choice*. Seattle, Wash.: Seal Press, 1987.

Blanche McCrary Boyd. *The Redneck Way of Knowledge*. New York: Alfred A. Knopf, 1982.

Lara Cardella. *Good Girls Don't Wear Trousers*. Translated from the Italian by Diana Di Carcaci. New York: Arcade Publishing, 1994.

Willa Cather. *Collected Short Fiction 1892-1912*. Introduction by Mildred R. Bennett. Lincoln, Nebr.: University of Nebraska Press, 1965.

Sandra Cisneros. *The House on Mango Street*. (1984). New York: Alfred A. Knopf, 1994.

Jane Duncan. *My Friend Annie*. New York: St. Martin's Press, 1961.

George Eliot. *The Mill on the Floss*. (1860). Edited by Carol C. Christ. New York: W. W. Norton & Co., 1994.

Leslie Feinberg. *Stone Butch Blues*. Ithaca, N.Y.: Firebrand Books, 1993.

Fannie Flagg. *Fried Green Tomatoes at the Whistlestop Café*. New York: Random House, 1987.

Radclyffe Hall. *The Well of Loneliness*. (1928). New York: Doubleday, 1990.

Edith Summer Kelly. *Weeds*. New York: Feminist Press, 1982.

E. M. Kerr. *Deliver Us From Evie*. New York: HarperCollins Publishers, 1995.

Jamaica Kincaid. *At the Bottom of the River*. New York: Penguin, 1992.

Maxine Hong Kingston. *The Woman Warrior: Memoirs of a Girlhood Among Ghosts*. New York: Random House, 1975.

Edith Konecky. *Allegra Maud Goldman*. New York: Harper & Row, Publishers, 1976.

Harper Lee. *To Kill a Mocking Bird*. New York: Popular Library, 1960.

Carson McCullers. *The Heart Is a Lonely Hunter*. (1940). New York: Bantam Books, 1988.

Carson McCullers. *The Member of the Wedding*. (1946). New York: Bantam Books, 1950.

Toni Morrison. *The Bluest Eye*. New York: McGraw-Hill Book Co., 1984.

Toni Morrison. *Sula*. New York: E. P. Dutton, 1987.

Alice Munro. *Lives of Girls and Women*. New York: New American Library, 1971.

Suniti Namjoshi. *Feminist Fables*. London: Sheba Feminist Publishers, 1981.

Grace Paley. *Later the Same Day*. New York: Farrar, Straus & Giroux, 1985.

Cora Sandel. *The Child Who Loved Roads: Selected Short Stories*. Translated and with an introduction by Barbara Wilson. Seattle, Wash.: Seal Press, 1988.

April Sinclair. *Coffee Makes You Black*. New York: Hyperion Press, 1994.

Linda Smukler. *Normal Sex*. Ithaca, N.Y.: Firebrand Books, 1994.

Jean Stafford. *The Mountain Lion*. (1947). New York: Farrar, Straus & Giroux, 1972.

Rose Tremain. *Sacred Country*. New York: Atheneum, 1992.

Virginia Woolf. *Orlando: a Biography* (1928). New York: Harcourt Brace Jovanovich, 1973.

MEMOIR AND AUTOBIOGRAPHY

Louisa May Alcott: Her Life, Letters and Journals. Edited by Ednah D. Cheney. Boston: Roberts Brothers, 1892.

Aman, the Story of a Somali Girl, as told to Virginia Lee Barnes and Janice Boddy. New York: Pantheon Books, 1994.

Box-Car Bertha. *Sister of the Road: The Autobiography of Box-Car Bertha*, as told to Dr. Ben L. Reitman. (1937). New York: Harper & Row, Publishers, 1975.

Simone de Beauvoir. *Memoirs of a Dutiful Daughter*. Translated from the French by James Kirkup. New York: Harper & Row, Publishers, 1959.

Annie Dillard. *An American Childhood*. New York: HarperCollins Publishers, 1987.

Maria Hinojosa. *Crews: Gang Members Talk to Maria Hinojosa*. New York: Harcourt Brace Jovanovich, 1995.

Teresa Jordan. *Riding the White Horse Home: A Western Family Album*. New York: Pantheon Books, 1993.

Anne LaBastille. *Woodswoman*. New York: E. P. Dutton, 1976.

Bia Lowe. *Wild Ride: Earthquakes, Sneezes and Other Thrills*. New York: HarperCollins Publishers, 1995.

Cynthia Ozick, *Art & Ardor*. New York: Alfred A. Knopf, 1983.

Grace Paley. *Grace Paley's Life Stories*. Edited by Judith Arcana. Champaign, Ill.: University of Illinois Press, 1993.

Elizabeth Stuart Phelps. *Chapters from a Life*. (1896). New York: Arno Press and Signal Lives, Reprint Services, 1980.

Minnie Bruce Pratt. *S/He*. Ithaca, N.Y.: Firebrand Books, 1995.

Olive Schreiner. *A Year on an African Farm*. New York: Viking Penguin, 1983.

Opal Whiteley. *The Story of Opal: The Journal of an Understanding Heart*. New York: Atlantic Monthly Press, 1920.

Frances Willard. *Glimpses of Fifty Years: The Autobiography of an American Woman*. (1889). Chicago: Source Book Press, 1970.

THEORY, ESSAYS, ETCETERA:

Lynne Mikel Brown and Carol Gilligan. *Meeting at the Crossroads: Women's Psychology and Girls' Development.* Cambridge, Mass.: Harvard University Press, 1992.

Susan K. Cahn. *Coming on Strong: Gender and Sexuality in Twentieth Century Women's Sport.* New York: Free Press, 1994.

Simone de Beauvoir. *The Second Sex.* (1953). Translated and edited by H. M. Parshley. New York: Alfred A. Knopf, 1989.

Carol Gilligan. *In a Different Voice: Psychological Theory and Women's Development.* Cambridge, Mass.: Harvard University Press, 1982.

Carol Gilligan, Annie G. Rogers, and Deborah L. Tolman. *Women, Girls and Psychotherapy: Reframing Resistance.* Binghamton, N.Y.: Harrington Park Press, 1991.

Emily Hancock. *The Girl Within.* New York: Fawcett Columbine, 1989.

Rachel T. Hare-Mustin and Jeanne Maracek. *Making a Difference: Psychology and Construction of Gender.* New Haven, Conn.: Yale University Press, 1990.

Carolyn G. Heilbrun. *Hamlet's Mother and Other Women.* New York: Ballantine Books, 1990. See especially, *"To the Lighthouse:* The New Story of Mother and Daughter" and "Alcott's *Little Women".*

Teresa Jordan. *Cowgirls: Women of the American West.* New York: Anchor Books, 1982.

Barbara A. Kerr. *Smart Girls, Gifted Women.* Columbus, Ohio: Ohio Publishing Co., 1985.

Sally Mann. *At Twelve: Portraits of Young Women.* Introduction by Anne Beattie. New York: Aperture, 1988.

Nicky Marone. *How to Father a Successful Daughter.* New York: McGraw-Hill Book Co., 1988.

Bobbie Anne Mason. *The Girl Sleuth: A Feminist Guide.* New York: Feminist Press, 1975.

Mary Pipher. *Reviving Ophelia: Saving the Selves of Adolescent Girls.* New York: Grosset Books, 1994.

Adrienne Rich. *Of Woman Born: Motherhood as Experience and Institution.* New York: W. W. Norton & Co., 1976.

Mira and David Sadker. *Failing at Fairness: How America's Schools Shortchange Girls.* New York: Charles Scribner's Sons and Maxwell Macmillan International Publishing Co., 1994.

ARTICLES

Lyn Mikel Brown. "Telling a Girl's Life: Self-Authorization as a Form of Resistance." In *Women, Girls and Psychotherapy: Reframing Resistance.* Binghamton, N.Y.: Haworth Press, 1991.

Stacy D'Erasmo. "Odd Girls Out: The Joys of Growing Up Strange." *Voice Literary Supplement* (June 1993).

Carol Gilligan, Annie G. Rogers, and Normi Noel. "Cartography of a Lost Time." Conference presentation, Harvard University Graduate School of Education, Cambridge, Mass., 1992-93.

Kristen Golden. "What Do Girls See?" *Ms.* (May/June 1994).

Marie Ingram. "Lester Rowntree." (1879-1979). "Part One: The Peripatetic Gilbert White" *(Hortus 31, vol. 8, no. 3);* "Part Two: Sanctuary: Conserving the Worthwhile" *(Hortus 32, vol. 8, no. 4);* and "Part Three: A Spirit of Keen Joy" *(Hortus 33, vol. 9, no. 1).*

Anne Scott MacLeod. "The *Caddie Woodlawn* Syndrome: American Girlhood in the Nineteenth Century." In *A Century of Childhood 1820-1920,* edited by Mary Lynn Stevens Heininger, Karin Calvert, Barbara Finkelstein, Kathy Vandell, Anne Scott MacLeod, and Harvey Green. Margaret Woodbury Strong Museum, Rochester, N.Y., 1984.

Sharon O'Brien. "Tomboyism and Adolescent Conflict: Three Nineteenth Century Case Studies." In *Women's Being, Women's Place: Female Identity and Vocation in American History,* edited by Mary Kelley. Boston: G. K. Hall & Co., 1979.

Annie G. Rogers. "Voice, Play and a Practice of Ordinary Courage in Girls' and Women's Lives." *Harvard Educational Review,* vol. 63, no. 3 (fall 1993).

Elizabeth Segel. "The *Gypsy Breynton* Series: Setting the Pattern for American Tomboy Heroines." *Children's Literature Association Quarterly,* vol. 14, no. 2 (summer 1989), pp. 67-71.

Elizabeth Segel. "Laura Ingalls Wilder's America: An Unflinching Assessment." *Children's Literature in Education,* vol. 8, no. 2 (1977).

Elizabeth Segel. "A Second Look: *Roller Skates.*" *Hornbook Magazine* (August 1979).

Elizabeth Segel. "Tomboy Taming and Gender-Role Socialization: The Evidence of Children's Books." In *Gender Roles Through the Life Span: A Multidisciplinary Perspective,* edited by Michael R. Stevenson. Muncie Ind.: Ball State University, 1994.

Jackie Vivelo. "The Mystery of Nancy Drew." *Ms.* (November/December 1992).

ANTHOLOGIES

Erica Bauermeister, Jesse Larsen, and Holly Smiths, eds. *5oo Great Books by Women: A Reader's Guide*. New York: Penguin Books, 1994.

Angela Carter, ed. *Wayward Girls and Wicked Women: An Anthology of Subversive Stories*. New York: Viking Penguin, 1989.

Judith Niemi and Barbara Wieser, eds. *Rivers Running Free: Stories of Adventurous Women*. Minneapolis, Minn.: Bergamot Books, 1987.

Ethel Johnston Phelps, ed. *The Maid of the North: Feminist Folk Tales from Around the World*. New York: Holt, Rinehart and Winston, 1981.

Lyn Reese, Jean Wilkinson, and Phyllis Sheon Koppelman, eds. *I Am on My Way Running: Women Speak on Coming of Age*. New York: Avon Books, 1983.

Lynne Yamaguchi and Karen Barber, eds. *Tomboys! Dyke Tales of Derring-Do*. Los Angeles, Calif.: Alyson Publications, 1995.

Credits